THE
REAL
STORY

Michael Bowman

Reality is always one jump ahead…

PROLOGUE

When I was little I believed that babies came via the mailman. Okay, some probably do, but now I'm grown up enough to know that reproduction isn't dependent on the postal service. When my mom was too young to know any better, somebody told her that God created everything in six days. She still believes that. My mom thinks evolution is a dirty word.

I guess we all know that people who believe in a six day creation are called *creationists*. If you're a creationist, hi. Maybe you can help me with something. As a spokesperson for God, can you tell me why He had to create the world and everything in just six days? I'm being serious here. Did some technical reason make it necessary to rush creation into six days, rather than spending, say, a few billion years on the job?

If the creation we're talking about is supposed to be a result of intelligent design, surely it would be more intelligent to design the world and everything g-r-a-d-u-a-l-l-y? To take *time* over it? That way, the designer gets to be involved in shaping and influencing the organisms being designed in an *ongoing* way, in *their* time. At the same time, those organisms get the chance to learn more t-h-o-r-o-u-g-h-l-y through their own efforts.

Does being religious mean being stupid? We'd have to be real stupid not to see that we're still being designed, and we still have a heck of a lot to learn. 'Creation' is still happening, right before our eyes. You can see it in everything, from genes mutating to people having new ideas.

Then there's the other anomaly of 'creation' being just a few thousand years old. You want to guess again? We measured the universe using real telescopes and it's billions of light years across and expanding fast. No, a light year is not a measurement of time; it's a measurement of the distance light travels in a year. (186,000 miles a second.) By measuring the distance that light has

1

traveled to us from the farthest stars, we know for a fact that the universe is actually 13.5 billion years old.

And another thing: Time is just as real a part of creation as everything else is; time is a fundamental and inseparable property of matter. Einstein said so. And that means whoever or whatever created the world, the universe and everything, also created time at the same, uh, time. Except for a few details involving relativity, time is constant, and we - me and Einstein - have every reason to think that it's remained constant since it began. So let's start getting Real, okay?

Design-over-time is a 13.5 billion years old fact. As another name for evolution, design-over-time is inseparable from the rest of science. To deny this 13.5 billion years evolution is to deny chemistry, physics, cosmology, medicine, technology, biology, and everything they touch. Also, by throwing out evolution you also throw out God.

How come? Well God supposedly designs and organizes everything systematically so it all works out the best way for everything and everyone, right? And that's exactly what evolution does. I'd call that pretty intelligent. Far from having completed everything in a six-day creation, the intelligence known as God, evolution or a self-organizing system, is constantly changing and improving itself, not only on the levels we're aware of, but on levels way below and way above our present ability to see or understand.

Even on the levels of 'creation' that we're aware of, this perpetual change and improvement is necessary for the existence of the fundamental elements and forces that all of science is based on. Without this perpetual change and improvement, the universe couldn't exist.

You don't need to look very hard to see God in all of that, but this is not the God of immature human invention. Not a God who demonstrates anger, vengefulness, impatience and other human failings. (That Old Testament God is so obviously the product of primitive imaginations, primeval fears and limited understanding.)

The 'God' of this constantly evolving, self-organizing universe appears to have taken us into account right from the very beginning when the universe was nothing but energy in its most basic form. Starting at that fundamental quantum level, it took billions of years of universal evolution to create the atoms that comprise our material bodies. Only that length of time allows for stars to form, then later explode in supernovae and spread their elements across space; elements that wind up as the vital components of these bodies.

2

The God of an evolving, self-organizing universe is also evident in the way everything is so predictable at the atomic level; predictable enough for us to understand reality at that level, and construct all of the conventional sciences on it before we progress to the more complicated subatomic level underlying it. In doing that, the universe represents a God that understands how minds grow, by presenting us not simply with a universe that opens up as minds open up, but with a reality that expands as our consciousness expands.

They say travel broadens the mind, right? Well this book is the story of my trip from a state of unawareness to one of growing enlightenment. I got on in a town called Asleep, passed through Wakefulness, and I'm still traveling.

To tell the truth I lifted that notion of a journey from something Ed said because I kinda like it. Here's what he actually said:

'Imagine life is you, going someplace new on a train. You don't know what's at your destination, or what you'll see and experience along the way. But you do get to make some choices about how you travel. You can choose to draw down the blinds and sleep through, in which case the journey will take forever because you'll miss out on the entire learning process. (If you don't know life's a learning process, your journey has hardly gotten started yet.) Or you can raise the blinds a little and only look out at the things you want to see, making this a very long and difficult trip. (What you choose to ignore now, you'll have to face up to later.) Or you can raise the blinds all the way, check everything out, get off the train at each station, become involved in what's out there and try to understand how things really are…'

I think there was more of that but I, uh, can't locate the tape it's on. (I spoke this book onto a million of these midget audio tapes but they all look the same. Sure I numbered 'em...except when I forgot...) Tape #1 begins with what happened at the river that night, though not being there I have no idea what really happened. But this is supposed to be a work of fiction, so here's how I imagine it went:

TAPE 1

Jeff Ackerley was on his knees, head bowed, sniffing the mouth of a whiskey bottle. He looked like he was praying. Someplace nearby was Roy King, smearing black vegetable dye on his private parts then sitting back to admire himself. Except that the darkness made him practically invisible, the same way it did Mike McClure, save for where the damp ground made contact with his bare buttocks and took off the dye.

"Why do we got to be naked?" McClure lisped through the mouth of the black hood Ackerley had told him to wear.

"Why do bears crap in the woods?" King said.

"Ain't no bears in these woods," McClure said, aiming a gap-toothed grin in King's direction.

"Peckerhead! It's so's we'll be naked as them Baptist jaybirds when we start kickin' up that holy water." There was no humor in Ackerley's voice.

" - An' they calls it religion," King chipped in.

"Religion my ass!" Ackerley tilted the whiskey bottle against his mouth.

McClure watched an unsteady line of tiny yellow lights trail downward from where a white wooden spire loomed against the night sky across the narrow valley. In the gully below, black river water waited, lazy and soundless. The religion word worried McClure. Sure, Ackerley had said those people were crazy anyhow, messing around in the river at night. He'd said nobody would give a damn if somebody went in there to liven things up some, running around in their camouflaged birthday suits. Hell, you couldn't even see the censored items with that color on, in the dark and all.

McClure's thoughts were cut short when Willie Stevenson, all done relieving himself, emerged from the night and stood over them scratching his dyed groin.

"'Bout fuck'n time," Ackerley told him and got to his feet; in his boots they were the only part of him not naked. "OK, let's get this thing done."

They found their baseball bats and set off down the slope, self-conscious despite the camouflage. Ackerley had counted twelve lights from this vantage point on the ridge. He figured they'd be led by the preacher whose heavy-duty flashlight beam it would be that now caught in ripples that spread out before him as he waded, waist deep, into the dark water below. Ackerley's pulse quickened. He was aware of King's bat being struck repeatedly against the palm of his hand...and then he was just one of four blackened figures, naked

4

yet not naked, coming out of the night without a sound other than the beat of their feet on the ground.

Ackerley leapt from the riverbank, his bat held out widthwise before him, and struck the first victim. High-stepping over him in a wave of mud-stirred water, he swung the bat at a second startled man. The screaming began.

Roy King's bat made a hollow *pop* against a young black man's head. The handle of the bat came around into the man's face in the same movement. King kicked him aside and punched the old man dressed in white shirt and black pants who'd grabbed the bat. The old man fell back with a splash into a crown of spray that showered wet against King's face and left it mottled black and white. Blinking, King looked around for another home run to hit.

The congregation was in retreat, making it easier for Michael McClure to do nothing he'd regret later. He stood waist-deep in the river, waving his bat around his head and yelling like a redskin, watching the Baptists scramble from the water up the opposite bank. He became aware of the cold water gripping his privates and looked down to see the white water-mark where the dye had washed off.

Then he screamed again - with shock this time because a face had come up at him from under the murky brown swirl, its eyes half-open, one of them squashy and red. A hand grasped his leg.

Willie Stevenson hung back, watching to see what the others were doing: Roy King was swinging his bat against the surface of the water and whooping. McClure knelt on the riverbank, busy with a victim. All of the lanterns were gone now, yet Willie could see that not all of the Baptists had fled in the same direction. Most had turned around and made their escape the way they'd come, up the rise to the church; all except for one girl who'd run towards the coat she'd left on the bank. She'd paid for that coat out of her meager wages at the hypermart in Jefferson; her mother would not forgive her for leaving it.

Willie saw Ackerley splashing towards her through the shallows. With what little natural light there was he watched Ackerley's black-streaked backside emerge from the river scant feet behind the girl, saw him lunge, heard the girl's scream cut short. She was on the ground, face-down under Ackerley, both of them struggling.

On the opposite bank, muffled sounds reached across the water to McClure: somebody grunting or sobbing maybe. He peered hard into the dark, saw a lighter patch of movement and knew that Ackerley had caught one of those girls...

TAPE 2

Now let's talk about me. My name is Laurie Hendricks. I was born and raised in a poor neighborhood of Tennessee where my dad was a miner. We didn't have books in the house other than a Bible and some ancient magazines so my writing got off to a slow start. I guess I'm still recovering from that.

What I did have though was a colorful imagination - I used to make up stupid little stories and stuff - so when my dad died I got a job on the local paper; only as the gopher at first, but that developed through taking calls for the advertising into me collecting material for editorials, and finally writing them.

Heck no, these were not like the real editorials you read in big city papers; I was just filling the spaces between the advertisements.

So like I said earlier, this book is compiled from a collection of tiny audio tapes I made - snippets of stuff I recorded over time. (I just happened to use one of those miniature recording machines for my job on the paper.) Some of the sections in here are just a few lines long, others run to a few pages. That's why it doesn't read like an ordinary old book, but who said it had to?

That's enough preamble. When an anonymous woman called The Star and said a girl had gotten assaulted and a young man beaten up, it was the best news I'd heard in months. A crazy local minister had taken it on himself to tarnish the fine, upstanding name of the community with his moonlight baptisms. Not being religious - except with money - I figured it was okay for Baptists to get baptized. Not so, my caller said, especially when the minister was dipping white and black folks of mixed genders together and all of them damn near close to naked. When I asked how close she got downright indignant (she already sounded pretty drunk) but before I could get to the names and addresses she hung up.

Well hell, folks called us all the time with wacky stories, not that I believed that holy orgy malarkey; at best there'd be a wet T show with God on the side, though it would be a little more than that by the time I'd gotten through with it. I put the phone down and headed straight for the Sheriff's office.

Yeah, okay, I guess that makes me sound kind of cynical, but I wasn't born that way. As a kid I used to wish life could be like those down-homey scenes of Americana that Norman Rockwell painted for the cover of The Saturday Evening Post magazine back in the last century. My folks still had piles of dusty old National Geographic and The Post from when my Uncle Will lived

6

with us, and me being the only child and kind of quiet, I spent a lot of time in my room reading those. But it was those Rockwell covers from the late 1940s and early 1950s that got a hold of me. They made those times look so safe, secure and cozy. Just remembering the magic in those folksy scenes still gives me an ache of nostalgia. To me that was life without all of the complications. In a crazy kind of way that was probably why I grew up to be a disillusioned small town hack who thought reporting 'the truth' meant exposing people's failings. I'd most likely still be doing that if Ed hadn't started me on the slow and often painful journey towards getting Real.

If I were to describe Ed in a few words, the guy you'd picture would be your idea of some guy who was nothing like Ed. Yeah, he was kind of good looking if appearances are all you're interested in. No, he wasn't rich or successful - not in the way you mean. To me in those early days of our relationship he was a guy whose books I left lying around in my car so people would know how smart I was: science books, philosophy tomes, heavy ideas.

Ed had been a physics professor at a famous university once upon a time. Okay, so he was older than me, and yes I did worry about that at first, but later I almost stopped seeing Ed; all I saw were Ed's ideas.

You never saw someone as their ideas? Well how else do people see Jesus Christ or Mohammed or The Buddha? (Or, come to that, Hitler, Pol pot and Jack the Ripper?) Those guys are not remembered for how they looked, but for their *ideas*. Ideas are what put us top of the animal tree. Ideas separate us from other apes. Ideas drive human progress and aspirations. Our best ideas are the best thing about us. You know what I'm saying.

But when you're all done congratulating yourself, remember that our capacity for ideas only gives us the *potential* to change things for the better. The tragedy is that with all of our bright ideas we still have war, inequality, hatred, poverty, terrorism, greed, envy, homicide, aggression, injustice, misery, etc. The same old problems we always had.

You probably heard some of the reasons why already - it's in our nature; we're just savages underneath, it's the fault of the devil and so on. But you didn't hear Ed's take on this. It goes to the heart of why, with all of our smart thinking and good intentions, technological progress, increased wealth and everything, we just can't seem to rid ourselves of those age-old problems, even in our own back yard.

According to Ed, we won't ever eradicate those problems until we accept that it's not some marginalized criminal fraternity that causes all of the bad things; it's ordinary people like you and me trying so hard to make *good* things happen for ourselves.

The so-called 'good' things I'm talking about here are happiness and security for ourselves and our family; greater personal prosperity; more 'love'; the freedom to practice our moral and religious beliefs, and stuff like that. (Write your own list of 'good' things.)

So how can wanting these good things cause all of the bad things? Well think about it. The things we all want never come for free. We have to *compete* with each other for a job, a roof over our head, love, security, freedom. But we're never content with just those basics; we always have to have a better job and an ever-rising paycheck; a bigger roof over our head; an ongoing supply of what we call love; security in the form of lethal personal weaponry or, in broader terms, fabulously expensive nuclear weapons. Even our 'freedom' comes at a price because it's the freedom to do and to have what *we* want, in a world where everybody else wants that same freedom.

Just having to compete for the 'good' things reveals a dark side that's in each of us: a self-serving 'I want' side that's constantly telling us we have a God-given right to those good things. But because the most fundamental of those 'God-given' rights is to reproduce ourselves, there's no reasoning with this dark side.

This 'right' to reproduce ourselves is the root of all our problems. It underpins everything. As the engine room of our 'I want' dark side, it's why we demand more 'prosperity' to give ourselves and our offspring an ever better living standard. That demand leads to sprawling social structures to suit our notions of what this 'better living standard' should be. Yet in spreading ourselves out to accommodate all of these extra offspring and give them this 'better' living, we plunder every material resource, trash nature and trample the entire goddam planet - and each other if we get in the way.

We tell ourselves we're creating better technology and improved lifestyles by being so eager to grab these 'good' things, but mostly all that happens is we accumulate more 'I want' stuff whilst creating mountains of short-lived, fashionable junk. The need for all of this 'I want' stuff actually controls us.

I'm not done here yet because the 'love' we're all so desperate to have is driven by this same self-interested 'I want' dark side, the result of a mindless biological imperative that has us all by the short hairs. (Nobody called God ever needed to say 'Go forth and multiply'; organisms were doing that since the first cell split in two.) For many misguided people that's all the excuse they

8

need to behave like dumb animals. For millions of others, their understanding of 'love' is mostly hormone-powered lust with a candy coating.

This candy-coated lust is then dressed up to satisfy a delusion of religion or morality. Too often there isn't even a candy coating; the market for raw lust is growing like a fungus.

Then there's our precious freedom. Huh? The 'freedom' to be more equal than somebody else? The 'freedom' to prove you're better at grabbing what *you* want? The 'freedom' to treat concepts like 'kindness' and 'compassion' as luxuries if and when you decide you can afford them? The more repressive among us don't see this as freedom but as moral degeneracy, profligacy and greed. They may be repressive but they got that right. The more determined we are in our demand for the 'good' things *we* have a God-given right to, the more we grab and hold onto them, the *meaner* we become. Out of this 'I want' meanness come jealousy, envy, greed, insecurity, aggression and all of our other undesirable traits.

That's only half of this equation, because even while we're all greedily, aggressively grabbing and competing to get what *we* want, we pretend we're nice, honest, hard-working folks, and that what we're doing is not just good and right and fair, it's admirable. We're reasonable, generous, caring folks. Hey, we have responsibilities to those we care about. We're an upstanding homemaker, a breadwinner, a civilized member of the community, proud to uphold the fine traditions that made this country great, blah blah. But when push comes to shove, and the stakes get high enough, we can be as mean, ruthless, even homicidal as the next guy. It all depends on what's at stake, and maybe what we can get away with.

This Jekyll and Hyde behavior is far worse than hypocrisy; it amounts to a dangerous kind of psychosis that won't allow your nice, homely Dr. Jekyll side to see this as an unfair description of you. Underneath that veneer of self-deception, your ruthless Mr. Hyde side looks at life as a non-stop competition for survival, where the health and welfare of ME & MINE always come first.

In reality, the 'good' things we all want are 'good' only because they'll help us survive long enough to reproduce. And our selfish determination to have those 'good' things is what causes all of our problems.

Keep reading and you'll discover there's a heck of a lot more to selfishness than you ever realized. Selfishness has a majority influence on everything we think and do - in personal relationships, in business, in the way we see ourselves and even how we perceive reality. Selfishness affects our every thought and deed. But because our dark 'I want' side is so powerful and so ancient, so fundamental to how our body and mind function, it deludes us into seeing much of our selfishness as 'right' and 'normal'.

This is why global warming, chronic inequality, greed, strife, war and everything else that's bad, are never *our* fault. It's why we keep on creating more of the same old problems, more of the same eternal conflicts of interest, bad feeling, or worse if we don't get what *we* want. Where else do dissatisfaction, jealousy and envy originate - especially if we see others getting something we're not? If we decide they're getting something that belongs to us, why'd you think we feel cheated, unjustly treated, unequal? It's because ME & MINE are losing out. Then we get angry and resentful, and that causes arguments, antagonism and aggression. This problem goes beyond material possessions to include all of our relationships, our deepest feelings and our moral and religious beliefs, so naturally it creates the kind of problems that can blossom into war, terrorism and the like.

All of the 'love' that's supposed to make the world go round, is in reality self-interest, and we're blind to how completely it controls us. After millions of years of being this way, the delusion has become more than just a part of us, it's our prime motivation. Self-interest is always just below the surface, waiting for the main chance, constantly monitoring the pros and cons, the odds, the benefits, the profits and losses, looking for openings that'll benefit ME & MINE FIRST.

Making matters worse is that some of us are born physically and/or mentally better at looking out for ourselves than others. Add the ME & MINE FIRST dictum to that, and you get all of the other inequalities in the world, with extremes like a billionaire in a first world economy and a beggar in the third world. These inequalities fuel the fires of all our other problems. Selfishness has made us our own worst enemy.

Sure, many of us are capable of kindness, generosity, even compassion - to a degree. But when those virtues are not reserved for people we care about, they're fickle things. They really have to fight for their survival in a world where 'I want' rules. All too often, if we do do anything for somebody else, it's only after we decided our ME & MINE FIRST account can afford it.

Okay. So far I only sketched a rough outline of this thing because there's a hell of a lot more to it. The fundamental problem of selfishness goes as deep as we do and then some. According to Ed, it's a symptom of mistaking ourselves for apes, and originates way below the conscious level. Like it or not, we resemble other apes in so many fundamental and obvious ways. We even share most of our genes with them, so to try and dismiss our evolutionary links to them is just willful ignorance. Our own bodies are living testimony to our ape origins and so is our behavior.

Ed said that even creationists who refuse to accept evolution as fact, are convinced that they and the body they walk around in are one and the same person. By identifying so completely with that body's feelings, wants, needs, drives and hungers, they prove their kinship to apes. The meaning and purpose of their life, and yours, is decided by those feelings, wants, needs, drives and hungers; they developed from simple biological cause-and-effect feedback mechanisms with only one purpose: survival. Many millions of years later, that mindless but utterly determined survival activity – created entirely by the interaction of atoms - is now shaped into what we call our body, nervous system and brain. Yet because our conscious awareness is interfaced so tightly with those atoms, we believe we and it are one and the same.

You don't need a college degree to appreciate that while *you* have conscious awareness, atoms don't. There's no significant difference between the structure and composition of the atoms in this book, and those in your body, your nervous system and your brain. Not one atom in your entire body has any consciousness whatsoever, okay?

Why do you assume that *you* and those atoms are somehow 'the same'? It's because that assumption came naturally to your primitive ancestors. It got handed down through the millennia, and you inherited it. That assumption is the reason why atoms with no conscious awareness are getting away with telling *us* how to think and feel about everything, including ourselves. But that's not the worst of it. In Ed's words, 'fundamentally non-conscious, material components are limiting our *conscious* view of reality to their *non-conscious* view of reality.'

The title of this book is The Real Story because we are not really these bodies; they're no more us than the clothes we wear. Our Real selves are *consciousness*, period. Being human is a point where the reality of material things and the Reality of consciousness meet. Those two realities - the material and the conscious - are both evolving, each in their own very different way, and we personify the results of this two-sided evolution.

As consciousness, we're not a product of this world's narrow material dimensions. Our only reason for being here in a material body is to learn that our Real nature is infinitely more than material.

If you're religious you probably already heard that a body is only a temporary vehicle for the Real you. Yet by identifying this body's feelings, wants, needs, drives and hungers as 'yours', you're allowing yourself to be deluded, not just about what *you* are, but about what *reality* is.

Look around, examine your senses, your feelings - that's reality *only* so far as those senses and feelings allow your conscious awareness to perceive it. There's a lot more to reality than those senses and feelings are capable of telling you about, but while you're in a material body you don't get to know about it.

As consciousness, our entire grasp on reality depends on our *conscious* perception of things, but in a material monkey suit our conscious view has never had the opportunity to perceive anything that wasn't obscured by atoms shaped into eyes, ears, nerves, a brain, a body. As a result, our hopes, aspirations and ideas are mostly a result of our developing consciousness trying to make sense of those survival-based feelings, wants, needs, drives and hungers. They're a result of the material experiences that made the brain our mind resides in the shape it is and the way it works. Our hopes, aspirations and ideas are products of the reasons *why* this brain developed from a primitive nervous system, *how* it came to be in a body, and *how* that body became the consequence of a few billion years of biological trial, error, cause and effect.

Can you imagine what those few billion years of biological evolution, in this delusional version of 'reality', have done for our hopes, dreams, aspirations and ideas? Hell, you don't need to imagine; these same hopes, dreams, aspirations and ideas are killing people every day.

Sure, if you insist on denying evolution as a fact of life, you can pretend all of what I just said is wrong because we're not products of a few billion years of biological trial, error, cause and effect, so there's no basis for our aggressive, competitive, selfish, ape-like traits. You'll look at an ape and pronounce that it was that way since God created it 6,000 years ago, and it'll always be that way. But when the ape in question happens to be human, maybe you ought to wonder why God created it with so many faults.

Some of the things I say in this book suggest that material reality is a delusion, but you don't have to take my word for that. Science has proved beyond question that materiality is not made from solid objects. Even the most so-called solid matter is actually waves of energy that depend for their existence on more dimensions of reality than the four we're familiar with.

12

That's science fact, but it's not the way you see reality, right? Even further from our understanding of reality is the fact that the solid objects we think we see, are only solid in our mind. Because of the true nature of material phenomena, we 'think' materiality into existence. Our consciousness organizes countless constantly shifting patterns in energy fields into what we recognize as 'things'.

Our biggest misconception of reality - the one I'll talk about most in this book - is how we live our lives not for our Real, consciously aware selves, but for the microscopic units of inheritance - *genes* - that copy themselves inside of these bodies, then persuade us to pass those copies on in new bodies. By allowing ourselves to be slaves to the gene replication and reproduction process - even though we believe our life has a higher purpose - we still try to live as the body we occupy, governed by *its* feelings, wants, needs, drives and hungers.

Growing out of our delusions is a long, slow, complex and often uncomfortable process. Anybody who tells you otherwise is compounding your delusions. The only reason why this sounds simple is because I'm using plain words that even my mom can understand. If I explained it in the kind of words Ed used, it would sound more authoritative but you'd need a tow truck to pull you out from between the lines.

TAPE 3

The Sheriff's office was in Passmore, a dead little town on the edge of what used to be a thriving Appalachia mining community. I left my car in the Rich-Mart parking lot and went to meet Sheriff Hughes, a big man with a big gut, thinning silver-blond hair and gray-blue eyes. I'd not met him prior to this, but he took my hand in both of his and came on like my long-lost father, except for the way his eyes frisked me. (Some people are lucky enough to have fathers like that.)

"Sheriff Hughes," I began, "I hear some Baptists had themselves a little trouble at the river..."

"Aw now hey, I only use *Sheriff Hughes* for fillin' out official correspondence and stuff. Call me Neil, y'hear?" You should've seen his stupid grin. Really.

"Well I guess it's the official version I'm here for, Sheriff," I told him.

"And you'll go away and put that in your paper, word for word, as usual?" Still grinning.

Faking innocence I told him I was not at liberty to write up my copy word for word, there being hardly enough space left for shorthand after the advertisements got placed. Self-restraint was part of my unwritten contract of employment. I smiled sweetly and produced my tape recorder like a rabbit from a hat. The recorder had been running all the while, but you know me. (Well you soon will.)

"Sheriff, my story will contain only the words on this recording tape." I meant after I changed their sequence and added others to them. "Now what can you tell me about the Baptist assaults?"

"Shoot, Laurie, I can't release any information just as yet." With a big, slow smile he added, "You knew I was gonna say that, right?"

"So are you treating this as a religious problem with a color problem side-order?"

He feigned dismay. "Hey, we don't want folks outside thinkin' we got us a color problem here, understand what I'm sayin'?"

"You mean after that other business awhile back? The black man who got his home torched up the Creek Road?"

His eyes went all squinty. "That was a plain old accident. Shit happens."

"You mean nobody got caught. You think maybe the same nobody made this new accident happen?"

Hughes' grin twitched. "Now Laurie, the Mayor would bust a gut I go rakin' over those ashes."

"Especially the 'nobody got caught' part, right?" I wiggled two fingers to emphasize the important words. "Any lead on these new assailants."

"Knowin' who did it ain't the important thing, Laurie. What matters is that we're out there lookin' for 'em."

Hughes winked and let go a self-satisfied laugh as the door opened and an unhappy woman of around thirty-five years walked in looking ten years older. Instantly Hughes' smile died, then the rest of his face went the same way as if he'd reached into the sub-cutaneous layer and brought out the face he used at home. I heard Hughes' deputy call to her, too late, that the Sheriff was busy. I also heard him call her Mrs. Hughes. Maybe even before I heard her speak I knew she was the anonymous voice on the phone that had brought me to Passmore. Hughes slid off the desk and slunk around behind for what little protection it gave, and I left with zip for my trouble.

Then I sat in my car and rewound my fruitless conversation with Hughes. While I was doing that, Mrs. Hughes came out and crossed the street to look

14

in the thrift store window. I could see from her reflection that she was looking at me, and the same female intuition that had informed her who I was, now told me she was just itching to talk to me but couldn't figure out how to without everybody knowing about it. I watched her go in her bag and do a little rummaging, then she walked along the street towards me and, as she passed, dropped a slip of paper through my open window - the window that didn't close all the way because the winder was busted. On the paper she'd scrawled 'Pull around by the trash'. This was real cloak and dagger stuff. Now all I had to do was trickle the car across the Rich-Mart lot so the red-brick bulk of the trash dump hid me from view. When I leaned over and pushed open the door, she got in without looking round.

"You're from The Star," she said warily. Then she saw my tape recorder. "Oh-ho no, I won't have my voice on that."

I made a big thing of switching the machine off, assuring her that confidentiality was one of my middle names. Naturally I didn't really switch it off. With me, as with real life, nothing is ever off the record. After I thanked her for her earlier call I couldn't shut her up.

"…I feel it my civic duty to bring these sordid goings-on out in the open. People have a right to the truth, however distasteful." Her mouth smiled at me obliquely with what was meant to be conspiratorial sisterhood. I imagined that same look on the faces of truth-loving Puritans as they watched witches crisping over open fires.

"So what is the truth, Mrs. Hughes?"

Her eyes narrowed. "Why, that so-called minister, stirring up earthly passions. Getting people stripped down to their…their underclothes, in the dead of night and everything. And him - " She paused for breath, her eyes glassy, thin lips twitching as she lingered over the images, " - him laying his black hands on them."

"You reckon the Baptists brought the assault on themselves?"

"My God yes, they surely did."

"The girl was asking to be raped, huh?"

She recoiled. "Are you trying to put words in my mouth?"

"How do you feel about Baptists?"

"I'm not against Baptists as such…life itself is a baptism."

"Oh surely, but those people got in over their heads - that what you're saying? It sounds like they got themselves beat up pretty much when the marines hit the beach."

"That is not how I would express it."

"I believe that kind of analogy appears in the bible, Mrs. Hughes." I was watching her with my eyebrows up and my mouth open slightly, nodding like I do. I could see she secretly liked the combative comparison.

"The man responsible should not have picked so strong an opponent as The Almighty."

"You're saying he was outpunched by God."

"Well...yes, I suppose he was."

That was when she said the name of the minister who performed the baptisms. It was John - as in *John the Baptist*, but the coincidence didn't register with me there and then.

"Think the preacher should retire - from the good fight I mean, after that knockdown?"

"He should be stripped of his authority. The people of this town can't sit by and let such things happen under their noses."

"You mean the way they did when that black person's home burned down? Know the thing I mean - couple of years back? Can you tell me anything about that? Not in your capacity as the Sheriff's wife, obviously. I meant do you have any personal feelings?"

At the magic word *Sheriff* she seemed to look right through the Rich-Mart wall into her husband's office. Softly she said, "You're damn right I do."

Just when I thought she was about to indict Hughes himself, she looked at me again with tears in her eyes. Then she just got out of the car and walked away without looking back.

Now I'm going to talk some more about getting Real, because after a few million years thinking we're material bodies, with survival and reproduction as our primary objectives, learning to think of yourself as a visiting consciousness will take what's often called a quantum leap by folks who have no idea what a *quantum* is. (I'll tell you later.) But once you take that leap, so many other things start making sense - like the notion of your body existing only to help you evolve consciously. What I'm hoping to do in this book is to give anyone who's ready an extra incentive to believe in their Real, conscious self as something much more than the sum of their genes. To anybody else this will probably sound kind of subversive, and that's exactly what it is.

For instance, although we live together in communities, underneath we're separated by a fundamental barrier created by looking out for our genes and putting the demands of ME & MINE first. You mightn't think of yourself as being in competition with other people and their family genes, but this 'my' genes before 'your' genes dictum exists for all species; it's the element of competition that drives the evolution of biological life - but only until consciousness recognizes itself as the Real reason for all of this, and appreciates that competition is a barrier between each of us and genuine equality/unity.

As human beings we're a confused mixture of the conscious and the genetic, an immaterial awareness residing temporarily in an unaware, uncaring bio-machine. And while our conscious self would like to develop the cooperation concept into something more, the genetic components are forever dropping wrenches into our efforts. Like when somebody threatens our happiness and/or security. Depending on how we're feeling, what's at stake and maybe whether we're carrying a weapon, this 'my genes before your genes' dictum overrules our better self. Yep, this very same 'my genes before your genes' thing really does cause all of our problems. That's what we're here to fix. Being human ain't easy. Nobody said it would be.

The instinct to survive first and foremost as material bodies of genes is why, instead of moving forward as a united species of enlightened beings, we're still working, first and always, to get the best deal for ME and MY GENES. Practically all of the thoughts/feelings that you experience are affected by that consideration.

Genetic life began with competition between the very first replicating molecules and went on to build the body you have now. In living as, and for, these genetic bodies, we've unsuspectingly built our world around a reality that's geared to selfishly ensuring the welfare of genes. Our Real, conscious selves are not naturally competitive. We only become competitive by assuming we're an extension of a body/nervous system/brain, never suspecting that 'our' body is really the property of genes, with an irresistible agenda its own, developed over millions of years of blood, sweat and mayhem? That agenda is to survive to replicate and reproduce genes, period. (There's a tape later detailing how replication works.)

How do we pass genetic selfishness on to future generations? The same way we create those generations: *Sex*. Genes evolved nervous systems and brains into bodies just to keep those bodies alive long enough to reproduce their genes through sex. From day one, life on this planet had to protect and perpetuate itself or it would not have survived. So selfishness and sex became genes' primary weapons for replacing and reproducing themselves. That's why being selfish for our genes is the major driving force behind just about everything we do. And because our very material existence has always been governed by selfishness, we're mostly unaware we're being selfish.

We reason that the development of human consciousness allows us to rise above selfish urges created by our biological origins. Consciously and unconsciously, we refuse to see ourselves as we really are; that wouldn't help our genes any and we know it. Besides, it's hard to be the problem, and see the problem.

Now I've gotten to the sharp end of selfishness and there's no way around this so I'll just say it, okay? The embodiment of selfishness, and genes' primary weapon for getting themselves reproduced, is what's commonly called *love*. Genetic survival is why the sensations, the emotions, the crazy behavior and delusional ideas responsible for what we think of as love have such a powerful and comprehensive influence on us.

In biological terms there's nothing mysterious about love. The same irresistible yet mindless chemical processes that evolved to keep plankton, beetles, lizards and human bodies alive long enough to reproduce, also designed in them equally irresistible - 'selfish' - sensations and urges to ensure reproduction happens. That's the only reason why we think love has to involve sex, reproduction and emotions.

After millions of years of social structure and habit built on that biological conditioning, we've come to believe that the impulses created by chemistry copying itself, are central to *our* existence, as *consciousness*. Obsessed, controlled and deluded this way, we've shaped our reality around biological feedback mechanisms that act like a hardwired electrochemical cattle prod, driving us to reproduce.'

Of course there's such a thing as Real love, but it's a billion light years from the delusion that restricts itself only to the people who we select as the objects of our fickle 'love'. Real love bears no resemblance to a mindless biomechanical survival instinct that favors some people over others because of their genetic makeup. Real love is totally immaterial in origin, free of chemically derived preferences and moods, sexual desires or hormonally generated emotions, ideas or delusions.

Only the truly deluded could imagine that a love representing perfect selflessness and the apex of conscious evolution, was the same as a hormone-driven survival instinct. Two such conflicting concepts are fundamentally incompatible. And yet, as a combination of material and conscious evolutions,

18

each of us is a living personification of this fundamental incompatibility. I guess that helps to explain why we're the way we are, but let me spell it out for you.

Under the name of 'love', the same selfishness that evolved to ensure the continuity of genes, went on to influence our consciousness in the creation of romantic relationships, having offspring, and making families. By doing that, this self-interested biological love plays an essential role in human evolution. It gives our evolving consciousness a way to figure itself out. (We do that by seeing our Real, conscious selves *in relation to* this so-called material 'reality', thus learning that we're not the same as it.)

The sole purpose of biological love, genetic evolution, the biological process and the entire material universe is to help our consciousness evolve. Yet by diverting all of our time and energy to satisfying the demands of genes, we've developed self-delusion to a fine art. We imagine that the epitome of selfishness - the gene replicating and reproducing institution we call love - is the very opposite of selfishness. Because of our primitive origins, we even imagine that this deluded height of selfishness is a gift from God. We've gotten used to everything being this way. To us, this way is 'right' only because we're unaware there is another way.

Our problem (okay, our opportunity) is to first make ourselves see through the layers of illusion and delusion created by a history of living on behalf of what we think of as 'our' biology. Maybe then we'll recognize the difference between that biological self, and our Real self. Maybe then we'll also see that genes, selfishness, sex and reproduction are the means to an end that transcends all of them.

TAPE 4

To say we're too close to the experiences of sex, relationships, romance, having families - life itself - to think about them objectively, is a major understatement. We're too involved in the *small r reality* created by genes looking out for their own interests for our consciousness to see itself as a phenomenon beyond the laws of physics and chemistry. As a result, we think romantic relationships and their reproductive consequences are all our idea.

Somebody out there is saying: "Hold on one second. Genes may be mindless, but we're not. Surely sex and reproduction and kids become our idea if we put our minds to making them happen?"

Besides ignoring everything I said so far, the questioner is missing the entire point of our existence: to evolve as our Real, conscious self. We're not here to work for genes and their bodies, they're here to work for us. Get that straight, okay? The only reason why we act out this biological charade is because genes and their bodies were here before we were. That's how genes got to make the rules for how we think of 'ourselves', for why we think we're here, and for how we behave.

I'm going to build what I call a *Reality Window* into this book just here so I can step out for a moment to say a little more about genes. (It's just a gimmick but it breaks the monotony.) Genes respond to changes inside and outside of our bodies by adapting them to survive in the world. Those ongoing adaptations are called evolution. The genes, and the organisms they build that don't adapt well enough, don't survive and don't evolve. That's what survival of the fittest is all about.

Strange as it seems, genes didn't evolve bodies for us. Neither genes nor their bodies, nervous systems or brains know 'we' exist. They don't even know *they* exist. That's only one reason why what's good and right for bodies/brains evolved by genes, for genes, is not good and right for us as evolving consciousness. See?

Heck, if I were talking about any other kind of control on your freedom - hypnosis, narcotics, a despotic ideology or some form of brainwashing - you'd be right with me on this. Well, those freedom inhibitors are all part of gene control. But because the mindless chemistry influencing your Real, conscious self also happens to be responsible for sex, reproduction, pride, vanity, competitiveness and ignorance, you'd rather carry on doing what genes want.

It's okay, I understand your resistance to ideas that question your assumed reason for living. Before I met Ed, I thought of myself as my body. I thought 'thinking' was what my brain did. Science said me and my brain are the same, and I went right along with that. When Ed told me consciousness is something 'Real' that exists in its own right, I thought it was just philosophical bullshit. To me, 'reality' began and ended with material things that I could get a hold of. And having him describe holy cows like falling in love and having kids as some kind of insidious control, everything in me resisted. Man, I did not want to hear it. The earth was flat and I liked it that way.

That stuff about small r reality and capital R Reality for instance. It sounds kind of stupid now, but he pointed to a spider. 'Think how much more meaning you see in everything than a spider does,' he said. That's because you're more conscious than a spider is, and yet that spider is just as convinced as you that its version of reality is as real as things ever get.' He meant there's a bigger reality than spiders know about, just as there's a bigger Reality than we know about, and the more conscious we become, the more of that bigger Reality we perceive.

Side note: It's hard to appreciate that there is a bigger Reality than you can perceive, or that some people can perceive it when you can't, but it's true. Two people can have vastly different views of the same things, simply because one has a more highly evolved consciousness. More about that later.

Sure, humans have evolved a bigger brain than spiders, but brains don't perceive reality - *consciousness* is what determines the contents of your reality. Brains are growing - evolving - all the time. In general terms, the bigger and more complex they get, the more consciousness they can accommodate…and the more reality that consciousness is able to perceive.

Even you must be able to appreciate that it isn't genes reading and understanding this. It's not a body built by genes, or the eyes built by genes, or even a brain built by genes. Without consciousness, all those biological components would amount to is a cadaver. For that reason I'm going to redefine 'life' itself by saying that without consciousness, nothing is 'alive'. (More about that later too. More about *everything* later.)

Before Ed, I never even heard about stuff like this. (I guess I was lucky in having parents who never tried to feed me the same lame-brain convictions they grew up with.) After my formative years spent inside a bubble of solitude picking over notions in magazines that I didn't really understand, Ed unlocked a few doors in my mind and turned on a few lights. Eventually I realized that without him, I might've gone my whole life cherishing a collection of short-sighted dogmas, prejudices and assumptions.

But once Ed opened my eyes, the problems began. The notion of seeing things for Real immediately seemed like a threat to everything I valued, by which I mean all of the things that genes built this body, nervous system and brain to value. Like you, maybe, I used to believe it was a kind of magic that brings two people together and causes the love thing and the sex thing, leads to kids and so on. To many folks those are holy institutions. Thanks to Ed, I came to realize that biology is neither magic nor holy. It's plain, dumb physics and chemistry. The incessant, nagging demands of bodies and brains 'feel' so overwhelmingly important, they have us convinced they must be right and necessary. 'Surely it can't be wrong if it feels so right!' And we're only too eager to pile moral, intellectual or religious arguments behind what hormones make us do.

TAPE 5

I guess it would be fair to say that despising his wife was Sheriff Hughes' hobby, and one he had plenty of opportunity to enjoy. After a hard day at the office he arrived home to meet a bow-wave of antagonism as she came into the kitchen holding her elbows protectively, ready for combat. Hughes pictured himself turning around and going straight out again to grab a bite at the diner, and was about to make the picture a reality when the front door slammed hard enough to shake the whole house. Footsteps ran up the stairs. Another door banged. The bass thump of rock music began pounding through the ceiling, then suddenly leapt in volume as the footsteps came back down the stairs.

Donna Hughes came into the kitchen without a word to anybody and threw open the refrigerator door, made her selection and disappeared. A moment later the door upstairs banged again, compressing the rock music to its bass vibration. Hughes whispered a profanity and went to the refrigerator. He took out a two-quart carton of milk and left the door open while he drank.

A white trickle bisected his chin and made him hunch over with his rump out, as if the carton was a saxophone, but too late for the drips to miss that much waistline.

The rock music leapt in volume again and a young woman's voice said, "She-*it!*" loudly and with feeling. The toilet flushed. Another door slammed.

Hughes' held a pinch of shirtfront away from his belly and looked down at it. "She-*it!*" he told the pinch. He could sponge it off but there'd be a wet mark to chill in the night air. God-*Jesus* that did it. He made up his mind to start a row he could ride out of the house on.

Right on cue the rock music ceased. Footsteps hammered down the stairs and the perfumed wraith of Donna Hughes would have passed through the kitchen in silence had she not become her father's excuse. When he stepped sideways to block her, she stopped, examining the plain white door of the closet beside her, a 'what the hell' set to her mouth.

"Where you goin'?"

Donna stared at the closet door.

"Took the Fifth, uh?"

"What's it to ya?"

"What's it to me is my house you're usin' like a motel. Hey! You listenin'? I won't be spoke to that way by a unpayin' guest, hear?"

She looked at him like he was an unpleasant accident. "So put me in jail."

"Now let me guess," he told her affectionately. "Some sleazeball is parked down the street, pickin' his nose and just waitin' to get in your panties, am I right?"

That was one step over the line for Catherine Hughes. "Jesus an' God in Heaven!" she fulminated.

It was the spark Hughes needed, but Donna had been in the crossfire too often to wait for peace to get declared. She slid past her father without stopping to tell them they were both crazy, because it would have made no difference, leaving Hughes slouched against the wall watching her neat backside until she was gone. Then he was gone too, leaving Catherine Hughes to watch the screen door swing shut and her husband's bulk fade into night, the color leaching out of his shirt as darkness filled the space where he'd been. She heard the cruiser start up, saw its red tail-lights float past the end of the driveway. Then she climbed the stairs, her bony fingers picking at each other's nails. From the open doorway of Donna's room she saw the shape of two bare feet cut out of talcum on the carpet, the glowing red eye of the stereo. Items of make-up were spread across the sheet that looked like a bad parachute landing. Suddenly Catherine Hughes needed to embrace martyrdom. It was that or self-recrimination, but she'd tried that and found it just didn't fit; she needed something for the less-fulfilled figure. It was time to unlock her bedside cupboard and commune with God through her illustrated bible, aided by her secret supply of holy vodka.

What I knew of Mrs. Catherine Hughes at that point would not have filled a small post-it note, and already I'd figured the wind had gone out of her and the Sheriff's marriage. Yet even people in unhappy relationships must have felt passion and desire for each other once. They must have told each other 'I love you' and meant it.

Why is love is so darned arbitrary and fickle? Because it's a million miles from the Real thing. Genetic love is about the day-to-day survival of these monkey suits, and the generation-to-generation transmission of their genes, both of which depend first and foremost on self-interest. Without that, there'd be nobody left to mix your genes with.

But I'm sidetracking myself. Actually I made this tape right after I talked with Mrs. Hughes in my car. As I watched her walk away I put the final touches to my Baptist story using one of Ed's books to rest my notepad on. That book was The Selfish Gene by Richard Dawkins, the famous British zoologist. Dawkins' book explains the science behind how selfishness came to figure in the lives of living organisms. You could say selfishness began when the single-molecule forerunners of today's DNA first began hooking up with each other. Then, as now, the attraction was no more about an idealized notion of eternal, undying, unselfish love than the attraction of the earth for a falling apple is. It was and is simply a result of mindless chemical interaction.

This same mindless chemical interaction is why we differentiate between people simply on the grounds of personal preference, genetic affiliation or hormonal whim. Well hey, even the dumbest animals are motivated by the same chemistry that we are. The big difference is, they're not capable of deluding themselves these chemical impulses are something more fanciful. The reason they don't call it love isn't because they're dumb animals who don't know any better. Fact is, we call it love because we're the dumb animals who don't know any better.

When Ed first explained that to me I laughed right in his face. I reasoned that our superior mind has taken our behavior into a whole other dimension than plain old gene replication. (I wasn't 'reasoning', I was indignant at the notion that me wanting kids was a result of chemistry making me selfish.) We were in a hot tub behind his cabin in the Rockies. It was snowing, I was a little drunk...Anyhow that was when he said selfishness isn't just about us looking out for ourselves, it also involves looking out for selected other people when we have something to gain for ourselves - like when we put our family before anyone else; even before ourselves sometimes.

Selfishness my ass! That sounded to me like the exact opposite.

Let's wheel Dawkins back in here. In his book The Selfish Gene he explains in great detail how genes, rather than ourselves or our relatives, are the real beneficiaries of selective selfishness. Because genes build bodies for no other reason than to replicate and reproduce genes, whatever you feel or imagine your motives are for giving you and your family priority over anyone else, you're actually doing it for your and their *genes*. Your family's genes are copies of your genes. The genes that built you are the same genes that built them. It's the future survival of those few *genes* that you're being so goddam selectively 'loving' for.

24

Disagree all you like lady, but you sure as hell know that when your and their health, wealth and happiness are threatened, you'll fight without mercy for your and their survival above anyone else's. You're blissfully unaware of the instincts and subconscious drivers manipulating you to prioritize people this way. You simply call it love.

Idiots and bigots aside, our intellect might tell us we're all equally valuable, but intellect ain't running genetic reality; it only imagines it is. Just like I imagined that hot tub in the Rockies. Truth is, Ed was fixing a flat on my medieval VW. It was late at night, and while he changed the wheel I was forced to listen to him explain this stuff with the kind of patience really smart people have. (Him being so smart sometimes made me angry because I felt inadequate.)

For instance I had to sit there and listen to him tell me about the common traits we all agree are 'bad' because they cause trouble for everybody: envy, greed, anger, resentment, jealousy, meanness, hyper-competitiveness, etc. Like I said upfront, we all experience these traits every day. We feel justified in having them because they help us survive as genetic vehicles. So even though we say these traits are bad, we make hypocritical excuses for them. We excuse our greed as 'getting what I need for MY survival.' Anger becomes 'ME being assertive for MYself.' Resentment decides 'an injustice has been committed against ME.' Revenge is 'ME getting justice for myself.' Jealousy turns into 'I want material equality for ME'. Ditto envy. We pretend our mean-mindedness is 'toughness' and kid ourselves it's admirable.

See what's really happening here? Self interest is telling us whether our behavior is 'good' or 'bad'. That's how 'good' and 'bad' come to depend on what we want, and can get away with. This is the self-interest that shaped our evolution. We've evolved a degree of cooperation, sure, but the survival of 'our' genes has remained our prime directive. Most times we only cooperate because of what we have to gain.

This is what created societies where some of us get to be more equal than others - that's what the freedom to compete in an open marketplace is all about. The better you are at competing, the better your survival chances. Instead of equality driven by kindness and compassion, we have inequality driven by survival. Our demand for the right to be free really means the right to be free to get what I can for ME and MINE, in a world where every other sucker is doing that. Worst of all, we go along with the tacit understanding that the inequalities in our genetic makeup create an automatic *right* to be unequal.

25

The competitive instinct keeping us unequal is programmed into bodies at gene level. So when, as part of this programming, self-interest causes friction, malice, divorce, murder, war or whatever, we nice ordinary folks don't feel responsible. No way Doris Day. We're just doing what we feel is our goddam right - looking out for ME & MINE first out of 'love'. Biomechanical components persuade us to compete on their behalf, and we go on doing it at the expense of our Real, conscious selves, or that much-talked-about but seldom seen thing, spirituality.

Speaking of which, didn't Jesus Christ say we should treat each other equally? There was no caveat about treating some people more equally just because they got the same genes we did. He meant unconditional equality for all, not your family first. Not selfishly prioritizing the people who don't even share any of your genes, but who you decided to mix yours with to create the next generation of your family.

Yes lady, I know - you can't help yourself. It's your hormones. Except that your 'can't help myself' attitude is what keeps the selfishness carousel going round. Ignorance is bad, but deliberate ignorance is stupid.

Ed showed me how, by allowing biology to dictate our priorities, we value all the wrong things in ourselves and each other. We conveniently ignore the fact that it's not some spiritual notion of love driving us to compete selfishly, often ruthlessly, for sexual partners, business opportunities, a bigger slice of whatever cake is on offer. And when we get those things, it's not spiritual love that makes us compete to keep them and get more of them, and in so doing create more greed, jealousy, envy, meanness, anger, resentment, misery, disharmony and dissatisfaction.

It's vital to remember that whether you're sitting in the bathtub, driving your car, or simply walking around in a monkey suit, each of those receptacles is just part of this material universe that surrounds the Real, conscious you. The monkey suit is a closer fit than your bathtub or your car, but don't be fooled - there's no magical, mystical difference between bathtubs, cars or monkey suits. Without the Real, conscious you, they and everything else are all just mindless molecular matter; nothing more than tools to help us evolve as consciousness. (Boy, even I'm getting tired of hearing me say that!)

And now you want to know all of the technical and scientific details of how an immaterial consciousness is able to occupy a material body and brain. How and why working through a material body puts major restrictions on consciousness. How those restrictions make us forget much of what we already learned before we got here, and all the rest of it. Well you're gonna have to wait. If I explained everything at once it would create a textual black hole and this book would disappear up its own ass, along with everything else in its gravitational field.

Okay then, smartass, so why do you think you're here? So mindless hormones can make you have babies? So you can bust your balls making money? Those stupid-level pastimes are just more examples of the Real, conscious you allowing yourself to be influenced by a mindless monkey suit. You're wired up tight to a bunch of urges and they're all screaming ME! ME! ME! They're swamping your awareness with instructions to strive for survival as a monkey: to eat, work, compete, have sex and all the rest of it.

'But surely I'll die if I don't?'

True enough. And while I could tell you that your conscious self - soul, spirit, call it what you like - is eternal, this is one of those things you only Really believe when you experience it personally. Until that happens, staying alive remains our most persistent urge. It's also why so many of us die before we should. The struggle we call life creates confusion, injustice, inequality and misery, yet we're the only ones making it this way. We've maybe heard there's a better afterlife, but DNA's 'here and now' life is so persuasive, we allow the monkey suit to control us.

In The Selfish Gene, Dawkins says that intelligent life comes of age when it discovers evolution. In a Star Trek movie somebody said intelligent life comes of age when it discovers warp drive. I've got a graduation saying of my own: You only come of age when you discover you're something infinitely more than a stupid monkey suit.

TAPE 6

Okay. Everybody knows there are genes for gayness, for criminality, for stupidity, etc., and that soon we'll be able to swap our 'flawed' genes for good ones and rebuild ourselves as perfect human beings, right? Sure it's bullshit, but people believe bullshit if it's scientific. Especially if those people also have a gene for believing bullshit.

This tape is about one of the rare times I persuaded Ed to come round my place for a trailer-home-cooked meal and we had sex - but only in a conversational sense. Even the meal was cooked in my mom's home, by her. Yes, I was trying to make an impression. My excuse for having him over was to help me write a genetic angle into my piece about the Baptists. I know this is one of the early tapes because I still had delusions about me and Ed doing something more interesting than talk. I sure didn't invite him round for a meal with wine so we could swap Bigfoot stories.

I had my midget tape recorder all ready, but old-fashioned Ed said I shouldn't write about genes if I didn't know what I was talking about. Fine by me. We'd finished eating and I figured we could now have 'dessert'. (We'd not had sexual congress up to this point in our relationship. Sustained eye-contact was as far as we'd gone.)

"Ed," I said, "we can talk about genes later. It's kind of heavy right after dinner."

"But Laurie, if you don't write your piece tonight…"

He was implying that I'd be too hungover in the morning. And then, suddenly, we were talking about God. With Ed these things just came up, don't ask me why.

Pouring more wine for myself I said, facetiously, "The old guy in the clouds?" I was thinking of that stuff on the Sistine Chapel ceiling, but what Ed had in mind was a version of God made from all of the consciousnesses in the universe, arranged in a hierarchy, the way corporations are. Sure he was serious. He said to picture this corporate hierarchy as being decided by how evolved each of its component parts is. The top executives of this corporate God would be the most conscious, exercising their influence from the top down - you know the way corporations are structured. He said if I didn't like that idea, the alternative is a universe determined entirely by chance. The Godless, soulless universe of science.

My response was that if scientists have hard evidence that everything happens by chance, why should I believe in a God that nobody ever saw? (I wasn't especially interested either way, I just felt combative. Well listen, I'd changed the sheets and everything. The bedroom still had a strange odor about it, but that's trailers, right?)

Ed put on his annoyingly calm smile for me. "So you think that because we don't see, smell, taste, hear or touch something, it can't exist? How about our thoughts and ideas? Don't they count as evidence?"

"'Hard' evidence. You left out the word 'hard'." I waited, wishing I were somebody else. Preferably somebody with a sex life.

"Thoughts and ideas are our mind outreaching the 'hard-evidence' of science," he insisted. "They're our way of handling immaterial things beyond senses that atoms and molecules - even those shaped into brains - have no way of perceiving."

While I tried not to think about that, he said that just because we can't see consciousness or ideas, that doesn't mean those things count for less than material things.

I refilled my glass. This could be a long night. I hoped it might get bumpy after Ed talked himself out - if I could last that long now he'd gotten onto how bodies are made from the same atoms that all of the 'dead' objects of this universe are made from - rocks, cars, computers; my dreams of getting laid. (I know what's kinda crude, but Jesus, I was only human.)

"Ed," I stopped him, for no other reason than being hormonally deranged. "Are you telling me our bodies are dead and we never knew?"

He laughed. "We don't say rocks, cars and computers are 'alive', yet their atoms are made from the same subatomic particles that our body and brain atoms are: protons, neutrons, electrons. Those particles don't change in some magical way just because they happen to be in human bodies and brains. What brings them to life for us is something uniquely extra - conscious awareness. Atoms are entirely 'mechanical'. Without consciousness, even the atoms and molecules in the phenomenally complex structure of a human brain would be part of the same essentially lifeless reality that rocks, cars and computers are.

But the reality of your mind, that's something entirely different. It's made from abstract concepts. Your consciousness turns those concepts into your *reasons* for being alive. It creates a reality of *ideas* about material things, beyond the reality made *from* material things. This unique ability puts consciousness a whole series of quantum jumps above materiality in the realness stakes."

You ever tried feeling horny with somebody who talks like that?

Donna Hughes, walking beside an empty highway at night with only the cold wind and her thoughts for company, was on her way to The Golden Triangle Bar & Grill, a mile or so outside of Passmore. She was going to meet a guy fourteen years older than her. He'd expect her to buy his drinks in exchange for the privilege of getting laid in his pickup. He'd stink of beer, tobacco smoke and bad personal hygiene. Know the scenario? Lucky you.

Donna grimaced and watched her breath drift off into the night, telling herself there were better things than all of that mechanical sex stuff. People only went through those motions because they couldn't control a bunch of stupid urges, and Donna knew all about those. Her expressive features grew a pained look now because those notions just stirred up the bottom-mud inside her. She'd arrive at The Triangle with a face that refused to smile, and be forced to rely on...

Jesus! Now she was having those crazy 'robot' thoughts again, imagining her body as a kind of automaton with a mess of mechanical parts underneath, kind of like the terminator. She felt herself watching from inside of it right now as it walked along in the dark without her help, while the real Donna, in her mind, was thinking these thoughts. She didn't know how this weird notion had gotten into her head, yet there were times when her real self looked in the mirror at her body and imagined it really did belong to a stranger she didn't much like. When the robot got a sniff of something it wanted, those powerful urges took over, and she found herself feeling and doing stuff she hated. Some of those things made her disgusted with herself.

A car sped by, buffeting her with its slipstream. She caught the tail end of a whoop and watched its rear lights grow smaller. She pushed the hair away from the robot's face and sucked in a long breath of the cool night air. She'd never heard of anybody thinking about themself this way, but the fact was she was fed up of being controlled by this - she looked down at her legs and her feet - this *dummy!*

She could hear the music trapped inside The Triangle even before she rounded the bend in the road and saw, beyond the familiar black tree-shapes, the glowing yellowy-red sign criss-crossed by telephone wires. Her stomach jumped at the sight. Up ahead the neon buzzed while the low building undulated towards her, the faulty G tube making the sign read 'olden Triangle'. She passed the same old queue of beer crates and garbage cans, a few parked pickups.

Her footsteps sounded hard on the road, then softer on the dirt out front, echoing back at her in counterpoint to the country music seeping out, brash as the glaring neon. And she realized there was something strange about tonight. This was the first time she'd really thought about the robot thing for more than a few moments, and now she couldn't get it out of her mind. For all that she disliked what her body made her do, the robot was a kind of protective shell in places like The Triangle. She just went on autopilot and let it do its thing.

Except that tonight was different. It felt as though she was about to walk in The Triangle as her other self: the shy, desperately uncertain Donna. And she was scared.

30

A few dark miles away there was I, gazing at one of Ed's books that lay open on my kitchen table. The book had a spaghetti worm dried hard on the page next to: *Plato*. Yep, a philosophy tome, dense enough to stop a nuclear blast. I'd been flipping through in search of pictures and found that famous inscription from the Temple of Apollo at Delphi (in Greece, Europe): *Know Thyself*. Plato, the ancient Greek philosopher, ascribed that saying to The Seven Wise Men - also Greek - each of who contributed a wise saying. (I guess the wise women in those days kept their mouth shut.)

I'd gone in my kitchenette out of frustration and was taking slow, deep breaths with my nose in the wineglass. It's called rebreathing; you're meant to use a paper bag, but did you ever try drinking wine from a paper bag? Okay.

Then Ed appeared beside me, examining the spaghetti worm. "'Think you know yourself?"

"Intimately," I said. It was more than he did. Becoming petulant now, I went back to the table and pushed my picked-over plate aside, re-refilled my glass and turned on the TV out of habit, determined not to listen to Ed explain all of that stuff about how I was actually just a collection of biomechanical parts that evolved so genes could replicate and reproduce themselves. Well heck, that would've been enough for most guys!

"But Laurie," he droned on, "biology is just hardware. Where's your real, conscious self in all of that?"

I nearly asked why didn't he come inside and find out, but even I'm not that unsubtle. Besides, I guess Ed was talking dirty enough for us both with that replicating and reproducing stuff.

Inside The Triangle, Donna struggled to reconcile her real self, in her mind, with her robot body. She felt as if the wires had come loose between her and it, so her robot body was no longer within her control. Its heart pumped faster. The skin tightened across its face. Its nipples clenched and she felt it shiver, suddenly wanting the ladies' room, feeling nauseous.

As this disjointed Donna stood, uncertain and exposed, a hand traced the shape of her buttock. She turned to look into Jeff Ackerley's face.

"Go get me a beer," was all he said.

The only person Donna had ever been in The Triangle was the street-smart Donna. Now there was no fearless body language, only a freshly peeled vulnerability as she crossed the floor, aware of turning heads and scavenging eyes. She felt like she'd hot-wired a stranger as the counter met her ribs and she looked around for the barkeep, the heat and color seeping up her neck and into her face. Donna Hughes, blushing! This was another first.

And then a face new to Donna came down the business side of the counter. He was young, real good looking and athletic - all the things the other Donna would have come on to. To confuse matters, unlike most of the guys she got checked-out by in here, he was looking at her eyes.

"What can I get for you?" Nice and friendly.

"Two beers...thankyou kindly."

She sensed a body behind her and found Jeff studying the new barman with dark interest.

"You know him?"

"Huh?" Donna played innocent and hung on his arm until their beers arrived. She studied her reflection in the mirrored tiles in back of the bar, saw Donna the Triangle regular. Everybody knew who and what she was. Tonight, the only person who didn't know Donna was herself.

By now Ed and me were beyond foreplay and into the hard-core. According to him, the notion that we can re-create little copies of ourselves when we reproduce is just more delusion. All we do is contribute half the chemical instructions for building another gene replicating facility. (A body.) Some of the genes we contribute never actually did anything for us; they came from our grandparents or their parents and just sat around inside us waiting for the next bus out. Even the few genes we do pass on get so shuffled and recombined every-which-way with some other sucker's genes, the idea that they can somehow reproduce the person we are is nuts.

"Ed," I told him, "if you're so smart, why'd you only bring one bottle?" I intended getting so loaded I no longer cared about the sex thing. I gave him a glazed look and drained the last of my wine, wondering if I'd ever get to be part of this reproducing business.

He held up the empty bottle and shook his head. "Around twenty-five thousand genes."

"Huh?"

"That's all you get to build an entire body complete with a nervous system and a brain - the works. After half of those build your body, the rest have to organize the one hundred *billion* cells of your nervous system, most of which are in your brain. Those cells need to form countless *trillions* of link-ups to work efficiently."

"Meaning?" I faked a yawn, imagining other things I could be faking.

32

"Meaning you can't pass on a copy of your personality to your offspring through genetic inheritance - just a few stock physiological similarities, a predisposition for some diseases, stuff like that. You might pass on the odd behavioral trait, but recreating a copy of yourself? Forget it. We're all individuals, shaped by a lifetime of unique personal experience, and that's even before you factor in experiences gathered from *previous* lives…"

Margin Note: Reincarnation is no weirder than creationism, *and* it makes a whole lot more sense, but we'll get to that on a later tape.

"So how d'you account for kids acting like their parents?" (What I meant was, why don't we just go in the bedroom, undress each other and see what happens next?)

He shrugged. "Kids only mimic parental behavior by observation. Their own unique mind is constantly absorbing sensory information and incorporating it into their mental and behavioral repertoire. Naturally some will pick up their parents' mannerisms, attitudes and what have you. Above all of that, though, their developing minds are copying one thing first and foremost."

"The Simpsons."

"Nearly right. They're copying how to survive as an organism built by genes, for genes. They're being indoctrinated into the thinking and behavior patterns of a society that evolved around, because of, and for, the genetic replication and reproduction process."

Wow!

The Triangle was crowded now, loud with music and voices, hot with bodies. While Jeff Ackerley leaned on her shoulder, arguing vehemently with somebody through a hailstorm of spittle and expletives, Donna was wishing there was someone she could talk to about how she felt. All that Jeff cared about was, did they go outside now, or get on the outside of a few more beers first? But the real Donna didn't want to go outside, not now and not later. She'd had enough of being used, by Jeff Ackerley or anyone else.

In desperation she turned to look through the smoke for the barkeep. Just seeing him and his relaxed movements, his calm, open face, made her feel better. It was not a sexual thing, just kind of nice. For one magic moment she was oblivious to Jeff watching her, resentment tightening his mouth, the vein in his forehead standing out like a safety valve ready to blow.

With no warning he reached out and took her wrist in a grip so fierce, Donna dropped the bottle. She resisted and stood her ground just long enough to make the point before letting herself be pulled across the room. Triangle regulars had gotten used to Donna being taken outside. Hell, some of them had taken her outside themselves. Even so, Donna was shocked that this could still happen despite being the exact opposite of what she wanted. But she went. In the front of his pickup, with the mixed odor of beer, tobacco-smoke and Jeff's unwashed body filling the robot's nostrils, the real Donna stared into the darkness and assured herself and the robot that this would never happen to either of them again.

TAPE 7

Willie Stevenson was fixing his ancient Camaro, lying under it with his legs protruding when he heard a car pull up at the street-end of the driveway. A door snicked open, footsteps approached and stopped to let Willie see black boots below cop's pants.

"Looks like a real nasty accident," Hughes' voice said. "You still alive, boy?"

'Even dead I'd be more alive than you, shithead,' Willie thought, watching the feet and legs amble to the front porch and disappear up the steps.

On the porch Hughes removed his hat and peered through the screen. He saw no sign of life, but counting Willie's wreck there were three cars in the driveway so that meant everybody was home - or bits of them were. The Mayor's voice was because it had gotten him over here, and he'd just seen Willie's legs. That left all of Maxine's parts. Hughes rubbed the side of his nose with his hat-brim and ambled around to the rear of the house.

The Mayor was the kind of person who abraded you down the phone wire, then did it all over again when you got round there. He started in on Hughes before he was all the way in the house.

"'They brought it on themselves!'" He shot the Sheriff a look of disbelief. "This is - an' I quote - 'As told to our reporter by Mrs. Catherine Hughes, a Passmore resident and wife of local Sheriff Neil Hughes.' Readin' further - now tell me if you recognize this quote: 'We don't want folks outside thinking we got us a color problem here.'"

The Mayor waited for some sign of contrition, but Hughes just stood there examining his knuckles while the tip of his tongue rescued morsels of breakfast from between his teeth.

"As if some boys bustin' up a religious meetin', rapin' a young white woman and beatin' the holy crap out of some black kid was not enough, we got the
34

Sheriff an' his wife writin' about it for our God-damn local funny paper!" He turned The Star around and held it aloft to make the point.

Hughes pushed a hand through his hair and hid behind his supercilious grin. "Hey now listen, Bobby - "

But Stevenson was not done. He'd yet to reach the best part. "No Neil, you listen. 'Sheriff Hughes was not at liberty to divulge the identity of the victims, but admitted that knowing who did it ain't so important as that we're out there lookin' for 'em.' Jesus, Deputy Dawg would be proud of that line!"

Hughes, trying to retain his dignity, said, "Let me see that there..."

The Mayor ignored him. "Now what do you intend doin' about this business?"

Hughes slid his wide backside into a too-dainty-for-comfort rustic chair that matched the other dainty rustic chairs that in turn matched the paper-rack and the breadcrock and almost matched the plastic veneer on the kitchen-units. Looking like a bear on a kiddy-seat he eyed The Star, then raised an eyebrow in a question mark.

"Come on now, Bobby, that ain't nothin'. You know The Star, just gettin' folks fired up as per usual." The facile grin said he was taking this thing as lightly as he did everything else.

"God-Jesus Sheriff! As if this problem wasn't enough, when their reporter brings up this town's ancient history, guess who tells her: 'The Mayor would bust a gut for us to go rakin' over those cold ashes because it don't make anybody look good.'? Just when everybody had forgot that business."

Everybody but Hughes. Two years earlier, as he'd stood and watched the home of that local family burn to the ground, he'd known it was a clear case of arson. The perpetrator was still at large - as yours truly had reminded him. The fact that Sheriff Hughes knew exactly who torched the house seemed irrelevant to their present problem, but it would soon offer a solution.

Lying on her bed upstairs almost directly above the two men, Maxine, the Mayor's wife, could hear their conversation as a meaningless hum. She was resting between thoughts, letting her fingers explore her abdomen like echo-locators, imagining she could sense the emptiness inside her.

She got up and let herself be drawn to the three-faced chiffonier mirror to compare herself in each of its faces. Leaning close to look into a hazel-eyed reflection, she examined a fine cleavage, the delicate freckles set off by her pale green satin slip. Posed this way, her belly concealed by the underhang of satin, hips narrowed by perspective, she almost liked what she saw.

Now I'm opening this Window on Reality to reveal Maxine's secret: a lack of functioning ovaries and the fruits thereof. All that Maxine had was an unloving Mayor for a husband and an unsatisfying affair with Sheriff Hughes. What she wanted was the one thing she couldn't have: a baby. Like you (and me at that time), Maxine believed that wanting a baby was entirely her idea.

This brings me back to Ed's 'Whose idea is reproduction anyhow' angle, which was another reason why I dumped him for being too right.

"Aren't you even just a little bit curious," he asked, "about a mechanism without mind or sentience that forces you to participate in a chemical process under the delusion that it's all your idea?"

I had to admit that no, I wasn't curious. But this was Ed, remember - the guy who made reproduction sound like a crime, and me feel like an accomplice.

"You're happy to let some mindless mechanism decide that all of this should happen to you?"

"Hell Ed, don't you know reproduction is an instinct?" I told him.

"And what is instinct? Something that happens without knowing it's happening, like avalanches and meteor storms. Where's your conscious free will while this instinct is running?"

I tried a different tack. "Okay, so maybe it's all God's idea. You remember - 'Go forth and multiply'?"

He assured me that genetic organisms never needed encouragement from God; evolution made sure that multiplying was their favorite sport a few billion years before simple minds came up with the notion of God. He advised me to quit revering reproduction as sacred, reminding me how the cold, mechanical physics laws in back of biology create physical needs, urges, inclinations and preferences. He did a real good job of making what I always thought was the most human behavior sound like a computer program.

But he was right. Laws of physics are just a bunch of don't-give-a-damn atoms and couldn't-care-less molecules. And I'm telling you this so you'll see what Ed tried to make me see: The crazy notion of somebody called God wanting us all to go forth and multiply is hokum. We're meant to differentiate between what genes make us do, and what our Real, conscious self should be doing…otherwise there's just no point in being *able* to differentiate.

Our consciousness is the only part of us that can be called genuinely human because it's all that amounts to something more than mindless components; the only force in the entire universe that can operate outside of physics laws.

Side Note: The reason why some of this book sounds anti-human is because, after countless generations as vehicles for genes, we've made sex, romantic love, kids and families the end in itself. It's no easy task to recognize that we're pure consciousness, just passing through this material level of 'reality' in our evolution as something infinitely more than material.

In fact you're probably stuck so deep in the 'sex, romance, kids and families' rut, your response to this will be: 'Okay, what's so goddam special about being more consciously aware anyhow?' Well I'll tell you. Unlike anything else you've got in material reality, you get to take your conscious awareness with you when you check out…

TAPE 8

As conscious beings, the genetic process isn't our birthright, it's our burden, and we insult ourselves by succumbing to mechanical urges that tempt us into willing submission for genes just because we enjoy the sensations. So maybe now's the time to unzip your genes down to their molecules so you know exactly what we're dealing with.

A human body is made from a thousand billion cells. Floating around amongst the old tires, rusting bedframes and sewage in the center of each cell is the stuff genes are made from. (It has the initials DNA, which is lucky because deoxyribonucleic acid would take my mom a week to pronounce.)

DNA is a long, complicated twin chain of molecules called a double helix. These two chains of molecules - nucleotides - are joined by hydrogen bonds, okay? The nucleotides pair up all the way along the DNA stairway in an arrangement called base pairs, coiled around each other in the shape of those spiral stairways people put in arty loft-conversions. The twin backbones of this structure are made from sugar phosphate molecules called 'deoxyribose'. (I guess they're still working on sugar-free ones.)

In a double helix there are three thousand million nucleotides, but only four different kinds. Their initials are A, T, C and G. These bases pair up all the way along the DNA spiral. A always pairs with T, C always pairs with G. You might get A-T, then C-G, then G-C, followed by T-A, and so on. I'll throw in the full names of these four bases for free. A is Adenine, T is Thymine, C is Cytosine, and G is Good Golly Miss Molly.

Okay, so you were just resting your eyelids. G is for Guanine. A, T, C and G are actually proteins, and those three thousand million paired A-T, C-G bases contain our genes. The way those bases are arranged along the spiral stairway decides the genetic code - the genome. Practically every living organism on this planet has its very own personalized genome. (My mailman looks like he inherited a few lizard genes. Boy, he's weird!)

Here's the most important part. In a process called *mitosis,* the entire double helix splits right down the middle. Mitosis happens when your body's cells (with these DNA double helixes in their center) divide, some every few days. Now hey, when cells divide, the DNA spiral ladders - the genome - in the cells, divides also, as if somebody sawed all the way down through the rungs. This leaves two gaping halves, each with millions of those bases (A, T, C and G) just hanging there without a partner. But that's okay because each half then re-pairs itself by picking up new bases from spares already floating around in the cell, and it sticks these onto itself in the right A-T, or C-G sequence. So you get a whole lot of new double helixes, each containing the instructions for building a complete and exact version of you, the physical jerk. That was mitosis. But in *meiosis…*

You still out there? Anybody? *Mom?*

What the hell. In meiosis we're dealing with the sex cells in testes and ovaries…and suddenly you're interested. But unlike ordinary cells that divide in two, sex cells divide into four. Imagine the double helix ladders inside these sex cells splitting down the middle and half way along each side, so the coded sequence for building a physical jerk is now in four quarters, each with a quarter of the code from some body's double helix. This is real complicated stuff that I don't care to go into so late at night, but it's what decides whether you'll become male or female.

I had to lie down with ice-cubes on my face after reading up on that stuff. (The ice-cubes were in a martini.) For any kids reading, here's a Disneyfied version of how genes originally began replicating. (They're bound to make me delete the Disney reference, then they'll go make the movie and I won't get a mention.) They'll cast somebody from the Arnie Schwarzenegger school of drama as one of the very first big replicator molecules. He'll be swimming around in the primeval soup, and whenever he finds a smaller, body-building nucleotide that'll pair up with one of his, he'll grab it and go, "Hey you little mother, stick with me and we'll take over the world."

No problema…except one. Ever since those early days, DNA molecules have been splitting in two during mitosis. Each half has re-paired with more

38

nucleotides in the correct sequence and made a complete new DNA molecule the way I described. And yet - ah-ha! - just occasionally tiny mistakes occur, and we get an inaccurately copied DNA molecule.

These mistakes happen because imperfections are a working part of evolution, life, you, and everything that exists. Whether you believe life happened by chance or was created by God, absolute perfection would be sterility. No change. The Real concept of perfection actually contains imperfections. Sounds paradoxical, but who said perfection had to be perfect? And anyhow, without imperfections how would we recognize the concept of perfection, or feel a need to strive for it? (Am I talking too much? Just say.) All chemical interaction is a function of this inbuilt imperfection, so genes have to adapt their replicating to accommodate imperfections.

But let's lighten up and talk about cancer, bright red hair, and folks who don't listen when you talk to them - just some of the consequences of genes messing up when they copy themselves inside people. (Hey you carrot-tops, just kidding. Some people think bright red hair is perfectly normal, hokay?)

Seriously, genetic replication is such a hyper-complicated process at microbiological level that wrenches do sometimes get in the works. In three billion separate bits of genetic information on a human genome, that's serious. Every minute of your DNA-life, hundreds of those delicate A-T, C-G bases on the genome get damaged. Most of these errors are corrected when the genomes split and reform during mitosis. But when a mistake isn't corrected by mitosis, we call it a *mutation*.

Just here your genes would be wetting their pants if they could read, because sometimes, instead of causing cancer or red hair, a mutation gets built into the next generation and improves things. That's how evolution happens. I have a sneaking suspicion that some mutations might be important in another way also. Why? Because wrongly copied genes could help to force rightly copied genes to work even harder to compensate. For instance, without mutated genes that cause cancer, genes that fight cancer wouldn't have needed to evolve…kind of thing.

Remember this is a mega-complicated process, in a world where so many different influences are coming at us all the time. Mother Nature doesn't just select for something, she also selects against things. With that in mind, think what would happen if we sent the micro-biological equivalent of the Special Forces into the human genome to blast all mutations. There'd be no downsides left for nature to select upsides to fight against. Not only would

Mother Nature think it safe to quit fighting, she'd lose the ability to fight anything unexpected.

What do I know? I'm no gene expert (mine are all faded to hell and ripped around the knees), but I can see that even the simple-seeming 'improvements' we make to genes will have consequences we can't foresee. We might have a long time to regret our haste, or we could wind up following the dinosaurs.

So there you are. It's because genes constantly modify bodies and brains in response to countless little influences that what we have now, instead of genes still floating mindlessly around in the primeval soup-de-jour, replicating themselves stupid, is genes floating mindlessly around inside 'you', replicating themselves, stupid. 3½ billion years of this mindless replicating caused protective membranes called cells to evolve around the DNA molecules. Those membranes gradually got tougher and more specialized, and became skins containing whole sub-continents of cells, in bodies with nerve networks that feel, hear, see, smell and taste, along with even later and more specialized nerve cells called brains to process those senses more efficiently.

I'll skip the details because I was out of town while this was happening, but when I got back, some of DNA's genes had bunched together in the shape of a durable yet delicate robot that some guy named Burroughs called the *soft machine*, made from bone, flesh, skin, blood, implants and drugs.

(Excuse me a second.) Hey! You in Poughkeepsie with the stupid grin. This is not funny. We're talking DNA - people win Nobel Prizes for this stuff!

TAPE 9

They don't give prizes for the kind of stuff I wrote in The Star. An emetic, maybe. Boy, the outsize ego of my ambition was so sick of being stuck in that shrunken-head of a job, I woke up mornings with a hangover when I hadn't even been drinking. Most mornings I didn't bother waking up. I still went in the office though.

It was that kind of a morning when I wrote my piece for the paper's previous issue proclaiming JOHN THE BAPTIST IN BRAWL. I'd decided not to build genes into the story; I didn't have the copy space. I settled instead for a few colorful lines peppered liberally with words like MAYHEM, RELIGION and RAPE. It wasn't the first time that particular trinity had shared the same bed. Now I needed an equally piquant follow-up for my Escape Portfolio. I was desperate to transplant my act to some metropolis or other - Manhattan, LA, Frisco. The Sargasso Sea would've been an improvement on Raiment County. (The Sargasso Sea is a mess of weed out in the Atlantic Ocean where eels breed, 'kay?)

Talking of eels, I figured that maybe a closer look at the Baptists would yield my next story. Checking around I discovered when their next session was scheduled, and so, a couple of days later, I drove out to the church thinking this was no time of year to be standing around in rivers just to be close to God. It could lead to a face to face meeting. But religious folks can be real determined. They lean on your doorbell for hours.

Ever see an outdoor baptism? I had me a grandstand view of this one from the church parking lot and barbecue area. I guessed John was the black guy standing thigh-deep in the river in his black pants, white shirtsleeves rolled to the elbow, eyes aimed heavenward as, one at a time, the men and women - I admit some were black and some white, yet none anywhere near naked except under their clothes - waded into the murky brown swirl to get dunked. There was no frenzied activity or rolling eyes and groans of ecstasy. Nothing you'd be scared to let the kids watch on TV. (They wouldn't have been interested - there was no sex, violence or profanity.)

Then I had the totally crazy notion that maybe there was copy in raising a few goose-bumps of my own. It meant getting religion for all of thirty seconds but I could handle that. My generous employer would recompense me for the cost of removing the river-stains from my jeans. (Like fun!) So, trying to appear religiously inconspicuous, I stumbled down the embankment and insinuated myself into the group of as-yet unbaptized. Already I was freezing cold and wild horses were dragging me, but nobody batted a lid when I took my turn and felt that private shock of cold water where the light of day seldom sets foot as the river crept up my, uh, well I guess it's okay to say ass - it is in the Bible.

I had my mini tape-recorder with me - it goes wherever I go - but I couldn't just walk in there waving it in John the Baptist's face. Religion requires subterfuge. With no pockets in my shirt I had to - don't laugh - insinuate the recorder inside my bra. I figured that clasping my bosom real tight during immersion would keep things dry, but boy, when I resurfaced I looked like I had me a boob job and one of my implants had gone tectonic.

So that was my baptism. I still didn't understand just what had gotten Mrs. Hughes and the Baptist beaters so annoyed. All I learned was that John was predicting the coming of a messiah, but so what? I figured Baptist ministers felt traditionally obliged to do that. You know - 'He who comes after me, whose shoes I'm not fit to undo, He'll baptize the generation of vipers' and all of that stuff. It's right there in the Gospels. God was 'Getting set to purge the ground and gather His wheat, to burn the chaff in that fire.'

Okay, so you're not familiar with the New Testament. Neither was I. Discounting those childhood bible readings with Mrs. Samson in that musty old chapel in my home town, I'm probably the least religious person you ever read about. But now I had me a follow up story to my Baptist piece I thought it would be a real smart idea to do a Second Coming send-up, and I began planning that as I drove to Ed's, soaking wet and ready for a hot bath and a big whiskey to warm me up. Under the banner: MESSIAH TO STAGE COMEBACK, I'd build my follow-up story around the minister's actual words, with my baptism - *from your on-the-spot reporter* - adding credibility. Folks in my unwashed neck of the woods were gonna eat it up.

I told Ed about it while he filled his tub for me, then I sent him off to get the whiskey, closed the bathroom door, stripped and climbed in, and boy did that water feel good. I laid back and called through closed eyes: "Hey professor, where's my medicine?" I knew he wouldn't come in the bathroom. Not Ed.

"Right here."

I opened my eyes to find him standing beside me with the whiskey. "You decent?"

"Jesus Ed, you're supposed to ask that before you come in!"

The guy was aggravatingly unfazed. Well sure I tried to console myself with the thought that he'd been around and seen most things, but I still felt kind of stupid trying to cover my modesty while simultaneously accepting the drink. And would he go away? Would he hell. He stayed right there in the bathroom, slouched by the window, going on about some crazy thing or other. (Naturally I recall what it was because I'm writing this book.) It was about how our brain doesn't create our mind.

I'll say one thing for Ed - he never, and I mean ever, talked about trivial things. He'd do anything to avoid having a normal conversation. And yes, I admit that this brain/mind argument is actually a very big deal.

Ed was arguing against all of the world's neuroscientists (that's brain scientists to you) who insist that our brain is what creates our mind. But that, according to Ed, is like saying light is the objects it illuminates. (Think on it for a week or two.)

42

Anyhow there I was, hunkered down in a kind of fetal cringe, willing him to leave, and it was simply to offset my embarrassment that I said, real nonchalantly, "Uh, okay, so how come MRI scans show different parts of brains lighting up when somebody's thinking?" (In fact I called them atomic scanning machines and edited MRI in later - what did I know?)

"Magnetic resonance imaging doesn't prove brain activity makes consciousness," he said. "Couldn't it be the other way around? Couldn't brain activity just as easily be a consequence of conscious activity?"

Time-out: Even scientists admit that nobody understands consciousness. But in the next breath they say brains make it. Fact is, they just don't know.

So let's get this thing clear. For brains to make consciousness implies that tiny amounts of chemicals and electricity can understand and appreciate the same things we do, in the same way we do.

Imagine that - biochemical machinery sharing your hopes, dreams and aspirations. If you knew what chemicals and electricity actually are and how they work, you'd understand how nutty that notion is.

Brains are exactly like computers in that their components are entirely material. They're nothing but atoms. (Yes, atoms reduce to smaller components, and down at quantum levels those components behave very weirdly. But weird behavior in fundamentally mindless bits of matter does not create consciousness. Besides, up here on the atomic level of reality we live in, the weirdness disappears altogether.)

No matter how small or complicated the behavior of these components in brains, it's no more mystical than minute nuts and bolts fitting together, no more magical than switches being tripped or levers being pulled to adjust the tiny amounts of electricity and chemicals in the interactions.

Right. So atoms can't think; they can't know what they're doing, or how, or why. Or what the consequences are gonna be. Or what those consequences might mean to somebody who's conscious, okay?

Okay. So what Ed was saying is, our hopes, dreams and aspirations have to be made from fundamentally different stuff than material components, otherwise how could we know there was a difference between our conscious hopes, dreams and aspirations, and the material things we hope *for*, dream *about*, and aspire *to*?

He even went one better and said hopes, dreams and aspirations are *more* real than material things, because material things can't think about themselves, whereas we can.

Anyhow I finished my whiskey, and what did Ed do? He came over and took the empty glass right out of my hand. He was pretty good about it though - he managed to get an eyeful whilst giving the impression it was nothing to write home about. Boy, I never did understand that guy.

TAPE 10

Mayor Stevenson and Sheriff Hughes were sitting in the Sheriff's cruiser on the back-road between Rosewall and Passmore, surrounded by rolling hills of beech and sugar-maple, sycamore and cedar. Beyond these hills, banks of faded-blue mountains were misty in the morning light. It was not sunny light; those blue mountains were sullen under an overcast sky the color of exhaust emissions. The Mayor rolled down the window and sniffed the cool pungency of moist earth and dew-laden greenery, angry at having to come all the way out here for some privacy. Even on the rare days when Maxine wasn't at the Mayoral residence, you could bet Willie would be sneaking around someplace. At the Sheriff's office was DeSoto, his ears like grain-chutes. And the Sheriff's own family were at his house, though the Mayor didn't like going there; something about the atmosphere. Nor could you stand in the street and talk, for the same reason you couldn't sit in a car at the roadside and do it: people walking by were just so damn nosey. Usually they'd stop with the excuse of talking about the abundance of dog-mess on the sidewalk when they'd just stepped on the only turd in Raiment County. Or to ask when was somebody gonna come and tow away the truck that had been rusting to a series of bright red holes right there on the lot next to Calhoun's house? Except these days they'd want to know what was being done about the Baptist attack.

Stevenson narrowed his chestnut-brown eyes, his unhappy gaze lost somewhere in the misty distance. In his mind's eye he saw the headline of The Star shouting MESSIAH TO STAGE COMEBACK. He felt the kind of weariness that usually came later in the day. He looked at Hughes' profile for a clue to where the conversation might begin.

"Folks need to see somethin' constructive come out of this trouble, Neil." He pictured the single-parent mother of the assaulted girl, her eyes sharp and dangerous as she reminded him that people didn't have enough paid work to keep them out of trouble. She and her big mouth would both be making it known loudly that she was looking for a quick result. The black kid's people would too, whoever they were.

44

As the Mayor turned back to gaze into the distance, the scent of the morning reached into a corner of his memory and reminded him of a happier time in his life so far back it was practically imaginary: a scene from the times he and Maxine shared before her plumbing problem engineered a rift between them. Of walking together in these hills one fall, kicking leaves like kids. Suddenly all choked up, he realized these memories usually stayed buried deep in his subconscious. And then he thought of the landfill, of all things, and instantly channeled his aggravation into the knowledge that he had a son who wouldn't take his advice and go join the army, and would instead probably shame him by taking a job on the landfill that would come to Passmore if he, the Mayor, had anything to do with it, objectors or no. For reasons of re-election he hadn't yet made it clear which side of the landfill argument he supported, nor would he until the last minute. But hell, even the idea of having somebody else's garbage dumped in their backyard would seem appealing when folks started taking home a wage again.

At length he said, "It has to go right, dammit, else things could get more out of hand than they already are." After another strung-out pause he added, "I guess I don't know exactly who I want to blame most - the boys who roughed-up the Baptists, the Baptists theirselves, or that preacher fella." He stole a look at Hughes, hoping this conversation wouldn't all be one-sided. "You got an opinion, or do I get to carry this thing all by myself?"

Hughes rolled his head in the Mayor's direction, a sly curl on the smirk. "Seems like you just put your finger right on it, Bobby." The Sheriff watched Stevenson through half-closed eyes, awaiting a request for enlightenment.

But Stevenson was too impatient for games. "What the hell you talkin' about?"

Hughes gazed out through the windshield and tried to look worldly-wise. "Seems to me none o' this here circus would've gotten on the road without John the goddam Baptist stirrin' folks up with his Bible talk, an' he's still out there doin' it." Again he waited, knowing the Mayor was driving himself, and expecting him to run alongside at the same pace. Well shit on that.

But Stevenson was thinking along the same lines. The real mischief had come out of that preacher's mouth. Hughes was right. Nobody would've gotten themselves raped if that preacher had not attracted so much attention to the Baptists. The good ol' boys with baseball sticks were not to blame; they were only reacting with the same annoyance everybody felt. That was the only way they knew how to protest against what they saw as blasphemy.

Stevenson felt his chin and realized that he'd neglected to shave that morning. Blasphemy, sure. Well hey, that Second Coming piece in The Star was more blasphemy. He shut his eyes, took a slow, unsteady breath, then let it out in a long, quiet sigh, after which he flicked a sideways glance at Hughes, who was picking at his teeth with a matchstick.

"Okay, so it's all down to the preacher - so what now?"

Hughes reached for the doorhandle and shoved the door with his foot until it stayed open. With his hand up on the outside of the roof he looked at Stevenson's ear and said, "No preacher, no problem." Then he got out of the cruiser, hitched up his pants, tucked his shirt in, breathed deeply of the damp morning air, cleared his throat and stretched his arms. He considered the notion that John the Baptist might comfortably absorb the blame for everything that had happened. Even his own wife would probably sanction such a conclusion. All he had to do now was complete the sale to Stevenson, and today would have gotten off to a satisfactory start.

The Mayor got out of the cruiser and stood with his arm across the roof so he could continue looking out to where the blue mist on the mountains merged with the sky.

"Neil, I said - "

"Hey, Bobby, I'm thinkin' on it, 'kay?"

"Well just make sure you're not thinkin' on anything that could cause more trouble. He's still a church minister, even if he has gotten derailed some. I know your style Neil."

Despite Hughes' thick skin, Stevenson could see that being torn off a strip had gotten through. There was a new hardness about Hughes' eyes. Even his eternal grin seemed frozen onto his mouth.

Presently Hughes said, "Give me credit for somethin'. I wasn't fixin' to go lynch anybody."

"Keep in mind he didn't infringe any law as such," the Mayor said.

No he didn't, thought Hughes, and that's why somebody's gonna have to infringe one for him.

A moment passed by in silence save for the call of birds and the sound of Hughes' boot making circles in the dirt.

The Mayor looked over at him and said with care, "Well I'm countin' on you to do whatever is necessary…as the law." Then he blew through his nose and turned his attention back to a panoramic scene so free of blemish, it might never have felt the hand of man. A more capable gardener than he'd ever be had created that vista, its forms and colors, so perfectly it didn't even need tending - until that same hand of man went in there and messed things up.

He knew the landfill wouldn't affect any of that beauty, sited where a strip mine had played out; where things had gotten screwed long before he was Mayor. Why couldn't the landfill's detractors see that? Come Summer there'd be millions of tourists in mountains and valleys just like these only a few miles over the hazy horizon. Mayor Stevenson could see them in his mind, clogging up the roads and polluting everything with their vehicles and their litter. Yet in doing all of that they'd be spending money.

Visitors to the Smokies never got around to its poor relation Raiment, let alone Passmore and the surrounding countryside. There were old industrial scars on the people as well as the land. There was no facility for tourists. But enticing just a small share of those dollars into this part of Raiment…Jesus H. Christ, wouldn't that be something!

TAPE 11

For Sheriff Hughes, looking into the tobacco-brown eyes of Jeff Ackerley was like seeing a slimmer mirror-image of himself. Resistance to the notion of any similarity between himself and this local example of low-life precluded further consideration of the anomaly. He didn't like the way Ackerley chose to stare right back into his eyes either, as if knowing how uncomfortable it made Hughes. He was doing that now, the leering smirk slashed across his face like a wound echoing Hughes' own grin.

Hughes knew Jeff was responsible for setting that fire under the Winston place. Hughes was also pretty damn certain Jeff was guilty of this new attack on the Baptists. Hughes couldn't comprehend the need to hate someone just because they were a different color, though in Ackerley's case it had nothing to do with color; it was just plain wickedness. It added a dark tinge to the peculiar sense of camaraderie that Hughes felt existed between them.

They were on Ackerley's veranda, Ackerley lounging in an old leather armchair tilted over on its hind legs, horsehair stuffing poking out through rents in the hide so it looked like the skin of a mummified Pharaoh. Hughes hung around one of the roof supports, its green paint mottled like an old apple where the undercoat of preserver showed through, but only above dog-height. Below that, a dark patina of grease had been worked into the paint-molecules to give the appearance of a structure subject to the rise and fall of a tidal river.

Jeff Ackerley's pa had bred Rottweilers, and Jeff inherited a posse of them. For a while they'd been kind of entertaining. They ran off and caught rodents and rabbits and barked loud enough to scare away The Horsemen of The Apocalypse whenever they came near the house. The Rottweilers were primarily to ensure nobody snook up behind the Ackerley place and got a look at the marijuana crop. Yet one by one the dogs died, as all creatures do, particularly if they're not looked after properly. Ackerley was the only animal here now.

"Folks gonna talk, seein' the Sheriff round my place," Ackerley said in a light-brown voice that matched his eyes.

For a moment they shared a silence punctuated only by the sound of Ackerley chipping at the beech arm of his chair with a kitchen knife. He was waiting for Hughes to get to the point, and didn't much care how long it took.

Hughes was beginning to think that the reason he hadn't pursued Jeff Ackerley for the Winston torching was because he liked the guy, asshole or no. Hughes checked his belly wasn't sagging too far over his belt and belched demonstratively. "Mayor's real anxious for to catch whoever did that stuff t'the Baptists." He made it sound like idle conversation.

"That right?"

Hughes screwed up his face to show his dilemma. "See we got this here vaginal swab from the girl who got raped. Body fluids from that there swab give us a DNA profile - know what that is?"

"I know." Ackerley thoughtfully scraped dirt out from under a fingernail with the point of the knife, then began sticking the point rhythmically into the chair-arm.

"Well anyhow I'm lookin' to bring a few people in for tests so's we can compare blood-product fluids and match profiles with what's on that swab, 'cept that doesn't have to be the reason why I come out here to see you, Jeff. I need help with a troublesome religious matter an' I figured you might be the man for the job, seein' as how you're experienced in these things."

He looked Ackerley right in the eye. "Lord helps them who help theirself, and that's what I'm givin' you the chance to do." He kept the grin in check to make the point that this could still become serious if Ackerley didn't abide by the rules.

"Meanin'?"

"Meanin' we got ourselves a preacher with a drug habit, an' you can help him out."

48

Hughes knew Ackerley had no choice but to accept. Besides, Ackerley had shown his eagerness to disrupt the Baptists once just for the hell of it. Hughes' proposition would be his opportunity to do it again to avoid going to jail for rape and assault. Hughes unbuckled his belt and made a big production of tucking his shirt back into his pants.

"Don't s'pose you got a beer?"

Ackerley jabbed the chair-arm twice more, then leaned over and stuck the knife in the board floor. He hauled himself to his feet. "'Think I might be able to accommodate you, Sheriff. I'm a great believer in keepin' up bad habits."

The statement reminded Hughes of something familiar he couldn't quite place.

Driving away from the house later, Hughes realized that Ackerley's remark was an exact match for one of the many doubtful wisdoms his own father used to utter. Hughes was not prone, as some folks are, to picking up and adopting their parents' old sayings. But Jeff Ackerley was. Until the age of twenty-seven, when his mother died, Jeff had often heard her use that particular one. She'd told him that being 'a great believer in keepin' up bad habits' was something his daddy used to say. Jeff's daddy had died when Jeff was just a few years old. He couldn't recall ever hearing him say the things she credited him with. He had no idea she was referring not to William Ackerley, her husband, but to Jeff's natural father whose family name was Hughes. The very same Hughes whose wife, sixteen months earlier, had given birth to a boy and named him Neil.

It's funny. When guys are not doing what you want them to, you want them to. And when they are doing what you want them to, you don't want them to. That was something else I learned about myself thanks to Ed.

I was halfway through his bottle of whiskey, camped out on the rug by his fire inside a tent of a towel that I'd climbed out the tub into, wishing he'd be a boy scout. But then I'd only have resisted his advances. Naturally I didn't blame myself for being so darn capricious; it was all Ed's fault. That's guys for you - always in the wrong.

I looked over at Ed, standing by the bookshelves, and decided he'd earned a little of my interest in his pet subject. I asked him hey, if we really are just little pieces of a bigger, all-knowing consciousness, how come we act like we're monkeys? Surely an all-knowing consciousness would know better? I was just making idle conversation, but Ed, being Ed, figured he should begin by

49

explaining why materiality is illusory, so I had to edit savagely to get a half-way intelligible answer to my question.

Okay. Forget about the material universe for a moment; think of consciousness as something that exists in its own right and just happens to be immaterial. (I guess that's the hardest part of this, you never having known anything that wasn't material.) Consciousness in its unadulterated state is simply awareness, knowingness, sentience, you name it. I could even say that consciousness doesn't need a material environment to exist, though the absence of a material environment would make things kind of pointless. Why? Because consciousness wants to continually relearn – to re-evolve – and for that, consciousness creates a material environment to evolve *in*. A material environment that is itself evolving. See that? These monkey suits are a tiny part of that evolving material environment; on this planet, being human is just one of the many evolutionary levels that consciousness is on.

To see this requires a shift in viewpoint. (As consciousness, you're uniquely equipped to make that shift.) Instead of looking at life from inside of a monkey suit, you can look at life from outside of materiality. Go on and try it. I dare you...

Margin Note: In case you were wondering, or even if you were not, no part of the overall consciousness ever becomes detached; we all of us maintain a connection with The Whole: what Ed referred to as the corporate consciousness. Happy with that, or would you rather stay a monkey?

"For consciousness to operate through the medium of a human being," Ed said, "requires a kind of multi-level, multi-dimensional interface between itself and the electrochemical components of a body/brain. This interface takes the form of a series of consciousness layers that overlay our physical body. These layers – sometimes called subtle bodies - are composed of much finer, less tangible stuff than atoms. Finer even than the fundamental particles that make atoms, because they're different frequencies of *energy*, but not the same kind of energy that atoms are made from; these refined bodies are made from *consciousness* energy."

Now mom, an 'interface' is where two different kinds of equipment fit together, okay? Well this conscious/material interface allows your Real, immaterial self to operate through a material body/brain as if it's part of that body/brain, yet at the same time remain separate from it - like a car's clutch mechanism links the engine with the gears I guess. (Be clear that I'm talking about your consciousness here, not your mind. A mind happens when

50

consciousness operates through a body/brain interface. A mind is a combination of consciousness and material components.) No, this isn't confusing; explaining it is.

Ed said a hell of a lot more on this subject than I want to go into just here. For instance, as these material bodies, nervous systems and brains evolve, the earlier and more primitive components in them don't simply disappear; they're built on top of, or adapted, or just sidelined and maybe found a use for later. As a result we get various evolutionary levels working alongside each other. (Simple example: the thin outer part of your brain, the neocortex that does your higher thinking, is a lot more highly evolved than the amygdala right in the middle, which handles your most basic emotions, 'kay? And yet those two different areas can't work without each other.)

Fine. Yet while we think of all that as our physical self, none of it could operate - or even exist - without our conscious self. Our conscious self is not contained in our brain, it's composed of that series of more refined 'bodies' (made from consciousness energy) that permeate and surround us. These subtle bodies interface the evolutionary levels of our physical body and brain, and the whole thing evolves as an interconnected unit.

At the time I didn't know what the bleep Ed was talking about. I told him I still felt a little chilly and maybe he should come sit by the fire and finish telling me why this monkey suit of mine feels so much like it's really me. Big hint. He still didn't sit down though, just kind of hovered around the place, hands in his pants pockets, shoulders kind of hunched, looking awkward…the way he used to.

"So you want to know about feelings, yes?"

No, I wanted to know why mine were going noplace.

"Feelings are sensations created by atoms banging around inside your body. Your consciousness confuses itself with those, and you interpret the result as a mixed up combination of physical and mental experiences. Some of those you call emotions. Emotions are the effect of electrochemical activity creating conscious ideas about that activity."

Hands up who thinks atoms can experience emotions. Yeah, you're right - that would be as nutty as thinking atoms can be conscious. What atoms in nervous systems and brains can do though, like he said god-dammit, is cause sensations that I respond to and interact with. The result of this interaction are feelings of pleasure, pain, depression, disappointment, hope, whatever. But for any of those interactions or sensations in nerves and brains to actually mean something, you need an extra factor capable of giving them meaning. You need consciousness.

This was when Ed raised the question of control. How much of my behavior was the result of those electrochemical interactions in my body and brain, and how much was a result of my conscious decisions? In plain English, was I running my own life, or was I only reacting to the demands of a stupid body and brain? Naturally he reminded me there are millions of years of genetic influence working on me; thousands of years of social conditioning; an existence where I'd only ever known the incessant demands of a body and brain machined only for their own survival.

Remember Donna's 'robot' problem? Ed said we all have that same identity problem. While we're in this chemical suit, we're convinced that chemicals wanting things, is us wanting things, so we mistakenly identify ourselves with the sensations they create as part of a mindless biological process. Instead of using what could be our conscious free will independently of what this genetic body wants, we wind up thinking and acting for the benefit of chemicals that can't even begin to appreciate concepts like consciousness and free will.

The whiskey slipped down my gullet, the edge of that towel crept lower on my shoulder, and Ed talked about nervous systems evolving to make bodies operate more efficiently for genes. He said that as bodies evolved and nervous systems got more complicated, the nerve signals became a network that needed a control center to coordinate all of the inputs and outputs. So brains began forming. And suddenly genetic DNA was in a different ballgame. (I guess he meant evolution's version of *suddenly*, measured in ocean floors getting pushed up to make mountain ranges, kind of thing.)

"Tell me about the different ballgame," I said, my cheeks feeling rosy. My face was kind of flushed too.

"Okay. By growing a brain from its own nerves, DNA's body got itself a powerful data processor. But the mind in that brain was still too primitive to distinguish between its simple thoughts and the sensations in its body. It still can't, hence our emotions..."

"Hey, just hold on a goddam second." I threatened him with my glass, oblivious to the contents slopping on the rug. "So okay then, how come minds and bodies feel so much like they're a part of each other if we're supposed to treat 'em as separate, huh?"

"Well think about it. You wouldn't be too effective a survivor if your consciousness wasn't glued so tight to that body and brain. Most people aren't

52

ready to handle the notion of separateness anyhow. You have to evolve so you can learn to make that body and brain behave less selfishly. Consciousness *per se* is free of selfishness; it's a body and brain that make consciousness behave selfishly. The more trouble we have distinguishing our conscious self from this body, the more evolving we still have to do."

I rebuilt my drink from more of the 'loose molecules' called liquid. (Boy, is that an apt description!) I was so loose I almost understood what Ed was saying about feelings created by mindless chemical activity, and how those become the currency we value ourselves and each other by when we base our value-judgments on the way chemicals make us 'feel' - about what they want - rather than what we as conscious minds think and know. No wonder we still have the same problems we always did.

Sitting by the fire, my face glowing like a solar flare, something inside of me fluttered at the sound of his voice, the way he inflected his syllables to accentuate a point, but that didn't stop me getting mad at the way he talked as though we were discussing pond life instead of red-blooded people with real desires and longings.

But you're siding with who I was then, right? You still won't accept that mindless feelings and urges are keeping your consciousness from evolving. You still think this sounds cold and inhuman, yeah? I sure did. Hell, I didn't want my feelings reduced, I wanted them increased! (The nice ones anyhow.) My feelings were the most real part of me. They made life worth living.

It was when he said that we *deliberately* encourage situations where emotions can get the better of our mental judgment that I fulminated.

"Jesus Ed, my emotions *steer* my judgment! I *think* in emotions for God's sake!" I knew I was yelling. Worse, I knew I was acting the way he was describing...

"Laurie, physical feelings are reassuring only because they've been running our lives for the whole of human evolution. Being a slave to your body's urges is how genes get what *they* want, and not knowing better, you imagine that's what *you* want." (I know - he did keep on saying the same things. I guess he figured I was so dumb he had to.)

Sitting there confused, my face burning and my eyes prickling, I was having trouble taming that damn towel, I can tell you. It seemed to represent the insurmountable barrier between us. That, and his patronizing manner. Incidentally did you ever notice that people are better looking when you've had a drink or three? The fact that he looked so good was doing nothing to calm my heaving hormones. The last thing I recall him saying was something about pleasure receptors...

TAPE 12

The tire-marks from Ackerley's pickup were still visible from the night of the attack on the Baptists. He parked up over them and sat in the pickup in silence save for the banging in his head, swigging from a bottle of JD. Then he took a flashlight and gloves and got out, looking beyond the trees to the river, the bridge, the little white church on top of the knoll opposite, 'like somethin' off of a f'kin Christmas card'. Above him a chill breeze whispered in the branches, but down on the ground everything smelled damp and green.

A heavy hangover that throbbed in the sides of his brain and brought an empty ache just below his heart made him irritable, ready to lose his temper with anything that didn't behave the way he wanted it to. Like when he made to close the pickup door and it swung open again. For that inanimate-object felony he whirled and brought his knee up hard against the sheet metal, but the satisfaction of hearing the door close tight was swamped by the pain, and he danced away, lashing viciously at the dark foliage, cursing the world before wilting to a motionless daze in the eye of his own frustration. Getting mad was not enjoyable with a dying-rat-feeling in your body from lack of food, an overdose of tobacco, no exercise, old alcohol circulating in your bloodstream and shrunken, dehydrated brain-cells decaying so fast, he was practically conscious of them going, like tiny light bulbs winking out.

He set off through the trees, staying in cover all the way to the edge of the meadow where the treeline ended in the same magnolia bush from where he and the others had watched the small band of Baptists. Here he stopped to check the bulge was still in the pocket of his camouflaged jacket. He'd felt for it before leaving the pickup, then again walking through the trees, but mild paranoia was part of the joy of self-abuse.

A gust of night wind ran up the slope and flicked his sand-colored cow-lick, and his eyes watered even though it wasn't so cold. He wanted to do something...what was it? He'd begun crossing the pasture before he remembered what it was and stopped to take a leak, his head rotating like a police cruiser light to check he was unobserved while the breeze blew urine back onto his feet with a pattering sound. He turned his back to the shallow river at the bottom of the slope and swore again, zippered up, checked his pocket a fourth time and let gravity draw him down the grassy incline to the embankment where he'd raped a stranger smelling of soap in the dark. At the bridge he sensed the physical presence of the black water sliding soundlessly past the wooden supports, its swirl filling the air with the odor of weed and, from upstream, the sharper smell of livestock. But up on the bridge a fresher airstream prepared him for his task, and made him look up to the top of the hill where the paler outline of the church floated like a ghost above the black cutout backdrop of pines. As he pulled on the work-gloves he tried to imagine how this would go, but so slow were his thoughts that all they could match was the speed of his actions...

Now forty-five minutes had passed, the job was done, he was back on the bridge, his plan complete as a memory of his actions. He was smirking under the pain in his temples over how he'd walked right in the church, not needing the tire-iron to force the aged door because it was unlocked. How the sudden rush of indefinable, memory-jerking pungency had billowed out as the door swung open onto cool darkness, disturbing a dust-and-spice aroma of wood that had experienced God-knew how many years of vociferous devotion; the rich elixir of human hopes and fears exuded by generations of worshippers that had become part of the building. But Jesus Christ, he was only imagining that crap. There was no unseen power making him scared of getting discovered; that stink was just oldness.

Next he'd needed somewhere to hide the incriminating evidence. Most folk roundabouts had already hung the preacher for his talk of a second coming. He'd supplied the rope and put it around his own neck, and was only waiting for the chair to get kicked out from under, a job that Jeff Ackerley was more than happy to help with.

Ackerley had found a plain white shirt hanging beside a broom above a pair of mildewed tennis shoes in a curtained-off closet. His gaze had followed the flashlight beam as it skittered over benches and walls and come to rest on an ancient black-wood pulpit. His dark shadow positioned itself behind this, knowing he could just as easily have left the prize in that broom-cupboard, tucked in a shoe or the shirt, but that wouldn't have the same symbolic power to indict as this fine piece of religious furniture, more lectern than pulpit, its once-sharp corners worn round and raw by a succession of ministers and their flocks, the nicks and scars softened by time.

The pulpit's sloping lid had raised up on its hinge with a squeak of protest, and from a pile of prayer-books wafted a concentrated odor of sanctity that caught in Ackerley's throat. (He cleared it again now at the thought.) The pulpit had been just too obvious; not even a junked-up preacher would leave his stash right there next to the holy goddam bible...or maybe he would.

Ackerley had rubbed his eyes with a rough-gloved hand to appease his headache, trying to think. He'd taken off the gloves and felt for the packet burning a hole in his pocket, spread it on the black bible so his shaking fingers could tease open the inner plastic wrapper. Jesus, with the flashlight laid on its side, creating shadows in all the wrong places, he couldn't see shit! Now sprinkle a few specks on these books. Do some more on the wooden bottom. *Holy fuck!* Don't blow on the - !

Right, that was done. Creative incrimination they called it. The preacher wouldn't know this stuff from spider shit. In a couple of days the old guy's prints would be all over the evidence. Ackerley resealed the plastic inside the paper wrapping and reached under the pulpit, feeling untreated wood and the castellation of dovetail, and then, right at the back, a cleft behind the compartment: just wide enough for the evidence when wrapped in the shirt to ensure a snug fit...

The cool river air on the bridge evaporated perspiration on Ackerley's face. He'd done it. His small world was whole again, its integrity secure. His temples still throbbed, the cold air ached in his sinuses, and by the time he got behind the wheel of the pickup he was all out of breath. He felt the parcel shelf for his smokes and lit one, careful to keep his head down so the light wouldn't show. Next he reached under the seat for the JD, uncorked it, drew on the cigarette and stuck the bottle against his mouth.

Thunk! The hard glass neck banged against his front teeth, splashing charcoal-filtered Tennessee spirit down his chin and making him swear profanely through a cloud of smoke. He ran his tongue across the teeth; there was no damage so he swigged more delicately, lowered the bottle and belched, enjoying the fumes in his nose. Even hungover, the inrush of nicotine and booze was invigorating. His vision became distorted by tears; the throbbing in his head worsened. Through a mist of sour mash vapor and smoke he replaced the cork and bent over to put the bottle under the seat, but straightening up saw tiny white stars. The darkness outside seemed to close in around the edges of his vision and his skull tightened. But hell, he wasn't about to let shit like that spoil his night. The drive to The Triangle would be an effort of concentration now his headache had settled-in, and no amount of drinking would cover its effects, but Christ, it wouldn't be for want of trying.

56

TAPE 13

The morning after drinking all of Ed's whiskey I awoke in his bed wearing his 'pajamas': a giant UCLA sweatshirt and a pair of his jogging pants. Ed is six-two, I'm five-two, so overnight I'd become the incredible shrinking woman. You can see me now, right? Well quit looking, dammit; I already had enough problems with that hangover and waking in a man's bed. (So okay, Ed spent the night on the couch-cushions downstairs.)

"And your maid dressed me in your clothes and put me to bed, yeah?" I challenged him in the kitchen, wondering aloud why I wasn't smelling ham and eggs. Even vegan ham and eggs would've sufficed (Ed is vegan) though behind the levity I was pretty embarrassed for all kinds of reasons. I'd been wearing a bathsheet and nothing else. Then there were natural bodily functions that could let a girl down, not to mention the rag-doll awkwardness of him manhandling the next best thing to a corpse. You ever tried undressing a dead person? Go dig one up and try it.

While me and my headache slouched around the kitchen I fantasized over what would happen if he had taken advantage of me. Hey, we all indulge in these private *what-ifs*, childish, disgusting or hilarious though they might be. This morning I allowed my fantasies to drift into the love part of the psychosis spectrum. I even glanced mentally in the direction of motherhood. Boy, I must have been in a state because those notions began to surface in my conversation, from where everything just went downhill.

Especially when Ed decided to de-confuse the difference between Real love (as in divine) and our biological excuse for love (as in sex). It was a bad time, me half-wishing we'd done something the night before, and consequently half-frustrated that we hadn't. That developed into the half of me that wished we had done something privately blaming Ed for the fact that we hadn't. Now throw in the lerve thing, by which I mean the sex thing that wasn't happening between us - for which I blamed him also - and top it all off with my fantasized broodiness, when all I was actually nursing was a new-born hangover...

He'd just reminded me that love - the urge that ensures genes get replicated and reproduced - is a self-serving process, and that we'd only knowingly and willingly allow ourselves to be part of it if the process itself was controlling us. Real love, he said, only happens when you quit letting yourself be pushed around by a body/brain. Only then will all of the problems created by this selective mating mania, the hormonal holocaust, the entire gene-survival fiasco, begin to disappear. Break free of the genetic delusion, and other people will become genuinely as important and as valuable as YOU AND YOURS. I mean *all* other people, *all* of the time, not just when it suits you. Hell, you *know* that. You only pretend you don't so you can carry on being selectively selfish.

But this is me talking after deciding to get Real. At the time I railed at Ed's notion of reproduction as biological control.

"The hell you say. How can it control me if I'm a willing party to it?" Damn right I was taking it personally.

"But you only became a willing party *after* the urge got a hold of you. And you're still not thinking this through. Your heightened consciousness is the only factor, sexual or otherwise, that makes you different from other animals. It alone enables you to appreciate that biochemical reasons for behavior are entirely different from consciously thought-out reasons. You do see that difference, right?"

Sure I did, but what did seeing things his way have to do with it?

"Your extra consciousness is no advantage at all unless you use it to *modify* your behavior, sexual or otherwise? If you're going to do exactly what other animals do, what makes you different from them?"

"Bullshit! (This was me again.) Are you saying that all of the complexity my mind brings to relationships doesn't make me different from other animals?" I think I was shaking with exasperation, but Ed - he was like Neo in The Matrix when he fights fifty guys with one hand without even breaking into a sweat. Boy, was *that* off-pissing!

"So," he persisted, "How did your mind make your sexual urges and behavior more 'meaningful' than for other animals? How is it different for you than for them? Is there a different motive? Is it acted out in a different way? No, and no. Even saying that you engage in sexual behavior when *you* choose to is a delusion, because all you're doing is re-scheduling those same sexual urges. Ditto contraception. You're not modifying the urge, you're modifying yourself to fit the urge. The only self you're helping is one that genes evolved for themselves."

I was hungover, angry *and* confused. And then he went off about why, if biological love is so goddam 'spiritual', don't people just fall in love and stay there? The answer? This genetic sex thing is a complete free-for-all, otherwise it wouldn't work. There'd be no biological life period. Genetic sex evolved to be as cross-fertilization-crazy as those little mothers could make it.

That's what competition is all about. In this jungle the monkeys compete with each other for partners they hope will give their own genes a better chance next time. And they've devised some real sneaky ways of ensuring that their own personal set of genes gets a good start.

Fact: Women can only have one offspring a year, while men can send their genes down the pipe with every woman they have sex with, day in and night out. Women know this consciously *and* as genetic organisms, so they've evolved ways to compensate for such a one-sided situation. Women became more discriminating than men about their partners-in-sex. More keen to seek out men with high-quality genes (brawn/brain), and/or the material security to ensure their genes-as-offspring get (a) a good start, and (b) to inherit those same high-quality genes. Apparently the maternal instinct spent millions of years evolving female genes to be their own quality control because of this biological differences in their half of the reproductive process. But as the laws of physics in back of instinct are still mindless, Ed suggested that only when women's consciousness becomes more aware of itself as something more than a means of gene reproduction, will this world become a better place for us as conscious organisms.

Sure, men will have to grow up too. The ones who dump their wives for younger and/or more genetically fertile women, for instance; sometimes a whole string of the latter, one after the other. Or all at the same time if the guy has enough time and/or money. Most women get a gleam in their eye (or both eyes if they've got 'em) at the sight of a materially successful man. Those guys spell security, a better chance in life and more likelihood of helping pass on into future generations the genes of women they have offspring with. Even fantasizing on what you don't have but would like to, is part of the process: it's practice. (Women need practice to try and even up the reproductive odds caused by the nine month lay-off.) I guess that's how DNA-as-women got to be so sneaky. Even the not-so-smart ones. When it goes beyond fantasy, women are capable of cheating on their partners just as eagerly as men do - maybe moreso - to get a better deal for their own genes in any offspring they create.

Adding to this later when I'd done some thinking on my own account, I figured the crazy circus we call lerve is infinitely more complicated than Ed explained it. Things don't always work like his examples because our clever minds bring a whole other reality to the game. But you're still thinking 'That isn't me', right? Nobody wants to recognize themselves for what they really are; we wouldn't like ourselves if we did, so we live in a delusion where nobody thinks of themself as especially selfish, mean or competitive. It's always the other guy. Except it isn't. The genetic replication and reproduction process works the same in everybody. That really is a bio-robot you're walking around in. It really is programmed to look out for the components that built it. And it really does make us selfish and mean and competitive - until *we* decide otherwise.

I just wrote down here 'global warming' without thinking. Is global warming caused by people being selfish and mean and competitive? Well what the hell else is it caused by? Ordinary folks like you and me, electing governments of other ordinary folks to look out for our national best interests. Where does a 'national best interest' originate? In each and every one of us looking out for our own genetic ass, in a world where everybody else is doing the same thing. We're not doing it to help each other. Looking out for ourselves just happens to work better if we all do it together as a club, a town, a state or a nation.

Why don't we all do it as a united planet? Because of international economic competition. And this is before you even start to talk about competition between religions and belief systems; that too is caused by being selfish and competitive for our genes. Deluding ourselves otherwise only helps maintain the injustices and inequalities in the world. It'll continue doing that unless and until the Real, conscious YOU does something to change it. Only the Real, conscious YOU makes the difference between bio-robot and something more. How much more is entirely up to YOU.

When Ackerley left the pickup out front of The Triangle Bar & Grill, the air was filled with soft, cobwebby rain that formed a red and yellow halo round the neon sign. Inside, Mike McClure turned on his seat and stayed facing Ackerley but looking down at his own boots. Beside him, Roy King remained hunched over the bar, watching Ackerley's reflection morosely in the mirrored tiles. Ackerley went directly to the jukebox, leaned over it so the light caught the hollows of his face and bumped the cabinet in a well-practiced movement that brought on the next selection; it was Dolly Parton, but what the hell? He'd succeeded in spoiling somebody's listening pleasure. McClure sensed a bad scene coming and ambled to the far end of the room to play some solitary pool.

At close on half after ten the door opened and Donna Hughes appeared, pale-faced and big-eyed. She'd just walked the mile or so from home along the dark highway, too preoccupied with her thoughts to be aware of the journey.

Outside a Doberman in a pickup had scared her, ramming its drooly snout through the narrow gap of a cranked-down window trying to get at her.

Before leaving home she'd reached a decision that had been brewing for days. Only after she was out of the house and on her way, with no sound but the robot's solitary footsteps and the cold night air on its face, did she begin analyzing her true reasons for going to The Triangle tonight. She wondered how much struggle the robot would put up when the time came. She'd known how to act like it all those years; surely she could turn things around and make it do the same for her? But then the dog startled her and broke the shell around her resolve. Now it was too late to back out, and the contents of her stomach churned as if a great big hand was squeezing the robot's insides.

Ackerley latched onto her straight away, yet instead of shying away, Donna stood her ground. The shaking in her legs made her angry at her old self but heightened her determination.

From around Roy King's back appeared the good-looking barkeep, his open face a ray of sunlight beside Jeff Ackerley's saturnine features.

"Beer, thankyou kindly," Donna said past Ackerley's ear, her sweet smile like a slap in his waxen face.

"Two," Ackerley said.

When the barkeep put two beers on the counter next to her, Donna looked deliberately into his eyes and was struck by their clarity. Something about him made her feel strange but reassured. There was that comfortable hint of a smile, exciting her and making her glow both together. Making her want to shiver, but not in the tacky old way. Looking at him, she felt she was seeing someone more real than she was. How could that be?

When Ackerley reached for his bottle, Donna was surprised to hear herself say, "I ain't buyin' your beer. I ain't payin' for you no more."

Ackerley snorted with incredulity, his narrowed eyes like a theatrical villain's. Subversive forces were at work here. He tried to see them through half-closed eyes while battle-fatigued brain cells formed defensive positions against this unexpected assault.

While Donna appeared cool and full of herself, it was taking more control than she knew she had to contain the shaking. She looked down at her chest, certain that the hammering in there was visible. Only John the Baptist's words about a messiah, printed in that copy of The Star she'd kept and re-read over and over, prevented her fainting away on the spot. She so wanted to believe those words. If it could happen once, why not a second time? People needed a messiah now just as much as that first time. Maybe moreso. But when she sought out the barkeep again for courage, Ackerley saw where her gaze was directed and the anger geysered in his brain.

"*Whore!*" The word came out before he had gathered enough wind for it, so he swallowed, rolled his eyes and tried again.

"You f'kin' dirty *whore!*" This time everybody in The Triangle heard him.

Now it was Donna's turn to lose her temper, instantly and completely. Before either of them knew it, she'd slapped the bottle from his hand so it flew across the counter and bounced against the mirrored tiles.

Her shaking had reached Richter scale intensity, but she flushed with new courage, felt it filling out the robot's farthest corners like air plumping out a balloon.

Ackerley stood blinking. Until this moment he'd had things all his own way in this relationship, and suddenly Donna Hughes was a stranger who had shamed and humiliated him, and Jesus, he was going to make her pay for that whether she bought the beer or not.

As if in slow-motion Donna watched his hand come at her. She was able to examine the blackened crescents of its nails before the fingers gripped her upper arm and started to squeeze: a merciless, inhuman grip with all his strength in it. Robot's arm or no, the tears jumped out, overflowed and ran down her face until they hung on an open mouth from which no sound would come. She writhed, expecting to hear the bone snap, the sleeve and flesh shred together between his fingers. In an agonized dream her free hand tried to prize him off, all sensation concentrated in that one place. Her knees started to give way for real this time...

Sometime later she became aware of walking an uncertain line that would lead eventually to the ladies' room. She couldn't feel her legs, didn't know that Michael McClure had Ackerley by the neck in as tight a one-handed grip as Ackerley had held her. Ackerley could neither breathe nor speak while McClure bent him backwards over the counter. In doing that he had pushed Roy King off his barstool so King now stood and watched, along with everyone else in the place. Donna missed the nice-looking barkeep calmly cleaning up after the fracas, observing McClure and Ackerley over his shoulder in the mirrored tiles as the juke-box played Stand By Your Man for the fifth or maybe sixth time that night.

Ackerley was gone when Donna emerged from the ladies' room. McClure offered to take her home but she told him no-thankyou, she'd rather walk; she was none too polite, unaware he'd been her Galahad. While McClure would get over the snub, he decided that maybe a sound social move would be to stop hanging out with Jeff Ackerley.

TAPE 14

The preacher's eyes were the brightest blue Andy DeSoto had ever seen. This was quite a celebrity Hughes had just brought in: the famous John the Baptist, proclaimer of the Second Coming - according to The Star. Whatever, the guy looked scared, which was understandable in the circumstances.

Andy always wondered how apprehended suspects must be feeling inside, but he was thinking of all the TV cop shows he'd seen because hardly anybody ever came into this office, guilty or innocent. He surmised that even the most ruthless TV felon had to experience some remorse or regret. The fact that they were only actors made no difference because, after all, they were acting out real situations that actually happened. That's what Andy DeSoto thought anyhow.

How a prisoner must feel was one of his many on-going procedural conjectures. He assumed the very sight of official police accoutrements - the uniform, cruiser, cuffs, and later the police-house and paperwork, the cells and, maybe most potent of all, the cold and unfeeling statements of intent in that alien, officious atmosphere - all of that could sap your soul.

Another of his conjectures centered on the treatment you gave to a detainee - again TV-generated. If you didn't just afford them the common courtesies, didn't just respect their basic human rights, didn't only observe correct police formality, but in addition communicated that you were genuinely interested in trying to empathize with them, that would go a long way towards making their problems, and your job, one heck of a sight easier. If ever he felt himself forgetting these considerations, he only had to remember how the very sight of cops had scared him as a kid. That fear had stayed with him into adulthood and still scared him even now he was a cop. Nobody knew about that and never would. Along with his other little conjectures, his innate fear of his own job gave him much food for thought.

Having Hughes for a boss did little to ease DeSoto's natural discomfort around cops, and would have done even less for his opinion of people generally but for a basic liking Andy DeSoto felt for his fellow man. He wouldn't have referred to it as compassion exactly; it was more an acceptance of what human beings were, warts and all. Even with that knowledge, DeSoto found he could get along with most of them, and actually liked most of them. He sometimes wondered if he was in the right job.

When Hughes had walked in with the preacher, DeSoto thought the black man had come to reiterate his protest at that trouble the week before, or maybe to complain that no progress had been made in finding those responsible for the attack. Then DeSoto saw that he was holding his venous hands clasped before him in that preacherly way because he was cuffed. Further inspection, just for the record, revealed he had on a white collarless shirt under his black jacket, elasticized running pants, and plain black shoes without socks. Then Hughes tossed a package on the desk, along with another white shirt, and smirked for the black man's benefit.

"Show John the Baptist here to our bridal suite Andy an' get me some coffee 'cause I could sure use some."

DeSoto was still gawping. "What he do?"

"He got hisself caught is what he done."

DeSoto led the minister through the door marked *cells*, over which Hughes had stuck a sign reading, 'Abandon hope all who enter here.' DeSoto wondered if John saw the sign as he passed through into the short passageway beyond and waited for the iron-barred door to one of the cells to be opened for him so he could step inside and stand in silence facing the wall until the door was closed and locked. Then he turned and looked into DeSoto's brown eyes with his own blue ones, as if waiting for DeSoto to say something, which he didn't, even though he wanted to.

Back in the front office with the holding room door closed, DeSoto got on with the coffee and without looking at Hughes said, "I thought he was the injured party?"

Hughes didn't answer. He was examining without interest the opened package he'd brought in, moving something around inside the brown paper with the tip of a pen. He'd know what this stuff was even before he'd found it hidden in the church. Now he was looking to see if any was gone. Then he looked at the wall where the window was, and finally at DeSoto.

"This here substance better get sent to the analyst in Zeno. Record it an' everything."

DeSoto came over for a closer look. Inside the package was a smaller plastic wrapper containing white powder that resembled flour maybe, or chalk dust. Hell, it could even be talcum powder. What would Hughes have brought that

64

in for? DeSoto bent closer and sniffed it before the light came on in his head and he was glad he hadn't actually asked Hughes what it was.

"This stuff *his?*" It would never have occurred to DeSoto that it might be drugs if not for all those TV cop shows.

Hughes drank his coffee down in one go and took his cup to the sink next door to wash it just for something to waste a little more time while he thought about what to say to the Mayor. There'd been an anonymous phone call (from Ackerley) telling him where to find the drugs inside the church. He'd even found traces inside the goddam pulpit where the preacher stood to deliver his sermons. The evidence and the circumstances would be taken at face value, however incredible they seemed. Whatever the Mayor believed about John and the drugs, or about anything else to do with this business, he'd have to be blind not to see that the end justified the means. But just in case he chose not to see, Hughes had figured a way to remove any doubts about the preacher's guilt.

On his way out of the office Hughes paused in an exaggerated pose of thoughtfulness. DeSoto knew Hughes well enough to figure that this method-acting school of police work was designed to communicate some kind of message, though what it might be he couldn't figure.

"Get that done right off Andy, uh?"

"How'd you get him with it?"

Hughes considered the ceiling, then gave DeSoto a shrewd look. "You never hear of a confidential informant?"

Andy DeSoto made a screwed-up face. "This stuff really *cocaine?*"

Hughes just smirked. Outside in the car he checked his breast pocket for the other little polythene sachet Ackerley had given him. In this one was the second, and conclusive, part of John's guilt: a dot of lysergic acid diethylamide, which even my mom knows is LSD. Hughes started the motor and looked in the mirror, seeing his narrowed eyes crinkle at the corner from a look of serious disbelief at what he'd discovered in the church on Knobby Hill. This was the look he was practicing for when he told his story. Then he put the shift into drive and headed in the direction of the Mayor's wife's house, where the Mayor also happened to live.

All of the problems between me and Ed were a result of what he described as my 'obsession with the physical'. Okay. I admit it. I was just like everybody else. Those crazy urges had me by the short hairs. I was just another drunk who doesn't appreciate he's drunk. (When you think about it, living your life as replicating proteins, for replicating proteins, is a kind of intoxication.) And yet at the same time I was scared that if we got some heavy thing going, I might just go and do something pathetic like fall in lerve, and maybe never get out of hicksville. So began my secret conviction that I was saving myself for something better. It was probably true. Maybe I used to look on Ed as a disposable accessory; a fill-in till I could move on to greener grass in pastures new and find somebody richer and more go-getting. Maybe I'd have some kids eventually, but with somebody as dollar-successful as I wanted to be. Hell, maybe a lot of things. Maybe that even fits with what Ed said about people selecting who to love because they're working for their biology. But this is me talking to you now, whereas at the time I was convinced that being able to choose who I loved was part of what made me uniquely human. The person I chose to love would be equally unique.

I was wrong - again. The physical factors we think are so important in selecting who to love are nothing whatever to do with any Real, compassionate, unselfish, divine kind of love. Nor is there anything unique about the physical parts of human beings that we do all of this selecting between.

To begin with, all physical human uniqueness is illusory - I don't mean in some weird mystical sense, I mean there is no physical uniqueness. Our visible features are made from some of the same hundred or so chemical elements that everything else in this universe is. Faces and bodies only appear different from each other because of excruciatingly, ridiculously, phenomenally small differences in the way atoms are arranged. There's not one unique atom in the entire human race. In every species the physical components have to be as interchangeable as lego, the differences between them so incredibly slight, so trivial, so arbitrary, that any difference becomes meaningless - otherwise the genetic replicating and reproducing process wouldn't work.

Look at the way other species are attracted to each other. There's nothing conscious about it; everything is decided by physical factors - the sight of color or plumage, symbolic movements, the draw of pheromones; it's all mechanical and instinctive, way below thinking level. All evolved by utterly mindless genes.

Attraction is mostly physical for us too, for the same reason. It's driven almost entirely by biochemical components making decisions for themselves. Yet because we're able to think about what these components make us do, we

66

imagine we're making conscious choices between meaningful differences using our free will. By making the demands of bodies/brains practically a full time job, our thinking is directed almost exclusively downward to the dumb level of biochemical components. Our uniquely conscious mind is playing Cinderella to a stupid monkey suit.

You don't think so? So how come you can get turned on sexually by the sight of somebody you never even met before? That's just plain, down-home lust. The machinery is moving in totally un-mysterious ways and taking you with it. Physical attraction, sex, maternal/paternal instincts, the entire reproductive process, is just your head being coerced by your hormones.

The problem is, this selective genetic 'love' automatically downgrades everybody you don't select. Would love be so conditional, selective and arbitrary if it were not built around a selfish agenda? Hell no. All of those factors are created by genes trying to get the best deal for themselves. Which is why you try to get the best deal for yours.

Besides, Real love doesn't need sex, so you wouldn't be interested anyhow. Real love only ever has a chance to enter the equation when you quit being a dork for DNA.

I guess I feel so strongly about this because painful hindsight informs me I blamed Ed for gradually removing all of the reasons for why I should continue trying to make a relationship out of us. He knew I meant a physical relationship. I guess that's why he left. One of us had to, and it sure as hell wasn't going to be me.

Now I feel the mother of all martinis coming on, but rather than sit and mope over Ed I'm going to tell you what happened when Donna Hughes walked through a fine mist of rain over to the jailhouse that evening with sandwiches for the prisoner. Lately Donna had nothing much to do with her evenings except watch TV, listen to music or read. Mostly she found herself sitting in her bedroom wondering what the hell she was going to do with the rest of her life, and the same subject rose to the surface of her mind, demanding attention. That subject was in the preacher's words, printed in that copy of The Star she had hidden in her closet. Those words were all that prevented her going crazy.

She walked in on Andy DeSoto, who said "Hi there Donna" more brightly than he'd told anybody hi there for a long time. Her appearance at the office was as rare as Christmas in July...or Mrs. Hughes herself coming in. Now there was a woman whose nervous glances made DeSoto damned uncomfortable. Did she think he was unaware of her watching him, kind of in the way a shy girl might cast furtive looks? It was especially embarrassing when the Sheriff was in the room. Donna, though, was something else.

"Hey Andy," Donna greeted him and dumped the brownpaper bag on his desk. "Sheriff said to bring these, 'kay?"

DeSoto went all stiffly casual and came around the front of his desk so he could enjoy the maximum view of Donna before she ran off again. "Yeah, he said you'd be over. Nothin' doin' tonight?" He saw that she wore tight jeans that showed off her slim legs, and a baggy waterproof walking jacket that didn't show off anything but her face.

Then she pushed the hood back and DeSoto saw that her cheeks were bright and shiny and her eyes even moreso, the lashes kind of sparkly with airborne moisture. And right now she smelled to DeSoto of mist, but real nice, fresh mist, and another odor that was probably her skin now it was warmed up with the walk. Maybe that was why DeSoto was a little breathless, trying to breathe in that odor without her noticing. He peeked in the bag she'd brought, but briefly so he could resume looking at Donna.

"Who, me?" Donna gazed idly around the office for something to be interested in but found nothing. "So who you holdin' in the jail?"

Andy frowned at her. "You don't know?" The way he said it brought her eyes to his.

"Sheriff don't tell me his business. So who?"

Now DeSoto had her interest he intended to keep it. "Have a seat and drink some coffee. I got some cake. So he didn't say nuthin' uh? Don't want things stirred up I guess." He went to the coffee-pot and let his hands feel their way through most of the work while his eyes stayed on Donna. "I was kind've surprised when your daddy brought this prisoner in." He watched her eyes to time the revelation. "So guess."

"C'mon Andy, who?"

"We got us John the Baptist in there."

His grin faded at Donna's cartoon look of amazement. She started blinking, eyes popping. Her mouth even dropped open. Donna took a long moment gathering herself together before she could speak.

"What he do?" Now she was a completely different person.

DeSoto went silent. He stopped looking at Donna so he could concentrate on the coffee.

"Andy? What did he do for God's sake?"

68

DeSoto looked guarded. "Well I'm not sure I ought to say anythin' 'bout that, Donna. Sheriff didn't exactly say this thing was any great secret, but he didn't say I was to broadcast it neither. I can't have you of all people runnin' back home sayin' I told you somethin' nobody should know about. You know what your daddy's like." Seeing the new sheen of tears on her eyes only confused him further.

"Come on and just tell me." Her voice was higher and uneven, breaking around the edges.

"Hey now, take it easy, Donna." He saw the way she was eyeing the holding-room door, like she was just aiming to go on in there and ask him herself. Then DeSoto was relieved to see that she'd relaxed a little, searching in her pocket for something, a handkerchief maybe. There it was. He sighed and poured the coffee, trying to watch her and it simultaneously. He brought it over and waited until she'd wiped her nose.

She sniffed. "Andy, can I see him?"

DeSoto's alarm returned. "Hey, I can't let you in there, you know that."

"Why can't you?"

"Aw shoot, you know he's the prisoner, that's why. The Sheriff would have me in there if he found out."

"But prisoners are allowed to get visits."

"What d'you want to see *him* for?" DeSoto looked pained, knowing he'd decided to let her in the tank, and that if Hughes himself walked in while his daughter was fraternizing with the preacher there'd be all kinds of hell to pay.

Donna examined his face. Could she tell Andy DeSoto? Why should she?

"I just want to see what he looks like, is all."

DeSoto eyed the clock, then checked his watch for no sensible reason. When Donna stood up and put her coffee cup down on the chair it was both a signal and an instruction. Reluctantly he led her to the holding-room door. There seemed no reason why she shouldn't see John. He was in a locked cell and not dangerous.

Inside the dim corridor DeSoto checked the preacher was decent. And there he was, sitting on the bench and just looking right back at DeSoto, expressionless, his big eyes glazed like a fish. Still feeling awkward, DeSoto stood back to let Donna look in at John through the bars.

So here they were: a black Baptist minister who proclaimed the Second Coming was coming, suspected of drug possession, sitting quiet in his cell; a young white woman, and her the Sheriff's daughter too, just standing there at the bars and staring in at him as though he had two heads; and DeSoto, Sheriff's deputy, just waiting and watching them both watching each other. The situation was just…well hell, it was *strange* was all. Nobody spoke or moved for long moments, unless you counted John's eyes moving listlessly from Donna to DeSoto and back again. In fact there was a great deal of eye-movement between the three of them.

"Can I ask him somethin'?" Donna said without looking away from John.

DeSoto's features flexed thoughtfully. "I guess."

Donna's voice was sympathetic. "What was it made you say all of that stuff in the paper? You know - about a messiah comin'. Why'd you say that?"

DeSoto felt a new discomfort now the situation had grown a religious limb, though it was a perfectly reasonable thing to ask bearing in mind what he had said. But that didn't stop DeSoto goose-bumping or his stomach tightening. He even opened his mouth to object, except that there was nothing to object to.

Donna took a hold of one bar of John's cell carefully, as if it might break. "Please mister, I have to know. It's real important."

Something stirred in John's eyes. "Why, girl?" The inner workings seemed to adjust behind his face so it lost a little of its stiffness.

That was the first time either DeSoto or Donna had heard John's voice, and it was shocking for its quiet power. (No, really. Writers' egos make them think they can describe anything and everything, but I doubt if I could do justice to John's voice. Maybe if you were to imagine Abe Lincoln's statue in Washington suddenly speaking, that might do it.) I think Donna started shaking then while she studied his face and tried to think. She was trying so hard to think that nothing would come.

"Do you care?" John asked, still looking at her.

"Yeah, I care," Donna managed to say.

To DeSoto it sounded as though she really did.

"How much?"

Again she was lost for words.

"Enough to accept Him? Enough to go to Him, and welcome Him? To serve and pray to God with Him, as He does? To let him show you where and how you went wrong, so you can start to put it right? Do you care enough to put your heart and soul in all of those things?"

Suddenly Donna had too much to think about, and knew neither where nor how to begin. DeSoto likewise, and John hadn't even been talking to him.

70

Donna saw that both her hands were now gripping the bars and trembling, and the tremors went all the way up her arms. Other tremors started in her legs. There was hotness around her eyes. DeSoto's too.

John had asked her something else.

"What?"

"I said what's your name?"

"Don - " She cleared the catch in her throat. "Donna Hughes."

"Donna, you do truly believe He'll come?"

"Yes I do." Her voice made an echo inside her mind, as if she were listening to the reverberations for a hint of untruth.

"And will you be ready to welcome your Messiah when He comes, Donna?"

That was harder to answer, and she held back for a second, eyes closed. "Yes I will," she answered finally. Believing she would caused a single tear to trickle down the side of her nose like a river.

John's eyes and voice softened together. "That's why I said what I said - so you'd know to be ready, okay?"

Donna nodded and let her chin drop onto her chest. The meeting was at an end, and she let a thoughtful DeSoto take her out of there.

TAPE 15

At twenty after seven on Thursday morning Andy DeSoto let himself back into the office, walked through to the door where the sign said *Abandon hope all who enter here*, unlocked it and went in the holding room to find his prisoner dead still, tucked into a corner of his cot, head back against the wall, eyes wide, red-rimmed and staring. His jacket was off and there was unpleasant streaking down the bib of his white shirt, which was pulled all the way out of his pants; they were similarly soiled over their front and down the legs. One of his shoes was off to reveal a bare black foot. (I only mention the color because DeSoto noticed it.)

At the sight of all this mess DeSoto felt his heart start to rise up in his throat, wondering what in hell had happened during the night. He stopped still to think, afraid that any decision he made could be the wrong one. The place smelled of stale vomit, sure, but DeSoto smelled other things besides. He visualized himself cleaning the place out with a mop and bucket and strong disinfectant and screwed his face up accordingly, only this aroma wouldn't ever go away completely. He knew it.

Now he was at the bars, close enough for a good look, and *Jesus!* The preacher really was a terrible sight - as if he'd been drinking all night or something. As though he'd gotten himself a pass out and been down The Triangle with the other soaks, then been brought back by his buddies and left at the door to find his own way inside. At least he'd had the decency to close the door on himself. DeSoto tried it - still locked - and felt stupid. He snorted and crouched down to search for a bottle. He couldn't possibly have missed something so obvious when frisking John the previous day. He hadn't made too thorough a job of it. The guy was a church minister; they didn't usually pack artillery or bottles - did they? No, he was positive that he had left John with only the clothes he came in the previous night when he locked up. Sure he did, but Hughes would still have a whole heap of stuff to say about this.

DeSoto checked his watch; there might just be time to get the place cleaned out before the Sheriff arrived. Then he thought further and winced. The preacher himself needed a bath and a change of clothes. And this stink! Yeah, there'd be one almighty whiff of pine - if they had any in the place. Shit, it was not the best morning he'd had this week. Finally he forced himself to unlock the cell and go inside. And now, scrutinizing the mess close-to, he recognized food in the vomit and decided his own stomach was in the first stages of a puke. Something soft underfoot made him look down...

Aw forget it. (This is making *me* feel sick!)

Let's fast-forward to where DeSoto locates John's missing shoe: John's sitting on it, okay? But there were other, more puzzling signs: like scratch marks on the wall behind John's head. Not just there, but all the way up. DeSoto went closer and saw they started way up at the window: lots of 'em, with dark red in them. Good Christ, there were scratch marks on the *ceiling!* When he looked at John's fingernails they were all of them either broken off or blackened, not just with bruising under the remaining nails, but with lumps of coagulated blood on the finger-ends. What in God's name had the preacher been doing?

A sudden surge of new anxiety fountained in DeSoto's chest. He leaned over John so he could examine the gaping eyes, about to test for signs of breathing first, and, failing that, a heartbeat, thinking 'Oh shit, maybe the preacher's - ?'

Then DeSoto was lying on his back on the cell floor with a numb cheek, listening to a high-pitched screeching and things crashing against solid objects - like walls that didn't give any but sure made a real unpleasant sound when bone bounced off of them: that distinctively soft-hard, hollow *bonk!*

DeSoto got to his feet in a hurry with smelly slime on his hands and pants, but too late to stop the preacher from making a far-from-clean getaway in which half of him seemed to want to take the iron doorframe along for company. The sickening sound of his face hitting the metal made DeSoto gasp.

Although he was right behind John and could have touched him if he stretched out his arm, the preacher would have been impossible to get a hold of. It was like the guy was working at twice normal speed, trying to fight off an army of invisible assailants coming at him from every side, the arms and legs all working at once, his head too. And all the while that shrill, frenzied screeching. DeSoto had never seen or heard anything like this before, ever, and he was scared.

Almost together they passed through the office, the preacher connecting with practically every item of furniture and whatever was on it, drawing DeSoto after him like a hurricane sucking a ball of debris after it. The deputy had to fight his way through the snowstorm of paper caught up in the whirlwind of files and books, telephones and electric fans, even a filing cabinet with its doors shooting open like big square fists. John hit most of them as if he were oblivious to pain.

Then he went through the glass panel of the door to Hughes' inner sanctum, bounced off the frame and changed direction instantly, like a pinball. Now there were flying drops of blood mixed in with everything else, and DeSoto made a titanic effort and lunged, only to find empty space till the floor came up and banged the wind out of him. He looked up to see John go out through the street door with a terrible bang that might have been from his face against the unyielding wood. Dazed himself, DeSoto began the next leg of the chase on his hands and knees before he was up and running again.

Outside the morning was sharp and fresh, but DeSoto's surroundings were just a blur. He didn't see the unmended crater in the sidewalk until his knee jarred and seemed to bend backwards, nearly but not quite pitching him on his face again.

John was still windmilling, about to hit the road. DeSoto thought it lucky there was no traffic this early. Except, that was, for the truck driven by Vince Lomas. Vince had just re-stocked the Texaco station's Pepsi machine and was accelerating out of town, one hand and both eyes on the radio tuner when John the Baptist connected with the front nearside fender and wrapped around it like a TV cartoon character might, his arms and legs jerking straight out, splatting against bits of superstructure (which were anything but super). The impact was so loud and close, DeSoto instantly shrank into himself and slumped on the sidewalk, deflated by the shock. Thinking about it later, he decided it was the only time he'd ever known anybody killed by Pepsi-Cola.

TAPE 16

Ed taught me there are different kinds of reality, but being so smart(assed) I guess you still think there's only one. You'd take a piece of rock and a conscious mind and tell me they both share the same reality. Now go look up the word *klutz*.

Okay, stop doing that and start remembering that consciousness gives you access to a Reality that's infinitely wider, deeper, more comprehensive and every-which-way more *Real* than the small r reality of material things. And what do we monkeys do with our amazing consciousness? We use it to compete with each other. To try and impress each other. To aggrandize ourselves. By concentrating practically all of our attention on physical things, we're giving preference to the mindless evolution of genes and throwing our amazing conscious potential down the john. But if we were to quit being so goddam concerned with making money, staying young-looking and trying to better each other, we'd evolve a hell of a lot faster, both physically *and* consciously.

Now I want to talk about how we could screw up the evolution of our Real, conscious selves just by monkeying with genes.

Before Darwin caught on to evolution in 1859, people had all kinds of nutty notions about what we are and where we came from. Most of us still have nutty notions, only now we've factored genes into the nuttiness, and decided our evolution is inefficient compared with how much more *competitive* we could be after some genetic monkeying.

Recall I talked about our personal 'bad' traits magically becoming 'good' when they help with our survival? Hyper-competitiveness is one of those two-faced traits. Human beings are the most hyper-competitive of all genetic organisms, driven by a mad mix of financial, emotional, intellectual, personal and corporate desires. Everything we do is increasingly competition-based. It even operates through religions.

Too often, different religions clash not because people have different gods, or because they have different ideas about the same God, but because

74

competing as genetic organisms creates *material* differences. Tribal feuding over territory, resources and rights, even mindless attacks on somebody else's religious ideas, are caused by the root fear of not surviving in a material world where everybody competes for resources. Trying to survive as genes, for genes, makes us all crazy, so obviously our crazy ideas about religion and God make matters worse.

Remember the cutting edge of what we're talking about here - *selfishness*. Remember *why* we're selfish - so our own personal genes will have a better chance of replicating and reproducing themselves. Competition is core to reproduction. Bodies, nervous systems and brains have evolved around competition. Sure it's all a matter of mindless survival engineering for genes, but when our conscious mind gets involved, competition becomes the motivation behind the 'I want' factor that drives us to reproduce. You don't think of the urge to reproduce as selfish or competitive, but there's a clear, direct link between genes' robotic survival behavior, and our conscious decision to reproduce. It's all about getting OUR own personal genes into the next generation.

It's hard to see as selfish or competitive because everybody is so eager to do it, and it happens with so little conscious effort on our part. (The fact that we're in these bodies only to help us evolve as consciousness never enters our thoughts, right? The only thinking involved in procreation is to make sure we get what we want from it.) Though one place you'll see plenty of selfish, thought-out determination is in folks driven by the genetic urge to procreate, but who can't because of some natural defect.

We think it's just great if medical science can help those folks have kids, because having kids is what genes build bodies to do. So when somebody with reproductive problems says they have a right to medical help because hey, having kids is *natural,* what they actually mean is, it's natural to be controlled by mindless, billion-years-old urges. Those urges have convinced them that being selfish for their genetic ass is *natural.* The word *natural* in this context is another excuse for ME, ME, ME. But because everybody does it for this same ME, ME, ME reason, we think that makes everything ok.

Tinkering with genes to enable otherwise infertile people to reproduce, is no different than tinkering with genes to enable them to select their unborn offspring's hair and eye color to go with the designer nursery. It's no different than the reason why people have plastic surgery to make themselves more physically attractive. It's all about taking personal notions of what I WANT for ME to ever greater extremes, because we can. (Why does anyone want to be more physically attractive? At bottom, to get laid. To make themselves more equal in the reproduction race...for their genes.) People who do these things for vanity reasons are riding on the exact same underlying motive as the folks who screen unborn offspring to improve their appearance or their survival chances: we're helping ourselves compete as genetic organisms, to ensure OUR personal set of genes gets a better deal.

I guess you've forgotten that this is the same selfish, gene-centered competition that winds up causing wars, inequality, poverty, hatred, greed, competition, pride, lust, homicide and all the rest of it.

But monkeying with genes to select the gender of kids before they're born, or their hair and eye color - that's only the start of a slippery slope. So is selecting the genes of the unborn for some idealized body type. The slippery slope gets steeper later when unwanted genes will be screened out so everybody appears 'perfect'. Except the only perfect they'll be is assholes. You're already so vain you think this book is about you, right? (Sorry 'bout that Carly.) The boundaries of what's acceptable will gradually be pushed back by us competing as genes, for genes, until who knows what? Cloning becomes natural and acceptable? Farming fetuses for new organs becomes natural and acceptable? Combining human and animal genes to create servants – or even 'interesting' partners - becomes natural and acceptable? What?

Question. What happens when everybody feels justified in demanding the selfish 'right' to whatever *they* want, simply for the good of their genetic ass? *Answer.* Our standards of morality, decency, common sense and humanity wind up being decided by what each of us wants for the good of our genetic ass.

When we insist that genetic tinkering to give us what we want is natural, what we really mean is *acceptable.* Acceptability driven entirely by self-interest. By what ME AND MY genes want. Genetic competition is why so many things that were once unnatural and unacceptable are now natural and acceptable, and standards continue falling. Quit kidding yourself they won't.

Hell, of course you don't want to see yourself this way; it's not in your interests as a gene machine. You probably think it sounds more like The Matrix all the time, but I'm not making it up. This is how things have always been for us. Good v Evil is consciousness fighting its genetically deluded self. We, the evolving consciousness that's merely passing through a genetic body on the way to someplace more enlightened, only benefit by what we learn from interacting with this material reality, and with each other along the way. Genes and their bodies are just part of the means to a very different end to all of this. They're how we learn to evolve consciously by developing a *less* competitive, *less* selfish way of life.

But seeing all of this for what it Really is takes some exceptionally clear thinking. And that's just the beginning. The hard part is learning to quit being selfish for what you always thought of as yourself.

TAPE 17

This tape begins with me wondering why Mrs. Catherine Hughes was not wetting her britches to bring me the glad tidings about the deceased minister. I got the news from Charlie, The Star's gofer. He had it hot from his daddy, who heard it off a friend in Rockdale whose wife got to calling all of her friends with the news. By the time I came to hear about it, practically half the western hemisphere knew a truck had creamed J the B. When I dropped in the Sheriff's office I found DeSoto, that well-known extinct automobile, holding the fort alone. His ability to divulge information had also gone extinct.

"Hey Andrew," I told him, "you remember me."

"Certainly I do, sure, an' I still got nothing to tell you, Sheriff's orders."

"But it was hit'n run, right?"

"Can't say nuthin' 'bout that. I mean no, it was not."

"The driver was on parole?"

"Look, Miss, uh - ?"

"Hoover. J. E. Hoover."

"Okay Miss Hoo…aw, hey, I've been told to hold this thing down, y'know? Low profile."

I sighed. "This ain't my day is it Andrew?"

He sighed also. "You an' me both."

"Hey Andrew - you can call me John Edgar, okay?" I don't think DeSoto had a sense of humor that day. Maybe he didn't ever - who noo?

Hear that? Already I was beginning to sound like a New Yorker. Except that it wasn't a New York Times reporter because those guys get stories, and all I was getting was frustrated.

Apparently DeSoto was still waiting for the Sheriff to return from the Mayor's where he'd been for a long time. From the stink in that place I didn't blame him. There was a guy reglazing a door and a general atmosphere of untidiness and disarray that made me wonder if the circus had hit the Sheriff's office for one night only.

Anyhow while Hughes was at the Mayor's I decided to pay a visit to the informant who had let me down this time and would henceforth no longer be credited in my articles.

The door of the Hughes household was answered by a homey-but-pretty teenage girl with a lukewarm-but-genuine smile who seemed to take an instant-but-wary liking to me. She said she was Donna Hughes and took me into a front room that seemed reserved for guests and offered me some coffee, but I said no, I had enough sleepless nights as it was without compounding a felonious assault on my body with more of that stuff. She smiled again showing a good set of teeth. Somebody had looked after them, which isn't always the case in this locality.

While Donna went to fetch her ma I eyeballed the place. It was kind of stark except for overly-fussed touches like lace covers on the backs and arms of the chairs. (Those covers are called *anti-macassars* for anyone who didn't know, which included me at the time. The only reason I know now is because Mrs. Hughes told me while I was there. She was even more pretentious than I was.) She didn't seem any too communicative this time, but I assumed this opportunity to open her big mouth again would get her hormones dancing to my tune if our last meeting was anything to go on. I figured she had nothing better to use her hormones for than mischief anyhow.

Now there appeared in her eye something less than a friendly gleam. "And how can I help you, Miss - ? Pardon me, I forgot your name."

Now it was my turn to be insulted because she knew my goddam name as well as I did.

"Laurie Hendricks."

"You gave the people in this town quite a lashing with that last piece you wrote, Miss Hendricks."

This was a reprimand and I was expected to take it lying down or I wouldn't get anything new out of her. As it happened I didn't get anything period.

"I transcribed straight word-of-mouth quotes is all, Mrs. Hughes, lifted right off of magnetic recording tape. I can play it back to you or anyone else who might have forgotten what they really said."

Her eyelids closed halfway. "*Off-the-record.*" You recall saying that, Miss Hendricks? I certainly do. Can you explain how my half of our off-the-record conversation made it onto your front page?"

78

Naturally I played innocent but I could imagine her dilemma. On one hand she was dying to open her big mouth, while her other hand was trying to restrain the foot that she knew would get stuck in it.

"I guess that tape must've just kept right on playing and its contents somehow wound up in the article, it being on the same spool and all you understand."

She understood. "Surely. And next time you need information about anything that happens around here you better talk to my husband. He's the Sheriff - but of course you know that."

I would've gotten up to leave except that I hadn't been offered a seat to begin with. Okay, so I'd put an end to what had been a rewarding relationship; she'd rewarded me with information I wouldn't otherwise have gotten nearly so soon, and I rewarded her with a kick in the teeth. I got what was coming to me. It was all part of a journalist's day. At least I walked out of there knowing what an anti-macassar was. Maybe I'd use that in the next edition; I wasn't getting much else.

Now, while I go make some tea, then pour it down the john and fix myself a drink, you can read about me driving away from the Sheriff's house, looking in my mirror in time to see his company car swing into the slot I'd just vacated. That gave me an idea. As I hadn't spoken to the Mayor yet about J the B, it struck me that maybe he'd like to see his name in The Star. Mayor's need to get themselves re-elected; his picture in the paper might help folks recognize him when they saw him in the street at re-election time. Better yet, if he knew he was choosing between a picture of his face or the deceased minister's, I figured Mister Mayor would make the right choice instinctively. (I wouldn't need to remind him The Star didn't run pictures with what I wrote; my prose is graphic enough.)

The Mayor's white clapboard house was bigger, neater and better cared-for than the Sheriff's newer and meaner one (which looked as if it had been erected for the employee of a now-defunct mine operator, because it had). The Mayor's place also had a healthy growth of honeysuckle running up the front and over the porch, and the smell of that was the second thing that greeted me when I arrived.

The first thing was the sight of a far more exotic flower in the shape of Mrs. Stevenson, whom I didn't know from Eve then, but I sure soon found out about afterwards. Maxine was standing beside an elderly Japanese micro-car when she caught sight of me and decided to wait and see who I was. The carefully painted mouth smiled carefully so as not to stretch anything into wrinkles. The well-shaped eyebrows climbed a millimeter up her high, clear forehead as the serious eyes held mine. Though even as all of those receptivity signals were showing, the real Mrs. Stevenson was someplace else.

"Hello, can I help you?"

"I'm here to see the Mayor."

"Oh? Robby never said." She wasn't looking me up and down the way women do, sometimes without even moving their eyes. Instead she seemed to be trying to see through my face. Nothing unpleasant, more a desire to know who I was inside. I even quite liked the way she looked at me; it would have made me feel almost protective if I hadn't been so self-oriented.

"He's…around back." She half-turned to look back at the house but kept her eyes on me. "You just…it's alright, just go right on through."

I stepped away so she could open the car's tiny door and slide herself inside, which I admit she did most elegantly for her size. Don't get me wrong, she was no balloon, far from it. She was kind of succulent and full-bodied, which made me think of a slightly neglected hothouse plant like a rare orchid or something of the kind, left to its own devices.

While I watched her drive away, a red Chevy Camaro came backwards down the slipway, driven by a young man whose eyes seemed everywhere at once, but then I figured a person's eyes did that when they were driving a red Camaro backwards onto the street at fifty miles an hour. He watched me in his mirror as the car accelerated away with a fat-assed roar that started dogs barking and folks looking out their windows. Yep, that was the Mayor's son. An interesting family.

Mayor Stevenson came around the side of the house in answer to my three pushes on the doorbell. "Miss - ?"

"Hendricks."

"Yes of course." He walked me back round the side of the house saying, "We don't use the street door, kind of inconvenient, people coming in and out all the time."

I was wondering what could possibly have induced Mrs. Stevenson to get herself hitched to a turtle like the Mayor. I waited until I was inside the house and smelling coffee before I steered the conversation to the business in hand.

"Okay to use this?" I put the tape-recorder on the kitchen table. "Kind of habit."

"No, I have no objection to going on record, just so long as I get a copy of the tape. I'll pay for it of course." He smiled as he brought the coffee to the table. "Sit down why don't you." He sat opposite.

In my most businesslike, career-reporter's voice I said, "Mayor Stevenson, about the minister…"

He seemed surprised. "Minister?"

I looked at him sideways. "The one who was run down outside the jail? I made an appointment to come over here and discuss it with you?"

"Oh, that. There's really nothing I can tell you, Miss - ?"

"Hendricks. Laurie Hendricks." Did I imagine the little brick walls where his eyes should've been?

"Ah yes. From The Star."

At that point I sighed. I know because it's right here on tape. Maybe that was a bad day for me, maybe I had a hangover, maybe all kinds of things, but I just knew I'd get nowhere with this guy, and that blank look of his - well, it just triggered something in me.

"Incidentally," he said, " how'd you hear about that?"

"A mail-shot from the Coroner's office in Zeno." I got up and reached for my tape recorder. "Okay, Mayor Stevenson, you've been real helpful," I told him. "So next I intend to visit the county morgue with a staff photographer and shoot some stills of the deceased minister. Then I'll go see what the Coroner has to say. Then I'll check with the driver of the truck. Which, in case you've forgotten that too, was on the doorstep of Sheriff Hughes' jailhouse, a picture of which will also look good in The Star. And when I'm through with the truck-driver I'll talk with every other person I can think of who might possibly have information that my Star readers have a right to know. But even after all of that, I'll still have space on the front page for a few words about how helpful Mayor Stevenson was when I called on him. Okay?" He even got a sweet smile as a period mark.

Mayor Stevenson stared at the window in silence for what seemed like an hour. When he spoke, it was with the kind of reasonable voice homicidal maniacs use.

"I've been wanting to meet the person who scrapes the sidewalk for all of that lurid and fallacious garbage that appears in your excuse for a paper."

He only said 'lurid and fallacious' because he was being taped, but I heard something else in his voice that might've been dislike for me personally and it made me uncomfortable.

I decided to get annoyed myself. I told him if he objected so strongly to The Star's version of events, all he had to do was change his paper.

He sat back and regarded me with bleak eyes. "It ain't nothin' to do with the paper. It's your own twisted version of events."

That time there was enough unconcealed malice in his words to make the hairs tickle on the back of my neck, and I was starting to wonder about the folks in that town. What with junked-up preachers and blacked-up, club-wielding rednecks, it was no wonder city dwellers sometimes had a poor view of life between the interstates. Not that it didn't cut both ways, of course.

"Am I imagining this," I said, "or do you have something against me personally?" Maybe I oughtn't to have pushed it, but I can't help the way I was made.

"I don't think you want to know the answer to that," he said. He got up to show me I was leaving. He'd chosen the discretion that maybe he wouldn't have had I not been a reporter, but he packed so much inflexion and meaning into that simple line, it was all concentrated animosity. And I still had no idea why. Maybe he just didn't like lady reporters.

TAPE 18

A message was waiting on my answering machine when I got back to The Star office in Zeno. It was Donna Hughes. She wanted to see me and talk, so I called her and we fixed a meeting. No, I had no idea why she wanted to talk. It didn't matter, just so long as I got the lowdown on everything from her parents' marital problems, to who paid the driver of the truck to run down John the Baptist.

I'd met Donna just once a couple of days earlier in Passmore, but the overly made-up little fox who got off the bus in Zeno that Saturday morning was not the same homey Donna I'd expected. When she said it would be nice to go get a milkshake it took me by surprise. And what's wrong with milkshake? Nothing at all. The stronger the stimulant, the weaker the individual, right? But hey, I shouldn't have to come on like Superman lecturing six year olds. (I only consume copious quantities of gin to make me a more interesting character in this book.)

The guy making the shakes was an amateur who never heard of a martini shake. As I sat and watched Donna siphon off that froth I suddenly saw myself as a big sister who could listen to her attentively, and in her gratitude she'd regale me with copy. Then she lowered the shake-glass leaving a yellow clown's smile on either side of her mouth, and I glimpsed a part of my younger self I was trying to forget had ever existed.

I found myself examining her make-up and clothes, the way she'd fixed up her hair, thinking how much she reminded me of me before I fell on my feet a few years earlier (or was it my head?) and got sentenced to that job with The Star.

Why'd she want to see me? For advice on getting out of Passmore, Raiment County, the whole thing. She was not so naive as to imagine I'd loan her a hundred bucks and put her on a bus, later hearing she'd landed a job in PR or something. Sure, fairy tales happen, but they don't solve life's problems. Most times they only create new problems. That's something else I shouldn't have to lecture anyone about. (Boy, I must be in one of those moods.)

I sure didn't need to lecture somebody who lived in a place with cold running unemployment, a nutty mother and the local redneck Sheriff for a father. Not to mention Donna's *robot* thing. Except that as just another character in this book I didn't know what her problem was. When I asked she went all shy on me.

"I don't really know how to start off. See, you're not like the folks round hereabouts who never been anyplace and don't know things an' all. I guess that's the problem - I don't want to end up like them."

I didn't explain that I *was* like the folks round thereabouts. Instead I told her I understood how she felt. Boy, I did too.

"All of the folks I know around seem like life quit on 'em, y'know? I can't stay in Raiment the rest of my life, goin' nowhere. I got to get out." Her voice had that edge of despair you get when seeking important answers in an empty shake glass.

Tedious seconds slouched by while I watched her struggle with the exact same problem I'd had at her age. Trouble was I still had it, so did most kids in Raiment County: they wanted to get away. Some would wind up in the army, others would drift into a life of crime, while the extra smart ones would get themselves pregnant so they could be a single parent on welfare.

Then she began opening up. "Miss Hendricks, I was goin' out four-five times a week, down The Triangle bar on the Zeno Road, makin' out I was havin' a good time, 'cept I wasn't bein' myself. It was all a crazy kinda act I was puttin' on for everybody."

"So you felt kind of fake? We all do sometimes."

"But I *was* a fake." Now more earnest. "The real me was underneath but on the outside I felt like a - " She wondered if she ought to say whatever it was. "It sounds stupid, but like I was stuck inside a *robot?*"

Then, without warning: "Miss Hendricks, what you wrote 'bout the messiah and ever'thing? It's all true. I know it is. I talked with John the preacher…"

I looked incredulous. "Well sure it's true. I wrote it all down verbatim, just the way he said it, word for word."

She seemed relieved. "An' there really is a messiah comin'?"

Suddenly I didn't like the route this conversation was taking. Sisterly feelings are fine when you're getting something out of it and secretly recording the conversation; big sisters can be as sneaky as the next guy, but I wasn't getting anything. It was termination time.

"Hey," I said in the most sympathetic voice I could find, "call me Laurie, okay?"

"Okay…Laurie. Aw hey, it's real nice of you to let me just sit here an' all." And then she was blubbing.

I gave her my least soiled Kleenex and watched her dab and sniff. From there the conversation just got trivial the way they do when one party just got something off their chest, and the other party realized there's nothing in it for them. A little while later I put Donna on the bus and forgot about her, went back to my office and fell asleep, woke up, came home and replayed our conversation, wrote down a few select items from all of the junk that was lying around on the floor of my mind, drank some nourishing warm milk and hit the hay.

Yeah, that was a joke about the milk; twice in one day can start a pernicious habit. But now Donna's robot has come up again, listen: Except in sci-fi, Kafka or someplace, a character thinking they're a robot means either they have a screw loose or the writer does. That's what I thought then. Remember I was more skeptical than anybody you ever met, only skeptical is not the same as pig-headed, or dogmatic, or a horse's ass for dismissing the entire notion of a robot/human comparison without thinking on it. Not until later did I realize just how neatly the word *robot* encapsulates the problem everybody has.

At first I figured Donna was just growing through the hyper-unreality of teen-age, when you're like a wild horse filled with chemical urges you never experienced before. You see all the other crazy horses running around with a bee up their ass so you go chasing off with them. (You might love horses but they're pretty dumb compared with how smart you're supposed to be.) You assume you'll grow out of those mindless urges after teenage. You don't. They just cool and harden into the dumb-level knowledge that some things are more gratifying to chase than others.

Most folks spend the rest of their life chasing money, personal recognition, sex, power, security, designer labels or babies. The fact that you wouldn't dream of *not* chasing those things just shows what a mindless habit it all is. Even the brightest people use that mold of smart blancmange behind their eyes to think about the same old instinct-gratification behavior in some form or another.

You're going to get real mad with yourself when you realize what's going on. Or you'll more likely do what I did and reject the notion entirely. From the time I was old enough to ingest TV, my body/brain had me convinced I couldn't live without all the things other folks had. I was jealous of the guys with fame and fortune, and nothing makes you more hungry for personal recognition than seeing others enjoying the kind of success you're not. (Like I said, it doesn't have to be fame and fortune; it can be kids, or lerve, or peer-acceptance, or self-worth confirmation, or any of the other delusional things that genetic gratification creates.) If any of those are not forthcoming, you feel you're one gene machine who's not surviving well enough.

Hence the *monkey suit* descriptor. It's a perfectly valid way to describe these bodies/brains. Yes, it sounds dehumanizing, but hell, I'm not the one trying to make people less than they are by reducing them to material components the way science does. I'm the one who's saying we're *more*. Not some weird, hybrid kind of more, just more of the consciousness that makes you uniquely more than chemicals. This uniqueness is the true miracle of life, not the stupid biomachinery. That only seems like 'life' because we're so impressed with the way it rebuilds itself.

To think that chemicals can create that consciousness is like thinking a Xerox copying machine can create consciousness. Chemicals for making Xerox copies come out the ground. Ditto chemicals for making body/brain copies. That fact didn't change since DNA's extremely great grandparents began life on the planet of you apes, and DNA is still no more consciously aware it can build new bodies and brains than a robot production line is aware it can build Volkswagens or Nissans or Fords.

So remember: The one genuinely unique miracle of life is being *consciously aware* you're alive. (Can you imagine not 'knowing' you're alive? I bet some of you can.)

TAPE 19

Hearing Donna talk about John the Baptist reminded me how, a couple of days earlier, I'd threatened Mayor Stevenson with a visit to the county morgue for some unsavory pictures to color my deceased minister story. Fact is, The Star doesn't run editorial pictures. Besides, can you imagine a picture of a guy who just kissed a speeding truck! The Mayor obviously could, which was the general idea. Interviewing the Coroner was more bluff; there was no need after Stevenson admitted John was on something illegal. All I had to do now was mention drugs, and folks would imagine the worst and rush out to buy The Star because everybody just loves reading about scandal. As for grilling the truck driver, hell, he was going to say it was all the preacher's fault. Who wouldn't? The guy was dead and couldn't argue.

Even after the Mayor said John's death was an accident, that would become homicide when I implicated the preacher's unknown supplier. Maybe I'd even advocate a charge of attempted homicide be made law for pushers.

See, I even had a moral standpoint to baste my tale with. The next Star edition was going to burn a hole in the floor of your front porch. Under the banner JOHN THE BAPTIST LOSES HEAD I invented the story I'd hoped to get, but didn't, from DeSoto, Sheriff Hughes, Mrs. Hughes, Mayor Stevenson and/or Donna. I was just disappointed not to have some real dirt to shovel into it.

Speaking of dirt, there are folks who harbor the nutty notion that we can engineer immorality out of ourselves by replacing 'bad' genes with 'good' genes. The trouble with that notion is, morality doesn't come from a particular gene or a sequence of genes. Morality comes from *all* of our genes. Morality is the result of minds trying to make sense of what genetic bodies and brains make them do.

Ed summed genetic morality up neatly: For genetic bodies, 'good for survival' is *right*, and 'bad for survival' is *wrong*. For millions of years that kind of 'morality' has steered the evolution of genes and designed the organisms that genes build.

Even for the consciousness in a human brain, with all of its potential, millions of years of 'good for survival' being right and 'bad for survival' being wrong takes time to evolve out from under. That's why we still mostly allow ourselves to be pushed around by what a genetic body wants. We still tailor our morality to fit its mindless *material* demands.

But being so smartassed, we're convinced that our morality comes entirely from our *mind*, and that our consciousness is in control of our body's demands. We're so full of our runaway success on this tiny planet, and yet we still think of 'success' as a *material* thing. Material success is what 'being genetic' is all about. Striving for material success proves that our body still has more control over us than our mind does over it.

According to Ed, one reason why we have so much trouble seeing beyond this genetic version of reality is that we've nothing better to compare ourselves with, or to set this narrow version of reality against. All we've got is our own stupid past. We seem to have gotten so far ahead of other animals (and our earlier selves) intellectually, we imagine we're way ahead in moral terms also. Yet we still live inside the same survival parameters they do, based on the replication and reproduction of genes.

I already said that one of the major illnesses caused by being genetic is competitiveness. Because competition is central to genetic existence, even when it leads to extremes we think it's natural, normal, and right. It drives business, sport and play. It takes over leisure activities. Competitiveness rules relationships. It's working from the moment you're born. Competitiveness, often aggressive, seems as normal as chicken soup. Fighting as competition is normal. War as competition is normal. Murder as competition is normal.

Normal? Well sure. Those things happen too often, in too many places, and always did, to be considered *ab*normal. (You can think of other words to describe them but, statistically, abnormal ain't one of those words. That would be like saying death is abnormal.) We mightn't like stuff but that doesn't stop it being normal, all thanks to genetic evolution.

Fighting and war and murder are actually condoned and often even prized as functions of the survival process. That too sounds insane, yet how many billions of dollars are poured into arms manufacture, supporting, perpetrating and encouraging aggression, war, and murder? The arms industry is massive on Planet Psycho. It exemplifies how competition psychosis vigorously dissuades us from even beginning to recognize a selfless, altruistic alternative even if it walked up and embraced us like a long-lost brother. Instead, this psychosis makes us think that our brother is a competitor for the same resources we depend on for our survival.

But never forget that our fellow competitors are in the same boat we are; they too are the paradox of consciousness stuck inside flesh and blood machines that evolved to keep colonies of genes replicating. And laws made by ourselves-as-genes, *for* ourselves-as-genes, can never change such genetically 'normal' behavior.

But selfishness for genes makes us refuse to see that life really is this way. It lulls us into thinking that more materiality is our real evolution, and that it's making us 'better' human beings.

The question is, what is a 'better human being'? What is a human being period? What are we for? Why are we here at all? Most so-called human beings simply don't know. They just do things the way people always did them. Their only understanding of the concept 'better human being' really is one who's materially better off.

For developing nations desperate to catch up with the big guys, materialism is next to godliness. Mine more, burn more, consume more. Maybe the planet will survive, but hey, we've got more important things to worry about than the planet. We have to feed and house all of these new people we can't help producing.

And there it is again, precisely what's creating all of our problems: the need for genes to replicate and get themselves reproduced. The self-perpetuating process that we delude ourselves is our most important role, and governs everything we think we are and everything we feel we should do. The process that makes selfishness cooler, more complex and more insidious the longer we practice it.

The genes and their bodies that we're all making the rules for, are chemicals, the same as drugs are. Like other hard drugs, their effects - in this case aggressive competition - are addictive; unbelievably hard to kick when you've been addicted for as long as we have.

These chemicals are also an hallucinogenic, producing paranoid delusions that make the addiction seem natural and normal. But rather than try to elevate our behavior to a higher, more conscious level, we allow competition to reduce our conscious notions of existence to the same level as the mindless instinct that drives these bodies.

We've been obsessed with 'winners and losers' and 'survival of the fittest' for so long, we only see bodies/brains in competitive terms. Physical and mental qualities have become 'better' or 'worse' simply because of whether they make us materially successful as genetic survival machines above all other considerations, whatever we pretend to the otherwise. We value the genetic efficiency in our own bodies and brains in the exact same primitive way we value hard cash - for the way they help us compete as walking collectives of genes. This attitude - steered by materialism, from a mindless level way, way below our consciousness - is the one we're bringing to genetic engineering.

We already know that bodies, brains and minds were created by genes trying to copy themselves accurately. In those terms, the genetic engineering that we do is the same as genes manipulating us to manipulate *them*, to improve *their* evolution, in the society *they* built using the brains *they* evolved. Sounds weird, but to scientists, that's what we-as-genes reduce to. Worse yet, some gene manipulators see us as collectives of negotiable property, part of some corporate balance sheet rather than as conscious beings who just happen to be wearing monkey suits.

Some folks use the term 'bio-piracy' to describe the way gene manipulating corporations claim pieces of human genome for themselves, except that doesn't make it sound half as bad as it really is. *Bio-cannibalism* is closer. Remember how the Nazis tried to create a master race? Eugenics is one word for that. It means the extermination of anyone who isn't up to your personal idea of perfect. It's an obsession with *physical* standards, in the Nazi example taken to psychotic lengths. All that matters is how well your physical attributes measure up to some totally subjective standard.

Genetic engineering could be more dangerous than what the Nazis tried to do if it involves giving expensive designer labels to altered sequences of genes for the same reason we give anything else a designer label - money. The things that make us uniquely 'human' - our awareness, our memories, hopes, dreams and spiritual aspirations - are being treated not just as by-products of genetic components, but as an irrelevance, or even a nuisance when some of we 'humans' complain that all the wrong priorities are taking over.

Do you like the idea of mindless bits of biology being more highly regarded - in profit, developmental and experimental terms - than your and/or your offspring as whole human beings, just because somebody found a way to own, buy and sell sequences of genes? Already it's difficult to separate this profit motive downside from any claim to altruism in the body-brokering industry, and it'll get harder as the business gets bigger and more competitive. Too much money is riding on it.

What we now call genetic engineering is just the latest phase of our congenital inability to recognize any Real difference between the evolution of a genetic body/brain, and the evolution of ourselves as consciousness. Genetic engineering is a super-efficient way of ensuring that selfishness continues to overrule unselfishness as our prime motivation.

Let me just go through the workings-out on that for my mom. Mom, selfishness is caused by material considerations. It creates divisions between people. But *unselfishness* is exclusive to consciousness. Unselfishness is all that can ever cause us to evolve for Real. So monkeying with genes for what are fundamentally selfish reasons will only accelerate precisely what made us selfish in the first place: the selection of physical differences because they make some people better survivors than others.

In gradually taking over the job of natural selection from laws of physics, our Real purpose is not to become more selective for genes, but to do what only consciousness can do: be selective *for consciousness*. That does *not* mean manipulating an individual's brain to try and make them brighter. (Brain brightness is not consciousness because brains themselves aren't conscious.) That misconception leads to more selfishness, more inequality, more of the same old problems.

One way to avoid all of that is to prevent genetic manipulation for the wrong reasons. Powerful legislation and policing are needed to prevent corporate genetic profiteering. Or to stop the 'improvement' of individuals simply for vanity reasons, or 'designer' offspring, or for any reason that, at bottom, is a selfish reason. Manipulating genes for ME, ME, ME reasons can't ever be good.

What are the right reasons for manipulating genes? Wake up. There's only ever one right reason for doing anything, be it stem cell research, gene therapy, the works. That reason is to help us all grow as our Real, conscious selves.

Evolving as consciousness is our only genuinely 'natural' way forward. More natural than the first single-celled ancestors of these human bodies dividing and replicating. More natural than their descendants crawling out of the sea to live on land. Whether you think evolution is God's will, or just the natural development of a Godless universe, evolving as consciousness is the only natural progression for us, simply because all that we Really are is consciousness.

Here's a mental health warning to anyone who wants to do some Real evolving: When you start saying stuff like: "We don't really need a bigger house, a more expensive car, an even deeper deepfreeze," you can bet your buffalo-hide bedsocks that people will start to wonder about your sanity. Even though the sanity everybody's trying so desperately to hang on to is precisely what makes them all crazy. I called it *Competition Psychosis*, and you catch it from genes.

90

You thought The Alien was good at looking out for itself? I'll tell you a secret. On The Alien's home planet they use our TV broadcasts to write their training manuals.

TAPE 20

I made this tape for Donna because she'd gotten to thinking that the road out of nowheresville pointed to God. The truth was that all she knew about God came out of a bible - after it got a fundamentalist spin from her monumentally ignorant ma. Too many folks think a bible is a bunch of strict rules you should live your life by. That way you don't have to think for yourself about the most important issues. Bibles free you of responsibility, and that's perfect for anybody who isn't too bright. Those same people just happen to be the ones who're most susceptible to simplistic notions embedded in fundamentalist religion, but even intelligent folks are hobbled by religion. Because intelligence is not the same as consciousness, it can often share the same brain with dogma and not be aware of its influence.

When did God ever say for you to quit thinking for yourself? Never. Why'd God give you a free will? So your Real, conscious self can develop instead of stagnating inside a mental straight-jacket. But to do that, your free will needs strenuous regular exercise.

You know how religious some folks are about guns? Well guns are only dangerous because of people, and so is religion. When guns and religion come together, boy, that's the front line where the blood 'n' guts, hand-to-hand stuff happens, and people prove yet again that their religion is about material considerations, not spiritual ones.

I was about to open my Reality Window just here to talk about the crazy zealots who can't wait to die for their beliefs, but one of 'em strapped a goddam bomb to herself and blew the entire wall away. Jesus! And these people imagine they're doing that for God? F*** right off. They're due one hell of a surprise, because the only way you can 'do things for God' in this life is by doing things for others, and I mean good things. That's not religion, it's common sense, of an infinitely practical kind that reaches way beyond primitive human notions of God or life. (That's a taster for the tape on Practical Reality later.)

Most ordinary folks get sucked into cozy reassurances that they've got the only right spiritual answer, when the truth is, their religion is just a different frame for the same old material questions. Religion isn't a final answer to anything. The second you make it that, it stops evolving, and you along with it.

Well certainly religion has to evolve along with everything else, otherwise you spend a lifetime going noplace. Meaning you either got the wrong religion, or you're ignoring the Real questions that need answering because they're contrary to the dogmas in your religion.

Anyhow there was Donna with a heap of questions about God, and the one person she thought might have some answers had just suffered a fatal Pepsi overdose. That put me next in line as Donna's spiritual advisor. Hey, she could've done worse - I had no preconceived illusions about religion. (The only gods I was interested in then were fame, success, and money.) At least I can admit it now without using religion to disguise it as 'spiritual'.

Yes mister, I know religion isn't all bad, but the downsides of religion are worse than bad. Religion is *people*, and their thoughts and deeds create enough downsides to fill a Congressional Library of unholy bibles. Get your facts straight. Religion per se is a *human* creation, no matter what you thought to the contrary. As that, it's susceptible to all of the same failings we are. In many cases it's a blatant expression of those failings. Turn on your TV and see.

Now picture me, staring at my office diary that morning wishing I was home in a hot tub sipping a cold martini, or even vice-the-versa; I wasn't too fussy right then. 'Cept that I'd probably have felt guilty buying gin when I could've spent the money on something infinitely more intoxicating, like paying my phone bill. Hell, what did I need a phone for? Nobody ever called me unless it was to say they were about to write me saying they'd be cutting my phone off for non-payment of arrears.

Just by coincidence that was when my office phone rang. I know because it too is right here in my diary. A hot bathroom turned back into my office and I picked up the phone and kind of leaned my head against it with my elbow on the desk, and by coincidence heard Donna Hughes' pleasant if twangy voice already saying something about my next piece for The Star.

"...*the healer* - and was you gonna do a story on him?"

"What healer's this, Donna?"

"Ain't you heard 'bout how he just talks to folks and cures 'em of stuff? Cured Mister Webberley's bad back, an' Liza Tindall of the croup, an' he can even fix broken bones an' I thought if you was goin' up there to see him I could go along? I wouldn't get in the way...an' plenty of folks been up there," she coaxed. "I'm kinda nervous 'bout goin' by myself, and..."

"…And you want me along as company. Where's your healer at, Donna?"

"Over by Blackwater Creek an' take the back-road, only it kind've disappears an' you walk the rest."

I snorted. "Story of my life. Okay Donna, you got yourself a ride. Just be careful when we get up there is all; I've heard about these guys and their layin'-on of hands."

That produced a snigger. "Don't worry 'bout guys - I bin there an' back a few times." The way she said it left me with no doubts at all.

I picked Donna up a couple of streets from her parents' house as instructed around six in the evening, and though Blackwater Creek is no more than three miles away, the road is underclass and winds through country that gives every impression of being untouched by the wheel of man. Which is something of a miracle, seeing as how the place is practically within a Coke-can's throw of the most visited part of North America. But even at the height of the season tourists don't go out of their way to look at abandoned strip-mines posing as prime landfill site material. No wonder they call this area the wilderness, though it's more of an eyesore - one reason why Raiment County is not renowned for its roadsigns. If you're just looking to dump some refuse, anyplace will do.

By the time we reached Blackwater Creek the new moon was clearly visible in the deep blue evening sky, bright and waxen as a buffed bone as you might say if you were writing a stupid novel. Now we had to find the road leading up to the place this healer was doing his thing. The charcoal-shaded gloom was dead still and silent and filled with clouds of tiny biting things with wings, and you couldn't tell where solid objects end and shadows begin. When a Pontiac Firebird, looking like it rolled over a cliff and was rebuilt by an alien, goes by you very fast without any lights (at least none I could see) you start to wonder if this is such a great idea. We could disappear and never be heard of again.

"How you doing?" I asked Donna. She'd been sitting quiet as a mouse for the past couple of miles. She was wearing one of those hooded cotton shirts and the same second-skin jeans she had on in Zeno, so I figured she had to be freezing because I was, even with the heating full on, but I wasn't so old that I didn't remember how annoying it can be to keep on at somebody younger when they say they're okay. I was trying to see where the track fell away, intent on making sure we didn't fall away with it when Donna nudged my arm and I turned her way. The Firebird was parked down a cut in the trees. A few other assorted vehicles were scattered around down there also, but I only had an instant impression before we went by. I hit the brake.

"Well, nothing ventured," I said, and turned in behind the Firebird, then thought better of it and parked so we could make a quick getaway. Donna was all ready and waiting for me when I finished concealing my purse in the trunk under a pile of mildewed Star copies, and checking there was nothing else in the car worth breaking-in for. There never was, unless you counted me, and even then you wouldn't have gotten enough to feed a medium-sized dog.

Amazingly Donna was displaying none of the symptoms of hypothermia the way I would be before long. That kind of thing doesn't enamor you to teenagers. It also reminds you that at my age (twenty-five) some people in New Guinea and places are great-grandmothers. Of course those guys don't waste time chasing careers. They wouldn't have chased mine in case they caught it.

I closed my eyes momentarily and walked into Donna who was stopped on this open hillside where it joined with two or three others along a series of crooked seams. The landscape here resembled the horizontal mid-section of a very obese person, with little ripples of grassy fat falling away from the large central mounds of belly and thighs. There was even a darkly isolated clump of trees for pubic hair, except that was stuck on one of its knees, but you get the picture. Now put a gathering of maybe fifty people on a small bulge of mother earth's navel, and that was the scene. Whatever I'd expected, this didn't look like much of a story. But that's what I'd thought about the Baptists.

We came up on the rear of the gathering and I stopped to find my tape machine, then I realized Donna was gone when nobody answered my whispered question about what we should do now. I was supposed to be holding her hand, and now I felt like Gretel without Hansel. Searching the heads in front for Donna's pony-tail, I found the gap-toothed grin of who I later learned was Michael McClure pointed at me. Then somebody moved between us and I lost him.

When I found Donna she was standing beside McClure. Better yet, on the other side of Donna was a Tom Cruise stand-in who obviously knew Donna too. I moved in behind them and touched her elbow, and she just handed me a quiet little smile over her shoulder and faced front again. The Tom Cruise clone did the same. McClure though, he reached out and grasped my hand, shook it nicely, then went on beaming his hillbilly smile at me until Donna turned him around the right way. He did one last take then behaved himself.

94

The ignorant skeptic I was then didn't expect anything special to happen. But things were happening - little things. Standing on damp grass, on tippy-toe, trying to see over these heads to the healer, I noticed how unnaturally quiet it was - like the whole of life's aural overload of neurosis-inducing junk had been vacuumed right out of the air. There were a few stars. Venus was a tiny prick of brilliance over the crest of one of that fat-lady-landscape's enormous breasts, not far from the softer light of the moon. The mist was oozing out of the ground, making a blue haze around us.

Out front there were no cripples throwing away their crutches or leaping out of wheelchairs. The healer looked much the same as anybody else you'd see on the street in a town in Raiment County, but the look on the face of each one of those people on their way back to resume their place in the crowd made my eyes hot for no reason I could comprehend. I forgot how cold I was. I even forgot to switch on my tape-recorder, not that it would have heard anything.

I don't remember Michael McClure or his cute-looking friend leaving. All I recall is driving back to Passmore with Donna asleep beside me while I watched my headlights grope their way uncertainly around the twisting roads, my face glowing in the dark.

Later, back home at this very table, I wondered whether to write the evening up from a skeptical angle. Should I berate the dumb locals for being so gullible, or should I simply forget the whole thing?

I went to bed with the matter still unresolved, and no martini, please note - a minor miracle. It wasn't until next morning that I began seeing the bigger picture. It had started with John the Baptist losing his head, narcotically speaking. Now there was a healer working in a place called the wilderness. This was too much like a 'second coming' for comfort.

TAPE 21

While Laurie Hendricks was busy writing the above, Willie Stevenson was watching his favorite corner of the kitchen ceiling and listening to the muffled sounds of Maxine, upstairs in her bedroom, readying herself for one of her 'window-shopping expeditions' in Zeno - euphemism for a tryst with the Sheriff. This had Willie's mind's eye working overtime as he imagined Maxine get dressed. (Oh sure, he'd been through Maxine's clothes when she was out and knew what she wore underneath.) Now his eyelids half closed to better focus on Maxine, imagining his hands moving over her, only to have her turn on him with those gently reproachful eyes under the thin pencil lines of her arched eyebrows.

Without warning there came the distinctive *snick* as Maxine's bedroom door closed. She was coming down the stairs, her reassuringly firm steps bearing the combined weight of those images. Then she was at the foot of the stair, walking towards him.

"Hi hon." She paused before a glass cabinet to check her hair, one eye on Willie before she went over to him and put her chin on his shoulder, which it would just about reach. Her face clouded when she saw his tense profile.

"You alright?"

"'M'okay."

She prodded his ribs playfully. "You sure?"

"Said 'm okay, 'kay?"

"Uh-huh. Well darlin', you sound a little off-color." She rubbed his arm and searched her mind for a relevant commonality. "If he don't show any improvement we might have to send him to a certain healin' mystic..." At least that got his attention, kind of. She moved away, wondering if she ought to make them both some coffee so she could learn what was eating him. Hughes could hang out to dry awhile.

The breathing space gave Willie a moment to fit in a silent sigh before she turned on him again. He saw she had on the navy reefer jacket, unbuttoned over a white roll-neck. Maybe below that the lacey blue brassiere he'd imagined, taming her voluptuousness. He barely noticed the tan pants except in the way they set off the rest. The blue deck shoes didn't register at all. She was standing with hands on canted hips, maybe because she thought that would look good, one leg straight, the other knee bent, her head cocked. Her figure in these clothes was unreal; all except for her open face between its parted curtain of auburn hair.

"Now do I fix coffee for the both of us?" she asked, "or are you feelin' too introverted for conversation, an' I'd just be wastin' my precious time tryin' to discover what you ate this morning' that was so disagreeable."

Willie wiped his wrist against the side of his nose, challenged as always by her presence.

"So tell me about your mystic."

Willie could not recall mentioning the healer to Maxine. Maybe he'd come in drunk one time and felt like talking; he'd most likely used the healer to deflect her intrusion from his other behavior.

Maxine faced him and became a statue with the spoon in one raised hand balancing the coffee jar in the other. "Why is the simple business of gettin' you to talk about things like pullin' teeth, do you know?"

He acted the lost boy and shrugged. "Guy I know said this fella was doin' healin' on folks around, is all." He studied Maxine's seat while she got on making the coffee. She twitched her head so her hair fell this way and that around her collar and shoulders.

"And just where does he do this healin' of his?"

"Blackwater Creek."

"Does he have a job?"

"Nah. Kinda hermit."

"He on welfare?"

"Don't s'pose he'd be livin' in that beat-up old trailer in the woods if he had money."

Maxine folded her arms loosely around her waist because they wouldn't fit across her chest and wondered why Willie had a kind of catch in his voice when he talked about this healer. At least he was not so tense now. To hell with Neil Hughes; it didn't matter if she never saw him again. She wanted to spend a little time with Willie. She wanted to be with her *son*. The unspoken word caused a frisson inside of her.

"How does he go about healin'? What kind of things does he heal? Does he specialize?" The crazy notion of this healer curing her incurable complaint crossed her mind. Maybe he could walk on water too.

"All I know is he does what he does for free."

Maxine came over to him looking for a reason to be motherly. "Sure you're not sickenin' for somethin'?" Her cool palm felt his brow while her breast jiggled against his ribs. When he tried to duck away she grabbed his arm and persisted, taking his jaw gently between her finger and thumb so she could look more closely into his face.

"Let me see your tongue."

He struggled under her scrutiny, but not too vigorously.

She let go of his arm and took one of his hands in both of hers, watching it carefully for a silent moment. "I do believe you're trembling."

"I - hell, it's just a hangover Maxine." He rubbed his face roughly. "You never had a hangover?"

She remembered the coffee and went to bring him a cup, black and aromatic. Watching him drink she said, "I don't recall ever havin' a hangover in my entire life." Not a boast, an admission. She wanted to put her arms around him but made do with another touch on his forehead and the instruction that he go lie down awhile. Then instantly she was brisk and busy, tidying up the coffee things, looking around for anything that Willie might have left lying out of place or neglected to wash up. She checked her tiny wristwatch with the kitchen clock, glanced at her hair, and more closely at her face reflected in the glass cabinet before one last considered look at her stepson.

"Now you do like I told you, hon. Go on now." She paused at the door on her way out, a sweet smile of sympathy with pained eyebrows, then was gone.

Willie heard her car pull carefully away, thinking about what she and Hughes would be doing later. From an upstairs window he checked that his father's car was not on the driveway before going into his own room, undressing, and returning to Maxine's room to lie naked on her bed, imagining again...

Let's take a closer look at the wrong-headed notion that we can engineer immorality out of people by replacing 'bad' genes with 'good' genes. (To keep this simple we'll say immorality is a propensity for confusing right and wrong, either accidentally or on purpose.) So what part, if any, do our genes play in helping us decide the difference between right and wrong?

Okay. All of our physical parts come from the instructions contained in genes. But a goddam hand, a leg, a lung – or a brain - can't know if they're doing the right or wrong thing in a moral sense because they're just stupid atoms. 'Right' and 'wrong' to body parts is measured simply by how efficiently they work in the role they evolved for. Our entire understanding of right and wrong in a moral sense has to come from our conscious mind, otherwise how do we know if we're doing what's right or wrong?

And where does our conscious mind come from? Most scientists, philosophers, and maybe you, think our mind is created by - and so reducible to - our physical brain.

So the obvious conclusion here is, if your mind is created by your brain, your morality must also be created by your brain. And if your brain contains faulty genes, they're gonna somehow screw up your thinking and your understanding of right and wrong.

People (scientists, philosophers, and maybe you) who believe that our conscious mind is created by (and so reduces to) our physical brain, are called *reductionists*.

Okay. But now consider Ed's contention - that the Real, conscious you is *not* created by your brain. According to Ed, the Real, conscious you is only *influenced* by being in a brain (and, of course, a body). I'm calling this Ed's contention, but it's yours too if you believe you have a spirit, soul or whatever you want to call it. Hundreds of millions of people believe their spirit, or soul, is something more than just a manufactured by-product of their brain. Something eternal maybe. And as your consciousness happens to be an essential working part of your spirit/soul, that means you agree with Ed about your conscious mind *not* being a mere manufactured by-product of your brain.

What's the 'technical' difference between your spirit/soul and your conscious mind? Well, in Ed's contention, our 'mind' is the environment - the theater - where our visiting immaterial consciousness interacts with our material brain to create what we experience as our conscious awareness. We don't have all our own way in this conscious/brain interaction, simply because brains have an agenda of their own. Your brain's agenda is not to work for you as consciousness, it's to work for the survival of its body. I know that sounds peculiar, but to the material, utterly non-conscious components of a brain, 'you' - an immaterial consciousness - don't exist. The only connection 'you' can have with that non-conscious brain is through the way your free will influences it (and as a result, affects the behavior of its body).

Far from being dreamed up by a stupid brain, your consciousness - the Real you - originates someplace else, in an altogether other kind of Reality. While the major part of your Real, conscious self remains in that other Reality, the rest of you – the part in the monkey suit, is a 'stepped down' aspect of your more complete Real, conscious self. (Fact is, EVERYTHING in this material reality is a stepped down aspect of that other Reality. To say 'it's all just energy' sounds far too simplistic, although that happens to be true. I'll talk more about this - yep - later.)

As consciousness we're not simply different from these bodies and brains, we're not even part of material reality. (We're aware stuff that thinks, whereas bodies/brains - like everything in material reality - can't think and aren't aware.)

The crazy thing is that the overwhelming influence of these material bodies/brains makes us think that reality, with us as part of it, is material. As a result of that delusion, our understanding of the difference between right and wrong comes from how we think a material reality works, and how we think that we, as material beings, ought to fit into that reality.

To get Real, you have to begin thinking of bodies/brains as components that evolve on their own account as part of material reality. And while they're doing that, their evolution is being influenced by our immaterial consciousness, which is also evolving and simultaneously being influenced in return by a body/brain.

This 'parallel evolution' gives us our evolving view of reality as something still mostly material, and as a working part of that, our equally narrow view of morality, also as a mostly material consideration. (A 'parallel evolution' sounds kind of complicated but read it over and you'll see it's not.)

During this parallel evolution, your combined body/brain-consciousness develops habits, drives and instincts, neuroses and psychoses. Or, as Ed described them, 'patterns that form and register in our own personal energy template'. These patterns become part of the baggage an individual consciousness carries as it passes through a long succession of monkey suits; baggage that has to be offloaded as we gradually learn what the hell is Really going on.

Yeah, that got a little involved, but it comes down to the fact that our notions of 'right' and 'wrong' are mostly determined by our conscious selves being influenced by the material 'reality' our physical self is evolving in, rather than by our mind figuring things out in some 'impartial observer' kind of way.

Well think about it. From the moment we're born into a genetic monkey suit we begin learning that morality is part of reality, and reality part of morality. Our fledgling mind is told: 'The reality you're in is how things are, and to be accepted as part of it, this is how you must behave.' A huge responsibility rests with the people who begin teaching us this combined morality/reality from birth. (Parents, relatives, TV, schoolteachers, religious indoctrinators and just about anybody our hungry young minds come in contact with for long enough to be influenced by. We - human society - are the teachers of new generations.) Both separately or together, on purpose or accidentally, we, as teachers, all push *our* understanding of morality - as part of *our* understanding of reality - into gullible growing minds.

Being so angelic, you'll deny that as a result of the above process, we've all gotten used to thinking and acting, first and foremost, *not* as enlightened, spiritual beings that temporarily inhabit bodies/brains, but as genetic bodies/brains that can think (a little) and as a result still compete for survival as genetic bodies/brains in a material reality because we didn't learn any better. But that happens to be how things are.

100

If our lives were geared to being saintly there'd be no frenzied competing with everybody for everything. No 'my nation/religion/ideology against yours'. No neurotic race to plunder, spoil and waste on a global scale, etc.

Regardless of what society pays lip service to, it's the *genetic* way of thinking and acting that we pass on to the next generation through our actions. And the entire 'reality/morality' framework created by being genetic organisms is forced upon that next generation before they have mind enough to decide what and how to think for themselves. Before they figured out what they Really are.

Where else do you think racial, religious and other irrational hatreds come from, along with the prejudices, intolerances and dogmas that human beings always had? These things aren't just born in us, they have to be learnt. We only learn racial and religious intolerance, prejudice and fear from other people who are themselves racially and religiously intolerant, prejudiced and fearful. Don't imagine you're different.

So the question is, why don't the people we learn morality from during our critical early life, take more of the responsibility if we grow up with faulty morals? We all of us have a hand in instilling morality into growing minds, and we all should be prepared to stand up and take the rap for failing to get it right. Yet instead we're more than ready to chastise each other for our misdemeanors. Read the papers or watch TV - public chastisement is a global sport. Morals are a bunch of holier-than-thou accusations that we bounce off each other at every opportunity.

The *hypocrisy* word is appropriate here, because the real reason for this 'your morals are your own responsibility' problem is obvious: our 'morality' is designed to protect and serve the material security of mutually self-interested bodies of genes, rather than to help guide us as something *more* than genes. (To simplify that statement for my mom: We all got so used to looking out for ME AND MINE, we're not really interested in each other - or even ourselves - as anything that isn't advantageous to us as genetic organisms. The irrefutable evidence we have on genetic replication, evolution, natural selection, and human behavior as a whole, proves it. Even science says there's nothing real about us that isn't genetically inherited!)

Okay lady, so you don't buy that. It doesn't apply to you because you're the goddam Virgin Mary. Now shut up and keep reading, because here's how this age-old genetic way of thinking and acting gets passed on to each new generation:

A developing brain is like either a computer being assembled or a jungle growing, depending on what version of science or philosophy you go for. In that brain, your visiting consciousness has to begin figuring out anew what everything means.

This newly arrived Real you has a bunch of potentials, but whether those will be developed, and how, depends on three factors: One is the non-material baggage you brought with you. (Experiences from previous trips to materiality - the 'patterns registered in your personal energy template' as Ed called them. Two is the development capabilities of the material hardware you inherit genetically. Three is the information that'll feed from the world outside into your slowly forming brain and its resident consciousness as you both grow. Your mental abilities, talents, predilections - and morals - will all develop as a result of the interplay of those three factors.

Sensory inputs come from everything around you, but most influentially from other human beings, and although neither they nor you are aware of it, they're programming you, just like they were programmed by their teachers, who were programmed back into pre-history. This incoming information helps form pathways between brain cells, and relationships between groups of cells. The earlier and more persistent the information coming into your brain/mind, the deeper and longer-lasting the impressions it makes. While all of that's happening, the Real, conscious you in there is struggling to make sense of itself in relation to all of this heavy materiality.

After teenage, the incoming information from material reality that's helping shape your brain/mind, begins slowing down some; those brain pathways and brain cell relationships no longer form quite so readily. By then, the ways that you think, and what you think about, have become heavily biased in some directions to the exclusion of others. Most of your basic attitudes, preferences, beliefs and etc. are fixed by then.

And the Real, conscious you, caught up in all of this confusion? Heck, it's been indoctrinated into the attitudes, values and 'reality' of a species that never knew any way to live, or think, or act, other than as genetic replication and reproduction facilities.

Never forget that to genes, this is *their* body and brain. It's *their* exclusive means to just one end: *their* replication and reproduction. That's not a conscious process; if it were, it would maybe have some feeling for and some interest in you. But it isn't and it doesn't. And you, getting so wrapped up in your own personal genes' blind determination to keep the process going their way, is what makes you so determined to be selective for the genes you call YOUR self, YOUR family, YOUR offspring.

In the final analysis, genes are not to blame for immorality; genes only influence your conscious mind to choose selfish options. You can decide not to choose those options. It's your call.

TAPE 22

Now how's this for a sky: We have a mix of clouds including thin ones streaked with white, bulbous grays, and some almost black that dissolve into silver at their extremities. Over there in the distance the leached gray of precipitation has erased part of the landscape, while in another direction bright gold rays of sunlight - like God shining a giant flashlight on some wretched miscreant - dazzle on spots of the horizon.

Back down on earth, other, less predictable factors are playing in an assignation created by human hungers, driven by the participants' emotions. Nothing comes anywhere close to being quite so volatile nor so vexing as emotions; not the weather, not the seasons, neither discomfort nor variations of temperature, or even, for Sheriff Hughes, having to tolerate a mild case of hemorrhoids. But I'm sure not dwelling on that. (And I probably spelled it wrong anyhow.)

Hughes' eager anticipation of this meeting had affected his family, associates and strangers alike for a whole week. And now here he was, oblivious to the wheel moving in his hands and the sun-mottled tree shadows flickering across his eyes as he breathed Maxine's perfume, the whole of the right side of his body ringing with the closeness of her. The lightness in his chest, the nervous twittering in his gut, the anticipation of well-worn sensations that could never become familiar; these were Hughes' reality right now. Equally real were the images passing behind his eyes: selected parts of Maxine's anatomy, like dishes along the orange-lit hot-cabinet of a self-serve diner, each perceived only for the gratification he was about to derive from it consumption, rather than as part of a whole, living being. Now he figured he ought to say something to the ears part of her. They were also on the menu, though only as input devices through which he could prompt the right responses. He ought to be starting with that right now, except that he couldn't think of a goddam thing to say.

Maxine, on the other hand, was trying desperately to compose a suitably humane way of telling him their affair - oh God, was it really that? - was dead in the water. Affair her assets! (She imagined faking a puke.) It was hard to believe she had entered into this thing with, of all people, Neil Hughes! Why him? Be honest now. Maybe it was as down-home simple as having somebody, anybody, convince her she was still a woman, still desirable and worthwhile and - Oh stop it! Fact was, she'd been stupid to ever let this thing get started.

But why all this reflecting now? Nothing had changed. She hadn't suddenly discovered any hidden trove of feeling for Robby. Perhaps these things all had their allotted time to run, and her stupid time with Hughes had simply run out? More likely she'd just come to her senses and seen what an asshole he was.

Reflecting this way, she was mildly surprised to feel no more guilt or concern for being adulterous than she would for a minor traffic violation. What the hell? If Robby learned about her and Hughes his pride would sting and that was all. What was his pride but a misplaced feeling of self-importance? That was no hurt at all compared to the permanent agony she endured every day of her life.

Maxine had long ago made an unconscious ritual out of disguising the emptiness left by the removal of her plumbing. She could look like any other woman in the street but that still didn't erase the cripple's hyper-self-consciousness. There was a stiffness in the way she held herself, always aware of her secret, knowing that it wasn't her fault, yet still blaming herself. Then she was angry again because it was so damnably unfair that such a secret had created another just to soothe itself, and that second secret had gotten so shabby.

Her mind was flitting around like a butterfly. Maybe she'd visit the body parlor in Zeno after all, rather than only using it as an alibi for Robby. Alibis were one thing she'd never eased-up on. Maybe one day she'd start to take chances just to keep the dogs of boredom at bay. Maybe she'd become inured to the danger of discovery, like a junkie needing ever more potent forms of opiate to achieve the same high.

Was it just her imagination that everything was different this time? Did the atmosphere inside the car really seem denser, able to communicate far more subtly than plain old H_2O? Maybe it would react to every expression her face made, each breath she took, the slightest movement of her fingers.

She looked down at her hands, one gripping her purse, the other lying self-consciously along her thigh. Maybe her thoughts would get into this atmosphere and tell him how she felt; communicate the emotions she wanted his sympathy and understanding for but couldn't put into words. Not that he'd appreciate how she felt. Not him. But she had to try because that was her reason for persuading him to make this country detour between the place she parked her car and the motel.

She tried to see his face from her eye-corner but doubted she could manage it without attracting his attention, and that was the last thing she wanted before she'd fashioned a reasoned argument. She had to be ready for anything he came back at her with. How would he react? He couldn't possibly get upset, not Neil Hughes. That would be too genteel. Sarcastic maybe. Vindictive? He might try to get back at her in some babyish way. Babyish - oh, that was him absolutely. Oh God!

Then a little of the lightness she'd left the house with came back, and through a flash of insight she recognized it as a product of two conflicting sides of the same coin. One side was the knowledge that she had the power to cut him loose if she chose. (Oh God! He would still be *around*. Still call in to see Robby...) On the other side of the coin was the notion that she could just as easily choose not to cut him loose. Before she left the house this power of choice had lifted her spirits, but now it was turning her in circles, with still no rejection speech ready.

While the moments passed slow and sick for her, Hughes was awash with the fullness of himself, warm and lazy and content that she was his property, to do with as he pleased. His eyes left the road and swung across to the knees, then up to the chest. The sweater was having a real hard time containing everything she had crammed inside it, and he took the image with him back to the road ahead, seeking a place to stop.

Damn him! He was doing that sucking-out thing again. Looking at her in the vampire way he did, trying to bleed her of life-force...like a big, fat leech! Well he was not going to do it anymore. She pulled the front of the reefer closed but it sprang open the moment she let go the lapels. She stayed hyper-conscious of herself, staring directly ahead, listening to his breathing kind of tight and shaky until, a couple of miles further on, he made a left down a dirt road, then after a quarter-mile more slowed to walking pace.

When they stopped, she'd get out quickly and stay on her side of the car while she told him it was over. It was going to work out just fine. Even though her heart was pounding it would be okay. Good or bad, everything had to end sometime.

With the cruiser far enough along the dirt road to be out of sight of the highway, Hughes cut the motor so they could roll to a silent halt, though even before the wheels ceased turning he was on her, his hand delving under the jacket to grasp his prize...

Except that Maxine had located the doorhandle, pulled on it, was out of the car. Without looking back she went to stand a few yards off, trying to calm her jittery heartbeat. She could taste the awkward guilt, like waiting to read an obituary to the next of kin for a death that she had caused. When she turned he was ambling towards her, hands in his pants pockets, grinning because she'd eluded him in there. He was sniffing the air, probably trying to decide on a gameplan.

Despite the all-purpose grin, Hughes was mildly annoyed. He'd only stopped for a quick feel-up; this was no place for anything more. He wanted to get to their usual motel on the other side of Zeno. Hell, what was Maxine doing wasting precious time here when they could be stripping threads?

He was two yards away when she said, "Stop...stop there."

Like his car he rolled to a gentle stop, looking bemused. "Well alright. You come on over here t'me."

With absolutely no idea what she would say, Maxine opened her mouth, and out came: "I want - I want to say something." She hoped the pitch of her voice and her solemn face would give the game away, and that he would realize what was coming and say something she could build on.

"Oh yeah? 'Bout what?" Was all he said. It was no help.

She tasted the words "It's all over between us" in her mind, but said, "We don't ever talk. Can you tell me why that is?"

He grinned more broadly. "Maybe we got better things to do than talk."

She was suddenly angry. "Good God, Sheriff, people need to talk, don't you know that?"

His eyebrows went up slowly. "Hey, I like it when you call me *Sheriff.*" He didn't. He just wanted her to quit being difficult.

She turned away, exasperated because Hughes was taking control again. My God but he was good at that. It was always him, whatever they did together, which was not something she wanted to think about now...

"Come on back so's we can talk an' drive at the same time," he said, and started ambling back to the car.

She listened until he got in, leaving her just standing there, stiff and exposed. The bastard had taken control of what should have been her decision.

106

"Hey!"

She looked back to see him start the engine. This was farcical, just like their relationship. She strode to the passenger door and got in, knowing it was now or never. Studying the door's inner face she said, "I'd appreciate you just letting me out in Zeno." Her casualness made him turn.

"Just like that, huh?" He hit the gas so the car jerked savagely in reverse and they hit the highway with a squeal of tires, but then he eased off and drove slowly, saying nothing, keeping her guessing.

That ought to have been all there was to it. He would drop her at the mall and she'd get in her car and drive away from whatever they'd shared - if you could call what he did sharing. Maxine knew it had been a one-way thing from both sides. He must see they'd only taken from each other. He'd taken more than his fair share without giving much, so had more to lose. But heavens, there had never once been any pretense of...

"Well," he said, "I'm waitin' for you to get the conversation goin'."

She looked right at him, conscious for the first time of a difference between his grins and his smirks. The grins meant Neil Hughes was pleased with his life, whereas the smirks were for when he thought he had just done something to keep it that way. God-damn the supercilious bastard! He was just playing her along until she calmed down. She couldn't figure out how he had bettered her without even trying. Not angry now, she was just disappointed. Was she so easy to manipulate?

"You want to talk," he said. "So talk if you want, I'm listenin'. Or were we communicatin' all along without me knowin'?" He snapped a glance at her, then back ahead. "Hey, I'll bet that's it. You bin kind've telepathizin' with me, ain't you?" And he slapped her knee, letting go with one of his self-satisfied laughs as final proof that the matter was closed.

Well alright, so maybe it was for the present time. She had to admit she was relieved in a way. Maybe her show of defiance would make him think a little more in future. Take a little more care with her. Make an effort to understand how she felt. A couple of miles down the road she thought: then again, maybe it wouldn't...

TAPE 23

I wrote *Veel Mistuan Bobli* on this tape. It's Venusian for 'Have a nice day.' (Seriously, if my handwriting deteriorates any further it'll need subtitles.) The annotation is actually a reminder to me: 'Need Christian bible'. It was to help me write my Second Coming story. Well sure I could've loaned Ed's bible, but I was not going round there after our little disagreement over his lack of ambition. Okay, *my* disagreement; Ed was not the disagreeing type. He'd agree to disagree and wait for you to grow up. He had some waiting to do with me, believe it!

I thought of borrowing the old family bible from my mom, except it weighs more than I do; it still contains copies of the original stone tablets. (That wasn't funny, but boy, I get mad sometimes when I think of Ed. Mad with me I mean.)

What I was not about to do was *buy* a goddam bible. I wouldn't have known a King James from a Cecile B De Mille anyhow, and I sure wasn't gonna splurge on a collection of fairy tales when I only wanted a few pages from the New Testament. So I just went in a bookstore and delved. I'd already figured that religion says nothing about God but a hell of a lot about people when I eventually sat down to work on my next Star piece: a tasteless, blasphemous allegory of small-town America, and maybe the world, at the start of a new century. While the iceberg dissolved in my titanic martini, and under the banner SECOND COMING EXCLUSIVE - YOU READ IT HERE FIRST, I wrote: 'Believe it folks, this could surely be how it began 2000 years ago in Galilee, near Jordan. Quiet gatherings of devotees around a holy man and an atmosphere you can bottle and sell in church.' And so on in my usual style. Folks who read The Star were so dumb, they wouldn't have noticed I was thumbing my nose at them with my tongue in my cheek even if I'd run a picture of myself doing it. Not that I was writing it for them; this particular piece was more material for my Escape Portfolio; I wanted prospective big city employers to see it as sharp social comment, designed to make people think about themselves.

There was a time when I'd thought my journalistic endeavors no deeper than the paper they were printed on, and now here I was, combing the Webster's for words like 'allegory', convinced I was writing a ticket not just to my literary departure from anonymity but my literal one as well. I even began imagining my earlier work had been intentionally allegorical too, rather than plain parasitic.

Being ignorant of what the bible had to say about the Second Coming, I read up on how JC is supposed to've told everybody not to be deceived when all the false prophets show up, acting the savior and talking miracles.

108

You know those guys. Some come up to you in the street and go: "Hi man, I'm the messiah." Sometimes they carry a concealed weapon, or ask do you want/have any drugs. They all have the same problem - keeping their messianic status to themself.

Most of these crazy people (that's another politically incorrect way of saying neurologically independent) don't realize they're crazy. The miracle is how they get so many so-called 'sane' folks following 'em, believing they're anything but just plain nuts. And listen, somebody calling themself a 'guru' doesn't change any of the above. All religious fanatics claim to know what's on God's mind. Even I might be partway convinced by those guys if they said that God advocated brotherly (and sisterly) love, peace on earth, equality of the sexes and colors, etc., instead of all that divisive, repressive stuff, often with a terrorism sideline.

What else do holy books have to say about the Second Coming? That before it happens there'll be wars between nations - so what's new? There'll be famines. Yeah, I saw those on TV. More old news. Pestilences? Well think about it: AIDS. Cancer. Heart disease. Except those are ongoing too, not some sudden precursor. And hey - we can even expect a showing from The Antichrist himself, aka the devil (according to Islamic tradition anyhow). Ask me, he was here all along. And finally, it says, comes the end of the world, which is the only thing we didn't have yet despite trying real hard. Bibles talk about hell and damnation, fire and brimstone, a last judgment and all of that technicolor frightener stuff. Just what I was looking for. Holy books beat Hollywood every time. The only real revelation in scriptures is that people will believe anything if somebody tells them God said it. A millennium or three later, what self-respecting religious nut would dare contest THE WORD OF GOD?

Just seeing those words in capitals scares ya, huh? It's supposed to. The only way all of that end-of-the-world stuff could become a reality is if you nuts don't get Real and quit being so goddam genetic.

Okay, I might as well admit it. The same night I wrote that Second Coming piece, I did something I'd not done for years out of sheer frustration. It was shameful and afterwards I couldn't sleep for thinking about it. I prayed. (I almost said 'for God's sake', 'cept that like most prayers it was entirely for my sake.) Shameful behavior for a confirmed atheist and materialistic cynic who'd seen all the wonderful things religion could do for people - hypocrisy, ethnic cleansing, genocide. And don't forget the guy in Noblesville, Indiana, using performing parrots to help him spread The Lord's Word. I swear it's the gospel truth!

Me - *praying!* That's how desperate I was to escape from oblivionsville. My prayers were for my career so I guess I was really praying to mammon, the god of genetic survival. I'd never once known big G get anyone out of a tight spot, but money seemed to work most times. Sure I knew calling on the god of money was stupid, but religion makes people do stupid things.

Some folks go through their whole life never giving religion a thought, then suddenly they're in deep excrement and who do they call? No, not Ghostbusters. It's *God.* Yep, even though the last time they thought of God was in Sunday School a hundred years ago. (In which case the evangelists would say you have no right to call out the fire department if you didn't pay your taxes.)

Anyhow despite everything I said so far, millions of people outside of this book are determined to believe that human notions of right and wrong sprang fully-formed from someone called God. That's in the same class of delusion as sex being something we do because we choose to, rather than something that genes make us do to perpetuate them.

On one of these tapes is a piece about where religious notions originated. If you keep reading you'll come to it. It explains in more depth how, millions of years before rudimentary brains appeared, genetic organisms 'knew' sure as eggs make chickens that whatever's good for genetic replication is right, and whatever's bad for replication is wrong. That core 'morality', built on the accurate replication and reproduction of genes and the one we hand on to successive generations, is not a morality we want to recognize, yet without such an uncompromising agenda, the components these bodies and brains are made of would never have gotten started, and they sure wouldn't have survived this long.

That core genetic morality is why we labor to make our genes the center of our personal world, and why our notions of survival all come down to material wealth that can help us maintain our physical health, so our genes can replicate accurately.

The prescribed formula for ensuring our material health, wealth and survival, is reflected in a few stark basics that are pretty much the same in all societies and religions. Just read the 10 Christian commandments and you got those basics. Being conscious, we only appreciate how these basics - in the form of religions, family values, social laws and justice systems - work for us as

110

consciousness in a monkey suit. We forget how the foundations of those basics evolved before what we call 'consciousness' appeared, just to protect genes.

For instance, the religious instruction 'thou shall not kill' is fundamental to keeping genes alive. Not coveting, being adulterous with, or stealing wives, asses and other possessions? That's about protecting the personal property that helps keep YOUR genes healthy. Breaking these property rules means upsetting the replicating and reproducing efficiency of genes in all kinds of ways: by threatening the material security of family units and tribal groups that radiate from the center of interest: genes. Genetic organisms all had these 'rights and wrongs' in instinct-form long before Moses went up the mountain and got stoned.

Am I being serious? Damn right I am. But what if, instead of this genetic 'morality', we had a Real morality? One that came directly from consciousness acting as the front office for our soul? We'd make a religion out of being equally unselfish with everybody.

Yes, mister, I know you hate being told to dump all of your dangerously outdated misconceptions and delusions. You want 'reality' to stay confined to the notions that grew up on this material world. You're so genetic, you're not even going to read any more of this book. What's that, lady? You're going to set a legal precedent and sue me for defamation of the human race? Fine. Now go back in your box and I'll get you some clean straw.

TAPE 24

Harve's Gun 'n' Tackle store was situated on the section of Passmore's main street where some shops still traded. Harve's place occupied a flat roofed building erected in the 1930s from a picture some local constructor had clipped from a magazine, then built with no consideration for the aesthetic sensitivities of structural or human neighbors alike. There was one small merchandise window, each side of which was embedded an iron fitment for the grill that went up at the end of a working day, and stayed there through Sundays. In that window, surrounded by faded promotional cards, was one dusty old Winchester pump that would never see another round pass along its barrel. A more up-to-date version, under lock and key inside, had latterly begun to appeal to Harve, the store's proprietor, as a means of avoiding further disillusionment with life in general.

Sheriff Hughes rolled the cruiser silently around the rear of the low white building and stopped beside Harve's Studebaker President. The Studebaker was exactly as it had been abandoned three years earlier, the key still in the ignition. The buttercup-yellow automobile, complete with whitewalls, had been left out to grass the day Harve had his driver's license taken away forever by a State Trooper who came to Passmore personally to collect it. Harve had gotten a lifetime's ban after he caused the death of the trooper's sidekick in an auto-accident: Harve had pulled onto the highway in front of their vehicle, which had crashed trying to avoid him, killing the driver into the bargain. The Studebaker didn't receive a scratch. That was a miracle twice over because Harvey Brown, firearms dealer and sometime hunter, who enjoyed driving and loved his beautifully-maintained anachronism on wheels, had been registered officially blind in nineteen eighty-seven. (Don't ask me how come he still had a driver's license when the accident happened; I only write this stuff.)

Hughes rapped on the rear screen door, which was also the entrance to the Browns' home, but got no answer. He certainly had no intention of walking right in after the time he'd done that and found Mrs. Brown stripped to the waist, washing herself in the kitchen sink. Worse was how she'd calmly turned and looked at him for a few lazy seconds, like he wasn't important enough to worry about, then just carried on with her toilet, leaving Hughes much reduced in stature. Thereafter, whenever he found himself in Rosemary Brown's company, the same disquieting sense of unimportance stole through him. (Rosemary Brown was either part or whole Cheyenne Indian, but Hughes had never quite finished formulating exactly why that didn't help matters. All he knew was that it must be a contributory factor to his discomfort. Those people were not like other folks. They were even harder to figure than blacks.)

Hughes picked his way through empty cartons to walk back round to the store's street entrance. There he pushed open the door and was met by a billow of spicy air. Suspended from the ceiling-beams, creating a secretive gloom all their own, were articles beloved of men of the outdoors, and Hughes inhaled the deeply satisfying pot-pourri of waxed cotton, fishing gear and gun-lubricant. He ambled through to the rear of the grotto-like retail area and found Harvey Brown in the workshop, winding thread round minute colored feathers on a jewel-like dry-fly lure.

It intrigued the hell out of Hughes that Harve could do such detailed work with his poor eyesight, even using those glasses with the telescope-lenses. Maybe he did most of it by touch, though with the fly up there under his nose he was more likely working by smell! (These were Harve's close-work glasses. He had another set for everyday, and a third that used to be his driving glasses but now only gathered what small deposits of dust that collected in the Studebaker's glove compartment. Really. Go look if you don't believe me.)

Okay, so this is Harve Brown, five-feet-square with a white block of crew-cut head and beard to match. The same Harve who didn't bother to look up when Hughes came in because he knew who it was by the slow and heavy tread on the linoleum, and the way Hughes tried to sniff everything out of the air as he came through.

"Sheriff." Harve's nasal address was neither friendly nor unfriendly.

"Well now how you doin' Harve?" Hughes' voice dropped a few decibels in the presence of weaponry.

"Badly," said Harve. The word was matter-of-fact and emotionless.

Hughes' grin widened. Sometimes it was hard to know if Harve was being serious, moreso because it was hard to know Harve Brown period. The only time he ever smiled was when doing some extra close work, and that was a grin of concentration.

"Done much drivin' lately?" Hughes said.

Harve's eyeballs didn't once flicker from their work. He said nothing.

"Yeah," Hughes said softly for reorientation and went back through into the store to do more sniffing. "Okay I loose off a few rounds out back?" he called, just loud enough not to disturb the atmosphere, bending over the wired-glass counter to peer down at an assortment of handguns with small white price-tags strung on their trigger-guards. When Harve didn't reply, Hughes tried the lid of the counter - locked - then went behind it to study the dark and purposeful shotguns chained into a rack on the wall. Just looking at them made his teeth ache, his hands itch to heft their machine-perfect shapes. All were lubricated and ready for use, but then Harve had little else to do with his time other than look after merchandise that nobody bought.

Hughes turned to search for the key to the chain and found Harve standing beside him, the little round glasses pushed up over his eyebrows.

"Which one?"

Hughes' own eyes narrowed to change the emphasis of his smirk. "Somethin' mean."

Harve already had the key in his hand, undid the padlock and extricated a pre-owned, all-black, semi-automatic Colt that nobody would ever come in the store and buy - not unless a local war broke out.

Hughes took it from him, sniffed it and said, "Al*right.*"

"This a purchase or you just wastin' time?"

"Well now Harve, that's what I'm here findin' out ain't it?"

Harve would have to clean the weapon after Hughes was through, but like I already said, there was little else for him to do. He went back to his work and Hughes strolled through the store and down a passageway that led to the same back-kitchen he'd caught Mrs. Brown in that time. Another door led off the side to a claustrophobic weapons gallery. Hughes looked back along the passageway, paused by the kitchen door to listen and, hearing no sound, nudged the door open a few inches with his knee. Purely for his own amusement he imagined finding Mrs. Brown squatting over a bucket this time, but the room was empty. After he looked around and sniffed, he closed the door again and stopped to insert the clip.

So. On an earlier tape I likened your developing brain to a jungle. Imagine that - a living, growing, seething rainforest of chemistry and small electrical storms inside your head, complete with spider monkeys, macaws, pythons, guys with chainsaws - the works. Like a mist hanging in amongst all of that is the conscious YOU, and while the conscious YOU is learning and evolving in response to the messages coming into the animal and vegetable life in this jungle from the world outside, you're simultaneously turning that rainforest/brain into what you'd call 'civilization' as you evolve. This personal evolution is a two-way civilizing process. This rainforest/brain is a tiny, condensed corner of the material universe, made from the same few basic elements everything else is. By consciously civilizing your brain as you evolve (by thinking, then turning those thoughts into actions) you influence not only your own conscious evolution and the monkey suit's, but the evolution of an ever-increasing proportion of the planet around you, its flora and fauna, other humans, and - in time - even the neighboring universe.

Like Ed said, material reality was created (and is being constantly recreated) by consciousness solely for the purpose of learning and relearning. While that happens on a scale too big and complicated to imagine, this little corner of the universe comes increasingly under the control of human consciousness, and that leaves us with a big responsibility. (Which those dumb guys with chainsaws are ignoring, and they're only the tip of the iceberg. What's an iceberg? Another endangered species.)

Earlier I said that as consciousness, we're not stuck in the 'here and now' of atoms in the brain we occupy. Nor are we ruled by the same iron hand of physics laws that hold this material universe together. By being outside of physics laws, consciousness is free to do what it wants - or would be if not for the relative material constraints of a monkey suit made from atoms – more of which in a moment.

See, when we use our memory of the past and imagine different presents and futures - then turn those imagined scenarios into real actions - our consciousness is exploring and exploiting *creative* possibilities. The better we become at doing that, the further our consciousness evolves, and the more creative possibilities it can explore. So by being creative - now read this carefully - we're reducing the element of randomness in the way the electrochemical components of our body/brain behave. That amounts to reducing the randomness in a small piece of the universe.

You can see for yourself how evolution has reduced randomness, noplace moreso than in human brains. In ordering randomness into the hyper-complexity of brain cells and their countless interconnections, evolution creates a vehicle for consciousness to operate in the material universe. (Not forgetting that consciousness itself oversees evolution.)

I know I'm getting ahead of myself with some of this stuff, so you'll maybe need to refer back later, okay? Knowing you, you won't bother. It's okay - I wouldn't either.

But wait. Immature human consciousness would be a loose cannon without a material brain to constrain it. It would run wild and cause trouble the way any immature agent does. There'd be chaos. Learning discipline is partly what our time in a monkey suit, on this level of material reality, is about. We evolve until our consciousness learns to use that freedom responsibly, over and above the demands of genes. The more responsible we become, the less constraint we need, and the more ability we have to influence our environment until eventually we figure that a material universe is the medium we're meant to be creative with as part of our conscious evolution.

Even the most primitive life-forms with minimal amounts of consciousness are low-level 'creative' in having a tiny degree of influence over their biology and surroundings. But while they do it entirely on behalf of their genes, we can choose to be creative for Real, unselfish reasons. That might sound dull compared with satisfying your senses through material gratification, but, as enlightened folks have said all along, the sensations involved in material gratification are momentary and insignificant compared with the advantages of being Real, which are permanent.

When early hominids (primitive humans) came down from trees and began living on the plains, that dramatically changed the way the components of their bodies/brains evolved. Well sure their decision was governed mostly by what their bodies wanted. Their simple minds had to operate inside a brain whose shape, function and purpose had all been dictated by genes looking out for themselves. Yet by being forced to think for the survival of genetic bodies, the consciousness in those minds was also developing in its own right - something that genes could never have 'foreseen'. This growing consciousness was gradually, if unknowingly, increasing its influence over the components in brains and bodies as a normal and natural part of evolution. Consciousness was evolving not simply so it could go on being selfish for genetic bodies/brains, but so consciousness could evolve as consciousness.

Because we're still devoting practically all of our thinking to what's best for DNA and its body/brain, this looped message will keep repeating at regular intervals: The only way to be sure it's *you* choosing your life and your future (instead of a mindless bunch of chemicals choosing for themselves, with you just going along) is to be *unselfish*.

...Boy, I've lost the thread of this story again. It's easy to do when transcribing from audio tape and somebody hammers on the goddam door, or the phone goes, or your drink needs rebuilding and you're trying to watch TV with one of your other eyes and forget to hit the pause button...

While I'm trying to find my place again I'll open another Reality Window to say that I talk about consciousness being separate from, and different than, material reality, only to keep things simple. Fact is, all notions of separateness are entirely relative and subjective. Nothing is separate from anything else; you only think things are separate because your senses and brain don't let you perceive them otherwise.

For instance you'd say you're definitely separate from the objects around you, and they from each other, right? You can even measure the gaps between you and them. But those gaps only appear empty because your senses of perception are not sensitive enough to perceive what's really there. When physicists probe smaller than the gaps that you can see, feel, hear, smell, taste, and even *think* are between things, they see that everything in so-called material reality is part of the *same* thing, called a *continuum* (a continuous thing). Physicists describe it in terms of countless mega-small parts - *quanta* - or as one mega-big thing - *space-time*. (I'll get around to explaining all of that stuff soon. Yes it does have some relevance to you, fish-head.)

116

TAPE 25

Rosemary Brown brought her washing basket into the kitchen from the back yard. She leaned over to put it on a chair and gasped at the incisive pain in her lower back, her face a well-tried mask of pain. The pain itself was just pain; the fact that it might prevent her walking to the wilderness was the real problem. She looked out the window, over the roof of the barn and her pig-pen, her features relaxing at the sight of white clouds that made comforting crowd-shapes against a blue sky. The sky was heaven, the clouds were the spirits of her ancestors riding celestial plains in search of sacred buffalo.

Sure they were, she told herself with a sniff. For Rosemary the realist that stuff was just bullshit. Life was about real things. Life was about people. People were what made you the person you were, shaped your personality, made your pleasure and your pain. Rosemary hoped the healer might fix the other pain in her life: her relationship with Harve. That was what first took Rosemary into the wilderness.

She pictured the healer now, his mesmeric eyes, the sense of - she closed her own eyes because this was the scary part - of his gaze having somehow found an inner Rosemary. That gaze had dissolved whatever held the inner Rosemary secure inside her. Scary because she'd felt the sensation of being set free; she'd seemed to lift up and soar across a vast empty sky inside of this gross and clumsy self. Later she'd woken in her chair at home, unable to recall walking back from the wilderness.

The dreams began later, and even though they were too blurry to remember on waking, their narrative symbolism impressed on her the notion that she was at the center of something and somehow important. Later, that notion adjusted to suggest that *people* were the center - of the world, of life, of everything, together and separately.

To Rosemary the realist these hyper-real dream experiences, though unsettling, contained a truth she could not deny. Further trips into the wilderness had generated more dreams, and these modified the original notion into a conviction that the only responsibility she and other people had was *to each other*. The dreams had interpreted the spirit of Heammawihio in terms of *her* reality - the reality of *people*. The dreams had underscored her conviction that people were the only place where spirit mattered.

A muffled stream of gunfire in the closed range shattered her reverie. The thought of Sheriff Hughes caused the corners of her small, plump mouth to turn down even more than they did naturally. She closed her eyes and flexed her back, resisting the thought that even Hughes was part of her responsibility. She disliked the man. She didn't trust him. But she realized that she was waiting for him to change, when the plain fact was that it was just as much *her* responsibility to change for *him*.

She nodded slowly and hoisted the basket of washing carefully onto her hip, making small, twisting movements with her spine as she crossed the room, exploring the nerve messages before she dared load the drier. At a sound behind her she turned to find Harve standing in the doorway, glasses held before his face with one hand while the stubby forefinger and thumb of the other worked at his closed eyes. The gunfire came again as she turned away and began filling the drier, aware of Harve's bulk between her and the shots.

She'd stopped loving Harve in the old way years ago. Her only feelings for him were just dried husks of things now, held in place by habit; distant echoes of the old affection. But she turned to look at him again, as ever hoping for a flicker of that old love, a sign in herself that she could still feel something for him; or a sign from him that he could for her. He must have noticed the inactivity because he looked in her direction; it was hard to know how clearly he could see even at this close range, and even harder to guess what he was thinking. Despondency enveloped Rosemary. Harve was her closest responsibility. Surely that meant she ought to *feel* something for him? To *care* for him? But how did you care for someone who no longer cared for you? And why would you want to?

For my next trick I'm going to make reality disappear. Say goodbye to the solid-object world of buildings and cars and rocks, of people, animals, plants and the rest. Even the unsolid stuff like air and water.

Having this familiar, solid-object reality in your face since the day you were born, naturally you think the more solid it is, the more real it is.

Now forget how you think things are. The truth is, even the most solid objects in this small r reality are *not* solid. There's no such thing as 'solid'; materialism is a concept created by consciousness. The entire material universe is just energy orchestrated into a kind of superior holographic movie-set for minds to role-play in.

Ever see an atom under a microscope? Me neither, but all of the so-called 'real' objects in life are made from atoms. Atoms are particles of stuff with more particles (electrons) orbiting them. Magnify the particles in the atom's

118

center (protons and neutrons) and you find they're made from even smaller particles, with the quirky name *quark*. (A physicist borrowed the name quark from James Joyce. It could just as easily have been *dork.)* These subatomic particles (sub-atom-ic = below atom size) are handled by very tiny guys called *quantum mechanics.*

Just kidding. This is me trying to demystify quantum mechanics, which is like popular mechanics but not so popular because this machinery is too small to see. *Quantum* comes from quantity: an amount. A quantum is the smallest amount of *energy* that physicists can get a handle on. As for *mechanics,* that also has the usual meaning. Here it refers to the fact that these tiny quantities of energy called quanta (that's the plural of quantum) are the *mechanism* - the nuts 'n' bolts - comprising everything in the material universe.

When you look real close at the so-called 'solid' objects of reality, and the forces (like gravity, electricity and magnetism) holding them together, and even when you look at the spaces between those things, you see they're all made from the same basic components: these tiny quanta of energy, glued together in different ways to make different things.

How can tiny amounts of energy be solid objects? I'm coming to that. We didn't finish getting smaller yet. Some quantum physicists think that all of these quanta of energy comprising everything in the universe, might themselves be composed of incredibly tiny pieces of vibrating string! Oh yeah. This notion is called *Superstring Theory,* and these strings are supposed to be 100 billion billion times smaller than even the protons in the center of atoms!

Crazy as that sounds, you'd be the first to agree how un-crazy it is if you were smart and educated and interested enough to learn quantum physics. Besides, even before this string notion was thought of, Einstein figured that everything in the known universe can be described as energy. $E = mc2$ is the formula he came up with whilst trying to understand some difficult relatives. (E is the energy contained inside material things. M is their mass. C is the speed of light - 186,000 miles a second. And that tiny 2 means you multiply the mass by the light speed to get your answer.)

Answer to what? To the fact that energy equals mass. (For simplicity, think of mass as weight, okay?

Now go work out the Yang-Mills field equations for mass/energy in 11 dimensional spacetime while I fix myself a drink.)

Okay. The weirdest sounding thing about superstring theory is the *string* shape all of this energy is supposed to reduce to. Physicists say there's a logical physics-and-math type reason for that shape, a result of which I'll translate into plain English (or whatever language you're reading this in).

At the impossibly tiny string level of 'reality', the strings vibrate at different frequencies, and these different frequencies determine the countless different *qualities* of so-called 'real' things - all of their shapes, colors, sounds, smells, tastes, behaviors, and everything else about them. It's kind of like different vibrations made by guitar strings producing different qualities of sound (except this is much more complicated). These different frequencies of vibrating energy make all of the quantum-sized particles - quarks, electrons, etc - that form everything we know about. The quarks then lump together in threes to make the protons and neutrons in the center of atoms, while electrons orbit that center.

The number of protons forming an atom's center, with an equal number of orbiting electrons, determine what kind of atom it is, right? The atoms then bunch up into molecules, and the molecules crowd together to form recognizable objects.

And then there's M-theory, because there are 5 different superstring theories, all of which seemed to conflict until physicists realized that all 5 are just different aspects of the same overall theory: M-theory.

Follow all of that? Just don't be too impressed; superstrings are just a theory, and theories are only the kettle. Proving them is the fish. When you theorize about stuff this small there's no way you can demonstrate it as fact because the technology hasn't been invented yet.

In a tiny editing suite in the news division at CNLB-TV Media, Memphis, minute reflections of monitor footage flickered across the surface of Rudolph Deeks' eyes. In his ears came the rapid-fire delivery of an anchorman someplace, the cutting-edge of his voice chopping a report into digestible slivers. Deeks, intent on the screen, had clean forgotten about a bite of information placed in the memory chip of his personal organizer just ten minutes ago after consultation with his boss. A letter (enclosed with a copy of The Star) had arrived in the mail at CNLB that morning from someone named Lauren Hendricks, a 'reporter' doing time on an adrag in someplace called Zeno, a small town that had died and gotten buried in Raiment County, itself lost somewhere in the state. Lauren Hendricks was looking for a media job in the city, and to showcase her talents had put together a few lines of conspicuously affected prose describing events surrounding the effects a healer was having on local people, which she'd made the mistake of describing as a 'Country Second Coming'.

Lauren Hendricks would not be landing a job with the News Division of CNLB, and not simply because the company wasn't looking to take on a new reporter just then.

First, a sub-editor would need to like what the applicant had written, and the one who'd gotten the job of not considering Lauren Hendricks in this instance happened to see the Christian Bible as a verbatim set of user-instructions from God. And Lauren Hendricks, through disrespectful paraphrase, had committed sacrilege.

Second, Lauren Hendricks did not have enough news-gathering experience in a metropolitan environment: not much of a reason, but this was a buyer's market.

And third, Lauren Hendricks had written something so far-fetched-sounding as to be complete fantasy. In fact Lauren Hendricks' job application would have gone straight in the trash but for the fact that a reporter/cameraman news team - of which Rudolph Deeks was the former - had already been assigned coverage of a siege by members of a fringe religious sect not too far from Boone, North Carolina. And Boone being just over the state line, it was deemed okay for Deeks and his partner, Phil Bonelli, to check out Laurie Hendricks' story of events in Raiment County - just in case.

So far as Deeks was concerned, the 'country second coming' story was something the locals had cooked up to try and pull a few tourists from the Great Smokey Mountains National Park next door. That, or a product of the same Spring madness that had prompted the good folks holed up in a house near Boone to open up with automatic weapons on two State policemen, just because one of the siege members happened to be under sixteen years of age and pregnant. And a HIV-positive registered drug user who also happened to be on parole. Whatever, Deeks and Bonelli had their assignment. They would drive out to Charlotte the following day and later stop off in hicksville.

Biologists talk as if evolution and natural selection began when the first DNA molecules appeared on this planet a couple or so billion years back. But way before that, nature had to select the universe, the galaxy, the solar system and this planet.

Remember those tiny quanta of energy that make up everything in this universe? (That's me reminding me. I just got up.) Well, before there was a universe here, one popular notion is that all of the separate and different bits of energy that comprise everything, were compressed into one phenomenally small and dense point called a *singularity*. A singularity, mom, is something so small and dense that I can't describe it, and you couldn't imagine it even if I did. What was there before this singularity? Ask me later. First, hold onto your hernia because according to the big end of science (stuff like astrophysics, cosmology and campanology), about fourteen billion years back, all of the pent-up energy in that tiny singularity exploded in what's called the *Big Bag* - if your 'n' key just decided not to work. (Otherwise it's known as the Big Bang.)

Superstring theory says the energy from that original singularity didn't just explode with a Big Bang. Instead, out of the singularity came a universe with 10 dimensions! That's something else you can't imagine because we always figured we live in a universe of 4 dimensions. When you measure something you check (1) the length, (2) the width, (3) the heighth, and - if you're smart - you check (4) the time. (If you still have trouble thinking of time as a dimension, that doesn't even begin to hint at the trouble you'd have trying to imagine another 6 dimensions of space. It would be like trying to imagine the aroma of frying onions as a measurement of distance.)

Our 4 familiar dimensions are reckoned to've happened as a result of that original 10-D universe cracking up soon after it formed, making a universe in two parts: one part with 6 dimensions, the other part - ours - with 4. (The universe cracking up is supposed to've caused the Big Bang in the first place.) The 6 dimensions shriveled up and shrank, so their share of the energy from the Big Bang became amazingly compressed into incredibly small spaces that are hidden someplace in our familiar 4-D universe.

I know this is headache country, but just try to imagine all of the hugely compressed energy inside that tiny (and impossibly heavy) singularity before it suddenly exploded in the Big Bang and became the universe. Even if it was only atom sized, it would weigh millions of tons, and that's the easy part to imagine. The hard part is to imagine *where* it was.

Before this universe-creating singularity exploded, there were none of the tiny quanta that formed the objects of so-called reality. Those were still nothing but a twinkle in the singularity's eye. There were no laws of physics, because there was nothing physical to apply laws to. There wasn't even time. (I guess nothing existed that could be described as changeable, and if nothing changes, you have nothing to measure time by. That's an intriguing concept I'll clear up later.)

In this Big Bang version of creation, scientists say that time, space, matter, everything, began when that singularity exploded in the Big Bang.

Where was Ed's corporate hierarchy of consciousnesses while all of this was happening? I'm working up to that. This is still an explanation of *material* reality.

So. In the very first fractions of a second of the Big Bang, the energy from that cataclysmic explosion began to spread outward and cool, forming into little points of energy - quanta - of various kinds (the quarks, dorks, and other fundamental particles). As this new thing called 'spacetime' (time and space combined) dragged on (the first few seconds), some of those quantum points/particles bunched together to make the bigger nucleons (protons and neutrons) that form the center of atoms. Some time after that these quantum points of energy cooled and built themselves into forces and chemical elements. (Some of the heavier, denser elements had to wait a billion or more years until stars formed and manufactured them through nuclear activity, then blew up in supernovae and sent these denser atoms out into space to eventually wind up as parts of other objects - monkey suits for instance.) After that, the evolution of the universe just got on and did its thing, and genetic organisms finally evolved on this planet.

There are other ideas about how the universe began. Like the Big Bounce. In this notion an earlier universe contracted down on itself all the way to a tiny point - something like the singularity that began the Big Bang - then expanded again into what we have now. I personally like the Big Bounce idea, although the rest of the above explanation stays the same.

Now about building a light-saber...No, delete that. Every nut will want one. Look what happened with guns. (When *are* you monkeys gonna grow up?)

TAPE 26

The way my CV was treated at CNLB was an example of how yours truly Lauren G.N. (for Getting Nowhere) Hendricks' mailshot for stardom crashed and burned. I didn't hear from any of the other people I mailed either. Hell, my writing ain't *that* bad! You read Jackie Collins? Or Barbara T. Bradford? How about the English Lord, Archer? What you're reading now is no worse than their stuff. I could run a small planet on what those guys make!

Don't tell me - I should've gone to see potential employers personally and sold myself, except that my boss wouldn't give me any time off, me being The

Star's ace reporter. Besides, vacations had a habit of turning into something more permanent while you were away.

Anyhow that was the background to why I was pretty pissed when I recorded this item. I'd gone into the wilderness up by Blackwater Creek, intent on producing more superb journalism for my escape portfolio, only to find the news-gathering team from CNLB sucking all the juice from what should've been my healer exclusive. Their big fancy Jeep was parked right by the healer's trailer at the base of the green hillside that was now turning into a picnic-area and campsite, their camera drawing whoever they pointed it at like it had some irresistible pheromone painted on it.

Boy, was I mad. Here were guys doing what I wished I was doing, with all of that technology and money behind them, and probably making more in a week than I made in a year at The Star. They'd gotten my mailshot and airlifted a team in. Naturally I'd have done the same in their place, but that didn't stop me being mad.

This was my first glimpse of Rudy Deeks, front man for the news-team from CNLB. The guy was cool and aloof-looking, professional, successful. Hell, he was what I desperately wanted to be. What Deeks allowed to get sucked into that mike and that camera would wind up on TV, and mister, I had to swallow all of my frustration at being stuck in nowheresville. Then I found myself in conversation with Deeks, and it was weird the way we got on, as if we'd known each other for months.

"The guy's eyes are remarkable," he said. "I never saw such a penetrating gaze."

Deeks was watching the healer but talking to me. That was when I realized Deeks was good to look at. Being with him was kind of comfortable too. And it also helps when the person you're talking to doesn't wait for you to avert your eyes so they can weigh your breasts visually. Guys imagine you can't feel that happening, but guys imagine a lot of things that have little in common with reality. Even Deeks' name was starting to sound not quite so dorky.

"Uh, oh yeah," I concurred. "He does have interesting eyes - I think. I never got that close." As a matter of fact I felt stupid for being kind've short-sighted. (Nobody knew because I was too vain to wear glasses, and I sure didn't like the idea of contacts.)

At that, Deeks picked up the camera and let me look through it at the healer, which was like me and he were standing nose to nose. It's something I never did again. In fact after that I made a point of not looking at him directly.

124

I won't embroider that explanation here, but I will say Deeks was very polite about the way I practically emasculated him with that goddam camera because I swear the healer actually looked right back at me through the lens! He was fifty yards away, yet he *knew!* That was how I learned why those folks who went up to see him came away with a dreamy look on their face.

After I told Deeks who I was, I was flattered to learn he'd heard of me - until he told me how he heard, and what CNLB policy was on ignoring cold calls. And right here I could bluff and say hey, by then it didn't come as so big a disappointment. I'd figured that as time goes by and you get older and wiser, you see a fuller and more accurate picture of how things are, instead of how you'd like them to be. Except that's not how it was at all. Suddenly I was a mixture of suicidal and homicidal all over again. The only fuller and more accurate picture I was seeing was of the brick wall between me and a real job in the news media.

Okay, now I want you to feel the wall, the table, your head. Solid, right? So how can they be nothing but vibrating energy? The answer is, because of the hugely powerful way some of those bits of energy attract each other, and the equally powerful way some repel each other. Explosive forces (eg: atom bombs) are produced by separating the nucleons in the center of uranium atoms. (Uranium is one of the 100+ atomic elements that everything in the universe is made from.) Boy, do those little nucleons hate being separated!

While I rebuild this drink I'll tell you about the 4 fundamental *forces* holding all of those chemical elements together: the electromagnetic force; the strong atomic force; the weak atomic force; and gravity.

You'll recall from my earlier lecture that the energy in different kinds of quanta forms the smallest particles like quarks and electrons (which build into atoms to make the 'real' things we see, hear, feel, taste and smell). Well, this energy also forms itself into other kinds of quantum particles that comprise the fundamental forces that hold everything together. The *strong nuclear force* holds protons and neutrons together in the center of atoms. The *weak nuclear force* is responsible for stuff like the behavior of electrons, and for the radioactive decay that makes geiger counters click. The *electromagnetic force* is in the form of electricity, magnetism, light and stuff like that. And then there's *gravity*, as in Einstein's famous General Theory of Relativity. (Migraine-inducing stuff concerning matter/energy and the curvature of spacetime, which also describes how the force of gravity holds all the planets, stars and galaxies in the shape of the universe.)

But there's a problem. To tie up all of the loose ends in physics, physicists need to understand how the behavior of particles at the small (quantum) end of things, fits in with the behavior of things at the big end of things (gravity, planets, stars and galaxies). In other words, mom, they need to find one single, unifying theory that explains how gravity holds planets and stars in space, as part of the *same* theory for the way the other forces hold tiny particles together as atoms. They were hoping the string notion would give them this theory, but string has gone kind of slack lately.

Now listen. I could explain all kinds of interesting things, such as how the quarks (that form the protons and neutrons in the nuclei of atoms) are held together by other quantum particles called gluons in the Yang-Mills field. I could sprinkle around a few words like lepton and boson, and describe how electrons (leptons) and photons (individual quanta of light) interact. That's called quantum electrodynamics. Right.

But you're wondering what the f*** does this stuff actually have to do with *your* everyday life?

Well surprise, surprise, this *is* your life I'm talking about here. *All* of your problems are caused by you not appreciating what your so-called 'life' really is.

Look around. *What* is doing the looking? Not your eyes, not your ocular nerves nor your brain because - as I explained - those are made from the same dumb-level components that other material things in the universe are. Eyes and brains can no more see on their own account than eyeglasses can. The only thing that *knows* it's looking is your conscious awareness. All the rest is just packaging.

The entire outfit is just something YOU put on when you're born, and take off again when YOU move to the next stage of existence. (You don't keep the goddam packaging when you get a gift, you recycle it - unless you're one of those nutty people who hoard garbage.)

Let's go in real close to where material reality meets the conscious you at the quantum level. For you at this crucial interface, reality isn't strings, quarks, nucleons, atoms, or even the solid objects made from those. Reality is you *being conscious* of the effects of the forces holding those particles together. All of the sensory 'realness' about material reality is in your mind.

For you as consciousness, the sensations of 'solidity' and 'touch' come second-hand, not as actual 'physical' feeling, but as *ideas*. All the physical sensations happen exclusively in a material body's nervous system and brain. The immaterially conscious 'you' interfaces that material monkey suit through the series of subtle 'bodies' I talked about. These are varying densities of consciousness. At their finer levels they're your conscious awareness. At their denser levels they're the sensations in your nervous system. This way, the immaterial energy of your Real, conscious self can work with the dense material energy of a monkey suit. All of it is just energy at bottom.

Great. But if consciousness is *more* Real than material reality, how come neither microscopes nor telescopes ever show conscious Reality?

Well, interestingly, that's all they ever do show. What you're seeing right now is not a material picture of the things around you. A material picture would have no consciousness. It would be just a bunch of stupid atoms.

The picture of material reality that you see is actually built up from the way your consciousness interprets the way one lot of subatomic particles, glued together to make eyes and nerves and a brain, interact with a lot of other subatomic particles bunched together to make light. You're 'seeing' a conscious, knowing, self-aware interpretation of something that has no consciousness, knows nothing, and isn't self-aware. You only ever 'see' material reality through the medium of conscious awareness.

Conversely, the only way to ever 'see' consciousness itself is through the way it influences, and is influenced by, a material body/brain interacting with the material reality around it. As your consciousness evolves, you come to see materiality differently - not because material reality changes as your consciousness evolves, but because your consciousness gradually learns to 'see' different aspects of the continuum of materiality, and to relate to it in new ways.

The reason why things are set up this way is so you (and everybody else) can interact with material reality. Your consciousness does that by causing material changes in your brain and your body, which then cause changes in material objects around you. That amounts to you consciously manipulating the physical laws that hold this material universe together. And by manipulating those, you're being creative with the 'reality' those laws represent, and it all comes down to how YOU choose to use that body and brain you're sitting inside of.

Think of your consciousness manipulating that brain like learning to play a musical instrument. A piano, say. First you can only hit the keys and make a discordant racket. (Even those dis-chords are your consciousness being 'creative' with otherwise mindless atoms shaped into a piano. Neither the racket nor the piano would have existed if their mindless atoms were left to their own devices.) But as you learn to play better, you make the notes produced by mindless atoms conform more and more to a pattern your consciousness calls music.

What's actually happening is that your consciousness is learning to play the 'instrument' of your brain by being creative with all of its otherwise mindless atoms, nucleons and quarks, and the resultant thoughts are the 'music'. Just by thinking, you're playing the energy particles - or even the superstrings if they exist - in your brain like an unimaginably awesome musical instrument!

Now let's just wait for my mom to catch up.

Good. As a new generation of readers has joined us, I'm going to continue showing you how physics, by encouraging you to think in material rather than conscious terms, creates a false view of yourself and everything around you. Let's start with something exciting, like gravity.

Huh? You don't find gravity exciting? Well there'd be no sex without gravity for one thing. (There'd be no *anything* without gravity.)

It's okay, I didn't find gravity interesting either until I realized gravity is just another way for mindless laws of physics to push the Real, conscious me around through a monkey suit. If somebody was continuously and ruthlessly pushing you around, you wouldn't stand there and let it happen, right? Well gravity and all of the other forces and chemical elements of material reality are doing just that, all of the time, by fooling you into doing just what the monkey suit wants. They're making you delude yourself about what *you* Really are.

It's not the universe's fault. The universe is only here to help you grow by providing a framework for your consciousness to work in. But if you let mindless physical laws tell you what to do and how to live through the urges and instincts and drives that genes evolved for their own benefit, that's like letting your car tell you what to do and how to live for its benefit. Yes sir, it's *exactly* the same. In both examples, the conscious YOU is meant to do the driving. Getting pushed around by urges is so dumb if you actually believe that's what YOU want!

In quantum mechanical terms, gravity is thought to be composed of quantum particles of energy called gravitons. (The same way that light is quantum particles called photons, and my drink is quantum particles called martinitons). Even more esoteric is the notion that each of these quantum particles of energy could be a particular mode of vibration along a piece of string. But whatever's happening, our consciousness only learns about these things as part of figuring out what we Really are.

128

Look around again. See the air? No, because it's too thin for human eyes to see (except in places where pollution has gone crazy). The air we breathe is made from quantum particles too, held together by the strong nuclear force as protons and neutrons in the middle of air atoms (mostly nitrogen and oxygen atoms). The nitrogen and oxygen atoms bunch up to make megazillions of molecules of stuff known collectively as *air*.

What does air have to do with gravity, or you understanding yourself?

Well, air just happens to be incredibly *more* dense than gravity. Gravitons are a lot smaller than even the protons and neutrons in an atom. And yet the force of gravity does something air could never do: it holds suns and planets in their positions relative to each other in galaxies, and galaxies in their positions relative to each other in space. Things in the universe don't come any bigger than galaxies, except for clusters of galaxies, which are also interpositioned and shaped by gravity. (Well okay, and clusters of galaxies form into even bigger superclusters.)

The question is, if gravity is so goddam thin, how can it hold an entire universe together?

On its own, it can't. But gravity is not on its own, it's inseparable from all of the other interconnected forces and particles in the universe, all of them arranged as interconnected and overlapping fields of energy.

On the subject of gravity, the planets of our solar system orbit the sun because their movement is governed by two things: one is their mass (the amount of energy in them) and the other is gravity. Any object with mass creates gravity. The more massive an object - a planet for instance - the more gravity it exerts on other objects. But what an object's gravity actually does - this is so cool - is to *distort the shape of space around that object*. The precise way that gravity distorts space round an object is by making that object act like a magnet. The more mass an object has, the more it attracts the stuff around it.

The most massive object in our solar system - the sun - is round, so it distorts space all around it, causing the planets to follow the distortion and orbit it. When space is distorted by objects with mass this way, the distortion affects anything material that passes through the distorted space, including the particles of light from other suns, aka stars, on their way to us from out in deep space. Light has to follow the shape of space created around objects that have enough gravity to cause distortions.

Hey, imagine the physical universe being made from differently colored pieces of playdo, each color representing a different quality of the universe's fundamental structure. One playdo color represents the quality of electromagnetism (an aspect of which is light), another playdo color the quality of time, another the quality of gravity, and so on. Now roll all of those qualities together so thoroughly they make one piece, so well-mixed you can't hardly tell the original colors/qualities apart and you've got the universe. You can't look at one color/quality without seeing all the others. You can't influence one color/quality without influencing all the others.

Now I'll repeat: You think this universe-sized combination of forces and elements is unimaginably powerful, right? Well you can overcome and control all of those dumb, mindless forces and elements just by refusing to do what the monkey suit wants. All you have to do is act unselfishly.

TAPE 27

Back in the wilderness the crowd was now rolling slowly down the side of that green hill like a quiet wave, Deeks and Bonelli surfing in and out of their midst doing interviews, with yours truly a twig tossing in their wake, scraping up for my no-account rag what few crumbs were left after the golden boys got their share. And the way some people went cross-eyed at the sight of a TV camera and a mike really got me mad. But what can you do when even the chance of a moment's fame means a lot in a place like Raiment County, where folks can hardly even afford to run an ego.

Deeks would fall in beside someone and wave his microphone like a goddam magic wand. When people realized they were on TV the mouths started flapping, they'd primp their hair and suddenly grow an inch taller.

Deeks would go: "And you are? Jethro. Yeah, hi. Why are you up here today?" And Jethro would look at his swollen nose in the lens and wonder out loud why he had come up there today. Or Deeks stuck the mike under another nose and told them why they were there: "You're here to be healed, right?" Sure they were. Or maybe they'd been healed and were striding boldly where before they could only hobble. I heard one guy tell Deeks it was a miracle.

"A *miracle?*" Deeks said with professional amazement.

"Yessir!" And who was gonna call the guy a liar?

"This your small son ma'am? You looking for anything in particular today? God? Did you find Him? You did? Thankyou ma'am."

Deeks to someone else: "Hi."

Local: "Hi yourself."

Deeks: "How you doin'?"

"Alright, thankin' you kindly."

"You local, sir?"

"Vienna."

"*Vienna - ?*"

"Vienna Illinois. Come f'the Smokies and wound up hereabouts."

I looked away for a second and Deeks was asking another fella, " - and that was how all of this thing got started? The healer just appeared one day and folks started coming up here to be with him?"

"That's how it was. Kinda just happened like things do."

"And is he part of a specific church or religion?"

"Don't rightly know 'bout that - I'm here with my heart."

"Your - "

"Angina. See that?" He rubbed his chest lovingly. "Sometimes that's real tight 'cross there, like a vise grippin'. Other times it's just a friendly squeeze."

"Thankyou very much, sir." And Deeks was off again, the mike a divining-rod twitching hopefully towards first one person then another, and in between times flicking from their mouth back to Deeks' depending whose turn it was to speak.

I loved watching those guys work, even though I hated it. Trouble was, after people had just basked in their moment of stardom, to have me offer them a tape recorder the size of a mouse-dropping and no camera was just plain insulting. But I still had my job to do, and that was where I had one over those media stars from the big city, because I knew the local people, by type if not personally, which meant I knew what they didn't have.

When folks are out there seeing what's being given away for free, such knowledge is very useful when you're aiming to communicate. I figured that all this was really about in many cases was a little light relief from the poor real lives some of these folks lived. I'm not saying any of them were up there because they believed my Star stuff about the healer being you-know-Who back for a second try. Maybe my stories seeded something in weaker minds, and probably gave the healer some publicity. At the time I couldn't have cared less whether the healer was Hannibal Lecter or Santa Clause, just so long as he made good copy.

So with the A-Team just ahead of me, I made a rearguard. My first catch was a balding, stooped man with tired-looking eyes.

"Laurie Hendricks from your local Star. You in work, sir?"

"Look at that." He showed me the black crescents of his nails. "Seven years, then the strip closed down an' I made freeman of the county."

"How you managin' now, sir?"

"Hell, Miss, I ain't. I'm retired sick."

"That why you came to see the healer?"

"This is where the gov'ment ought to come; they's the sick ones."

When I asked him why he said that, he gave me a 'come-on-now' look. "You seen any work round here lately? Even that landfill thing is just a big maybe."

"Landfill?"

"Hell lady, what's a little more garbage to a place like Raiment?"

"You're very kind for talkin' to me."

And that was how I first got wind of the landfill project. They were proposing to site it just outside of Passmore. I later learned that, like the man said, the landfill was still a maybe, and the Mayor and everybody were half-denying it would ever happen anyhow.

While I was wondering how to capitalize on a project that hadn't gotten the go-ahead yet, I stopped beside a youngish woman with a toddling girl who looked a might too thin and sickly to be trailing round the wilderness.

"'S'cuse me, ma'am. Laurie Hendricks for The Star. Do you have a special reason for coming to see the healer?"

She glanced down at her daughter, her eyes bleak when she looked up. "She's badly, so I thought, well, why not."

"Yeah, I know. Costs a fortune just to stay alive."

"Well that's right. I got us a ride up here but I didn't see him yet. We're still hopin'."

"Keep tryin', ma'am; you'll see him." I was wishing I believed my own publicity.

"Thankyou kindly. I hope so."

It was when I'd begun to lag behind the TV that I got to talk with an elderly gent who'd actually been touched by the healer. I probably only got him to myself because he was moving too slowly for the hotshots. He was so bent over I had to crouch in order to speak with him as we walked.

"Pardon me, sir, but have you come to see the healer?"

"I seen 'im!"

"You did?"

"Surely. Fixed me up real good. Never felt better in m'life!"

132

"Were you sick, d'you mind if I ask?"

"Sick an' tired, I was. Sick an' tired."

"With what?"

"Pain in my ass."

"S'cuse me?"

"Pain in my ass! You deef?"

"Uh, you saw him 'bout that? What happened?"

"Took it clean away is what happened!"

"He did?"

"Just said so didn't I? Maybe you should see 'im with your hearin'."

"So you're, uh, cured?"

"Sure thing. Never felt so good."

By then we had a high view of that track in the valley I came in on, which led to a kind of settlement: a few shacks and the healer's silver trailer arranged untidily by a small copse of mixed deciduous and conifer trees for shade, and, down in the bottom, the polluted stream called Blackwater Creek, except I could only see that by reputation.

There are lots of hollows like that hidden away in the hills around Passmore and such places, home to poor people, black and white (uh, meaning black or white) who scratch a livelihood somehow but just don't ask me how. I guess some of them are as poor as any you'll find in America if you take the time to go looking. But why would you want to? All you'd find is the downside of genetic competition: poverty and hardship and disillusionment.

I don't need to lecture you about how so many folks finish up in life's landfill. What somebody obviously does need lecturing about is how we all vote, with each selfish act, to keep that landfill open.

TAPE 28

I made this tape a couple of days later when I was at one of the loose ends that my life is woven together from. It's about pumpkin pie. (Okay, so it's about quantum physics, but you have to make stuff like this user-friendly or people quit reading - especially as I already made the incredibly tiny quantum end of reality sound complicated. Stay tuned because now I'm gonna make it sound just plain nuts.)

Quantum physics (aka quantum mechanics) deals with the tiny particles of energy (quanta) that combine to make everything in our material world, right?

Right. But those tiny particles don't act like they're part of any 'real' world. Some of the things they do have more in common with stuff like ghosts and time travel. Well ghosts, time travel and quantum particles only seem weird because most people don't understand them yet.

Just one of the many weird-seeming things about quantum particles is, they act like individual particles, and at the same time they act like they're part of an entire wave of particles.

Now you're thinking quantum physics is far too complicated for a dummy like you, but you're confusing 'complicated' with 'this stuff was never explained to me in plain words'. So here's the particles/waves thing explained in familiar terms.

Imagine a football game where one side appears to have only one player. Weirdly enough, he's running and passing and tackling as if he's part of a complete team, and the ball too is behaving as if there's a full team playing alongside of him. Even the opposing players are running and passing and getting pushed around as if they're playing against a full team. But all they can see is one guy. Well, that's the crazy kind of way things would happen if he was a quantum particle.

This is the 'reality' that your body, brain and everything else are made from. And you thought quantum physics didn't concern you? ("No Laurie, I'm just too dumb to give a damn one way or the other.")

According to string theory, quantum particles are neither particles nor waves, they're momentarily glimpsed 'notes' produced by those tiny vibrating strings of energy. That's unproved as yet so let's stay with the particles/waves anomaly. What it means is that instead of knowing precisely where a quantum particle will be, you can only ever guess where it'll probably be. (It actually means physicists can't figure out the exact position of these particles and, simultaneously, how fast they're moving.)

Why is that a problem? Because only by measuring a particle's exact position and speed both together can you *predict* its behavior precisely. Understanding matter so you can predict its behavior exactly is what physics is all about - or used to be before quanta were discovered.

In science we used to think that the smaller you go, the more precise you can be. By knowing precisely how things behave, you can make them behave the way *you* want them to, instead of having them do what the hell they like. But how do you control particles that are sometimes waves, when you can't even be sure of their precise position and speed simultaneously?

134

You drive a car? You have to know both the position and speed of your car together or you can't control it, right? Sure there's leeway, because driving doesn't require subatomic accuracy. How about performing micro-surgery? Knowing the exact position and speed of instruments in micro-surgery important? It is if you're the guinea-pig (sorry, patient) and the surgeon's using a laser scalpel.

Physicists eventually realized that these waves/particles of energy are not *real* waves or particles in the way we understand 'real', they're only *probabilities*. Material reality is just one big maybe. And having decided that 'maybe' is a fundamental, underlying property of everything in the universe, physicists had to come up with a way to describe it - the *Uncertainty Principle*.

Now let's cut the crap. The only reason why this sounds nutty is because the way we see things, is not how they actually are. All we ever saw was the tip of the reality iceberg.

For that reason, reality at quantum level is said to be *counterintuitive*, meaning it doesn't *feel* right, even though it's *more* right than the reality we've gotten used to. Experiencing the *less* right reality of clunky solid objects made from atoms is part of the delusion that our underevolved consciousness is beginning to overcome. We're learning to see through our old notions of reality, imposed on us by having to work through a monkey suit made from these same clunky atoms.

As consciousness, we don't exist in any material sense…but to fully appreciate all of the implications of that takes time. That's fine, because working through a monkey suit to discover those implications is the reason why we're here. This process of discovery is what drives our conscious evolution. Even the 'time' that it takes is part of the process.

Like I said, material reality is nothing but a façade, a medium for us work with to achieve more conscious growth. As consciousness we're here to learn who and what we Really are, right? And by seeing material reality as a 'maybe' thing, we're simply taking a natural step along the road of our own evolution as consciousness. As part of this upshift in our conscious evolution, the discovery of quantum reality is simply telling us there's a lot more to us than replicating and reproducing genes.

Okay. So now we're looking at material reality as energy that exists as what quantum physicists call probability waves. Everything you see (and hear, taste, smell, touch, etc.) is the result of countless numbers of these probability waves of particles that appear to us as things made from atoms.

That's easy to say, but *why* do wave-like patterns of interconnected energy at the quantum level appear to us as things made from atoms? It's because consciousness, interfacing a material monkey suit at this evolutionary level, sees materiality this way. Probability waves of particles are organized (by laws of physics) into bigger 'things' - quarks, nucleons and electrons, atoms, then molecules that amass into the recognizable objects of our reality. The bigger those objects get, the more predictable their behavior appears to us.

Now we've reached the important part of this tape: choice, and the free will factor. Think of probability waves/particles as a limitless number of potential alternative realities that might or might not happen. While we can't do anything about most of the alternative realities in the universe, the choices and decisions we make here on Earth can and do turn an ongoing series of those potential alternative realities into real events.

How do the choices we make turn probability waves/particles into real events?

Even though we perceive us and the world around us as tangible, material objects, our consciousness, as the environment of ideas, awareness and thought, is fundamentally free of materiality. This freedom enables us to see (and think about) ourselves *in relation to* the solid objects of material reality.

But we don't think about ourselves as conscious entities, right? We identify with our material body. So the 'self' we perceive in relation to our surroundings, is our material self. And the surroundings we mostly perceive our material self in relation to, are other people's material selves.

That's how we create desires, hopes and aspirations for ourselves in relation to those other people, and in relation to the other material things that affect us. We see possibilities, options and potentials for ourselves in relation to all of these material things. We can choose to turn those possibilities, options and potentials into actual events by consciously manipulating materially real things.

This is exactly what Ed was saying about learning to be creative with the material universe, by harnessing the possibilities inherent in material reality. Except that explaining this stuff has brought on one of my headaches, but let's take it a little further anyway before this martini runs dry.

The energy of probability waves doesn't simply fill the universe, it *is* the universe. The whole thing is interconnected in the way that a hologram is. Hell no, I'm not gonna explain what a hologram is (something to do with using lasers to split light and then recombining a scattered wave and a reference beam to form an interference pattern, kind of thing).

136

No, the wild thing about holograms is, they're composed of tiny pieces, and each one of those pieces can represent the complete image.

In a universe of interconnected probability waves that act like a great big hologram, the implication is that you can't do something in one part of the universe without affecting the rest, because subatomic particles all share an instant connection with each other! (You might even say they're interchangeable with each other, but I'm not going anywhere near that notion with this headache.)

Interestingly, this holographic notion is also supposed to apply to the way our brain works! (We used to think separate brain areas handled things like sight, taste, touch, ideas, understanding and etc. Now we know that these activities involve the whole brain.) Well sure they do. The brain exists to give consciousness a way into material reality (not merely to look out for the body it's in). Consciousness has been modifying brains for that purpose ever since nervous systems began evolving.

According to Ed, the energy frequencies of this instantaneous holographic style connectedness (both inside and outside of brains) operate outside of time and space, and that opens the door to the once-crazy possibility that past and future are both accessible in the here and now.

Reality Window: I guess stuff like this seems a million miles from our familiar old reality because we're used to a reality built on hard evidence. Without the hard evidence provided by 'solid-object' reality, our consciousness has nothing to push against. The only solidity is where we're coming from - our ignorant past. Ignorance is just too goddam reassuring. And as the embodiment of the ignorance of our own genetic past, we imagine that we have too much to lose, when in fact we have everything to gain.

I think a summation is in order here: Because of the origins of our bodies/brains, our ideas about reality stem from our need to survive as genetic organisms in a competitive world. (Reasoning: If you're not sure what's real, you're not gonna survive very long.) By allowing our lives to be governed almost entirely by this need to survive, we're confined to the dumb-level atomic version of reality where we only see a façade that hides a more accurate and Real picture.

The newly discovered probabilities/possibilities at quantum level are telling us that our old understanding of real was not just incomplete, it was wrong. Until now, we've only experienced a childishly obvious kind of reality more suited for mindless biology to flourish in. These new insights are a starting point for consciousness to begin figuring out what reality ought to mean in a *conscious* sense.

If the opposite of weird is 'sensible', then quantum waves/particles don't behave sensibly. But sensible things are only 'sensible' because they help us survive in material reality, as replication and reproduction vehicles for genes. Now it's time to start getting Real. The world, the universe, these monkey suits, everything we see, hear, smell taste and touch - is all an elaborate illusion created by the limited way we perceive patterns of energy. It's just a stage-set made to appear as the objects we experience.

At the very beginning of this universe, energy at the quantum level was all that existed. That energy was gradually organized into the atomic level of 'reality' by laws of physics. After things started to slow down and cool, and the predictable forces and elements formed, the opportunity came for material bodies to evolve on the atomic level; bodies with brains that later became vehicles for our consciousness.

Why'd it all happen that way? Because without the subjective predictability of this atomic level, the first vestiges of our visiting consciousness wouldn't have known their ass from a black hole. The atomic level is a necessary, safe, kindergarten stage from where our consciousness can learn about the more exotic subatomic and beyond. In time we'll figure that the fundamental (quantum) constituents of the universe are, as Ed said, a malleable extension of consciousness itself. An extension that was created by a much higher level of consciousness than ours.

Okay. That was as complicated as this book gets. If you're still with it, the rest is a piece of cake. Yep, the uncertainty principle also applies to cake. (Maybe you really can have it and eat it too.)

TAPE 29

In the wilderness the last of the sun was caught in the trees up by the summit of one of the hills behind us, which left that collection of dwellings in the bottom a might cool. I expected people to start drifting away for supper, but not a one of 'em took off. As McClure and his friend organized folks out front of the healer's trailer, I relocated Deeks to find out how they were getting on. He looked up from what he was doing and said hi in a real friendly way, so I said hi yourself and asked him how I should go about trying for a job like his.

138

"Go live in the city."

I noticed in passing what nice teeth he had, but lots of black folks have nice white teeth. Sorry, where was I at? So I found Deeks attractive. I used to find the aroma of barbecues attractive but no way would I let that get between me and my ambitions.

"I have no connections in the city," I told him.

Without looking away from what he was doing he said, "Make some."

"Maybe I'm trying to right now."

We shared an easy smile. Leastwise I did. "No, 's'okay," I told him, "I'm being pushy. Apologies all round." I surprised myself by meaning it. "Besides, I wouldn't wish me on my worst enemy…"

His eyes started to turn my way then thought better of it.

I looked over at the little silver trailer to think. The healer was standing by the front steps with McClure right beside him, crouched by the wheel like a pet dog. I couldn't see the other faithful follower - Donna's handsome friend - but guessed he'd be doing something useful the way I assumed those healer helpers did. Well hey, if I was playing the groupie to Deeks, what were those two guys doing? What were they after? At least I had my own best interests at heart, so what was in it for them?

This seemed like a good time to ask Deeks how he intended to 'tell the world' about what was happening here. I made the question sarcastic to get even for being embarrassed earlier.

Deeks threw the question right back at me, the way Ed would've: "How do you intend telling it for your readers?"

"Want a few tips, uh? Well let's see now…I guess telling this like it is won't do a lot for my Star readers. They're used to plenty of ketchup on their potatoes."

I couldn't believe how fake I sounded; it was a shock because I'd not listened to myself that way before. I had no idea why I'd suddenly started overhearing my own garbage. The knowing look in Deeks' eyes didn't help.

"So you'll tell it the way you think your readers want to hear it?" He didn't say it as a reprimand or an accusation, but that didn't stop me from hearing those.

"I didn't say that," I lied, knowing I couldn't have put it better myself. I think I might even have blushed, but that was just the result of being outdoors. "I just rework the facts so they're easier on the ear."

"*Ketchup?*"

"C'mon Deeks, that was a joke."

Except he knew that it wasn't. Worse, I knew he knew. I also knew Deeks was not the number-one fan of Laurie Hendricks, hack to the hicks. So when he excused himself and went off to do something more interesting than talk to me, I just stood there feeling guilty about the way I worked. It was part of the painful awakening I'd begun to experience, though it wouldn't have been half so painful had I not resisted it so vigorously.

A little while later I actually got to witness Deeks 'telling the world' what was happening here. You know how these news guys work. At the end of their report the front-man/woman with the mike turns to camera and ties everything up neatly. That was what Deeks did now. In close-up with the healer's trailer in the background - inside which was the real subject of this piece - I watched Deeks do the broadcast that was to bring many more hundreds of people flocking to this small corner of Raiment County. This is it:

"Today we've seen unusual events take place in this quiet backwater of Tennessee. Events that I doubt these people - some of whom have lived their entire lives hereabouts - would be any better at explaining than I am. And yet…(definitely paused for effect)…and yet they seem to know, in some indefinable way, exactly what is truly taking place in Raiment County. This is not simply people having their ailments banished by a healer, maybe through the simple act of faith, who knows? And not through the kind of devotion that simple, God-fearing people give to a figure who comforts them without seeking any recompense…who actually refuses offers of money or other benefits. Something else is present here today. Some intoxicating natural element, a definite sense of hope and optimism that unfortunately isn't able to be captured on camera. I've had people come up to me and try to explain just what that is, and each of them failed. But the important thing is, they know it's here. I know it too. You've heard them talking to me. You've seen the man they came to see. We've brought you the facts here today. Now it's for you to form your own opinions. This is Rudy Deeks in Raiment County Tennessee for CNLB News."

By that time - it must have been pushing eight - the sun was getting heavy, and a pleasant aroma of dew was just starting to ooze up through the grass; mixed with woodsmoke from the few ramshackle buildings round about, a real mellowness got mixed in with that earlier magic…

On another audio tape I just transcribed are my early thoughts on the landfill story. I must've come home and started on it that night. I probably mixed a drink, set myself right down here at this, my own private landfill, and came out with suggestions for lines like: 'Is Raiment about to get dumped on.' 'Trashville Tennessee.' And 'The Garbage State of the Nation.' It would be nice to scoop the dross like that off the surface of my mind before I start diving for the pearls, but mostly I just end up using dross because that's all there is.

Earlier I said that while we devote our lives to the demands of these genetic bodies, our 'free will' can't ever be truly free, and Real freedom will remain a delusion. Now I want to say more about that. (The hell I do; I'd rather go to a bar, drink tequila and make a damn fool of myself.)

People have always had a problem with the notion of 'free will'. Some got philosophical about how unfree they thought our will actually is and called it *determinism*. For determinists, every single event that ever happens is caused by earlier events. That would mean our every thought and deed is predetermined - pre-decided - by events that happened in the past. Even though determinism would involve too many separate events to ever keep a track of - especially in brains – on paper it does have a kind of logic to it. It can also be used to argue that God doesn't exist, except in our imagination. Why? Because traditionally, God is famous for spontaneity. He doesn't need to justify miracles with deterministic events. (Determinism was probably invented by skeptics to counter notions of God, religion, magic and stuff like that. Skeptics hate those kinda things, and I should know.) Matters only got worse when somebody went and invented *reductionism*, which you might recall is the strict reducing diet of scientists who say that everything reduces to the smallest material components we know about.

Reductionists used to think that everything was made from atoms, and nothing smaller existed. Their atoms behaved as predictably as nuts and bolts, supposedly making the universe run like clockwork. Brains too.

When determinists and reductionists started hitting the same bars together, they decided between them that the 'clockwork' machinery of our brains is what creates our conscious mind. That meant we can no more have original, spontaneous thoughts than a clock can. Every thought would be the direct result of a series of tiny mechanical actions caused by earlier tiny mechanical actions in our brain. Kiss your free will goodbye.

Most scientists and brain philosophers still believe brains make consciousness, without actually knowing what consciousness is, or how brain machinery makes it. They've replaced the clockwork notion with something similar but more complicated: the laws of physics. And we still have the same problem: If brain machinery reduces to particles created and governed by physics laws, how can a brain create a conscious will that's *free* of physics laws?

Not so fast say neuroscientists. We don't actually need a will that's free from the influence of physics laws. The staggering complexity of brain machinery gives us more than enough options to make it *seem as if* our will is free. These guys are determined to stick with reductionism, and brains that reduce to known material elements have to create consciousness, because any other explanation would contradict the laws of physics and leave the door wide open for God, and God-knows what other unscientific notions.

To make matters worse, scientists have now been given the quantum hand to play with. Our thoughts and deeds, along with our morals, hopes, dreams and aspirations, are still assumed to reduce to the atoms that comprise our brain, but now those atoms are built from the interactions between particles that travel in probability waves ruled by quantum uncertainty.

Scientists and philosophers don't know how consciousness works or how it's generated, but they can't just up and admit that. Human beings, scientists especially, are programmed against admitting ignorance. So they postulate ideas about how it *might* work, then throw a lot of facts at you that prove various things, but not that consciousness is made by brains. Quantum mechanics only complicates matters further, enabling them to rope in the unpredictable behavior of the quantum level to suggest that uncertainty itself might enable a brain to manufacture a consciousness free will. These guys have gone so far down the reductionist road, they've no room left to turn around. They've dumped determinism, only to replace it with *uncertain quantum determinism*.

TAPE 30

Before we move on I just want to say a few words about *chance*, otherwise known as *randomness*. Yes, it's pretty goddam important for all kinds of reasons, not the least of them being that Quantum physicists insist the entire universe is fundamentally random, that it all began by chance and has all been shaped by chance events. Oh, and as a result of this randomness we just happened along.

So first, what the hell are chance and randomness, Really? It's simply a lack of information about how things actually are.

While we're on this relatively uninformed human level of consciousness, events that appear to happen at random or by chance (aka luck) seem that way because we, the conscious onlooker, lack information about how all of those events relate to each other.

Understandable enough when you're dealing with quantum uncertainty, though even when atoms are organized into everyday objects, events involving them can still be seriously unpredictable simply because reality is so complicated, and we just don't know enough about stuff to prepare us for all of the things that might happen next.

Even if we could have all of the relevant information, things made from atoms would still behave unpredictably…because *we're* involved with them, and nothing is more unpredictable than us. (And we're nuts, which doesn't help any.)

Reality Window: As I'm talking about chance and luck, we have to bring religion into the conversation. Why? Because all of our notions of religion and God developed from primitive survival urges, when early human existence was at the mercy of random-seeming events. Developing brains hate random events, so they look for patterns in the way things happen in an effort to impose some kind of order and predictability in their world. But being primitive, they find answers in the most obvious things. And the most obvious answers are hardly ever the right ones – especially when you're primitive.

Even now most people still think a superior intelligence is in back of chance and luck (in the hope that nothing is really just random). Millions of us still offer worship, appeasement, sacrifice and whatever to God to try and swing His favors our way. Thinking that God must be something like us - what other way could we think? - we presume that the reasons we have for wanting things to be a certain way, within the logic/reality/purpose structure that we exist in, is the same logic/reality/purpose structure that God exists in. That's one way we design God in our image.

Ever hear of *Chaos Theory?* Chaos Theory is about things behaving unpredictably simply because their behavior is so damn *complicated,* not because it happens by chance or luck. Like the way water behaves when you splash it around. Boy, it goes everywhere. How could you ever possibly figure out where every single atom of water went, and which other atoms got in the way and how they all influenced each other? You couldn't, because you don't have the equipment to keep track of all those countless atoms. And yet they all behave according to known and understood laws of physics. Every one of those atoms is strictly controlled by physical laws; not one of them behaves by chance or luck.

In spite of probability waves and the uncertainty at quantum level, up here on the classical atomic level things are as down-home mechanical as if you sprayed a trillion microscopic nuts and bolts around. And like I said, on the atomic level we only think events happen by chance because we lack information about all of the countless past events that led to subsequent events. Fact is, most of us only know about a mega-pathetically small proportion of the total number of events happening in the world around us. We know even less about their potential consequences. This painfully limited awareness breeds notions of chance and luck.

Take accidents. An accident is something you didn't know was gonna happen because you were unaware of all the events leading up to it. But being a smartass, you'll realize that if you knew which events and their consequences were going to lead to accidents, accidents wouldn't be accidental, they'd be on purpose.

Yes lady, and if you knew which events were going to cause accidents, you could *avoid* those accidents by making *different* events happen. Except those new events might cause other events that you didn't know about, which in turn could cause accidents - but what do you care so long as you're not involved? (They say the talent for writing is a gift. I don't think anybody would want my talent for writing, even as a goddam gift.)

Whatever, we can overcome a little of our ignorance of events by using our limited knowledge of the past to predict what might happen in the future, otherwise nobody would be able to plan ahead. You'd have no idea what you or anybody else was going to do next. You'd keep walking in front of cars, or sticking your hand in the fire to see what flames feel like.

Having this picture of ongoing and future events just by remembering what happened in the past, is the pattern seeking notion I just mentioned. We all do it without even thinking about it. It's a part of the organizational way that brains work. Though even having a pretty good idea which events will lead to accidents doesn't mean you can change the events you have no control over.

There are ways to prevent shit happening though. Think about the events you do have control over and can do something about, which you deliberately choose to turn into unfortunate accidents for somebody else. I'm talking about the events you cause all the time by thinking 'what's in this for ME & MINE.'

144

Yep, the selfishness thing again. The luck of the world turns on whether each of us chooses to cause selfish events, or not.

What makes your luck good or bad? Whether or not it gives you what you want, right? But there's a double benefit if you prevent accidents happening for yourself *and* other people. If you influence your luck *and* theirs by reducing the number of bad events that happen to the both of you.

You know how this works because I just told you. You do it by the astute application of past event knowledge to ongoing events, to influence subsequent events, thus avoiding an accident.

A plain English example would be when you 'accidentally' shoot somebody half a dozen times and 'accidentally' wind up in the gas chamber, when instead you could've changed one simple event (taking possession of a gun) into another simple event (*not* taking possession of a gun) thereby avoiding not only somebody's 'accidental' death, but also removing the 'chance' of getting caught, and avoiding your own 'accidental' death as ordered by law.

So remember: The only bad 'people' things are caused by you *knowingly* acting selfishly. *Deliberately* screwing things up, not just for somebody else, but for yourself as well. You *pretend* shit happens by chance or bad luck, when the truth is that you deliberately choose to keep your awareness of the events you have some control over narrow for the sake of your ass. You make many of the important accidents in this world happen on purpose - *your* goddam purpose.

Now repeat after me: Anybody who takes possession of a gun, then complains that somebody got shot *by accident*, has no excuse. An entire world filled with people complaining that "It was him or me" can't make homicide right, and it never makes it 'accidental'. (I might even write that up in The Constitution when they make me President.)

TAPE 31

Tonight Jeff Ackerley was superman - the dark side from that old Superman 3 movie. His powers came courtesy of a volatile cocktail of Jack Daniel's and home-grown marijuana. Inside his pickup, the glowing instruments bottom-lighting his face into a demonic mask, Ackerley was on a crusade with justice and truth on his side: the justice of malice; the truth of hatred.

While the radio squawked country through a busted speaker, Ackerley let the vehicle do the driving, correcting its path only when necessary. The pickup was moving fast enough to cause everything inside the cabin that was not nailed down to fly around, and were it not for some deft bracing, Roy King and Willie Stevenson would have been flying around with it.

King's eyes were like back-lit marbles in the near-darkness, his small, plump lips pursed tight. He was sweating badly, which heated up the dormant bacteria already swarming in his unwashed clothes so he stank still more. There was fear-smell in there also, but to Willie it was just raw body-odor. It was making him nauseous.

"You know where the fuck's this turn?" King asked. Nobody answered.

Ackerley drew on his unshared joint with one hand while his other maintained a precarious hold on the wheel and their lives.

Willie was sweating too. Each time Ackerley sucked at the joint, Willie's eyes flickered between the hand on the wheel and the lighted road ahead. They'd missed the turn, but when Ackerley was in this mood all of his channels of communication were sealed. Willie pressed himself deeper into his uncomfortable position between the seats and rubbed at his eyes; they stung from trying to do Ackerley's seeing for him. He sneaked out a sigh, trying not to inhale King's stink.

Ackerley finished the joint and opened the door to toss the butt out, but took his eyes off the road for just that fraction too long…and suddenly there was nothing under the wheels. Willie's stomach ballooned in his chest. Wide-eyed, he watched the headlights cleave bushes and dazzle back from a tree, blinding them all. Then the suspension slammed up into its mounts, and Willie's coccyx connected with the steel floorpan. Either side of him, King and Ackerley bounced in synchro like strung-puppets, their heads hitting the roof with one combined *Dunk!* The planet lurched hard sideways one last time and everything stopped.

In the silence King said, out the side-window, "Thank the fuck we got that over with."

Then Ackerley let go a string of obscenities that would have stretched all the way back to Passmore. He got out, and by the sound of rain on leaves was taking a leak. When he returned he'd made a route-decision. He'd turn back in the direction they just came and blame the others into revealing where he went wrong. That done, a few more minutes saw them hit the turn-off over the bridge that led up to the settlement where the healer's trailer was.

Ackerley's plan was to repeat that of a couple of years earlier. It worked just fine then; the nigger's burning house had made a hell of a glow in the starry

146

sky. Ackerley's one disappointment was that his victim had gotten himself and his family out of there alive. No crispy dark meat that night. This time Ackerley had built a new factor into the plan which ought to put an end to these crazy messiah notions spreading around the county. The healer had better have the lucky touch with burns after this barbecue party.

A half mile from the healer's settlement he pulled off the track and let the pickup bury itself so deep in some bushes they had to fight their way out. Ackerley already had on his ski mask.

"Ok, gimme your bottle," he ordered King.

Reluctant, King handed over the booze and watched Ackerley unscrew the cap and tilt the bottle to the mouth of his mask. He replaced the cap and slipped the bottle in his own pocket. Before King could protest, Willie touched his arm, shook his head and passed King his own bottle. Willie had already swallowed enough to round off the corners; more would only impede his ability to look out for himself.

Ackerley had brought a rolled-up pair of old pants with him. When he unrolled them there was a Rich-Mart carrier-bag inside containing what looked to Willie like another full bottle. He heard liquid sloshing and thought Ackerley was just being his usual asshole self for keeping King's booze, until the smell reached him. Gasoline! The crazy bastard was going to burn the healer out of his trailer. The hell with that. Willie Stevenson was not so bored with life he was gonna get himself a murder rap. Not for Ackerley or anybody else, but especially not for Ackerley.

"You ain't serious!"

The panic in Willie's voice caught King's attention. He reached out and pulled the bag open before Ackerley pushed him away with an expletive that sprayed spittle on King's exposed lips. King only nodded and said, "Yeah, okay," as if the proceedings required his go-ahead.

"What's okay?" Willie accused them both. "Somebody's gonna fry an' it's just okay? You're cra - "

His protest was choked-off by Ackerley's fingers around his throat, gripping in an intoxicant-inspired fury.

"Just shut the fuck up, y'hear? You're in this an' that's it." The words were spat into his face point-blank.

Willie almost gagged on Ackerley's breath. Despite Willie's unwillingness to fight, even in self-defense, Ackerley was smaller and lighter and it seemed senseless to just stand there and let himself get choked. He got a hold of

Ackerley's wrist, surprised how strong the guy was for his scrawny build, and only managed to free himself after using both hands. Ackerley immediately forgot the transaction and walked off into the darkness.

King nudged Willie's arm. "Come on." He tried to sound encouraging, but Willie's heart and mind were not in this. There was nothing here but trouble for anybody.

This seems like a good place to introduce my Nobel Prize-winning General Theory of Reality: *Reality is what you think it is.* (I didn't get the prize yet - a miniaturized statue of an ego; maybe they mailed it to my mom's house and she's using it to keep the catflap shut. She hates snakes.)

So you disagree with my Reality Theory? You reckon that reality is real regardless of what we think it is? You reckon reality would still be just as real even if we didn't exist, right? Common sense, logic and sanity all tell you that must be true. And yet (flip your mind over and see this from another angle) it's just as true to say that if your conscious awareness didn't exist, you wouldn't know that anything existed. So your conscious awareness has to exist to make reality exist for you, okay?

Now you could say: 'But even if my conscious awareness didn't exist, there'd still be everybody else's conscious awareness to tell them reality existed.' Yeah, but *you* wouldn't know that because there'd be no 'you'. So it still holds that your conscious awareness has to exist to make any kind of reality exist for you.

I guess it's hard to grasp not existing when you already do exist. But now that your conscious awareness does exist, we can look at another statement: As our conscious awareness grows, things will get *more* real for us.

You want to disagree with that too? You reckon reality stays the same kind of real all the time? So remind yourself that when perception began in living organisms a few billion years ago, they were less aware than cheese is. Since then, living organisms, us included, have gotten less cheese-like in our conscious awareness of ourselves and the things around us. In other words, things have gradually gotten *more* real for us. This ain't just word-play; what the hell is reality if not the way you perceive things to be?

As we become more consciously aware, material reality itself changes. The universe is evolving constantly and we're part of that evolution. Reality doesn't stay the same kind of real however you look at it.

Even we, in our small ways, influence the shape of the material reality around us by making things go a certain way. And while we're influencing and

148

shaping this reality, it's influencing and shaping us. The way we use our minds, brains, senses and bodies, helps determine how they work. We help to steer their evolution in the direction we choose. The version of reality our minds, brains, senses and bodies feed back to us then helps to decide the direction of our conscious evolution by determining our thoughts, ideas, hopes, dreams and aspirations.

In simple language, our conscious decisions, and the actions that result from them, decide the kind of reality we live in, now and in the future. By making reality up as we go along this way, our evolution increasingly rides on the decisions we make. And what do those decisions all hinge on?

What things *mean* to us. The contents of material reality lack consciousness, so they don't mean anything to each other. But to us they mean what we can do with them, what we can change them into, what relationships those changes have with the changes we can make in other material things, or with the changes we can make in immaterial - conscious - things.) And because these monkey suits are also material things, what they mean to us, our relationship with them, and what we do with them, is a major part of this deal.

See, as soon as you start to think about material things - no matter how primitively - your relationship with them begins to change; not just because thinking inspires you to make changes in *them*, but because the very act of thinking about them causes the Real, conscious *you* to change. Your awareness of that Real, conscious self is reflected back at you from material things. (The same thing happens when your self-awareness is reflected back at you from non-material things - ideas - but in a more complicated way.)

Over evolutionary time this reflective process creates the difference between what a primordial snail 'thought' material things were, and what a present day human being thinks material things are. (Why do I stop at the human level of evolution? Because that's who I'm talking to.)

Okay. So while our consciousness gradually evolves by interacting with materiality (in conjunction with other consciousnesses), material things change also. (Rocks stop being just rocks and become weapons, tools, houses, TVs, automobiles, computers.) This process of making things more real for ourselves involves revising our notion of what we are and why we're here, as in *The Meaning of Life*. We have a lot of revising to do because our lack of conscious awareness of how things really are still results in so many wrong-headed notions, superstition, bigotry, narrow-mindedness and prejudice. Oh yeah, and war, inequality, poverty, hatred, greed, homicide, dissatisfaction, jealousy, envy, anger, treachery, misery, resentment - the list goes on. All of those downsides are a result of our misshapen notions about what 'reality' means.

As I keep reminding you, the factor driving our need to understand the difference between what's real and what isn't, is the same factor that creates all of our downsides: our misguided/incomplete notion that we are these genetic monkey suits, and (as a result of that misguided/incomplete notion) the determination to survive as monkey suits (albeit ones that can think a little) in material reality. We need to understand material events because they affect our survival, and in trying to survive, we give the material universe, and ourselves, meaning.

For a few million years, the 'meaning' of our life has been to survive. To most of us, that's still what life means. (Okay, so we don't think of it as survival, we think of it as happiness and security for ourselves and our families; greater personal prosperity; more 'love'; respect for our moral and religious beliefs, etc.)

On the dumb level that most of us operate, we're only interested in what our actions will 'mean' if they mean we get what *we* want. So by striving to make events behave predictably to help your survival, your consciousness is reducing the element of randomness - chance - in the way material events happen. Every decision you make and put into action reduces the element of chance inherent in material reality.

As we become more conscious, and our understanding of materiality - and our relationship with it - increases, there's less opportunity for material events to appear to happen by chance, accident or luck. Bear in mind, though, that it's not just a simple lack of information about the *physical* effects of our actions that creates the illusion of chance, accidents and luck; it's lack of *conscious* awareness of the *implications* of those actions: what they'll *mean* further down the line in a *conscious* sense.)

What do I mean by what they'll *mean*?

Well, things can only ever have *meaning* if there's a consciousness for them to mean something *to*. Without consciousness, the material universe wouldn't mean a goddam thing to anybody. It would just be a lot of mindless stuff interacting mindlessly, forever.

The *meaning* for consciousness is in why this mindless material stuff exists in the first place, why it interacts, why we interact with it, and what the implications of these interactions are for us as consciousness.

150

At the most basic level, we simply want to know what all of these material events will mean for our survival. See, by trying to figure out the element of randomness and uncertainty at the quantum level, science becomes an extension of our ongoing need to control events that affect our survival. (It's no crazy coincidence that in figuring reality out, we figure ourselves out.)

Another way to see this thing called 'chance' (the possibility that any one of a number of alternative events might happen) is in *knowing that we don't know* which of those alternatives will happen. Knowing and not knowing are all about being consciously aware. So the concept of chance wouldn't exist without conscious awareness. And hey, even the uncertainty in quantum events wouldn't be uncertain unless somebody conscious was unable to predict those quantum events, or to understand precisely why they happen the way they do. Well hell, you have to have some consciousness before you can be *uncertain* about things. Remove consciousness and you remove uncertainty. With no consciousness who'd care anyhow?

Willie could hear Ackerley crashing through the wooded undergrowth up ahead like a blind man. Every now and then would come a muffled oath as he walked into a tree or fell down; if his performance in the pickup was any guide, he might just do everybody a favor and break his goddam neck. Willie was trying not to think about what he was letting Ackerley involve him in. This was the healer they were hunting, and folks said things about the healer that both intrigued and worried Willie.

Behind him, Roy King was in Nam again, not that he was old enough to have been there a first time, but he'd convinced himself he would've been. From the safety of his imagination he would have volunteered. Now he had Ackerley's present position pin-pointed and could take him out with a single round. Then the bridge of King's nose connected with a bough that instantly turned his vision red, and he fell sideways into a rhododendron bush.

Moving silently between a juvenile King and a psychotic Ackerley, Willie stayed loose, waiting for his chance to fade into the night when the others were too busy making their mischief to notice. Then, unaccountably, he started thinking about Maxine and the way her tits would fill his hands to overflowing. Naturally he'd gotten to feel girls' tits before, but they'd been small and tight. Maybe Maxine's would be kind of, uh, spongy - like an old sofa with its springs gone. Maybe Maxine's jugs were harder when she was younger? Maybe -

"Ugh!"

A fist had punched him in the chest, though not hard enough to do any damage. Willie went hot and cold, smelled whiskey and gasoline.

"Quiet down, jerkoff. Where's fat man?"

"Back there some."

"Right here."

Willie heard a twig crack before King's bulk appeared beside him. The smell of stale sweat joined the other odors, and Willie turned away to inhale the night..

"Okay, git your ass in back of me and move out," Ackerley commanded. His animal instincts must have taken over because now he moved with more stealth. The lighter shapes of ground and sky beyond the wood's perimeter were close, and Ackerley's dark form was crouched over, moving towards the lights Willie could see about a quarter mile away: two tiny squares glowing yellow like eyes at the base of their sheltering chef's-hat-shaped clump of trees.

"Hey," King stage-whispered from the rear. "What if there's dogs?"

When no-one answered, Willie relayed the idea on to Ackerley. It seemed a fair question.

"Ain't no dogs," Ackerley rasped back. "Think I'm stupid?"

They came out of the trees in Indian file and when Ackerley broke into a trot, Willie did the same, planning his silent departure as he bounced along, wondering why he was bothering to crouch. He was determined to leave before Ackerley tossed the cocktail. Then the peculiar feeling returned, caused by what some people said about the man inside that trailer…that he was more than just a man. Shit! What *else* could he be? Willie balked, sneered the implication away, feeling angry at himself for even considering it. That the crazy bastard loping along a few yards in front intended to torch the trailer of a human being was enough; the other thing was inconceivable. The words 'homicide' and 'accessory' sounded in his head. His gut tightened at what could happen; that he should be trying to stop it yet instead was thinking only of his escape.

Out front of the aged silver cylinder of the healer's trailer, Ackerley knelt on the ground preparing his incendiary device, so intent on the task he didn't notice the Rich-Mart bag being lifted silently and carried away, ghost-like, on a gust of night breeze.

Willie was level with the end of the trailer. There was another lighted and draped window there, the trees just beyond it. When he looked back, Ackerley was at the trailer door. Although Willie couldn't make it out, he was trying to bind wire round the door-handle without the occupant hearing.

Then Ackerley's masked face lifted at a strange angle. He became immobile and seemed to be getting smaller. Willie frowned and screwed up his eyes, trying to see through the darkness. Ackerley was *collapsing*, just kind of deflating until his black-masked head was almost touching the grass. Then he keeled over and lay down, curled up in a fetal ball like somebody with a terrible pain in his gut. He was making stiff, jerky movements and small noises.

King watched this bizarre performance also. He and Willie stood frozen while the quaking figure grunted and wheezed for long moments until something sounded over by the nearest shack - maybe fifty yards off - reconnecting Willie to his senses. He ran back to Ackerley, but King got there first, took hold of Ackerley's throat and shook him. Closer, Willie realized Ackerley was doing all of the shaking, King going with it like a man holding a live cable. *Jesus!* Now Willie knew what was happening. Ackerley was -

"He's havin' a fuckin' *fit!*"

King looked up into Willie's masked face, his own eyes large and helpless through the jagged holes in his hood. "The fuck he is!" He seemed unable to let go of Ackerley.

But Willie's instinct for self-preservation was at maximum. He dropped down beside them and pulled Ackerley's hood off. You were supposed to try and keep epileptics from biting or swallowing their tongue or something. Hell, he was no medic, and King was next to useless in a crisis situation. Worse, the sounds he'd heard might mean somebody was coming.

Willie's own head was jerking from right to left, imagining figures appearing from out of the darkness. He looked at the trailer door, expecting that to fly open any second and the healer himself to - No, the handle was wired.

"Pick 'im up," he told King, who was watching his limp arms being shaken as if they belonged to someone else. When King didn't respond Willie tried single-handedly hoisting the seizured Ackerley off the ground, still locked in his traumatized fetal curl, but couldn't budge him. He grabbed a desperate hold of King's collar, pulled his face closer and croaked "*Pick - 'im - up!*" Now Willie was the one shaking - with nerves. He'd succeeded in galvanizing the stupefied King though.

With one hand King caught a hold of Ackerley's pants leg just above the knee, and with the other the front of his jacket, and hefted him as though he

153

were a log. Ackerley was still frozen in too awkward a shape to do anything but seriously inhibit their escape, but Willie turned King in the desired direction and pushed him that way, then wheeled to look behind. He imagined somebody was swishing through the grass just around the far side of the trailer.

His legs felt rubbery. He couldn't breath. His heart was hammering so hard it made his head nod. Through dancing orange circles he watched a face bob towards him out of the reddy-black darkness and recognized Mike McClure. The crazy guy was smiling! Willie couldn't make up his mind whether to be relieved or go on being scared because they'd been caught. They'd done nothing yet, but Jesus, the evidence was there okay.

He looked back for King and his burden but they were gone, so he turned to face McClure again. McClure had stopped also and was just standing, still and silent, hands in his combat-jacket pockets, grinning his lunatic grin. Willie watched McClure's mouth saying, "Why don't you take off th' mask, Willie?" His gappy lisp was almost as ridiculous as the way he'd walked up with his indifferent demeanor and recognized Willie, even in the ski-mask.

Willie tore the itchy hood off and realized the thing was ringing wet. He saw that McClure was no longer looking at him. McClure was looking right past him with a rapt expression, his grin softened to a stupid smile.

When Willie turned, the trailer's small door was open, spreading a yellow-bright mist of air out into the moonless dark. Willie didn't see the figure on the step for a moment because it didn't appear to be blocking the light. But that must have been because Willie was seeing the open doorway from an oblique angle. The motionless figure was looking out at the night as if alone. Something in the stance, the attitude of the head, said absolute aloneness. Willie noticed that most of all. Then Willie blinked, and the door was closing again, taking the light back inside with it.

Willie looked at McClure, who was backing away the way he'd come, into the night. Then Willie turned and ran, and kept going all the way to the pickup without once looking back.

TAPE 32

When you're scared of getting eaten you evolve quicker. That's a phrase I stole from Ed. He said predators were a major factor in the design of human bodies and brains. Millions of years of running scared helped determine the

154

shape and function of our bones, muscles, organs, nervous systems, brains and psyche. He also said our deep-rooted need to understand what scares us can point us towards superstition (God), or towards a more down-to-earth approach (science). The people who favor God have religion, but right here I want to talk about those who favor science, because they have *math*. (Mathematics. Numbers. Things that add up, okay?)

Scientists say that everything we see, hear, smell, taste and touch has to be measurable and describable with math or it doesn't count as real. And while religious folks use their scriptures to try and 'disprove' science, this thing can cut both ways, with scientists using math to 'disprove' anything that defies the term 'materially real', ie: stuff that can't be measured or otherwise quantified. (I guess scientists wouldn't admit that the very facility enabling them to use math - crazy old consciousness - can't itself be measured or quantified. Measuring brain activity, as I keep saying, is not the same thing at all.)

Reality Window: If the notion of math scares you, think of numbers standing for the *amounts* of stuff that things are made from. A ten ton rock is made from 10 tons of rock, so the whole rock is a 10. After that you can use numbers to describe a rock in as much detail as you like, weight-wise, ingredient-wise, behavior-wise, any-wise, all the way down to subatomic levels. You can even use math to describe the most complicated relationships between that rock and everything else around it, because numbers don't just describe amounts of stuff, they describe amounts of change in stuff. Numbers describe other factors also, but you get the picture.

Complicated? Math? Even in the simplest object you'll find an uncountable number of measurable amounts, especially down at the quantum level. In the whole universe there's too many numbers to imagine, all constantly changing and evolving in relation to each other. Complicated is too simple a word for it.

Making math infinitely more complicated is that it's inextricably tied up with life's biggest mystery: consciousness.

In case I failed to make it clear, scientists didn't invent math and numbers, they discovered them. Math was already embedded in material reality long before genetic monkey suits existed. So math isn't simply a way of representing everything in the universe with numbers; math *is* the universe, and vice-the-versa. The universe is one great big interactive, dynamic equation that scientists are nowhere near figuring out yet, whatever they think to the otherwise. The math that is the universe is way, way ahead of the people trying to figure it out.

Yeah, but *why* is math inextricably tied up with consciousness?

Think about this: Are universes built from numbers entirely by accident, even though numbers don't mean a damn to anything with no consciousness? Or did a conscious entity design the universe using numbers as a sublime key that only consciousness could turn to unlock the mysteries of physics, chemistry, medicine, technology and - who knows - maybe even consciousness itself? According to Ed, one reason for why the material universe is built from numbers is because the numbers are just waiting for organisms to evolve sufficiently to accommodate a consciousness with the ability to recognize the enormous significance of numbers.

Hey, that's only the half of it. Fact is, the universe that we know wouldn't exist, and neither would these monkey suits, if the numbers had been ever-so-slightly different. This sounds like a far out idea, but listen: some physicists think that if this universe had developed a tad differently, the necessary organism-building components couldn't have formed. (Everything had to be just right from the very start of the universe, to end up the way things are now.) This 'universe with everything just right for us' notion - called the *anthropic principle* - makes even some hard-nosed scientists think there could be a controlling intelligence at work.

Before the anthropic notion came up, scientists assumed that the laws of physics holding our universe together just 'happened' to be this way. To suddenly realize that hey, maybe things aren't so random and accidental after all, was just a little too much to handle for some people, so physicists had to invent another notion - the 'many universes' idea or *multiverse* - just to cover all of the other kinds of universe where things aren't 'just right for us', thus negating the uniqueness of that special anthropic principle, or us. A multiverse would be countless other universes, all of them slightly different from each other.

What happened was, a famous physicist named Feinman decided that fundamental particles (the ones that travel in probability waves) don't just go straight from one place to another. He said each of those particles takes every route possible in getting where it's going. Each of those possible routes is called a 'history' because each supposedly creates a slightly different universe with its own conditions.

But that's at the quantum mechanics level of reality. Up here on the atomic level of material reality, the probability factor is mostly cancelled down to just one actual route for every particle.

There are other unfathomable aspects to this stuff, but you probably quit reading awhile back so I may as well drop some in; I have nothing else going on right now.

A particle (or an entire wave of particles) with every possible history – go back and read what that means - is said to be in a superposition of states, meaning it can be in two or more places until you try and measure it. It seems that what actually stops particles in probability waves being in more than one place is somebody conscious looking at them. By looking at them (trying to see them in terms that we can understand and measure up here on the atomic level of reality), we cause the waves to 'collapse' into just one particle with either a definite location or a definite velocity. That's the way I understand it anyhow. Anything makes sense after a few martinis.

Anyhow, even though the anthropic notion and its counter-arguments help demonstrate what can be achieved when consciousness discovers math, it's beside the point I'm trying to make. Which is that a universe built from math is much more than just a lucky accident, or something for clever monkeys to while away their time trying to figure out. The purpose of a math-based universe is to enable evolving consciousness to outgrow the mindless material genetic vehicles it passes through, and to figure out what it Really is. Part of that is deciding what you *want* it to be. If all you want is a place where you can go on being a slave for genes, that's your choice. It just means you'll stay stupid for longer.

How far will people go to stay stupid? As far as they need to. They're only too willing to go along with scientific reasoning that says if you put enough mindless components together in the right way, you'll get consciousness. Other folks prefer another notion - that consciousness is present in absolutely everything, and, I guess, just needs a complex enough vehicle to manifest as the walking, talking, thinking consciousness we recognize in ourselves and each other.

Those two notions might sound the same, but real scientists would laugh at the idea of everything being conscious. (Then they contradict themselves by saying that consciousness actually comes in the same quantum-sized pieces that material things do, and they call those pieces qualia. We'll look at that later.) On the other hand religious folks would probably accept the idea that consciousness - or God anyhow - is in everything.

Some reductionists even question what consciousness is for. They say we could probably perform okay as genetic replication and reproduction platforms without needing all of the fancy extra mental firepower provided by this mysterious factor called consciousness. Yet another notion suggests that consciousness is a self-aware facility that evolved as a separate system from the reflex responses of genetic bodies to the world around them. In other words, self-awareness evolved because it gives genetic bodies better survival potential. Then self-awareness began seeing itself as something special and developed enough self-importance to become the thing that now calls itself *me*.

Still determined to be a genetic replicating platform? Even one that just happens to have accidentally evolved self-awareness to help genes replicate and reproduce more efficiently? Or do you want to be something fundamentally *more* than that?

For my money, the existence of math as an integral property of the material universe, is just one of the factors that underlines the fundamental more-ness of consciousness. Not only that, this conscious self-awareness gives us the unique ability to look at everything from a separate dimension *outside of* material reality. If our consciousness was not essentially separate from material reality, there'd be no way for us to see how material reality can be described in the immaterial terms of math. (Or to see that math, being symbolic of materiality, is a bridge between consciousness and materiality.) And like I said, without this fundamental separateness, we wouldn't be able to describe anything in amounts. There'd be no mathematical descriptions = no science, no physics, no chemistry, no medicine, no technology, no machinery…no evolution.

I guess if there was no math, the universe would be unquantifiable - which is maybe what we had before the Big Bang/Big Bounce.

TAPE 33

Spring in Appalachia can be pretty damn beautiful, even when I describe it. Picture endless lush, green, rolling, tree-covered mountains rising from mist-shrouded valleys, all of it stretching clear to every horizon. But like most other places on this planet, Appalachia is also people, molded by circumstance and shaped by other people, because that's how life works.

A deeper examination of the mist-shrouded valleys between those breath-catching ranges will reveal pockets of hardship and deprivation where people would be only too willing to exploit tourists to make life materially better for themselves. All they want is the opportunity.

Laurie Hendricks had begun to figure that out as she sat in her car at early evening and watched the few street-lights gleam on out-of-state pickups towing trailers, on winnebagos and late-model sedans with tents strung on their roofs and bikes glued on their rears, all of them trickling around the narrow streets of Passmore, their occupants' eyes seeking Ramada Inns, Old Smokey Pancake 'N' Pizza houses, all-nite breakfast joints and suchlike; and their kids' faces pressed up against the glass looking for McDonald's and Wendy's and Baskin Robbins. Boy, were they gonna be disappointed.

Reality Wingmirror: I've switched to a disembodied voice in third person because I feel like a change, okay? I'm still not Earnest Hemingway but I'm sure you'll agree anything's better than my usual prose style.

Yet Laurie was only half-seeing the extra tourists the healer had begun to attract; she was more interested in the local tradespeople going up the Town Hall steps, singly and purposefully. They, too, had obviously noted a slight upturn in the town's fortunes. Laurie was betting that had she been close enough to see into the eyes of those people going up the Town Hall steps, they would have had little dollar signs twinkling in them.

Laurie figured that Mayor Stevenson had arranged this meeting with her so he could give her material for a piece on how the tourists were affecting trade in this otherwise down-at-heel area. That had to be it. Maybe he wanted to congratulate her on that week's Star piece about the landfill, which had already appeared under the headline: TRASHVILLE TENNESSEE?, then gone on to explain how such a project, besides creating jobs, would also be something rather less than a tourist draw.

Stevenson had told her eight o'clock, and her watch said three minutes to. She figured the guy was probably punctual, so slipping the tape recorder in the pocket of her Burberry trenchcoat she checked her face in the mirror. The light was not flattering, but unless you had the money and the inclination for cosmetic surgery, you had to make do with what you were born with. (Aw hell, so the trenchcoat was an old, pre-owned government issue airman's from the surplus store in Zeno. The face was real though, unfortunately.)

Out of her eye-corner Laurie recognized the tall, stiff shape of the Mayor, right on time. Leaving her car, Laurie negotiated the traffic and called after him from half-way up the steps, but he ignored the call and carried on to the main entrance; only then did he stop and appear to be studying his nails, but was in fact watching Laurie's reflection in the door-glass as she came up behind him.

"Mister Mayor? I guess you didn't hear me call you."

Stevenson turned and threw a disdainful look in her face before his eyes went around her and took in the street below. He made no effort to hide the same antipathy he'd demonstrated at their last meeting. What the hell? If he was going to be an asshole, she'd be a pain in it. This was the new-style Laurie Hendricks who'd watched and listened as Deeks showed how it was done, but she'd learned more from Rudy Deeks than she appreciated. Her 'tell it like it is' motto was now tinged with a genuine desire to do just that.

"Where's the camera?" Stevenson said, still looking over her head at the traffic. "Didn't you say the people from that news station would be here? The *real* news people?"

Laurie had said no such thing. This was the Stevenson touch again.

"'Fraid you're gonna have to tell whatever you've got to me." She nodded at the traffic. "Folks do read The Star you know."

"These people didn't come here because of the defamatory fiction you put in that rag. They've got TV same as I have and they saw that report them fellas from the city did."

She knew the reason why he didn't raise a more powerful objection to her 'defamatory fiction' was because it was mostly true. The landfill had been Stevenson's trump card before any healer showed up, and no way was he just going to toss it in. Hell no, it would stay up his sleeve in case the game resumed.

"And where do you think the guys from the city got the idea of coming down here, Mister Mayor? From my Star expose of the healer."

"The plain truth is," Stevenson said, "that word gets out when a place is ripe for development. Passmore's openin' up despite and regardless of your efforts to the contrary. Tourist trade's finally gotten smart about what we have to offer."

"You did just say *ripe* didn't you Mister Mayor? You mean when they get downwind of the landfill? Can we go inside now please?"

They swapped penetrating looks while a horn blared as if to censure The Mayor's thoughts, then he raised his wrist and made a thing of looking at the time. "Well now, as the TV people didn't show, I guess I've nothing more to say to you, but I do have a meeting to chair."

Stevenson was obviously so confident in the town's - and his - rising popularity that he'd ceased to care about being rude. But Laurie was not through with him yet.

"Mister Mayor, before you go can you enlighten me about the agenda for tonight's meeting. How do the town's store owners plan to handle any new tourist opportunities?"

Stevenson looked at the traffic. "Naturally the best interests of this town are uppermost in my mind. Same goes for everyone with a commercial interest in Passmore." Some of the acid had actually drained from his voice. "More people visitin' naturally means we're going to do our best to serve them with the kind of hospitality this part of the country's rightly famous for."

"That's just fine, Mister Mayor, but what about the person these folks have really come to see? The healer?" Laurie tipped her head on one side and smiled sweetly.

Stevenson considered the question for a moment before blowing hard through his nose to expel his annoyance. "Okay," he said, as if about to make a deal, "Tell the readers of the little collection of advertisements you write for that in my opinion, these good people we see in our town this evening don't give a pig's whisker about any unwashed hippie no-account up in the hills. These folks took one look at this unspoilt countryside on their TV and went right upstairs to pack their bags."

Just as he was turning away Laurie interposed herself between him and the door. "Mayor Stevenson, what about the landfill we've all been hearing about? People are interested in working too. The landfill will bring jobs. Is that on tonight's agenda? Is it a real possibility? And where do you personally stand on the issue?"

Stevenson's eyes flashed knives. "I'm warnin' you, quit that shit you been puttin' out about this town's private life and its business affairs," he told her, biting back his anger. "And don't look so innocent. We got two young people hurt and a man dead. As for that healer crap, all you did was give an open invitation to any new-age dopehead who wants to come down here lookin' for a handout. Jesus Christ! We got enough home-grown scum of our own without advertisin' for more, y'hear me? This county's had more than it's fair share of hard times. People been waitin' too long for something better to happen, and now it is, they sure don't need you pissin' on it."

Scarcely able to contain her glee, Laurie willed him to keep going.

He kept going. "Further to that, I might as well tell you we got a tourist industry startin' here that's gonna be bigger than anything your pathetic little rag can handle, and when I got somethin' to say to all of those folks out there about how well we're doin', it'll be to the TV stations or a real newspaper, not somethin' that finishes up hangin' in my toilet." He looked around to make extra sure they were not being overheard before adding: "And if you don't leave that landfill thing alone, I'll personally see to it that a whole heap of trouble and grief gets dumped on you personally, you got that, lady?"

Triumphantly, Laurie took the tape-recorder from her pocket and showed it to him. "Oh I got *all* of that, thankyou kindly Mayor Stevenson." She put the recorder back in her pocket and kept her hand tight around it as she backed away. "And if those people at the TV station - it was CNLB by the way from Memphis - want to use the statement you just put out, that's fine by me."

She paused for a moment to enjoy the Mayor's face. Then he turned and the glass door swung shut behind his stiff figure, and Laurie watched him pass below the cheapening fluorescent lights in the foyer and disappear through a door on the left before she brought the tape-recorder close to her face and turned towards the street.

"That was Mayor Stevenson of Passmore talking candidly to Lauren Hendricks of The Star," she told the recorder conversationally. She ran the tape back for a moment to make sure it had recorded, then switched the machine off.

"Seems like I got you by the balls there, *Mister* Mayor. And thankyou."

Fifty feet away, in the stale atmosphere of a motorhome parked up in the street, the eyes watching from behind tinted one-way glass turned their attention to an audio snooperscope. "Yep, I guess you did," said a tired voice. "And thank*you* Lauren Hendricks of The Star."

The above was me pretending to be Laurie Hendricks the disembodied author. This is me pretending to be Laurie Hendricks reminding you that consciousness is the only phenomenon in the universe that's free of physics laws. One of the interesting things that means is that as our Real, conscious selves, we can step out of the monkey suit at death and walk away. I'm gonna look at that now…when I locate the tape it's on…

TAPE 34

This is the *time* tape. To conventional science, the time dimension is just as real as the material dimensions of length, width and height. Why? Because time as we're able to grasp it is composed of the events in those 3 material dimensions. The way those events happen in cause-and-effect sequence, from

162

past through future via the present – with events strung out one after another - is called *linear* time.

Aside: The reason why I'm spelling everything out is not because I don't credit you with an education. Like I said earlier, my mom will be reading this, and, well, you know moms. If you knew mine, you'd know exactly why I'm spelling it out.

The concept of linear time is fundamental to our understanding of small r reality. Sub-concepts like past, present, future, gradual, process, cause-and-effect - they're all time-derived and central to how we perceive reality. (The same goes for me wondering if I used up the last of the gin yesterday instead of tomorrow.)

But the small r reality that we perceive isn't the full story, right? While these genetic monkey suits appear to evolve as a result of material events, like everything else in this 4-dimensional reality (length, width, depth and *time*) there's a lot more going on that we're unaware of on our everyday level of awareness. You'd need to be truly nuts not to appreciate that appearances are not a true misrepresentation of how things actually are.

It was only the day before yesterday that we discovered the four fundamental forces - the electromagnetic force, the strong atomic force, the weak atomic force, and gravity - holding 'reality' together. Why didn't we know about those forces earlier? It wasn't simply because our senses and brains weren't able to perceive them. Human sense and brains still aren't able to do that, yet now we know about a heck of a lot more than just those four forces. The reason why we know so much more now is because we're all more conscious. Because our consciousness has evolved and learned to use a human brain/body more effectively.

Now about time. (You might just need to concentrate here.) On the small r level of material reality that we imagine our perceptions are confined to, each biological event appears to be the consequence of other biological events that happened earlier in time. And what is every single one of those biological events? Right - a tiny *change* in the relationships between material components.

Side note: I'm confining this to all of the changes in relationships between stuff on the atomic level of material reality because, as you now know, way down at quantum level, 'reality' goes bananas, and so does time. I could explain the details but only three people in the world would be interested enough to read it because it involves the relative kinetic energy between particles in superpositions of states, and stuff like that.

So anyhow, up here in our everyday version of reality, all of the events caused by interacting atoms are what time is made from. (What the hell else did you imagine time was made from - *minutes and seconds?)* Time isn't some kind've abstract 'other thing' that gets imposed on material components. It's the other way around: time is made from one big, uninterrupted sea of interconnected, universe-wide interactions between material components.

In case you missed it, I'm saying that what actually creates the concept we call time, is us - consciousness - perceiving the *changes* that happen in all of the separate components that comprise materiality in 3 spatial dimensions. (Changes caused by the interactions between quarks, nucleons, molecules and atoms that create people and objects and events.) Those changes don't just happen at the same time as time passing; they are what create the entire impression of time passing. And that, my dear Watson, is what makes time materially real, rather than an intangible framework for real events to happen inside. If not for the material events that cause change in our material universe, you wouldn't know that time had actually elapsed.

If you were to believe the scientific notion - that a continuous stream of events between material components in brains creates our consciousness - you'd also have to assume that an absence of material activity in brains would mean zero consciousness. But that's not how things Really are. Our consciousness doesn't depend for its existence on a continuous stream of material events. Our consciousness – from the inside of a monkey suit - merely perceives this particular level of existence as a continuous stream of materially real events.

Meaning that even when all material events cease in our brain and body (the events associated with being alive, that is), conscious activity continues. (It gets out of that dead body first of course. Who'd want to stay in a dead body?) Suddenly free of the material activity in a body and brain, does 'time' continue for consciousness? Sure it does, but (A) we're no longer talking about a consciousness that's being filtered through a genetic brain, and (B) nor are we talking about the kind of 'time' created by material events in 4-D reality. We're now talking about a kind of time created by *conscious* events: an any-which-way-you-like, controllable time that you can be creative with – once you relearn how.

Even when it's in a 'living' monkey suit, our consciousness can juggle the concept of time using imagination and memory, right? Imagination and memory might seem to exist in an altogether different kind of time from the

164

time created by external material events. Imagination and memory live in a totally flexible, negotiable 'time' that exists only in our mind. How can this purely conscious kind of time be real?

Well of course it can't - not in the accepted sense of what's 'real'. And yet – oh-*ho* – this totally flexible, negotiable 'time' existing only in our mind is where our immaterial imagination and memory begin to make materially real things happen. (You can't build an automobile, for example, unless you can imagine it first by being creative with your stored memories of material reality.) And as with that automobile, read ditto for everything else in the man-made world.

Fact is, all we're actually doing when we break free from a material body/brain (as in death) is climbing out of the material river of events that carries our consciousness along with it.

What kind of time is created by conscious events alone? That depends on how much control you have of conscious events. In other words, on how well you learned to control your Real self. (How highly evolved your consciousness is.) The degree of conscious control you learned will determine the kind of environment you find yourself in after you leave the material world. You won't be alone; you'll be sharing your immaterial environment with other consciousnesses, each with their own ideas. That's not Really a problem - you can have your own conscious environment to yourself if you want, or you can choose to join up with others. Maybe I should save more on that subject for a later tape…

Okay. Time as a linear concept is one of the factors that helped impose a narrow reality on us, and leads scientists (and maybe you) to assume that brains and consciousness are inseparable parts of the same reality. We even used to assume that thoughts themselves happened one after another, because that sounds and even feels logical, right? The only reason why it seems logical is because our 'logic' is based on linear time, where events only happen after, and as a result of, the earlier events that caused them.

Things are changing. Science is toying with the notion that reality mightn't be confined to a whole list of phenomena we're familiar with. They already know that thoughts don't happen one after another. Separate bits of the same thought are brought together from different parts of the brain. Like a movie being made, those separate bits aren't assembled in the same order we think them. Even in brains, time isn't what it seems.

The old linear notion of time is just one example of the fundamental difference between these material monkey suits and our Real, conscious selves.

The only way for us to become more conscious is by growing out of the habit of thinking of everything in the same ancient, outmoded *material* terms. (Especially the way we think about the part of us that does the thinking.)

If, in the future, brain scientists got together with physicists to try and write equations for the nature of consciousness using quantum calculations, their equations will be more like music than math. The math will demand the kind of intuition and imagination that lifts material considerations into higher dimensions than what we currently describe as 'material'.

Reality Window: I guess you could say consciousness is to brain activity, what dark matter and dark energy were to the behavior of the universe before anybody even knew that dark matter and dark energy existed. (I had a construction company build me this makeshift Reality Window in here after realizing I didn't mention dark matter or dark energy earlier. Dark matter and dark energy are thought to constitute maybe 95% of the known universe, but nobody actually knows what dark matter and dark energy are, because they're, uh, dark. We only know they exist because of how they affect the part of the universe we can see.)

As I'm feeling slightly 'poetic' this evening I'm gonna pick up the theme of music from just above and say that the energy inherent in those mega-mega-tiny, constantly vibrating quantum particles would create the notes of this symphony called material reality. (If there are such things as superstrings, that would make an even better analogy.) 'Symphony' is kind of misleading here because quantum energy still only describes material reality, whereas music is something that only consciousness can appreciate as music. Music itself is a kind of interface between materiality and consciousness.)

Let me clarify that: Where, how and why does sound become music, rather than meaningless noise created by material components banging together? Answer: In your mind. Composers use materially real instruments made from predictable molecules to create music, but those instruments themselves aren't the music. The vibrations in those molecules - even in the equally material molecules of your ears and your brain - aren't the music either. Only the *more-than*-material meanings and uniquely personalized interpretations that consciousness sees in the effects created by those vibrating molecules, are the music.

Math is 'language' (because its symbols express unambiguous meanings over and above the symbols themselves), and music is also 'language'. Music can even be written using math. But music doesn't have any fixed set of meanings;

166

the messages it communicates exist on more sublime levels than equations written in numbers (or in words). Music in our consciousness is simultaneously less tangible yet more emotive than any math.

Now we're back to what happens when our consciousness is creative with material reality. The more deliberate, conscious input goes into the creative manipulation of molecules called music, the less opportunity there is for those molecules to behave *randomly*.

Music 'began' as coarse vibrations that appealed more to your primitive ass than any higher, conscious aspirations. So when - stay with me on this - did the impacting of material elements start to change from plain noise into something more like music? Answer: When there was more conscious input involved. More consciousness can create more complex, more refined vibrations in molecules. More consciousness can also interpret those vibrations more subtly. As music evolves, it becomes less instinctive (less driven by non-conscious, material sensations) and becomes more intuitive (more consciously inspired). Less bottom-up, more top-down. The more randomness that consciousness removes from vibrations in material components, the more music emerges. This removal of randomness begins at *the* most subtle point of interface where consciousness meets, and is able to play the symphony of energy waves: *in your brain*.

Keep remembering this isn't a science book, because you wouldn't read one, and I sure wouldn't write one. This book is just me pointing out how everything in the material universe is only a background for you to appreciate your consciousness against. (The few technical terms in here are so you'll think I know what I'm talking about.)

TAPE 35

Now I'd like to tell you more about Ed, the one-time man in my life, the logger, the balancing influence. Ed the nice guy. Ed the one that got away and I never got over. The same Ed who got me thinking and interested in writing this kind of stuff. I just located a tape I made concerning him, and if I were not in such a good mood I'd drop it in the trash and pretend I never found it. But now I've started I'm going to make a hole for this errant snippet right here and build it into something relevant, the way he'd have wanted me to. (Owing to the way this book was put together - like a movie - some of the later tapes were transcribed before some of the earlier ones. Only after I had the whole thing in the can did I decide its sequence. This particular tape was made during a blue period.)

So I called him Ed the logger because that's what he did some of the time. The whole time I knew him though, Ed was the same constant kind of guy. By 'constant' I do not mean boring or tedious, even if I did think so then. (I thought a lot of stupid, short-sighted or just plain wrong things in those days.)

If Ed was influenced by the same selfish genetic survival urges everybody else is, it wasn't in a way you'd notice. (Unless a preference for his own company rather than mine can be called a survival urge.) Peace and quiet was Ed's ideal state. There were occasions when he'd tolerate my mindless mouth and, believe it or not, there were odd times when I felt a need for his peace and quiet. Those rare congruences exposed me to Ed's view of Reality.

But in the Ed days, all that my emotions ever did was to spoil things between us because they ran me. I don't just mean in a sexual way; it was more devious than that; my genes made me want money before monkey-business.

Right here is where I drew the drapes across my Reality Window so I could pause this tape and think about my feelings. Well hey, even I have feelings. I couldn't write about such things otherwise. Except now I know my feelings are products of a primitive past, whereas you think yours are handed down from heaven or someplace. Worse yet, you actually *feel* that your feelings are God's gift. But when you're in a monkey suit it's practically impossible to separate top-down thoughts from bottom-up feelings, aka 'emotions'.

I know - you don't go for that stuff about emotions being a survival mechanism evolved by genetic monkey suits to protect themselves. You're determined to let 'your' feelings get the better of you. They're all you've ever known in this life and you wouldn't know who to be without them. (You will eventually.)

If the instinct-derived sensations called 'emotions' could be neatly compartmentalized and attributed to the separate material components that cause them, you'd soon see which was doing what, and how this mindless biomachinery controls the conscious 'you'. But they can't be compartmentalized. They're all connected to each other through circuitry that's more interdependent and complicated than any wiring diagram you can imagine. Just trying to keep the non-conscious parts out of your conscious part, is like trying to keep fish out of the ocean.

Sound complicated? *Ha!* Even before you begin to access what you refer to as 'your' thoughts, those different evolutionary levels of your body and brain,

168

filled with self-willed yet mindless components, are working 26 hours a day, 372 days a year to get their own way, and their way is geared exclusively to you-know-what.

Genes were trying mindlessly for billions of years to get the replication and reproduction process perfected. Then minds came along and assumed they were part of that process. So by the time all of that effort gets to focus into a narrow beam at your point of awareness, you're convinced that the urges, needs and demands of those mindless components, are your *conscious* urges, needs, demands.

Boy, no wonder you're nuts. So nuts, you think you're sane! But the only way to become Really sane is to use your consciousness to control all of those mindless components in back of instinct and emotion.

Lucky for you there is one simple way you can begin to quit being selfish for genes. Refuse to be a passive audience at the movie of your own life. Start directing your own consciousness. Just be nice to people without wanting any kick-backs. I know that's a dizzying concept, but try it because it's a basic evolution exercise for your consciousness, and useful for anybody having trouble telling the difference between their Real self and DNA's stupid ass.

Hell no, it's not easy to go against instinct or emotion; if it were, it would take you a lot longer to learn what needs to be learned. The reward for all of this learning is that you eventually become your Real self. Then you'll find that one of the best things about actually *being* conscious is that you can finally come down from the trees and quit waving your bare ass in front of other monkeys. (You ever seen them do that at the zoo? That's what you do, only you put slightly more thought into it.)

Remembering how I used to be with Ed could make me feel ashamed, and sad, and pathetic, and maybe frustrated, and angry and wretched - if I let it. (None of that is anything to do with Ed, you understand; it's just me enjoying feeling sorry for myself.)

Don't concern yourself, I'm okay. The minute I start thinking about everything Ed did for me, without my realizing it at the time, and after all I didn't do for him and did realize it, I don't feel sorry for myself anymore; I just feel lousy. Now, it's not selfish emotions that make talking about Ed about as easy as having teeth pulled, it's recognizing there's a better version of me in here someplace; a version that Ed himself helped wake up. It only makes it worse remembering how I flushed him down the toilet. That's why I'm gonna stop talking about Ed now and watch some TV, and you're gonna join me.

You heard about how media sex and violence subverts minds? Sure, but it works in a more insidious way than either you or the people feeding you that stuff imagine. Not just on TV and in movies, but in any medium. And let's not forget real life for Christ's sake.

Sex and violence sound like old potatoes, but those activities are the basics of genetic evolution that we all grew up with, and as such are the most deep-rooted, persistent and hard-to-kick of all our bad habits. Nothing is more natural than sex and violence - except growing out of them. Fat chance of that happening with billions of dollars pouring into media versions of both.

Listen, who but a bunch of psychos would be outraged at themselves, protest about themselves, to themselves, over the inhuman treatment of each other they see perpetrated on TV news and in other media? Yet these same psychos continue thinking about, making, selling, living off, ingesting and enjoying fictionalized versions of exactly the same behavior, *as entertainment?*

Only a species of psychopaths would use depictions of murder, vengeance, rape, robbery, deceit and all of the other forms of inhumanity, in leisure activities. Or celebrate being such efficient survival machines for DNA in film and the printed word. (War movies, spy movies, international finance scam movies, westerns, ethnic conflict movies, etc., etc.) Even the inhabitants of Planet Psycho would only do that if they were driven to it by a compulsion controlling their mind.

My case rests.

It's done resting. Now I'll tell you what those activities in real life, then as entertainment in the media, really are. They're subliminal propaganda encouraging us to stay primitive. Using the very worst criminal excesses of behavior as entertainment is encouragement for our genetic selves and our offspring. Boy, the word insidious just ain't up to describing this. *Contrapuntal* would be a good word to describe it, if that word didn't mean something else entirely.

I'm gonna rest my heavy case again to remind you that an endless stream of money is poured into TV junk food for the mind, even though it's bad for our health. Pressure groups lobby for the crap to be taken out of food and water and language and everything else, but forget that far more dangerous ingredients go into 'entertainment' on that box in everybody's living room, kitchen, bedroom, dining room, den, patio, bathroom, treehouse, toilet, trailer, train, boat, plane. Everybody is saying, 'Just fill my head with pictures and sound, and no matter how puerile it is I'll eat it up'.

170

Think about the fact that the majority of audiences ain't Einsteins or saints. Many are kids, regardless of their age. The difference between real-life and entertainment might - *might* - be obvious to an Einstein or a saint, but that difference gets blurred for most adults, even of average intelligence, because they want it to blur. They actively want to suspend their disbelief that murder, vengeance, rape, war, deceit, death, and every other form of inhumanity used in the arts, is only 'entertainment' in order to enjoy it. But to impressionable kids and Mr. Below-Average intelligence, there's gotta be some dangerous confusion of entertainment and real life at a deep, *unconscious* level.

I rest another of my many cases. I should go find a porter.

I'd gone round to Ed's for something to eat - yeah, he could cook too, goddammit - on one of those nights when I felt I could tolerate Ed's peculiar insistence on relaxing quietly. (It wasn't peculiar at all; that's the kind of pejorative remark you use about something you disagree with - usually because you don't appreciate the benefits.)

While Ed was in the kitchen area putting together some Chinese concoction to remind me of my own culinary shortcomings, I snooped around for something to dampen my incipient boredom. As usual there were millions of books lying around but I didn't curl up by Ed's fire with one of them. I put the TV on. Well even Ed had a TV, unplugged till I went in; he used it to stack books on. And so there I was, surfing for lurid scandal or scenes of carnage when who did I see but Rudy Deeks! (I know it's an unbelievable coincidence, but this is a book remember.) I even called Ed in to see him, or rather what was behind him: that hillside in the wilderness where everybody was gathered quietly around the healer's trailer. I didn't see me because that day I was too busy trying to insinuate myself into Deeks' professional affections.

And now I've gone and reminded myself again how badly I treated Ed, sucking up to some newsman just because he was a newsman, and successful, and glamorous, but mostly because he might be able to help me. A newsman who, like Ed, turned out to be a nicer guy than I deserved. And I'm glad, because it just goes to show me how pathetic I used to be. So there!

Okay. According to these excuses for notes, seeing Deeks reminded me how, in the hyper-materialistic and mega-competitive world of Planet Psycho, TV news has to be as entertaining as the 'entertainment' it's competing with for its share of the money pie. The real versions of living and dying have to be entertainment just to keep up financially with the 'entertainment' versions of living and dying. Run a well-made docu-drama parallel with a news item on the same subject. The docu-drama is fiction, but it could easily be more convincing, more believable than the real stuff, especially to our Mr. Below-Average or the kid. Moreso if all the technical wizardry and editorial skill of 'entertainment' is packaged with the same conviction as news.

Which is real and which is Memorex? Double-moreso if the news it's competing with also has the same glitzy packaging as a sitcom or a soap, the same hard-sell treatment as a detergent, with bites slotted between the commercials right alongside everything else that appears to be real but ain't. Triple moreso when 'entertainment' is fashioned around the same social issues that already shape the news, the commercials, and just about everything else. At the end of all that you'd be forgiven for getting the messages about reality (news, sport, wildlife and so on) confused with more important messages about detergent and so on. They're all just little bites of the same thing.

What thing?

Yo! Finally I've reached my point: The same thing all those TV programs are, and movies are, and videos, and books, and newspapers, and etc., is *Life,* aka the genetic replication and reproduction system as you understand it. We're so easily confused about the difference between entertainment and reality because, genetically speaking, there is no difference. The *only* kind of real to genetic organisms is the ME and MINE FIRST kind. That's the same kind that news, commercials and entertainment are all aimed at with the same conviction. Separately and combined, those mediums are all doing the same job: reassuring and confirming for us exactly who and what we are: gene survival machines.

So yeah, good old Rudy Deeks, on Ed's TV, saying the actual words he said to all those people out there with me practically standing next to him. I must have been just off-camera - about where Ed's fireplace was. And guess what it reminded me of? That I was still pissed off about Deeks lifting my story right from under my goddam nose.

To be honest, that was the real reason I went round to Ed's - for consolation. Ed was expert at consolation, though not by stroking your ego. Ed's way was better and involved getting you to wake up. What do I mean by that?

Okay. You're dreaming that a monster is chasing you. Obviously you're scared, and when it catches up with you and there's noplace left to run and

172

things can't possibly get any worse, and you're about as scared as you ever could be...you wake up and find the monster is lying beside you because you married it. (Am I kidding? You tell me.) Seriously, if you ever had a dream like that you'll know what relief is. Boy, if only life would turn out to be a dream and we could wake up to find the relief was Real.

Well we can. Because the monsters in dreams and the monsters in what we call real life are all creations of our genetic past, living on through our stupidity and selfishness.

But anyhow there I was at Ed's, saying things like, "What the hell am I gonna do? I'm never gonna get out of this dump. I'm doomed. I might as well give up right now." And similar stuff. It really is incredible to think that I could've been so all-out pathetic and...Words fail me. (You're not supposed to say 'words fail me' when writing a book, but they do sometimes, believe me.)

Sure I had my pride - tons of it - but Ed was the one person I could act that way in front of because, well, I guess he had no pride or he wouldn't have associated with me. He'd probably grown out of the stubbornness, vanity or other illusions of self-importance that create pride before he ever got to know me.

But let me finish the monster analogy. (I love analogies.) Okay, so the monsters we have to wake up from are ourselves. By consciously striving to make a society free from the horrors and misery our monster-selves created for their survival, everybody's nightmares will end. The monsters will disappear. But the media is doing everything it can to keep those monsters alive with all of this gene-propaganda, and TV is the prime example because everybody has TV, even if they don't have much else. (Sorry you TV guys but you weren't to know. You're mature, responsible, successful, high-earning adults, devising all of that stuff for the sake of material gain, then broadcasting it at millions of people continuously.)

No, I singled out TV news because it's supposed to be real, and has more impact-value precisely because of its apparent realness. Nothing appeals to you-as-DNA quite like real living and dying. That's the stuff we spent the whole of evolution so far growing up on, so even though we have no idea what happens before life or after death, we sure as hell know a lot about what *causes* life and death: it's sex and violence.

This indictment doesn't just apply to TV news, but kind've like those little Windows I open occasionally in this book, TV happens to be a general window on ourselves. It lets us watch ourselves as we shape the world and ourselves in it. And in showing us those things, TV news, fiction, fantasy, the works, is educating us about what we *are*. All forms of media help educate us about how we shape the world, but what they show us must be the shape we *want* the world, and ourselves, to be in, otherwise we wouldn't behave the way we do. (And don't go blaming some other guy again; ain't nobody here but us monkeys.)

What we see and hear in the media is ingested as life-experience. Besides telling us what and who we think we are, it influences and encourages *what* and *how* we think. What and how we *believe*. And then, as a result, how we *act*. It's a pretty damn total effect.

Sex and violence on TV and in other media, not to mention real life itself, are fundamental survival options being run past us. Whatever you *think* you're thinking about those downsides, they're assuring you that this is actually how genetic organisms called people survive. Not by being moral, but by being selfish.

Our natural inclination ain't to be saintly in the face of life's adversities, it's to be selfish for our genes. Your mind automatically stores those selfish TV scenarios as life-guidance for later reference. Sure, you could well have a tendency to be tolerant, kind, maybe even a little unselfish - sometimes, up to a point - but this constant stream of selfish survival scenarios doesn't appeal to those tendencies. It encourages your ME FIRST survival urge.

What and how you think - even subconsciously - helps shape your physical brain. But even worse (or better, depending on you), your actions help decide the shape and function of your offspring's brain (because they inherit your genes). As genetic survival is a matter of getting by in a traditionally sex, violence, selfishness and competition-preoccupied world, the genes getting passed from parent to offspring will be selected because they *improve* a brain's ability to help its body survive in that kind of world - unless we make it a different world. But the media isn't helping any.

The media is the only education a lot of people have, after real life. Sometimes instead of it. Kids of all ages know real people are killing and screwing each other every-which-way out there. Then they see that same murder and procreation mayhem treated as entertainment.

Whatever you think that's doing to the audience's understanding of life and reality, seeing the world they're a part of behaving that way tells people to *be the same* - Mr. Below-average and kids especially. It's a practically irresistible

174

persuasive force, all the more effective because the *instinctive* need to be the same, and conform, is in everybody's genetic survival make-up.

So did I carry on being pathetic at Ed's that night? You bet. But being such nice people *and* brainy, Ed surely saw right through my lame act and only pretended he didn't for my sake. Sensitive people do things like that don't they? Thinking back, Ed probably figured he'd have to put me straight by a more devious route, knowing the kind've person I was.

When he said, "What's the longest thing you ever wrote?" I just carried on sulking and told him not to change the subject. I meant from me complaining.

"Same subject," he said. "So go on and tell me, what is the longest thing you ever wrote?"

I only bothered answering - I only bothered thinking about the question at all - because Ed was not the kind of a guy to ask meaningless questions. There was invariably a good reason behind things he said, no matter how tangential or flippant it sounded. That didn't prevent me from being tangential and flippant without any reason.

"Probably my Christmas list. I think I wrote down *gin* three times; it sure felt like it the morning after."

"Was it well-written?"

I gave him my drop-dead look. "You seen the Pulitzer Prize Second Class, Shopping List Section I got framed in my toilet?"

"Do you ever get interested in what you're writing?"

"Hey, what's with all this writing stuff?" But I knew. Ed was trying to help me over my disappointment at losing my exclusive story on the healer with the same technique he used to deal with all of my on-going frustrations and impatience at going nowhere with my life. It was working; I began to think about my writing. But then, we were talking about me, right? Ed was a clever guy because that was the real object of this exercise.

"Sure I get interested - my writing paid for the shopping."

"Interested enough to write something longer than a shopping list?"

I can picture him now, wearing the amused face that usually presaged bringing out into the open what he'd been stalking through the same wood that I hadn't been able to see for trees.

"Like a, uh, *book?*"

Well of course he was talking about writing a book; to him that was writing. He probably thought the hysterical verbiage I puked into The Star was an outlet for my venomous nature rather than anything even distantly related to literature. There were some things we were in agreement about.

While Ed kneeled down and stoked the stove, my gaze drifted up from the way his hair kind of curled over the back of his collar, to the TV - which I'd stopped absorbing after Deeks - and then to the books stacked on top, where ordinary people have a vase of flowers or a lamp or a picture of their genetic progeny. Or a lizard. (Not too many folks have a lizard on top of their TV so I may delete that.)

Anyhow I wound up staring absently at Ed's bookshelves rising to the ceiling and filling the wall because at that point I had two choices. Either I carried on being pathetic, hoping he'd nurse me along, or I swallowed my pride and helped him to help me. But that was too simple. When you're up against superior intellect, especially when it belongs to a too-nice guy who's trying to help you to help yourself, you have to play games. Well I did.

"Aw, words on the page have had their day. Even that thing is looking dated." I nodded at the TV. "I mean come on, they're practically on the verge of being able to plug your head straight into the goddam web."

Ed's mouth compressed. After he turned the TV off he slouched into the kitchen area to check on his concoctions, and I felt kind of hollow for having snubbed his offer of help, but what else could I do? At the time, I'd started to change just enough to feel bad for not having changed enough to behave better.

Later that evening, as they say in books, when I was sprawled on the sofa in front of the fire wondering if Ed would want me to stay the night, and which excuse I'd use not to, I relented with:

"So you think I should write a book about the healer?"

Ed carried on washing the dishes that I should've been doing in the kitchen. "Why not? You're on the spot. You have a unique opportunity to tell the healer's story from the inside like nobody else does."

"But those TV news guys are already telling it better than I could," I told him, knowing in my guts he was right, and that my protest was only half-true and just a way of getting him to explain further.

"No, they're doing you a favor by creating even more interest in this healer guy. When they pull out and move to a new story, that's when you pick up the ball."

Did I mention what a smartass Ed was? That he was always right? When somebody tells you what you already knew but are too pathetic and self-

176

pitying to work out for yourself, man, it's downright aggravating. It sounded like a half-reasonable idea, only I hadn't thought of it. But you already guessed I was jealous of Ed's mind, and that I was annoyed at him for not using it to make a lot of money.

"You like writing about people...right?"

"Only because I can't make a living from my shopping lists."

"And people are interested in the healer, right?"

"So?"

"So it would be a human interest story."

I sniggered. "Yeah, right. Except I need humans for that. This is Raiment County remember." When no reply came I had to develop the theme myself. Again. "Anyhow, I thought what I did at The Star was human interest."

"And I thought you wanted to leave The Star."

"Yeah, and I wouldn't say no to longer legs, but wanting and getting are two different words." (I didn't really say that, but if you can't make yourself sound sharp in your own goddam book, when can you?)

What I actually said was: "And I said I have to make a living."

"Write the book in your spare time."

This sounds like a leisurely conversation, and I sure appeared that way, having kicked off my shoes and poured myself across the sofa with my arms out above my head. Like that famous old painting, except I was dressed. But my mind was going so fast after what Ed was saying I was practically running to keep up.

"You crazy logger, what spare time?"

"Loafing around the office. Evenings. In the tub. Driving. Just talk it straight into that little machine of yours. Start by stringing together a few of your opuses from the paper and go from there."

As the sense of Ed's words hardened into conviction, I heard, "*Well?*" from someplace just behind me. I was startled as much by the soft tone of his voice as its close proximity before I realized how provocative I must look, couched in total abandon that way. I got up so fast to forestall his showing a little human interest of his own, you'd have thought I'd been stung.

"Thanks for the meal and advice," I told him while I got my coat from the chair in the kitchen, "but I do gotta go to work in the morning ya know." (I tend to talk that way when I'm trying to be tough.) And anyway it was practically nine-thirty and dark outside.

"I got more whiskey...you're welcome to stay awhile and help me drink it."

There was no threat involved and I knew it; Ed was just being nice. He knew I enjoyed an occasional drink - I wrote that with a straight face - though I suspect he only suggested it because it took the hard edge off of my pushy personality. And that night it would definitely have improved my mood.

Ed had no hidden motive, I mean it. But this is me now, talking about a time when all that my genes would let me see was a guy trying to persuade me to sit on his sofa and drink whiskey to the sound of a blazing fire so he could - well, I don't have to go on. Genes gotta do what genes gotta do, as they don't say but should. And mixing chromosomes with somebody as unambitious as Ed was not my idea of getting out of my dead-end life.

I did pause for effect on Ed's doorstep, my arms halfway in my coat Ed was helping me on with, trying to look as if I was thinking about his offer. In reality I was looking for more excuse to go.

I said, "Actually, log of my life, I should've been home hours ago thinking up a story about how the landfill could transform this area into a bed of roses for everybody." Knowing his thoughts on waste and hyper-consumerism, I hoped he'd approve of what I was going to write. I'd be writing it with him as my imaginary audience and editor.

Maybe it's just as well words on the page fail miserably to convey emotion in quite the same way my voice on this midget recording machine can (meaning like the emotions of a toaster-oven). No, seriously - if you knew just how many times I re-edited this piece to get all of the soul-searching out of it, wondering if I should've stayed that night, you'd know why there are salty-water stains (yeah, and gin) all over my notes. What the hell. Even if I had stayed it would've been for me, not Ed, so I know I did the right thing. I'm world-champion at being wise in hindsight.

TAPE 36

So you never thought of the news/entertainment industry as us, pumping out gene-survival propaganda at ourselves? Think again. News, entertainment and the arts mostly draw on the *conflict* inherent in life - sexual jousting, money, trade, envy, deceit, murder, greed, mayhem, death, competition – but always with an overwhelming emphasis on the *downsides* of how human beings experience life.

As our consciousness struggles to make sense of being on this planet, the media exploits and lives off the problems created by the struggle. But as the

178

ones responsible for the news/entertainment industry, we should be actively encouraging ourselves to work *against* the downsides and the conflicts inherent in real life. All communications media should be a vehicle for helping us understand ourselves better. Media should be an active part of the learning process, helping consciousness evolve, pushing higher values, etc.

But that would require the entire news/entertainment/media industry to stop feeding your instinctive appetites, and there's too much invested in entertainment as sensationalism to incentivize such a radical new approach. It's those very downsides that make much of news and entertainment so goddam 'newsworthy' and 'entertaining'. It would be like the tobacco industry telling you to quit smoking for the sake of your health.

Okay. In our 'civilized' society, movies about murder and mayhem are called works of 'art'. Our Real, conscious selves, driven by mindless chemicals to survive through bloody competition - an *art form?* A million silver tongued excuses don't stop there being something seriously weird about that. Hell, weird ain't the word. *Insane* is the word.

Here's another radical approach. For society to evolve for Real, we'd have to replace the value of money with something infinitely more valuable: each other. We all know that money is more valuable than people on Planet Psycho; we spend enough of it making goddam movies to remind us of that fact, then paying a lot more to 'enjoy' those movies.

But think: If little scenarios of fictionalized sex and violence can influence people (and if you think they can't, you obviously don't believe in concepts like encouragement, or setting examples, or coaching, or even education), then real, non-fictionalized sex and violence can influence people even more efficiently - simply by being real. Nothing has more impact than the real thing.

All the real versions of the real thing (sex, violence, emotions, relationships, human interaction) always draw bigger and more avid audiences than fictional spinoffs. But those don't seem to be enough for us loonies; we feel compelled to strive for greater realism when creating little fictions of material reality.

Another reason why real living and dying in the media is always more exciting than fiction, is because lifestyles that often end in homicide are supposed to be antisocial. We condemn them, immediately making them more exciting. Sex crimes, crimes of violence, the legalized mass murder called war - it's all big business for the media because people *want* to see it depicted. And the biggest problem is, all of this stuff is even more exciting on a level that we're not consciously aware of.

Remember that *all* of our material parts are built by chemicals to allow bodies to feel things, excitement included, exclusively as a survival aid. Not a *conscious* survival aid; excitement is mindless chemical activity. (Of course you can excite your physical self by thinking, but it ain't your thoughts themselves that *feel* excitement, it's only that body and its brain that feel excitement.)

Excitement caused by life and death, fictional or real, is designed to have an instant influence on chemical mechanisms. The latest development of those survival mechanism - a brain - evolved to make those mechanisms more efficient. That's why, while we're openly condemning the sex and violence, a lot of us are simultaneously eating it up. It's *meant* to enhance genetic survival.

Ask yourself why we imbibe both news and entertainment versions of sex, violence, competition and the rest so avidly. Ask yourself what's happening to us when we do. You might even come to the conclusion that witnessing sex (not just criminal offences, but the love charade, the entire lexicon of male/female chromosome jockeying and role playing), and violence (with all the shades of itself, from innocent-seeming competition-sports, all the way up to mass murder) - knowing all those things are the real thing - constantly reaffirms our heritage by reminding us not only what we do, but what *to* do. These are the things we've always done and still are doing, better and more efficiently and often just as readily as we always did. And because we still do them, and don't look like stopping, we obviously think there must be something okay about it. More delusion.

TAPE 37

Living in Zeno I was familiar with tourists swarming all over the 'outstanding natural beauty' of The Smokies whilst giving neighboring Raiment County a wide berth. Now I was seeing traffic with license plates from places as far apart as Maine is from California, and it was like watching fresh blood being pumped into arteries and veins that had long been starved of nutrient. Raiment was picking up its bedroll and walking, and the phenomenon was nowhere more evident than around the little town of Passmore. Despite my Trashville Tennessee article, the tourists were giving local residents a taste of what the National Park had enjoyed for years.

Yet even this early there was one obvious effect the locals were unanimous about: the profit effect. Whatever anybody says to the contrary, the first New World settlers met with the same effect.

180

Yeah, I know everybody imagines those early pioneers from England and places stepped onto these shores and were set upon by angry natives, but the natives only got angry because of shabby treatment from greedy landgrabbers.

Fact is, when the first out-of-towners appeared in their backyard, native Americans didn't reach for their tomahawks, they hung rugs and beads outside the teepee with marked-down prices and got right on with the business of trading.

The only real difference between natives and invaders was the color of their money. Neither side wanted to risk getting their own blood shed unless absolutely necessary because that's not an efficient way for genes to get themselves replicated/reproduced. Trade is safer than tribulation.

It was only when those invaders - sorry, settlers - realized they couldn't get what they wanted by trading (because they wanted it *all*), that they dropped their genteel, civilized manners and pretense of fair play and fell back on the same old tried and trusted methods: robbery and violence.

A lot of folks still rely on guns and robbery with violence, but now the really slick 'traders' use weapons far more advanced than those hand-held museum pieces. Sure, we still take what we want through force, but the process has gotten ultra subtle and devious; we've created societies where robbery with violence is now sublimated to figures on screens that change so fast, and interact so complicatedly, that even a goddam supercomputer couldn't work back and discover who robbed whom, how, when, and where. A lot of the time we don't even know we're being robbed. Underneath it's exactly the same thing it always was, except the weapons only look like weapons to people not wearing gene-colored glasses.

We have 'social structures' and 'laws' that are meant to outlaw arms as a form of trade agreement, yet still permit widespread use of the most dangerous weapon on Planet Psycho: the mind we've been hoodwinked into using against itself by genes. You thought insider dealing was sneaky? Grow up. The best con artists have nothing on DNA because they're all working *for* DNA and don't even know it!

But as I was saying, I saw how the healer was drawing tourists every place I went in search of material for the book I'd decided to put together, so I figured I'd go interview some of them. Of course I still had to scrape a column for The Star off my shoe each week but that was easy enough - I figured I could just dump the out-takes from this book in the paper under a sharp headline.

My first interview was with the Oberdorfs from Cincinnati. Mr. and Mrs. Oberdorf were long-standing Elvis fans; I guessed that from the way they talked about his Sun Record days in Memphis. Oh, and their three little girls being named Elvisa, Elviola and Elvisabeth. Mr. Oberdorf looked like your favorite bank manager but was actually in lingerie.

When I asked exactly why they were in this neck of the woods, he gave his wife a sideways glance and said something about the scenery, he guessed. He even showed me the guide-book as if I wouldn't believe it otherwise, only the guidebook didn't include Raiment County; instead there was just a blank space. It was an actual unretouched aerial photograph.

As an afterthought he said, "Say, isn't there some local fella up in the hills, been on TV? You know, The Healer? People come and see him in The Wilderness, is that right?"

Oberdorf was no actor. The healer was their sole reason for being there.

"Sure there's a healer. Mind telling me why you came down to see him?"

Oberdorf laughed nervously. "Oh, we didn't come specially because of *him*. I just heard he's a kind of local attraction. They say he, uh, heals folks."

"So the TV news people say." I knew Oberdorf hadn't seen any of the stuff I wrote in The Star because that would've kept more people away than it attracted.

I turned to Mrs. Oberdorf, who was augmenting her husband's comments through a language of half-smiles, raised eyebrows and little nods.

"You interested in the healer, Mrs. Oberdorf?"

She looked at her husband, then at me, then at her knees, then at my little tape-recorder, then at him again. "Well, he sounds kinda interesting…"

"You folks Christians?"

"Certainly we are," Oberdorf said. He looked at the three kids, who were watching something Christian on a portable TV. Beavis and Butthead I think it was. "But that's not why we're here."

I didn't blame them for walking around it; the healer phenomenon was not easy to quantify.

"That's okay," I volunteered. "I've seen him myself and it's pretty unique as experiences go, believe me."

That dispelled some of Oberdorf's timidity. "You did? How? I mean in what way unique?"

I tried not to look smug but failed, and fell back on: "It'd be easier if you just go on up and see for yourself." They said okay and I left feeling it was one of those no-news days. I never did care for Elvis myself. I much preferred his brother Sydney. Remember him? With the performing rabbits?

I next talked with a middle-aged couple traveling in a camper with a Vermont sticker on the tail, next to another sticker that said: 'I adopted a whale, what did you do?' But not feeling it was any of their business what I did with a whale I asked them point-blank did they come to see the healer.

"Yes indeed we did." The man fixed me with a defiantly sincere stare. "We're looking for truth. Are you a seeker after truth, sister?"

Yep - another nut. Hello, is anybody sane out there? When I asked why they'd come to see the healer, he turned up the volume of that stare.

"We try to go see as many enlightened heralders of the New Age as possible. We're going up there this afternoon as a matter of fact."

He asked if I was going up too, but I told him I had work to do which required that I leave right there and then, before his sincerity made me puke. After that I talked to some folks from Texas who were going into the wilderness the next day and wondered if there'd be a barbecue after the show. I suggested that maybe they should organize one and donate the proceeds to saving a whale, and that I could connect them with an interested party. I then had a brief verbal exchange with three self-confessed lesbians who were sitting around on camp-chairs outside this enormous pink and blue winnebago that resembled Flash Gordon's rocketship. I knew they were lesbians because their camper had a sticker too. It said: 'Honk your horn if you're gay.'

So far nobody had given me a believable reason why the healer was having this effect on people. If someone had told me right out they were down here because he was Jesus Christ come back for a second try, that would've given me something to be skeptical about (and something definite on which to hang my human interest story). But nobody did say that, and I wouldn't have believed it anyhow.

TAPE 38

It took me a couple of days to find this next tape. It was meant to run straight on from that stuff about the media but, as usual, I misplaced it, and decided instead to insert the one about the tourists. Boy, if this book were a movie, I'd get the oscar for innovative editing. Anyhow there's little point in us reforming news and entertainment - cutting the movie of life - whilst doing nothing about life itself. That's shooting the messenger for delivering the bad news, when the fact is that we are the subject of that bad news. Hell, we know how we behave, yet we pretend to be intelligent, sensitive, aware individuals. Caring parents. A species of conscientious, civilized human beings, progressing steadily and collectively towards a better world. (Remember my analogy about the same brain that thinks up life-saving advances in medicine as it's thinking up more efficient ways of killing?) Schizophrenic behavior? Not us. Must be some other guy.

If that kind of behavior were in a science fiction story, you'd say: 'Yep, she's right - this must be a planet of psychos'. Reading on, you'd have confirmation by discovering that the inhabitants of Planet Psycho build much of their so-called 'family entertainment' around the artfully disguised survival of the fittest instinct.

Let's have some examples. Wildlife productions featuring furry animals are too-obvious an example of survival through competition in the wild world, yet only slightly less obvious is family entertainment featuring human competition, which is us reasserting for ourselves and our kids that competition is good and right. Forget tiddlywinks, I'm talking about the real competition we all experience personally every day in real life, and make entertainment out of.

You've seen movies about beating the next guy to a job, or to the girl/guy, or to the draw, or to the gold, or to - yeah, you've seen it all. Sports movies. War movies. Westerns. Cop pics. Biblical epics. Cartoons. Musicals. Love stories. *All* movies are about genetic competition in its myriad subtle or blatant guises. Subliminal training films for life in geneland, made with the full cooperation of human consciousness. The only way to change it is to get your head straight and start seeing it for what it really is.

But more about kids, because they're the genetic offspring everybody's so desperate to survive for. Let me remind you that the TV and movie sex and violence that goes into your kid's head is one generation-as-DNA ensuring survival-propaganda stays healthy in the next generation-as-DNA. That propaganda is indoctrinating kids with the same instinctive old ME FIRST survival view of life. Survival of the fittest DNA-as-people.

You as a conscious entity might think that you appreciate some kind of distinction between comic-book violence, competitive sport, movie mayhem, TV-news homicide, killings on Wall Street, *et al.* But to you as genes, these are still all part of the same thing: the reality of genetic survival. And while all of this stuff is delivered daily in media that only has survival reality to report on, that'll be the *only* reality there is for kids of all ages. They'll continue to swallow

184

it at every meal and between meals, and it'll go on killing 'em in dangerous places like Iraq, L.A. and, it seems, just about everywhere there are people.

On the subject of megabucks, alias Dow and Jones, another popular ingredient of 'family' entertainment is trade, an important aspect of survival that kids learn from an early age. The earlier the better, some might say, right? Teach 'em the real value of money.

Relax. The 'life newsreel' we star in every day is doing that automatically, reminding us all that competition in trade is a vital survival weapon. Okay, stop cheering and think what the 'entertainment' portrayal of material goods and money being greater than the value of human life, is doing to junior minds. No wonder many of them actually become the people with misplaced values they saw in TV and movie 'entertainment'.

Oh yeah, and then there are *guns*. Jesus! More of that science fiction story set on Planet Psycho, only this time the nuts have weapons that blast holes in each other. Any nut can get hold of such a weapon. (Why'd ya think it's called Planet Psycho?) Think of all the many ways in which gene-survival propaganda in the form of gun-related violence appears in film and TV. Why is it so commonplace? Because you're all crazy. Sane people don't go near guns.

But let's make this more relevant to the real purpose of survival: replication and reproduction. The dating game is something everybody thinks is innocent, but dating is genes surviving through reproduction. It might seem harmless enough (if you forget everything I've said so far) until competition in one form or another gets involved, and the nuts and bolts of gene-survival machinery start to show through. People do get killed in the DNA reproduction business. I don't mean the people who get themselves into extreme interpersonal situations and end up with gunshot wounds. Those things have always been par for the course in the sex war, but I'm talking about WAR. What on earth did you imagine wars are about if not extreme examples of protecting and enhancing the gene replication and reproduction process in competing camps of gene survival machines?

Anybody with more than three brain cells can already read enough into this to make further explanation superfluous, but man, that ain't about to stop me. I'll just repeat that to kids of any age, seeing non-stop examples of the behavior I'm describing all around them, then seeing it again treated as entertainment, makes it look all too easy. And it's *condoned*. Sex, both in real life and as entertainment, is more than condoned - it's celebrated everywhere you look. Why? Because it keeps DNA reproducing along the same narrow evolutionary avenues, through the survival machines it evolved exclusively for that purpose.

Likewise guns, both in real life and entertainment, are celebrated. They, too, are everywhere. And like the mania around sex, guns must be an integral part of the perceived right way to behave because everybody's got at least one. Our fascination for 'em starts early and lasts as long as we do. (For some that ain't very long thanks to those guns everybody loves so much.)

Just don't give me that crap about sex, violence or anything else in the 'entertainment' media being 'social comment'; the only social comment being made is that people are making money by portraying human misery and human stupidity, then feeding it to other people.

Yes lady, certainly I'm a crazy reactionary dope-headed freak because I'm indicting life as you know it. I'm the bozo telling you entertainment fiction is really a form of subliminal propaganda designed to corrupt children of all ages. I'm telling you this subliminal, genetic kind of self-propaganda works infinitely harder, is infinitely more effective, it's effects infinitely longer-lasting than the amateur stuff we recognize as propaganda, because this kind is what the audience wants. This audience is *chemically programmed* to want it, and to want its children to want it. You already thought sex and violence on TV and places was damaging to kids? That's kids' stuff compared with the real situation.

Even if you don't want to believe what I'm saying here, do the next best thing and continue imagining you're reading a work of fiction. (Well hey, you read far crazier things than this every day in the goddam newspaper!)

Reading about this crazy planet called Psycho, you've suspended your disbelief to accommodate the notion that this gene-propaganda scam is real. You're letting yourself be horrified, if not for yourself then for the kids on Psycho who're getting indoctrinated. Their parents and guardians are doing squat to stop it. But still you keep reading - about what could happen if somebody *sane* - I don't know, maybe a bunch of escaped mutants or somebody - got inside the machinery and started feeding the kids *good* propaganda through the media.

I can already hear The Rockies and Gibraltar crumbling and tumbling respectively in the face of all the outraged vested interest purveying genetic reality to itself, but I'll carry on despite. What if kids were introduced to a *different* diet. One driven not by personal profit, but by genuine compassion, the sanctity of all life, and giving instead of grabbing?

The eternal excuse for not doing that is: 'But how do we portray the good things without showing their opposites?' Well like I just said, everything depends on what motivates you to make these 'entertainments'. While we continue using our consciousness to give survival priority to a bunch of stupid, body-shaped chemicals, nothing will change very fast.

But what if kids were actually shown the reality of this genetic scenario, instead of being processed automatically as an up-coming generation of replicating-molecule survival machines? They'd start seeing life for what it really is. They'd recognize Planet Psycho as a place where everybody is born with Competition Psychosis. Where everything is geared to one big virtual reality survival game. Maybe they'd decide it's time somebody did something about the sick and dangerous place where they have to 'get out there and hustle' just to survive. And if just one up-coming generation were taught what Really matters, they'd teach *their* kids.

Maybe you imagine you're already doing that? No you're not. That's just more of the mass delusion. Didn't any of what I've been saying sink in? The major change that's needed *can't* happen as just another facet of this I-know-it-all, self-congratulatory, ME & MINE FIRST delusion. It has to be done for OTHERS FIRST, not simply because they happen to be related to your ass.

The transition will be painful because it means changing more than just the media; it means changing *real life* into something better than gene-survival reality for the media to imitate.

Just think - your kids could be the first generation to use their talent not to cash-in on what we do to each other for genes, but to use entertainment constructively. They could learn to use the media and entertainment industry not as gene-survival propaganda, but to finally educate and enlighten us all *out of* the Gene Age, for the sake of our Real evolution. But first *you* have to wake up enough to stop force-feeding selfish survival reality to *them*.

If you did that, who knows what else might happen? I mean, hey, that's the kind of place J.C. might actually *want* to come back to!

TAPE 39

Harve Brown, proprietor of the Gun 'n' Tackle store in Passmore, no longer padlocked the chain that passed through the trigger-guards and open stocks of his weapons. He couldn't be bothered to go looking for the right glasses so he could fit that tiny key into its minute hole every time someone wanted to see a piece of ordnance - especially now things were moving so fast. Besides, nobody ever came to check if he was fulfilling his insurance obligations. Hell, he had better things to think about than insurance; he was getting customers.

"Hunting or home security?" Harve asked conversationally as he hoisted a hunting rifle from the rack; it had come in a few days ago, a replacement for the older model he had managed to offload to a guy from out east after discounting it to the bone.

"Same difference," said the gangling, gaunt-faced man.

Harve didn't know the man but he'd seen the gun-look in his eyes often enough. There was nothing humorous about guns and anybody who joked about them was either crazy or dangerous. Yeah, or both. As the man inspected the weapon, Harve looked across at two other men, one of them poking around the waterproofs and fishing-poles, the other trying on waders.

"Here f'the healer?" Harve asked while the man sighted along the barrel.

"How much?"

"Work somethin' out. Here to hunt, hm?"

The gaunt-faced man had stood around on a cold hillside while his even colder wife and her two mother-loving boys had been up to see the guy with the beard. He'd gotten time off from the plant and was now pretending he didn't have to go back, knowing in his heart there was no way he could ever work up the courage to take off on his own and lose himself in some forgotten backwoods. But he clung to the vain hope that he'd get up early one morning and sit in the car looking back at the house with its windows reflecting things he didn't understand - like her eyes - before going off to find himself. Was it all dreaming? Jesus, he was too close to the edge for it not to be a possibility, however narrow.

"How old is this stuff?" one of the men by the fishing gear called over. "These boots are perished."

The man waved a wader at Harve, who did have some pretty ancient stock that he had been loathe to dump in case he could offload it to impecunious locals and maybe recoup a little of his initial outlay.

"Try the new stock," Harve told him. "All discounted."

His myopic gaze centered on the brighter square of the window and he considered the changing times and attitudes of his customers, and how the more money they had, the less willing they were to part with it.

That thought settled in Harve's mind without disturbing the dust that had only recently started to cover the other, more fatalistic notion. New money

188

had begun trickling in and taken his mind off, well, the term *retirement* would suffice. The store just tipped the balance...for now. When stock went out, he got the same item in. He did his accounts, paid his taxes and service bills. He ate when he was hungry. When he needed to use the bathroom, he used the bathroom. When tired, he locked up and went to his bed. And if he didn't drop right off, he pored over back-numbers of his gun catalogues with an unseeing mind. Day followed night. He breathed and washed. None of it mattered much. Oh yeah, he had a wife around the place someplace, but she seemed more like someone in his past...

The gaunt-faced man bought the rifle and immediately wished he hadn't. He couldn't afford it, but in the heat of the moment the subterranean longing in him won. The man who had discovered the perished waders left without making a purchase and took his friend with him, also empty-handed. By that time there were two other men in the store, getting their senses provoked just by being in there; weighing up whether the cost of this jaunt to the backwoods left them enough spare to indulge those senses. Maybe in an old curiosity store like this you could unearth a genuine bargain, if you didn't mind being seen with equipment that was out of date.

Depending on your point of view, Harve's tiny workshop was either an impossibly untidy mess, or (this is the notion I prefer) minutiae in a silent cacophony of motionless frenzy. I don't know whether that's poetic or just plain gibberish. I do know this is where Harve took pieces of himself apart and put them back together again every day, symbolically speaking. Maybe on a deep level he was trying to reconstruct something of himself that was lost, or broken, or just run down. Who knows? (I sure don't; I'm only a woman.) Even Rosemary Brown never knew who the real Harve was.

Harve's unconscious probings into himself were not helped any by his eyesight, which couldn't have been much more than twenty-percent, the rest being made up from a few percent touch, smell and sound. The contribution made by more esoteric means is anybody's guess.

As this is getting too deep for me to write about with my headache, let's leave Harve for a while and switch to Rosemary Brown instead, because whereas Harve was shrinking in on himself, Rosemary was getting herself stretched spiritually by the healer.

Since I mentioned these two last time, Rosemary had decided Harve was a test of her new notions of personal responsibility. She felt the need to start thinking of herself as an extension of others, instead of vice-the-versa, and she still had much work to do in this department - especially where Harve was concerned. Though to be honest, Rosemary Brown didn't think of herself in the important-sounding terms I'm using, even in the privacy of her own mind. These were simply ideas and feelings she sensed the shape of.

Rosemary lay on the floor of the parlor behind the store with her feet under the table and her arms extended above her head, feeling for sensations in her spine while she stretched and twisted, a millimeter at a time, first to the left, then the right. Sometimes there was a dull ache, other times real pain, but throughout was a perverse kind of lethargic ecstasy of relief. Lying on her back this way, she would close her eyes and drift; that in turn lifted the weight off her thoughts the same way this position eased gravity's pressure on her vertebrae. The abrasive edges of life's components softened, her brainwaves changed and she drifted into an altered mental state. Sounds from outside, the voices from the store, seemed like they were underwater.

In this altered state of consciousness Rosemary imagined the two big opposites in her mind - love and guns - melting like the limp watch in that painting of Dali's called *The Persistence of Memory*, until the two images ran together as one. As the gun concept merged with the love concept she glimpsed the abstract notion that the gun had a legitimacy and inevitability because guns were a necessary twig on a branch of the evolutionary tree, put there only so conscious action could let that twig wither and die. Why? To teach people something they couldn't have learnt otherwise.

The revelation shined too brightly to look at for an instant, then the orgasm of insight faded. She was coming out of her dream-state, sinking into the clammy ocean of reality again. A tenuous shaft of the light followed her into the depths for a second: the conviction that she must pursue her uncompromising new ideas. Then she dropped all the way into wakefulness and the thought was gone, leaving her frustrated after understanding had been dangled before her so briefly.

With care she got up, waiting for her back to cry out. Miraculously, it felt okay. All that remained of her revelation was a fear that her old, self-centered, physical notion of love didn't measure up to the job she had to do on Harve. His love of guns had driven her to walk in the hills around Passmore, and latterly into the wilderness where she'd discovered a small group of people ranged silently around the man they called the healer. He'd be there now. On the spur she decided to go to him, to feel the calm certainty of purpose she felt near him. With her coat over her arm she opened the door to the passageway. Low voices sounded in the store. She went out the back of the single-story building, aware of the pleasantly ripe aroma of her pig-pen. Now it masked a newer odor: burnt hydrocarbons from the extra traffic going by. She twitched her back instinctively. Still quiescent.

As she rounded the corner of the squat whitewashed building she saw a man go in the store, another come out with a box of ammo. Harve wasn't bothering to wrap his goods anymore. Rosemary turned and walked by the store's blockhouse-like facade. A pickup had just pulled in and a man got out and went to look in the window. When Rosemary was a couple of yards from the door, it opened and someone guffawed from inside the gloom. As she passed by, Harve's short body and square white head emerged from between the stiffly-hanging jackets, leading a customer outside to better inspect a small black firearm. Harve looked right at Rosemary without any reaction, then back to his customer and said, "Personal protection, uh?"

"Sure thing," the man said, hefting the small handgun that gleamed like a strange captured insect. "This here's to protect me 'gainst ever'body else's personal protection!" He guffawed again.

Rosemary walked on, aware of the disparity between the person who'd brought all these visitors to Passmore, and the upsurge in sales at the Gun 'n' Tackle. These people were so immersed in the same numbing traditions of life and death that had written the country's code of behavior, that regardless of their state of mind, or lack of it, any one of them had the right to buy a gun. But it was no God-given right, it was a man-given right. Not God-fearing man, but man-fearing man.

TAPE 40

I named this the 'Life after death' tape because the notion of an afterlife (be it heaven, valhalla, paradise, the happy hunting ground, you name it) figures in most religions and cultures. But brain scientists say it's all just an illusion. They say that because brains evolved consciousness to help genes survive in an increasingly complex world, our illusion of an afterlife is a sneaky evolutionary design feature to make us think death isn't the end. (Genes already fooled us into thinking sexual reproduction is our idea; they could just as easily fool us into thinking an afterlife is also our idea, even if its only function is to make us feel better about the inevitable while we're alive.)

Even before you get to the afterlife you might have a near-death experience, but brain scientists say those happen when our brain is starved of oxygen, or maybe when the part of our brain where emotions happen is flooded with endorphins. (Endorphins are feelgood chemicals.) Feelings of euphoria, visions, memory reruns during a near-death experience - science says they're all just results of brain activity. They say we don't *really* leave our body.

To folks who don't believe in God, the above explanations probably sound plausible. But let's not forget that scientific plausibility wouldn't recognize itself if it traveled back a century, or forward a few years. Fact is, scientists know as much about an afterlife as most other folks do: zip. That's about the same amount they know about how brains 'create' consciousness. These guys would have you believe we're just dirt with big ideas. To them, your consciousness is made by a brain that evolved from star dirt, dumped into space by old suns. (It sure feels like that some mornings.)

To be fair, scientists have some great ideas, but reducing religion, God, an afterlife and life itself to products of dead star dirt ain't one of 'em.

Most folks think the afterlife must be someplace outside of material reality, where earthly desires, dollars and materialism don't exist. Others hope those things are there in abundance - a childish notion built on a lack of understanding of how this world works, never mind the next. When you finally get Real, you realize that religion is supposed to help you see through this selfish genetic circus and its delusions. There is no materialism before life and after death anyhow. You don't have a material body before life and after death. You're only issued one of these monkey suits to see how big a monkey you can make of yourself here in geneland! You're meant to prove you can be more than a stupid monkey *right here and right now*. That's the whole point of being here.

I guess this is as good a place as any to look at where human notions of God originated. Although most of it is straight-forward evolutionary science (to anyone not force-fed with religious propaganda) it usually takes a few billion years to explain. So I'm giving you the pocket version, which all started with the early ingredients of this newly created universe - the first building blocks of matter: quarks, protons, neutrons and stuff - all swirling about in space after the Big Bang, Big Bounce or whatever.

Each of those building blocks represented a question: "What am I?" As the new thing called 'time' went by, and the equally new laws of physics began organizing those different quarks, protons and neutrons into workable relationships, an ongoing stream of ever more complex questions (in the language of physics) was created, like: "Who stole my positron?" Or "What have I become now I've hooked up with another particle in a nucleus?" Or: "Can I have a meaningful relationship with a guy, produce a family, hold down a goddam career and find my true self, all at the same time?"

I think we accidentally skipped a couple of billion years with that last question, but with an ever-more-complex stream of ongoing 'questions', effects were caused, chains of events were linked in increasingly complicated ways, the universe evolved, and in amongst the life-forms that resulted we got primitive replicator molecules that later became vehicles for a consciousness that asks questions about every damn thing you can think of.

Asking questions about things that affect you is an important feature of surviving. Seeing things in relation to other things, then comparing the differences, is how we make value judgments about everything. (Unless we're stuck in a belief system that prevents us from questioning things - including God and religion.) Till now we've concentrated on asking questions for ourselves as genetic organisms. If the things around us affect us in some way, we try and change them to make life better for ME and MINE. We'll go on doing that until we evolve enough to see that changing things to make life better for ME and MY genes - even genes in the form of monkey suits - isn't the be-all and end-all of small r reality, never mind Reality.

But what does all of that have to do with our notion of God? I'll tell you after this next tape.

TAPE 41

Imagine you're in a room illuminated by the reflected light of Atlantic sea and sky. The room is palatially spartan, decorated with a chic mixture of items from pricey east coast boutiques, along with stuff you'd find washed up on the beach, all of it cast with painstaking abandon upon an azure ocean of hand-stained board floor. (I guess the interior decorator saw everything in here as flotsam and jetsam, of the kind you'd get from some fabulous private yacht wreck.) Beyond the windows, Hyannis is off the starboard bow, Cape Cod away to port, and Nantucket Island twenty nautical miles over the blue-gray horizon. The house is one of the properties belonging to Massachusetts senator Robert Miller Johnson, who happens to be rich. Senator Johnson's wife, Marylou Celia Stephanie, is also rich.

Today this particular Johnson residence is being used by Peter Paul Johnson, twenty-one years old son of Robert Miller Johnson and Marylou Celia Stephanie Johnson, nee Parker as in The Boston Parkers. Peter Paul - P.P. - is a Harvard man. He's sipping beer and not watching the football game on TV.

Beside P.P.'s deeply-cushioned rattan chair is a hard book on business-studies, and another entitled Wall Street Utopia. On top of these rests a can of beer covered in tiny, perfect droplets of condensation, while on the blue floorboards behind the chair is a large white towel. P.P. brought the towel from the bedroom where he took it to finish wiping vomit from his face earlier this morning before getting back into bed. P.P. was sick from an unhappy mingling of coke (as in cocaine) and white rum.

Susan Elizabeth V. Raleigh, who was asleep somewhere in the bed at the time, and probably still is, is P.P.'s girlfriend. Susan E. has the stronger stomach, so suffered none of the ill-effects of last night.

P.P. stared blankly out of the window, aware of the sickly tide-mark of garbage bobbing inside his forehead. He was pissed with life and existence, but what in hell had he to be pissed about?, P.P.'s father said in his mind. Didn't he have everything a young man could want? How many times had P.P. heard that accusation during his life?

He rubbed at the soft oval of his face and let the hand continue up through his mussed porcupine of dark brown hair. The TV remote slid off his thigh and landed face-down on the seaweed-colored rug that looked as if it were made from real seaweed; the channel changed to a picture of people gathered around one of those silver-aluminum trailers resembling a small airship. There was a guy standing out front of the crowd, obviously the center of attention before the anchorwoman stuck her predatorily pretty face that was mostly mouth into one corner of the screen and said something about "...growing crowds of curiosity seekers in what was once so quiet a part of Appalachia you thought it had been left for dead."

The camera tracked right after her as she walked in front of a gray panel-van with a satellite dish on the roof and XYZ-TV on the side.

A flattening of the sound-waves immediately behind P.P. made him turn to find Susan E. standing on the rumpled white towel, wearing his beach robe back-to-front for some unfathomable reason. She was watching the screen.

"Who was left for dead?" Susan E. asked with disinterest as she reached for P.P.'s beer, and the TV voice said: "...being visited by curious tourists from the National Park next door."

194

Susan E. took the beer over to stand at the window so she could examine her reflection, thinking about what she could buy for herself today. While her right foot smoothed over the upper surface of her left, she imagined herself in some death-defying new outfit, posturing mentally amidst her peer-group, marking their potential responses to her purchases on a scale of ten. While that was happening, another corner of her clever mind was compiling a list of things she'd seen and liked, matching those items with the scores on her peer-list, analyzing expense-recognition signals related to jealousy-quotients and envy-levels.

Which is not to say that such pointless notions meant Susan Elizabeth V. Raleigh was a few students short of a full faculty. On the contrary, there was an above-average number of efficient pathways in Susan E.'s brain. Trouble was, they all led to Susan E.

P.P.'s headache seemed to be worsening as the morning dragged on. The TV was not helping any.

" - we've all seen religious cults before, yet no-one here is being openly recruited, and dare I say, no money has been seen changing hands. If this sounds a little too good to be true - "

What the fuck was this fool going on about?

" - all of it centered on the person locals call *the healer*."

Just as P.P. began listening to what the TV voice was saying, the report ended and the sports news came on, clanging against that last item and making P.P. still more irritated. He reached for the changer and killed the TV.

The silence brought Susan E. back to the present. She came to look down at P.P. so she could tell him how dog-eared he looked. That was when P.P. saw his beer in her hand and wanted it. He started to raise the hem of her robe with his toe - until she stopped him - and decided he wanted more than beer.

An unspoken covenant of P.P.'s parents' relationship, and that of many 'sophisticated' people like them, is based on trading goods and services. In the circles that P.P. and Susan E. revolved in, a suitable mate demands the right background, your family's money, social standing, etc. Such family structures are built around getting the best for your genes. Emotional attachment is a secondary consideration.

As the only son of Senator Robert Johnson, P.P. had picked up this attitude from his father, who also believed that regardless of what reactionary spokespersons for the underclass say, life is not a welfare society. In this world you make your own luck; if you can't make enough you deserve to go under.

P.P. would almost certainly have become a straight Johnson clone but for a quirk of evolution that occurs from time to time. Like viruses that attack a body, an intruder sometimes appears in DNA's system that, instead of working for the ME FIRST factor, introduces unselfish change into the system. P.P. was unaware of his own conscious potential. Still a dork for DNA, he'd decided that Susan E. was not going to lift his beer and wave her tail under his nose without accepting the consequences. That was his coke she'd inhaled last evening, and this was his - well okay, his father's - house. Yes, alright, one of his father's houses.

When P.P. grabbed a corner of the robe Susan E. sort of had on, she tried to pull away and the robe parted to expose her tanned bottom from sunbathing naked on the private veranda.

She rounded on him, clutching the robe to her. "Don't, okay?"

"Come to papa."

"I doubt you're up to it - you weren't last night."

"How would you know - you were out cold."

"What was there to wait up for - some guy going down on the john?"

P.P. yanked at the robe, which jerked the beercan in her hand so cold liquid slopped on her bare foot. She let go the can. It fell heavily and made a notch in the blue board floor. Beer flew on impact and foamed around it.

P.P. was suddenly mad. "Jesus! What the fuck - ?"

But Susan E. was is no mood for this. She quietly took off the robe, compressed it into a ball and hurled it at P.P. as hard as she could. "So screw yourself," she told him quietly and, feet thudding on the boards, she stomped out of the room.

You probably saw people like Susan E. before - maybe when you look in a mirror? For her, being self-centered was a virtue. Protecting her own interests was a natural function of existence and should be her first consideration. To people like Susan E, that's simply being tough-minded. They'd say we should all aim to be like them, when the truth is, all they're interested in is getting what they want and keeping it.

On a more personal level to Susan E., the above syndrome manifested in her need to acquire expensive clothes under the excuse that your appearance was an important part of what you were. In fact her clothes and possessions were status displays, bonding signals aimed at the right potential gene-mixers of the opposite sex, and exclusion signals for anybody else. They were also a kind of security blanket and an inequality enforcement.

196

Susan E recognized that P.P. Johnson had not inherited any genes for political ruthlessness and statesmanlike cunning from his father the Senator. Maybe those had gotten themselves masked into being recessive by his mother's genes or something like that. Whatever, marriage into the family meant she would still have the money, influence and status, without the tedium of a strong-minded husband telling her what to do.

But more of that later. Let's continue looking at where the idea of God came from. I guess people who aren't religious think the God notion had the same humble origins we did - molecules that copy themselves, later to be called DNA, gradually evolving to create ever more complex gene collectives - bodies - that later grew nervous systems and brains. Some of the creatures with these early brains banded together in tribes, their instincts and primitive consciousness telling them they'd survive better within groups of their own kind. (There was safety in numbers, partners to mate with, and somebody else to blame for your own shortcomings.)

These forerunners of human beings had simple minds, but their primitive thoughts felt like an extension of their body - a slightly more aware version of the sensations they experienced in their ass. (Am I describing anybody you know?) They never even noticed religion and God sneaking into their lives. All they cared about was looking out for their ass and mating - which amounted to the same thing, besides being the reason why God snook into their lives.

See, these small tribes of proto-humans, competing for territory and the raw materials of survival, were naturally impressed by the powerful forces that affected reproduction and survival, and even meant the difference between life and death: the sun, moon, weather, seasons, etc. They imagined such powerful and incomprehensible forces were supernatural, wielded by beings with the only attributes these simple minds understood - their own - boosted to often cataclysmic levels. Later they figured these 'Gods' had a pecking order like they did, and behaved much the same way, with the same foibles and failings, only more cruelly or benevolently; more powerfully, ubiquitously, omnipotently. (Go buy a Webster's.)

Today we're so smartassed we have explanations for everything, but in those days, early human consciousness with its primitive imagination, hopes, aspirations, dreams, fears and etc., trying to figure out the big things in life - much the same ones we have now - used superstition to explain life, death, and their relationship with those Gods. And that was how our notions of God began - as the forces that govern material survival.

Even today that same primitive notion of God explains why people use religion in any way selfishly or divisively. It's still about material factors. (In the small r reality of life on this planet, *everything* has a material reason - until you quit working for genes.) That same primitive notion of God is also the reason why somebody questioning, disagreeing with, or worse, threatening the stability of your imagined relationship with God, elicits an unfriendly response.

After Susan E. left the house for her shopping trip, P.P. lounged around in the pool and thought over their scene, thankful in retrospect that he'd lacked the resolve to make more of it. Maybe it was a good thing they'd had a row; it meant there'd be something to make up later - worth a little aggravation because Susan E. was hot on making up.

Though not as bright as Susan E, P.P. was not so dumb that he hadn't figured life was a series of trade-offs, and Susan E always made him pay for the privilege of re-earning her favors. She always screwed him for what she got out of the transaction, regardless of what he got. And now he was thinking along those lines it occurred to him that their entire relationship was built on that premise.

Lying against the poolside with his shoulders resting on the rail and his arms stretched out along it in cruciform, he frowned at his legs wavering slowly up and back underwater, wondering why he'd not seen it before. Susan E. was slyer than he'd given her credit for. He didn't mind her being smarter than he was by a few blocks because of the cache of getting laid by a smarter woman who was also foxy as hell - but only when she felt like it. While he'd simply been having fun with her, she'd been - what? Seeing him in a much more calculating way? As a control exercise?

P.P. splashed his face and said, "Well fucking well!" So it had taken him till now to figure out just who was screwing whom. A chance argument because he'd swallowed some bad medicine, and a new side to their incorporation had emerged. Without the benefit of his father's philosophy in back of his mind he probably wouldn't have noticed it.

Jesus, if he took this new idea to its natural conclusion - marriage (well for Christ's sake, they fought enough) - she could screw him for a seven-figure alimony sum and a matching set of benefits.

He brought his rubber legs up together so his toes twinkled on the surface. This dawning awareness was unpleasant on an upset stomach, with a fuzzy head. His nose kept running as well but he hardly noticed that in the pool...and there was something else bothering him. That weird news item on TV. The memory of it had stayed in his mind and he didn't know why. Appalachia? Jesus, where exactly was that? How would you find such a place? Why would he want to? How come that stupid news item had gotten hooked into him? It made no sense, but nor did most things until you forced them to; until you really looked for your own version of sense in them.

That was a skill he'd learned by living with his father, but not from his father. With the Senator you had to appear to swim with the current of convention because, most of the time, you were going to be carried along by it anyway; in the Johnson household you were powerless to do otherwise. For that reason it came as a surprise when you realized you were not a slave to those conventions, but only wore them like a life-vest. Underneath you were free to be who you really were...except that P.P. was still waiting to discover who he really was.

Without understanding why, he suddenly wanted to go to Appalachia to see what the news item had been about. It didn't matter that it made no sense; it just felt like a good idea. Yeah. He'd take Susan E. and just go. Then he thought again. Why take Susan E. when she made him work so damn hard to earn a small place in her heart? Especially when he was having serious doubts about wanting to be in that heart?

In yet another sudden flash of insight he realized she was a lot like his father. Those people had stock-portfolios instead of hearts. Jesus, what in hell had unleashed such an avalanche of objectionable insights?

P.P. turned his back on them and pushed away from the pool rail, sinking under the surface to hang like a drowned man, eyes half-open and dreamy, baptizing away any reason why he shouldn't just get in his car and drive down to Appalachia. He was thinking underwater. He'd not done that before. Thinking that the sane and sensible reasons why he shouldn't go belonged to his father's way of doing things. That in itself was reason enough for going.

TAPE 42

From the TV in Donna's bedroom the voice said: "There are no bands playing here, yet something about this place people are calling The Wilderness feels like the first Woodstock, and I know - I was there."

Donna did not bother to look up because painting her toenails was a delicate operation. Sure it was kind of decadent but it wasn't harming anyone.

The TV voice said: "These kids were not even thought of when the first and best music love-in happened in a New York State backwater, but the same special feeling of peace and harmony is in this equally anonymous corner of Raiment County Tennessee."

Thoughts of The Triangle evaporated in the joyful haze that overtook Donna when she pictured the healer and felt the surge of love rush up through her. She let her eyes close and suspended her nail-painting so she could experience the full force of it, then slowly opened her eyes again and carried on, smiling to herself.

"...and all because of this man they call *the healer*."

At mention of his name Donna looked up to see a tall figure in blue jeans and a white tee-shirt touch his hand to the blond head of a small child who smiled sweetly up at him. So perfect, it could have been a moment from a commercial.

"He's said to be just a simple soul, living in a trailer here, and yet something about him - some are calling it an earth-magic, others a mystical charisma, and, would you believe, I've even heard the Second Coming mentioned - is bringing the crowds."

The reporter reached off, brought a hamburger into shot and smirked, self-satisfied. "No-ho, there are no loaves and fishes being passed around in this wilderness, though the healer has attracted local fast food merchandisers to this spot near the once-sleepy little town of Passmore just over the hill in back of me."

Donna hunched forward and flattened the tiny brush along the curve of her big toenail. The sight of that burger had made her feel hungry, but the boiled-candy odor of nail-polish counteracted the gastric activity, and she just licked her lips. She was almost done anyhow.

"The busy little money-bug is turning Passmore into a tiny tourist haven...it's a real pleasing sight. And boy have they been waiting for just something like this..."

"I surely have, Lord," said Donna with complete happiness.

Downstairs though, the Sheriff, cleaning his gun on the kitchen table, could hear that same TV program from two directions at once and he was getting angry in stereo. In his hands the disassembled weapon - a series of hard, finger-friendly planes - faded through to an image of Catherine, stretched out on the couch in the front room, still and back-straight as a marble statue, minute points of light and motion dancing in her unblinking fish-eyes. The

Sheriff was angry because he had successfully eradicated one holy nuisance from his town, only to have this god-damn healer take his place. Worse yet, the guy had gained access to Hughes' own home, invited by the two bitches he had to share it with!

Hughes put the small barrel to his eye and looked down it, seeing his own frustration in the empty cylinder. The situation was not helped any by all of these day-trippers pouring into his domain, clogging up the roads and using any handy piece of roadside as their own personal picnic pull-off, creating even more harassment for him; treating him like some god-damn minor public servant. They had no respect for his position. The way some of them eyed him up and down, grinning, it was almost as if he'd become just another piece of local color, part of the circus going on up in the wilderness. Well Jesus Christ! Neil Hughes had had enough of being treated like a lowly servant of the community. Folks used to look up to the Sheriff. Hell, they used to be in awe of him. Not any more. Something had happened to the friendly little town of Passmore lately, and it wasn't healthy. And God-*damn* Maxine Stevenson!

Hughes put the cylinder on the table and got up, slapping his chair out of the way. At the open doorway to the front room he stopped to watch the scenes flicker across the square of light and felt it feed his anger. He saw someone kneel before the tall figure who, to Hughes, appeared more like a high-school dropout or some other useless type than a magnetic draw for those crazy people. They obviously had nothing better to do with their time than waste it on this crap. A sharp finger of fury poked up through Hughes' anger, but cooled instantly to bitter sarcasm.

"Surprised you ain't up there washin' his god-damn feet."

Snapping out of her trance, Catherine Hughes looked around and blinked to focus on her husband, his face alive with reflected images of the healer. "What did you say?"

"You heard me." He turned to go back into the kitchen. "God-damn freak-show. Weak-minded sons-of-bitches."

When he was gone, Catherine watched the healer wander through the crowd with his eyes mostly lowered, raising them only to bestow one of his looks. Oh Lord, those eyes! Catherine Hughes had seen eyes like that, but never on a normal human being, only in devotional paintings; the Last Supper kind of picture. Christ healing the leper. Christ restoring the sight of the blind man. Christ inviting the crippled man to take up his bed and walk. There were many such pictures in her Illustrated Bible.

Catherine lowered her eyelids and her shaking head, guilty for nursing doubts. Could this possibly be Him? Could it really be happening on the doorstep of her town? Was she offending Him by having such doubts? Ought she to be up there with Him, doing something to help spread The Word? Wasn't this what she had prayed for? Begged Him for? Longed for in her very soul?

Her eyes flickered open. The Lord Himself would answer her questions through her Bible! Why in God's name hadn't she realized it before now? For years she had turned its pages, examined those lurid, but to her magical, illustrations - some naive artist's impression of life in biblical times. She had drawn cold comfort from those stories…

In the bedroom, by the side of her divan, was her red-and-gold-fiber-bound, machine-tooled copy of the Illustrated Watson Bible, waiting for her to draw near and open its pages to the truth her hungry soul craved. She selected a page at random; it was in Isaiah, chapter thirty-five. She read: '*The wilderness and the solitary place shall be glad for them.*' The Wilderness! '*And the desert shall rejoice and blossom as the rose, abundantly, and rejoice even with joy and singing.*'

Surely it couldn't be so simple as opening her Bible and finding a sign, just like that - could it? She began devouring the text, skipping through words and meanings that vaguely connected until she reached: '*…and they shall see the glory of the Lord, and the excellency of our God. Strengthen ye the weak hands, and confirm the feeble knees. Say to them that are of a fearful heart, be strong, fear not: behold, your God will come with vengeance, even God with a recompense; He will come and save you.*'

Catherine Hughes felt her throat constrict with emotion. She read further: '*Then the eyes of the blind shall be opened, and the ears of the deaf shall be unstopped. Then shall the lame man leap as an hart, and the tongue of the dumb sing: for in the wilderness shall waters break out, and streams in the desert.*'

At that her body was wracked with uncontrolled breaths that came in tearing rents, as if she were rushing into the wind and couldn't catch enough air to swallow. These words were from Isaiah. This was The Old Testament, meant to refer to the first time He came. The Second Coming was something she knew hardly anything about; only that it would herald the end of the world. Ideas filled her head, fighting each other. She read on: '*And the parched ground shall become a pool, and the thirsty land springs of water: in the habitation of dragons, where each lay, shall be grass with reeds and rushes…*'

By the end of chapter thirty-five the tears were streaming down Catherine's cheeks, running along the line of her jaw and dripping from her chin. Spots of gray appeared on the page. She felt the unbearable weight of holy conviction pressing down on her shoulders.

She didn't recall placing her bible back on the bedside cabinet, or taking the tiny key from its secret place under the hollow base of her reading-lamp. She tasted the intoxicating words of Isaiah even as the key tapped and probed against the lock before slipping into the keyhole. When her hand located the hard, cold circumference of the vodka bottle, she sat with great stillness on the edge of her bed, holding the bottle upright between her legs and staring blankly at the wall while her blind fingers unscrewed the cap. She raised the bottle to her mouth, then closed her eyes tight shut and drank, feeling the spirit of The Lord burn in her chest.

When Neil Hughes came up an hour later he brought his gun up with him and placed it on his own bedside table. His wife was dead asleep, snoring the way she always did after a session on the juice, but Hughes was not thinking about her stupid addictions as he undressed and slipped between the sheets of his own bed. He was considering how best to exercise more authority around his jurisdiction.

All of the riff-raff and disruptive types a crowd of out-of-staters invariably brought in their wake were going to feel the power of the law. There'd already been a break-in at the mill. Somebody else had lifted Dave Snodgrass's car stereo. It made no difference that Dave always left the window of his pickup rolled down (because the winder was busted); before the tourists came, folks around these parts could trust their neighbor, and this town wasn't going to tolerate criminal city ways.

Hughes reached out in the darkness and touched the cold gun. Hell but that felt good. Maybe it was time he started carrying a piece of heavy artillery in his cruiser. Something big and mean; a pump-action shotgun maybe, or even that semi-automatic rifle he'd tried out at Harve's...

Here's more of that earlier tape on the material origins of God. I want you to picture those early humans with minds someplace between a chimp's and a child's: Impressionable and fearful, imaginations untainted by education and so-called 'sophisticated' social experience. To those primitive consciousnesses, the Gods of nature were all-powerful decision-makers in everything that affected their material survival. So they thought up ways of pleasing those Gods with rituals (that later developed into formalized religious worship) to ask for the Gods' mercy, help, cooperation and favors. Those supposedly life-

and-death-deciding rituals to please their Gods grew into the reason why people stick with their 'own kind'.

See, your religion, its rituals and its rules, laws, commandments, became the way you lived your whole life. When you survived by beating off your competitors to win the raw materials of life - land, food, water or mates - you wanted you, your family and your tribe to have God's favors rather than somebody else and their tribe to have them. For that reason, these rituals later became secretive exclusion symbols of unity to help people survive, not just in the face of everything they couldn't understand (superstitious magic and demons and stuff) but against more down-to-earth threats from rival bands in their own neck of the woods. Those survival rituals eventually formed into major religions that, on a subconscious level, symbolized survival itself.

This might seem like a stupid question, but *why* did those primitive humans want to survive? For the same reason you or any other genetic organism wants to survive. Not because their consciousness tells them to (most genetic organisms don't have that much consciousness) but because genetic organisms, whatever else they might think of themselves as, are automated biomechanical systems programmed with the instinct to strive to maintain their own existence. Us too. Sure, being aware of the unhappy/uncertain/maybe painful consequences of dying gives us conscious reasons for wanting to survive, but a far more primitive and powerful reason, way below our conscious level, is driving us to maintain our existence as a physical body.

The trillions of atoms in bodies and brains exist as a result of the evolution of totally automated processes that behave according to laws of physics and chemistry. The urge to reproduce is part of that same automated program. Sex is *not* something you either initiate or decide with your mind. Any conscious 'reasoning' that seems to be involved comes only as a result of millions of years of trial and error in that automatic program, when all of the decisions to reproduce, and all of the reasons for reproduction, have already been made by mindless components. Your mind merely refines those decisions. (Though 'refined' is the last word I'd use for what's involved in reproduction.)

In material terms, gene replication has always been more important than the survival of individual organisms. (Genes being the only material part of us that gets passed on through heredity - the whole purpose of the genetic program.) So without ever realizing what they were doing, those early humans were making a religion out of an urge to survive, programmed into their bodies and

204

brains by millions of years of genes, mindlessly replicating and reproducing themselves.

And that's the pocket version of how religious dogma became an extension of the genetic survival instinct. Religious dogma prevented anybody changing what folks believed was the best way for their particular tribe/nation to survive and reproduce. Somebody coming along and messing with your beliefs, even now, is perceived - on levels you're not even aware of - as them messing with your survival.

Those primitive people never meant their 'religions' to bring us all together. There was no 'higher spiritual purpose' in it. (That concept got bolted on later and is mostly overruled by material considerations.) To those primitives, religion and God were ways of *separating* themselves from rival tribes, to protect what they had. And later, to protect their ideas about who they were. Their 'religion' was about *survival*. To see that process in action today, watch TV news. Those divisive religious notions are still working. They're handed on from generation to generation through indoctrination.

One reason for why the notion of religion as survival is still part of us, is because brains, and the consciousness in them, evolve differently. Being every-which-way more dynamic than brain matter, an evolving consciousness kind of drags the brain's evolution along behind it, forcing the brain to use consciousness in new and different ways. That in turn encourages brains to accommodate more consciousness.

A result of this process is that the unique-to-you, mostly symbolic picture of what reality means at the deepest and most profound levels, is being constantly modified by your imagination, thoughts, hopes and dreams about your relationship with the world around you.

This 'you/world' interaction is gradually changing not just the structure of your brain but the contents of your subconscious as well. Like I said, over millions of years, some of the brain machinery that used to interface early consciousness gradually got demoted to subconscious levels, and newer brain machinery replaced it. The more primitive components still operating in your brain work in conjunction with the newer ones - like the earlier parts of an old building getting gradually added-to through history. Evolution just builds right on top of those ancient foundations, incorporating some of the old stones, bones, refuse and whatever into the newer levels. Those ancient components are still interconnected, some still interactively influencing the way your mind works now, on levels below your conscious awareness. That's how the 'thoughts' that helped shape the brains of earlier human beings, have also helped to form the way your brain/consciousness interface works now.

We all share the same mental evolution and the same subconscious structure. According to a guy named Jung, our subconscious minds all share the same symbols for our fears, aspirations, hopes, dreams, and understanding of reality. Jung named these subconscious symbols 'archetypes'. The God notion is one of them.

That means the same survival motive behind religion, with the same inbuilt 'material provider' God archetype, is as fundamental for all of us as breathing and heartbeat. We may have cultural, social and personal differences, but those are only paintwork; these *archetypes* are what form the common basic structure of our understanding of reality. (Some folks prefer not to interpret these subconscious influences as notions of 'religion' and 'God', so the notions come out as other kinds of beliefs.)

No matter who we are, whatever our religion, our notions of God originated in the same place that our notions of reality did - in the evolution of these genetic bodies/brains. As we evolve and our consciousness grows, a natural development is to adjust our concepts of religion and God, the same way we adjust all of our other concepts, to accommodate a broader, more mature understanding of reality. Only that way will we cultivate a progressively more accurate picture of ourselves, where we should be going, and why. God, like any other idea that our mind interacts with, is a way of figuring ourselves out, okay? For that reason, as human consciousness evolves, our notions of religion and God should evolve too. But when somebody tells you God is this, period, and God said you must think and act the way we say, the result is the very opposite of evolution, growth and natural human development.

Okay, so...(juggles microtapes, knocks some off the goddam table, almost spills drink)...divisive religions are what you get if nothing fundamental has changed for your belief system in centuries or even millennia. (And by 'belief system' I mean your philosophy for living.) Instead of your ideas evolving, as all ideas must, you'll still be trying to live by those ancient, exclusionary elements in your religion. Perpetuating what keeps you distrustful of, and antagonistic towards other tribes/nations/belief systems. Your 'traditional' beliefs will encourage you to go on seeing the world from a narrow, localized perspective. You might even excuse that narrow religious perspective as 'purity' as you practice repression, inequality and barbarity. But that's going to change because everything does, sooner or later.

206

Even though we still live in the same materially competitive environment that spawned these divisive religions, it's getting smaller and more complicated all the time. Through modern communications we all know what each other has, and regardless of our religious differences, we all share the same basic human nature. So if somebody else has a better deal in life, we want in. Even the people who're scared of change can't resist evolution. It's inevitable. Resist change and you become isolated, then extinct.

Resisting change is what make religion dogmatic. The only non-dogmatic religion is one that says, 'Believe what you want to believe, not what somebody else wants you to believe.' Trouble with that is, it would mean giving people in general, and kids in particular, a choice, right? (Kids being the ones who get indoctrinated into their parents' beliefs, delusions, prejudices and hatreds.) That in turn would mean exposing kids to the ideas in back of other people's beliefs. Which would also mean parents and teachers being sane and reasonable and open minded. How can that happen when the people of every religion each think theirs is the one and only true religion, with the one and only true God?

Boy it's cold in my trailer since the heating quit! Know what the nicest part of writing a book like this is? Getting up and walking away. (Who said, 'Ditto reading it'?)

TAPE 43

Harve Brown sat at the parlor table and ate his supper in a cocoon of concentrated silence without once raising his eyes to either his wife or the big, dark-wood cabinet TV in the corner, its volume turned to zero. Things happening in the world didn't concern Harve. Not even these events taking place just a few miles down the road. Nor did he realize that if not for the central figure in those TV pictures, his business would be dead now, and him right along with it.

For Rosemary Brown, somewhere in the same room, the world had been turned upside-down by that TV figure. Before him, all she and Harve had left in common was the space they disturbed around the house. Now that Rosemary was seeing Harve in a new light, she'd come to some disturbing conclusions. She decided he'd become little more than a reflection of his store, a working part of his own rigid routine. His world was the empty sails of unfilled garments, the negative vibrations of weaponry.

She understood how, for Harve, this parlor was reduced to an annex of the retail area, and that she existed only as an instrument of mealtimes and maybe certain other functions that happened around Harve but were of little consequence to him. She saw how she was less important than his customers.

Right now Rosemary leaned against the old kitchen dresser and explored the status of her spine with the same small twisting movements that had become practically instinctive. She'd grown so used to the old aches they were now a normal part of feeling. She'd become her pain in the same way that Harve had become his store.

They'd both been overtaken by their material existence; she knew because the healer had showed her how to look at her material and spiritual selves separately. The healer taught her that her body was what the world had made, from its elements, while her spiritual self was eternal. For that reason, spiritual questions could never be satisfied by material answers. You had to use the spiritual part to *change* the material part; that in turn would enable the material part to help the spiritual part progress further into spirituality, or spiritual Reality. He seeded in her mind the notion that by refusing to let go of her old, material understanding of love, she was only prolonging the pain between her and Harve.

Coming to terms with all of this was hard for Rosemary. Her notion of love as something physical had gotten between her and Harve, had traveled with them for so long, dictating the terms of their relationship, slowly levering them apart over the years. She'd demanded the kind of gratification from that old love that she could feel and see - gratification of the senses. She'd expected too much of that physical love, when the truth was that it could never satisfy a spiritual need. But if that were true, there could be no such thing as physical love; the name was more than misleading, it was a lie.

It was the healer who finally made Rosemary understand that she amounted to much more than her physical demands. Through those, the illusion of that old love clouded her reason. That old love only masqueraded as a giving thing, only pretended to be selfless. It made you discriminate between the deserving and the undeserving on all of the wrong grounds: skin, or shapes under the skin, or promises of getting, or desires seeking fulfillment, or…But there were so many sides to that illusion. And even with this new insight, just questioning such long-established attitudes still scared her. She needed reassurance.

She came around the table and sat down in the hardback chair opposite Harve so she could look right into his eyes. She'd given up looking for

208

something specific; now she would be glad to see anything at all: impatience, annoyance. She knew that at this range Harve couldn't focus on her. What was he seeing when he did aim his gaze in her direction? A lighter circle in the surroundings? A face seen through frosted glass? If she kept still maybe he wouldn't see her at all. He'd most likely forget she was there. She could die in the chair, and only the dead-animal smell would give her away.

After she had sat and stared at him for a minute, Harve lifted his faded blue eyes to hers, but lowered them to his hands again without reaction, as though she was a window to an uninteresting view. But some unaccountable thing made Rosemary hold old her gaze on Harve's face until he looked up again with painful slowness, maybe…could it be…as though beginning to remember why he looked up the first time? What was he seeing? What was he thinking?

Rosemary couldn't know that, like her, Harve was struggling with himself, facing inward, trying to remember who he had been, who he was supposed to be now. To find and hold-on to what was left of an earlier self. But it was like staring at an old daguerreotype of that self, standing in a group of other people: the population of his memories, all of them fading fast. He had the feeling that as the chemical surface of that picture degraded and the people faded, he would fade with them. He would cease to exist.

Rosemary watched him press himself up from the table, a tired old man. Watched as he turned and made his way along the dark passage to his workshop. And suddenly, with no warning, a tiny spark of the old half-maternal, half-sexual feeling flashed inside her. It came out of nowhere, yet because it followed so close on the heels of those earlier thoughts, she was able to check herself, knowing it was part of the old trap set by physical needs. Lord, how effortless it was, this urge. But it was not a *giving* urge; this was an urge reaching out only for what it could *get*. This was a leftover from the animalistic reason for living that once filled her to bursting, running through the forest of her being like wildfire.

And then came a pang of bitterness at the thought, not new, that Harve's rejection of that old animal love had itself provoked her to seek an alternative. The bitterness went slowly out of her, became gratitude now she recognized these urges for what they were. Even as they encouraged her to succumb to that arbitrary habit of love, her soul knew better. For a long time it had been telling her there was more to love than that, and now that she was finally learning how to listen, she had to make Harve listen too…

So far we only looked at God from the bottom up, meaning from the 'genetic origins' angle. We've seen plenty of evidence for that version of God, created by our need to survive. Now let's go looking for the Real God.

And don't somebody say "There's no need to look for God - God is everything and everywhere." That's just a chicken-out for folks who can't think for themselves. God being in everything and everywhere never prevented shit happening, and you know why? It's because we're the only ones who can prevent it happening – by demonstrating genuine unselfishness and compassion for each other. Besides, we're not looking for a one-on-one with the material phenomena around us; we need something we can identify with, and emulate, on a conscious level.

Or maybe you're scared of getting up close and personal with God because somebody told you He has moods and a temper, like we do. God might get angry and punish you for being inquisitive. Maybe you think God has draconian rules and regulations and a death squad of angels just waiting to smite wrongdoers? Or worse, hand them over to the guy downstairs?

Relax. Like I told you, all of that fearsome God stuff was invented by primitive imaginations. It's a creation of confusion and insecurity, shaped not by understanding, compassion and wisdom, but by their absence. The Real God is a combination of all levels of consciousness, in whatever form it takes in this or any other universe.

Does that imply God is bad stuff as well as good? Damn right.

For example, a very primitive splinter of consciousness might reside in a suicide bomber. Somewhat further up the evolutionary scale you'll have another level of consciousness living in a worm, or maybe a cow. Much higher up the scale there are consciousnesses that don't need to be in what you'd recognize as a physical body. Everything with consciousness, on whatever level of awareness it evolved to, is a little piece of the overall consciousness that you might choose to call God.

I'm not saying that each of us is God. I'm saying the consciousness in every one of us, together with all of the consciousness in everything else, everywhere, adds up to God. That's how God gets to be composed of every shade of experience, of understanding, of awareness. It's this way because to be God, God has to BE every nuance of experience, every iota of understanding, every facet of awareness, otherwise there'd be Godless pockets of creation, right? This is also how God gets to BE every bit of ignorance, every shade of evil, and every color of all the other ways that consciousness

210

can be. Only by being all of those can God know what they are and what they mean.

Before I talk about how God can be all of those things at the same time, let's look at the notion that God is 'in' inanimate objects that aren't alive.

Start by thinking about the way consciousness interfaces inanimate objects. As consciousness, you already interface DNA's body and brain, right? So bring the idea of a computer into your mind, and make your brain tell its body to mold your conscious notion of a computer into an actual computer.

Okay. Now you've got an actual, physical computer that began entirely as conscious ideas. Now use the same consciousness-body/brain interface to program the computer.

Good. What you've got there is a non-conscious, material computer. It's programmed and running and turning out more non-conscious material stuff (in a form we can read). We - consciousness - have used entirely non-material ideas and concepts, and (via our human interface) built and run a completely material, non-conscious computer. We can even reverse the process by reading what the computer is spewing out, which amounts to turning non-conscious information (written data) back into conscious ideas in our mind.

See what happened? Non-material ideas became a material computer and its program, which then produced material data that our conscious mind turned back into non-material ideas. That was a simplified example of how we use our consciousness/body interface to be 'in' inanimate objects that aren't alive. (The reason why we had to go through that slow and primitive process is because material things – eg: computers - exist in a different set of *dimensions* from our consciousness. Consciousness exists in the abstract dimensions of ideas, understanding and awareness, whereas a computer exists in the mindless dimensions of this material universe, right? Right.)

Now let's do the advanced example of how consciousness can be 'in' inanimate objects that aren't alive. Recall what Ed said about human consciousness operating through what we perceive as our body. He described our consciousness as a series of more refined energy layers that correspond with our physical body/brain. These layers - called subtle bodies – are different frequencies of consciousness energy that sit one inside another, kind of like those cutesy Russian dolls.

You have a problem with these frequencies of consciousness? They're no weirder than a body being made from varying densities of energy (molecules, atoms, nucleons, quarks). And how weird is the scientific conclusion that all of material reality is just energy, probability waves that appear to us as things made from atoms? Better also remind yourself why they appear to us as things made from atoms? It's because a material body/brain allows our consciousness to appreciate only a tiny fraction of how things Really are.

Okay, so our consciousness is not just a vague cloud of knowingness inside a brain, it's actually a multi-dimensional series of dynamically interacting layers that interface a collection of electrochemical components (a body/brain) that you discard when you die. (Actually it's the *components* that 'die' because they no longer work together efficiently enough. Consciousness never dies.) While a low level frequency of this multi-dimensional consciousness 'is' the physical body as we see it, at higher frequencies our consciousness is invisible to us. We can be aware of higher frequencies because they're responsible for our emotional and mental states.

Thing is, consciousness doesn't need a body and brain; we only choose to be in them for educational purposes. (So we can evolve.) That said, we don't simply get to do what the hell we like with our consciousness – it is part of the corporate hierarchy after all, and there are company rules.

Though what I'm leading up to here is that, by dumping the low-frequency matter of a human body, either temporarily or permanently, consciousness at higher frequencies can insinuate itself into other forms of low-frequency matter if it wants to. (You might have already tried it, though now you're back inside a monkey suit you probably wouldn't remember. Though I guess not many people would be interested in 'becoming' a rock after experiencing the potential of 'being' human.)

Sure, this is all very interesting, but what would be considerably more useful during this trip to monkeyworld is not trying to interface your consciousness with rocks, but learning how to interface with other consciousnesses. And I mean without your material body/brain getting in the way and confusing matters. (You lost the thread? So read more thoughtfully.)

Listen, the only way we know that other consciousnesses (eg: in people) exist at all, is by communicating with them through the medium of a material body/brain. The notion of one consciousness communicating with another consciousness *without* the need for a material interface is usually called telepathy or extra sensory perception (ESP) or whatever. Those assume that you still need a material brain to send the communication, and another material brain to receive it. But that's not the same as communication between totally disembodied consciousnesses. Oh-ho no. For that, Ed said you'd need

212

to appreciate what being a disembodied consciousness is like. I guess the folks who've had near-death and temporary-death experiences know a little about that. (And, of course, folks who die and stay dead.)

Just try and imagine a disembodied consciousness attempting to communicate with people who only perceive consciousness through a very limited bodily interface made from atoms shaped into nerves, senses, a brain. Personally I can think of some damn good reasons why a disembodied consciousness would choose *not* to communicate. If one spoke directly to the folks I know, they'd either crap in their pants or start thinking they were Jesus Christ. I guess that's why we have mediums.

Now, let's assume for a moment that you believe in life after death, and that people can and do have conversations with the dead through mediums. From what you've heard, it sounds as if having died and left loved ones behind, there are people who want to communicate with them from their disembodied state. They want to tell them hey, I may be disembodied but I still exist! Quit grieving! And a million other things, mostly of a trivial nature because that's life for most people - even after death.

Note: They're disembodied in the sense that the material body they had on earth is gone. They still have a body after death, but it's composed of *conscious* material.

Okay, but in 'heaven', as on earth, people aren't all on the same conscious level. Some are more highly evolved. So while your dear departed might be all too eager to link up with you from the other side, there'll be others who, when they actually get in that situation, have a different take on things, and decide there's nothing to be gained from trying to communicate. After ridding themselves of that body/brain, they're suddenly gonna see a much bigger picture of Reality and maybe figure it's pointless or counter-productive to communicate with consciousness that's still in human form. I guess you'll just have to wait and see...

TAPE 44

If, as a good Christian soul, you had stood outside The Golden Triangle Bar and Grill on that warm night in May, listening to the steady throb of country music, you'd have noticed the mended neon sign proudly anointing the head of everybody who passed beneath its red and yellow light. You'd have registered surprise at another sign, newly erected, declaring *Families Welcome.*

(Until a short while ago you would never have considered The Golden Triangle a suitable establishment for families, and certainly not young children.)

Had you then been overpowered by ruffians and taken inside this den of sin against your will, your suspicions would have been verified by the sight of so many drinkers of alcohol and smokers of tobacco wallowing in sublime intemperance, etc.

When your eyes had adjusted to the gloom and the stratocumulus of smoke, you'd have been astonished to find everyone present - drug-dealers and addicts, parole breakers, escaped murderers and other fugitives from justice, the pitiful clutch of fallen women - watching TV with the sound turned off, because nobody was interested in listening to some jabbering TVpersonspeak; not when *the healer* was on, and they could watch him and still imbibe the strains of their other religion: country music.

The healer was theirs now. Hell boy, he was one of them! He brought them together as the underprivileged locals who were getting descended upon by so many strangers with money.

An out-of-stater at the bar counter, wearing a check-jacket strident enough to induce epilepsy, turned to a local man in a battered straw fedora and said, "He's really something, isn't he?"

The local man's lizard gaze remained fixed on the TV screen. He raised his beer to his face and drank slowly. Then, eyes narrowing, he said softly with a distinct hint of menace, "Mister, that there's our healer and don't you god-damn ferget it."

At that moment a cry of accomplishment went up at the far end of the long room. Two teenage men playing pool were the only ones in The Triangle not watching TV. Their intrusive voices brought a wall of hard faces their way. Somebody yelled, *"Quiet down!"* Others cleared their throats in agreement.

Over by the music-selector, fighting to keep the tremor out of his hand long enough to mine his nostril, Jeff Ackerley tried to bully another beer out of Roy King, whose sullen expression said he was tired of buying for somebody who treated him like garbage. It had seemed to make no difference to Ackerley that King had rescued him from an almost certain charge of attempted arson during their abortive sojourn to the healer's trailer that night. Since his marijuana crop failed from neglect, Ackerley had withdrawn into a tight little world occupied only by his frustrated sexual needs, rare visits to The Triangle and unpredictable fits of epilepsy. His eyes, red-and-yellow rimmed - like the

214

Triangle sign - and sunk deep as desert wells, rode above dark crescents wherein lurked small blue veins.

King, impervious to Ackerley's disdain, oblivious to his mood swings, indifferent to his poor personal hygiene, figured the guy had bought himself a one-way ticket down the chute to shitsville. He was not alone in this assessment. From his vantage-point behind the counter, Matt, the Triangle's part-time barkeep - when he wasn't working for the healer - also knew where this particular customer was headed.

Matt wandered over to Willie Stevenson, playing with his bottle of lite beer, so he could answer the question Willie had put to him before he went off to serve a customer.

"Sure, we could always use some extra help in the wilderness." He searched Willie's eyes for something, but Willie immediately looked away.

When Matt went back to his duties, Willie looked him up and down, wondering what kind of satisfaction a smart young guy working The Triangle could find as unpaid help for the healer. Willie was trying to find places for the pieces of a jigsaw-puzzle he had been carrying around in his head ever since the night he'd seen the healer standing there on the steps of that silver trailer like a visitor from another world. He wouldn't admit to a curiosity about that other world, or that it attracted him. (Other worlds had gravity that affected people though, didn't they?

That's what astrology was all about. Maxine had explained to him how even the gravitational influence of our little moon had the power to cause something as big as the ocean to behave the way it did.) Willie didn't believe that astrology hokum, yet seeing the healer that night exuding an inexplicable power composed of silence and stillness, Willie realized he had stored the experience away under 'unknown'. It was why he had engaged Matt in casual conversation. Now the guy was coming back and Willie caught himself liking him, but immediately quashed the feeling and replaced it with cynicism. The result was a discomfort that caused Willie's smile to flicker as uncertainly as neon gas through the old glass tubes of The Triangle's sign. Why was the guy being so friendly? Willie's eyes went up to the TV screen.

Matt turned to stare at the screen too. He knew who Willie Stevenson was from Donna. He'd seen Willie up there in the wilderness, a face in the crowd, his expression guarded but unable to conceal his interest. Matt had watched him stop still for long moments and peer into the distance at the healer. Willie's face had thought itself a blank mask, but the eyes had told the truth.

Matt drifted away to tend bar. When he came back to collect Willie's empty bottle he figured Willie had gone away to do some thinking of a kind he was not used to.

The Camaro's headlights swept around the corner of the Zeno Road along with a squeal from balding tires before the nose raised up with a waffling V8 roar to race the final hundred yards. Willie hit the brake and killed the lights to let the car creep up the ramp and stop, its pitted fender an inch from Maxine's tiny Honda. He switched off, got out, sneaked the door shut and walked soundlessly around the rear of the house in shadow. On the way he was met by a smell of cooking and felt his gastric juices begin to flow and his stomach yawn.

Willie had brought himself home to catch the supper run. His parents never ate breakfast together, and luncheon was every man for himself, but supper was another matter and always on time, prepared and cooked by the Mayor himself. That was fine by Maxine, for whom cooking was a rare chore rather than a pleasure.

But tonight, Willie's habit of peeking in at the kitchen window brought a surprise: his father and step-mother were standing together in front of the tiny TV that normally lived in Maxine's bedroom. They never watched TV during supper; that was one of his father's rules. Then he saw his father's arm was around Maxine, the palm of his hand resting comfortably on her shoulder, his fingers hanging over so they touched the bare flesh of her ample upper-arm. The Mayor was *touching* Maxine. They were *together!*

Then Willie was in the kitchen making a hell of a racket any way he could, unable to think or breathe. The Mayor only turned his head, a stupid, stupid grin plastered on his face. Maxine hadn't even bothered to acknowledge Willie's presence. When she did condescend to look at him, it was not Maxine. An alien presence had taken over her body and was looking at him through Maxine's once-accommodating eyes. It smiled at him using her sweet, bow-shaped lips that he had imagined, warm and moist against the private places of his body, except that now her pearly teeth threatened to tear at him.

"Why Willie, come here hon and see the healer." The freckled arm reached out at him, its long fingers twinkling like fleshy spider-legs. "Here baby - "

Baby! It was the very worst thing she could have said at that moment.

"Ready to eat, son?" the Mayor asked over Maxine's shoulder while his eyes feasted on the bosom welling up between the flappy lapels of that shiny blue

216

and white dress that Willie had seen in Maxine's closet but never on her. It looked old and dated, like something she'd been keeping for just this moment.

Willie's heart pounded like an angry fist. Beyond the Mayor's fingers on Maxine's arm, beyond the steady rise and fall of Maxine's breasts, Willie's gaze was drawn to the TV - a close-up of the healer. *He* had done this! It couldn't have happened without these flickering, holy-ghost images mesmerizing the two people Willie depended on for everything - as separated people, not as a couple! They couldn't help themselves. They were no longer in control of their own actions. On that screen, pale and silent, reconstituted from invisible waves in the ether, was the one who had somehow engineered this unacceptable change. *He* was to blame!

Then the enigmatic TV face, frightening in its private significance for Willie, lifted. The eyes came up to meet Willie's own, and instantly everything poured out through those televised eyes into him. Those eyes filled with his own burning tears of self-pity and rejection, both punishment and forgiveness for having sought to manipulate his own family.

It took Willie ten minutes' serious driving through the night to reach the spot by Blackwater Creek where he, King and Ackerley had set out from that night. The hollow in his stomach now a pit of acid-nerves, he started walking, retracing their route through the dark wood until he emerged into a weak slice of moonlight.

There was the trailer's softly luminous silver shape against its umbrella of dark elms, both its windows aglow as if watching him. Now he was away from the house and could think more clearly, he saw Maxine's face in his mind, eyes closed, lips moving in prayer while the Mayor gave it to her. To Willie, this inverted incest, with the father getting to act out the son's fantasies, was all the healer's doing. When Willie turned away and walked back into the trees, he was already working on a plan to repay the healer.

TAPE 45

On this tape we'll look at how God can be composed of every kind of experience, every level of understanding, every facet of awareness, as well as every bit of ignorance, every shade of evil, and every color of all the other ways that consciousness can be.

We already looked at God as a man-made by-product of the genetic survival instinct, and we looked at Ed's Corporate God notion, aka the hierarchy of consciousness. Plain common sense says you'd be crazy to stick with a man-made God invented by primitive fears and superstitions, but common sense is in short supply where religion is involved. While we occupy a monkey suit, the cause of those primitive fears and superstitions - the need to survive in a material world - is part of the package; its roots go deep into our subconscious where those primitive fears and superstitions are still very much alive and kicking.

Sure, we might harbor more sophisticated aspirations about ourselves, God and whatever, along with ideas like compassion, tolerance and cooperation, but those immaterial concepts are constantly undermined and overridden, often blatantly ignored in favor of more pressing material demands that obscure a Real view of God.

How can we escape these material demands, when our senses of perception and brain are made from atoms? From the deepest subconscious levels through our everyday consciousness, we're convinced reality is a material experience. We're incapable of imagining a reality that isn't material.

For that inescapable reason, even if we say God is a 'spiritual' experience (somehow more than material), our materially based perception of reality tells us that if we don't *feel* something *physical*, in our heart or gut (in the atoms our body/brain is made from), our experience of God isn't *'real'*.

Remember, we're in human form only because our consciousness isn't yet ready to recognize itself as an immaterial force; we need this material 'reality' to reflect our Real, immaterial self back at us so we can learn to recognize our Real, conscious selves as something *more* Real than materiality. The problem is, God as a man-made by-product of genetic survival prevents us from doing that.

The plain, unpalatable truth is that most of our ideas about God, even now, are no more than word of mouth hearsay that over the centuries have gotten embroidered by God-only-knows how many people into full scale religions. All we have is someone else's notion of what God is. We're prescribed a pre-packed, standardized, sanitized version of God, and we're not meant to think outside of that version. Deluded by material reality, we've come to expect too much of the God we created out of this material reality, and too little of our Real, conscious selves as aspects of an immaterial yet infinitely more Real God. That Real God is the one we're going to look at now. Ready?

We already know that an immensely powerful yet immaterial force exists in the universe. We experience it every day, yet need no blind leap of faith to believe in it. Yep - our own consciousness. It interfaces material reality, but it's *more* Real than materiality.

Do I need to explain that our conscious awareness of material reality is what gives it meaning and purpose? Or that only consciousness gives anything the potential to become *more* - more useful, more worthwhile, more *meaningful* - than it was before you thought about it? Okay then. So why do we demean ourselves by reducing all of the meaning, purpose and reason for our conscious existence, to the material level? Why do we try to satisfy these genetic bodies by enslaving our Real, conscious selves just to suit the demands of mindless biology?

Hell sure, you'll deny those things are true. You'll say something along the lines of: 'God is the meaning, purpose and reason for our existence,' and a million other empty phrases, but nothing that *means* anything or positively addresses the problems we make for ourselves and each other.

So let's dump the rhetoric and get Real about God by seeing the concrete proof of how God is working through every one of us all of the time. We'll also see how God can be immaterial yet simultaneously *more* Real than material things. How? By being an *idea*.

Start with the fact that there is nothing more (and nothing less) than ideas. Ideas are the most powerful things there are. Everything that exists represents a great big idea made from many smaller ideas. Ideas are free to expand and explore without inhibitions (unless somebody tries to limit them), and they're unique to consciousness.

So yes, I'm saying God is a great big idea made from many smaller ideas.

Now combine 'God as ideas' with the notion that each of us is a tiny aspect of God. What that combination gives us is a God comprising the collective ideas of every conscious being in this or any other universe. God as the entire environment of ideas. God as an unimaginably vast, inconceivably rich interactive network of awarenesses, materially indefinable (until we put our ideas into material form) yet total, accessible on whatever level your consciousness has reached.

Think of this God as ideas, aka the universe-wide corporate consciousness, as a force that's been around for, uh, well, forever. Big Bangs or whatever are no more than day following night for this God. As a result, the God of ideas has evolved limitless cumulative mental abilities. This is God as an unimaginably potent collective mind, a superconsciousness capable of stuff so far in advance of our understanding, it could be millions of years before we even get close to that understanding. The ability to create and influence material phenomena just by thinking would be a walk in the park for this corporate superconsciousness/God.

Yet at the same time, this God is also a combination of ideas that depend for their existence on the minds that have them. (By 'ideas' I also mean all of the knowledge, understanding and awareness in back of those ideas.) As all of those ideas in minds, all of that conscious knowledge, understanding and awareness, God becomes the most potent 'something' imaginable, without actually being any 'thing'.

As a little piece of this God, the Real, conscious you - the non-material environment of ideas - is able to grow and evolve into an increasingly bigger piece of God. This God is an entity of endless ideas that you're forever growing to accommodate. An infinite understanding that you're trying to become, to 'realize'. And in becoming that understanding as you continually become more of God, God also becomes more of you. There are no boundaries around pure ideas or pure consciousness. They all merge into one. The only thing preventing that merger are our own limitations.

All of the questions we ask about things began with the early components of the material universe, each representing the question: *"What am I?"* Those components represented self-interest in its simplest form because they represented materiality at its simplest.

Even when conscious organisms got around to asking that same question in more complicated ways, the question was still motivated by self-interest. You still want to know about things for the sake of your own survival.

Yet at the same time, as a little piece of evolving, universal consciousness, you're also asking questions on God's behalf. That amounts to God asking the same questions you are, through you. God, as all of the consciousness in the universe, is asking all of the questions they're asking. And you know what? You and they are all part of the ongoing, open-ended answer.

With all of the above in mind, think what happens when people use fossilized, materially-derived notions of religion and God for their own purposes. I mean the pretentious, self-important statements trapped in holy books, supposedly uttered by God Himself. Besides removing the ongoing, open-ended feature of our conscious evolution, those narrow attitudes can prevent us from asking new questions - about God, ourselves, anything.

Religion is famous for its refusal to allow its dogmas to change or be deviated from, for the survival reasons we looked at earlier. Name me another collection of ideas that have been preserved in amber as long as those of religion. And these are ideas people try to live by, for Christ's sake!

Can those unchanging rules and traditions help your consciousness evolve? No. They're a straight-jacket for helping people-as-genes get by in a material environment. That kind of religion actually works against the Real evolution of who it's meant to help. It's why so many people just love getting offended on God's behalf, or feel compelled to use their self-appointed status - God's Personal Offence-Taker - as a weapon against anybody with different religious ideas and opinions.   God as an evolving idea is just too big to fit inside minds narrowed by genetic ME & MINE FIRST survival considerations. And it's no good shutting this book and carrying on like you always did, because people who don't want to know, don't want to grow.

Consider this: The number 1 tenet of all serious religions forbids us to kill, and yet people have always been ready to do precisely that to uphold those very beliefs and what they represent. How'd you explain that most wars are fought by people who believe in a God who says that killing is the primary sin? The explanation is that people make their own rules to save their genetic ass.

Recall JC saying 'Turn the other cheek'? The only time I ever saw anybody do that was in a movie and it was only acting. Incidentally, 'turning the other cheek' has a multiplicity of sub-meanings. One is about opening up to new ideas. (Think about it.) Likewise when JC said not to go around beating up on people and suchlike, he meant even people who don't agree with your ideas about God. He said, 'Love thy neighbor' too. He meant unconditionally. If your own particular religion's spokespersons for Reality said something contradictory to those things, boy, you got the wrong spokesperson and the wrong reality.

Now read these words for me: Religious intolerance. Religious bigotry. Religious dogma. Religious indoctrination. Religious propaganda. Religious persecution. Religious war. (Feel free to add a few religious words of your own.) Take that religious prefix away and you're left with some excellent examples of how religion helps DNA-as-people do their genes' dirty work. That list of ancient social ills was with us long before prefixes were invented, religious or otherwise. Could those ills hinder an *evolving* relationship with the idea of God? You bet your ass they could. (Or the one you covet that belongs to your neighbor.)

Religion can also be a vindictive and vengeful indictment of other people's beliefs, their behavior, their very existence! Killing other people for God, or inciting that in others, getting offended for God, expressing God's disapproval - those are just authoritative-sounding excuses for looking out for yourself-as-DNA, or the tribe, nation or whatever you're affiliated to for your survival.

There are folks with minds so narrow you can hear the two sides shut together if somebody suggests that organisms still trying to clean the primordial slime off their shoes, mightn't yet have the complete answer to the Ultimate Question. Somehow you know those folks aren't too interested in compassion, sympathy, charity or tolerance, even when those words are right there in their own scriptures.

Most of us are totally ignorant of what comes before birth or after death (and not too sure of what's going on during life), yet we're conceited enough to imagine *our* religion gives us access to the only true God.

Now just hold on while I get this Reality Window open. (I gave it a lick of paint to hide the rot and the darn thing's stuck)...There. See that bright idea on the horizon? Well take off those goddam gene-colored glasses! That idea uniting *all* classes, races, creeds, colors and flavors? Helping us all evolve together as enlightened consciousness? Does your religion do that, or is it a stupid dogma that ain't even house-trained?

TAPE 46

Many of the folks who came to hear the healer went away disappointed or angry because they didn't want to hear the Real truth; all they wanted was confirmation of what they already believed. For others he might as well have been speaking in Esperanto. For them, it wasn't simply a case of 'none so deaf as those who will not hear,' but of those who don't know *how* to hear...because the healer was using the language of big R Reality.

To understand that language you have to think beyond your old notions of small r material reality. Quit trying to think about these words with your heart, sex organs, feet, instincts, political leanings, religious superstitions, wallet, or any other genetic diversion. Imagine you're reading this not as the monkey suit that genes built for themselves, but as a visiting consciousness that's merely observing.

Helpful hint: the moment you feel any disagreement with or antagonism for what I'm saying, ask yourself - "Am I disagreeing/being antagonistic because Henhouse is saying something to threaten the security of my genetic body/brain, or those of my genetic relatives? Or am I disagreeing because the

Real, conscious me genuinely thinks that what's being said is disadvantageous to the human race as something *more* than genes?"

What's up, squarehead? Can't fit a few new ideas in because all of that genetic furniture (tradition, myth, superstition, habit and the rest) is cluttering up your mind? So have a mental garage sale. Dump the junk. Think of yourself as a computer whose memory is filled with old, outdated files that need deleting, then hit 'delete'. Otherwise you'll stop learning, growing and evolving. Or did you stop already? You got the one right answer and all of the others are wrong? If that's you, mister, you're going noplace. You probably won't even bother reading this because you already know everything.

For everyone else, the big R Reality the healer was promoting exists regardless of everything we know and love in the small r reality of geneland. Big R Reality was around long before you and your beliefs, and would still exist even if you and your beliefs, this planet and everything on it had never existed.

Imagine an ancient 'old master' painted in oils. Since the original artist made that statement, countless others have daubed at it, trying to make it look the way they see things, so now the picture is so obscured, the original artist's statement has become unrecognizable. Well that's how notions about big R Reality, as expressed by a few genuine messengers over the millennia, have gotten confused and perverted by this genetic, small r reality. Then along comes the healer and puts a present-day slant on things. (There's no need for the message itself to change because the principles of Reality don't change.) But nor do people looking out for their ass, their thought processes clogged by ingrained layers of dogma, superstition and misinformation. Most folks coming to see the healer already had their likes and dislikes set in holy concrete. When you traveled maybe a few hundred miles to check out somebody you saw on TV who reputedly has the charisma to gather and hold a crowd with just a few quiet words, it's kind of aggravating to discover that some of the things he's saying challenge your most deeply-held beliefs and fundamentalist motivations.

The healer's version of Reality ran straight into all of the prejudices and illusions that being a dork for DNA had piled up inside everybody. Folks had become blind to the simple truth that Reality is not about materiality and being genetic. But the message is nothing in word form; it has to be turned into *deeds*. Words amount to squat without selfless actions: Kindness. Generosity. Charity. All of that stuff. Sure they sound like old hat, but they work the same wonders they always did. I don't mean the watered-down versions that most folks imagine is kindness, generosity, charity and what have you, where the ultimate beneficiary turns out to be ME or MINE. Remember what we're talking about here: something that transcends material gain.

I probably said this before - maybe I got a gene for repeating myself - but one of the craziest traits human beings exhibit is to cry out for progress, change for the better, a future we can feel confident about. Then somebody explains how to get and keep those things and what do we do? We react with our ass instead of our head...

The tape ends kind've abruptly just there (I fell asleep) so I'm gonna open this pocket bible again, jump in with both feet and analyze the whole thing in evolutionary biological terms.

The hell I am! With this headache? Instead I'm going to ask some awkward questions. Let's say you genuinely want your relationship with God to be spiritual and not just an excuse to be selfish for your genes. So how do you justify prioritizing YOU and YOURS over and above other people? How is that 'spiritual'? Selfishly prioritizing yourself and your offspring is the cause of all humanity's problems, so how do you explain the fact that it conflicts with religious tenets about unselfishness, brotherhood, compassion, etc., supposedly advocated by God?

The simple (minded) way to slide around those questions (you probably don't even appreciate their implications) is to say that this is all God's idea. Blame your selfish behavior on God. God created us, God wants it to be this way. It's part of God's Masterplan, beyond our comprehension, and who are we to question Him? I bet you also imagine 'go forth and multiply' means the same as 'love they neighbor'!

Get Real! If you're going forth and multiplying for God, why, instead of selfishly prioritizing *your* offspring through personal vested interest, don't you put the same value on *everybody?* If you're doing all of this procreating because God said so, where did all of this selfish MY, ME, MINE stuff come from?

The truth is, you're not doing any of it for God. You prove that by demanding offspring as a personal right, then prioritizing them over anybody else just because YOU had them and they're YOURS. This mindless urge to reproduce and be selfish for genes is NOT about you having a spiritual relationship with God, it's the exact opposite: It's you making up your own rules, religious and otherwise, so you can continue being a slave to your stupid hormones.

224

But as I was saying, can you imagine the healer, trying to translate the higher practicalities of Reality into this small r reality? He had him a communication problem even before he opened his mouth. Ever tried explaining color to a congenitally blind person? Well this isn't about using your eyes to see color, it's about learning to see through the delusions you're born into.

We like to imagine we have ideas about things before we act, because that's a vital part of what makes us human (unlike 'lower' animals who act from instinct and primitive urges). 'Having ideas' means translating the stuff of material reality into thought-form so we can be creative with them. In thought-form, material objects become what they were all along without our realizing it - not separate things but all part of the same idea.

If that sounds weird, recall that material things are all part of the same thing at bottom: *energy*. When they're outside of you, the material objects made from this energy seem like solid 'things'. But when you translate the material objects of 4-D reality into idea form, they become mutable and malleable. The only limit on what you can do with material objects in your conscious environment, is your imagination. And it's precisely because they're all part of the *same* idea that you can figure out new ways to relate them to each other.

What idea is everything part of? *Consciousness*, evolving into more refined dimensions of Reality where I, ME, MINE considerations don't intrude, and genetic just rhymes with pathetic.

Talk of higher, more refined dimensions of Reality will still sound like baloney for some people, so think: How does the football game get to be a two dimensional display on your TV? You don't see those moving pictures getting sucked into the camera, or flying through the air to your TV. And what about satellite broadcasts? They get bounced back from out there in space for Christ's sake, and no wires or anything! Those moving, three-D pictures of a real four-D football game would have been black magic or witchcraft (other words for ignorance) a few years back. Imagine - burned at the stake for watching the televised Superbowl.

The Real witchcraft ain't in the technology; that's just laws of physics, and they don't create technology on their own. The Real witchcraft is all in the *consciousness* that manipulates physics laws to create the technology. Those TV pictures that you can't see or hear till they're decoded by your receiver are kind of like capital R Reality, which is also invisible until you have enough consciousness to decode it. Get enough Reality and you'll learn how to separate your consciousness from your genetic ass. Your Real, conscious self will begin to outgrow the need for the restrictions of DNA's chemical monkey outfit, or the material dimensions it confines your understanding to.

Going back to the healer, even Jesus Christ couldn't please all of the people all of the time, they were too busy pleasing themselves. (In my experience, pleasing just one of the people some of the time is a minor miracle.) Which reminds me of a lady I overheard at the wilderness.

This is America, and anyplace there's a regular crowd there are also burgers, hotdogs, ice-cream, popcorn, newspapers, sex, drugs, rock 'n' roll, and god-only-knows what else, and it's all for sale. Anyhow the lady I overheard, who was grossly fat, had just been to get a look at the healer. Carefully managing to overhear what she told her equally fat husband, it transpired that she was not entirely satisfied with the experience.

"He didn't give me what I wanted," she told him.

"Uh? No chili-dogs?"

"Shut your mouth. I just been to get my fortune told by the healer-man and he didn't even know my starsign!"

I'm no seer, but even I knew her starsign: it was Fatso the Flabmonster. I could just see the headline on my next Star piece: SLOB STUMPS SEER.

Then off she went again straightaway on an infinitely more important mission - to find the chili-dog man.

All kinds of people were visiting the wilderness. I guess it was like those original Sermons On The Mount, or do I mean Christ talking to the multitudes? We also had a few of the other things they had for the first Coming: folks peddling handicrafts, others doing drugs, or lighting illegal barbecues, or running crap-games. There were even a few hookers. The whole thing had become a money-making exercise, so-called free enterprise being the American Way.

Maybe you were one of those opportunist entrepreneurs? If so, you'll know there was no need for any miraculous sharing-out of loaves and fishes – but maybe that was just as well; the people hawking all the food and drink would've had something to say about it - especially after the healer had his helpers talk those hawkers into providing trash cans and disposal sacks and stuff for all the garbage. (That junk would have choked a landfill all of its own.)

Speaking of landfills, the healer had a few things to say about the way we waste the earth's resources. He probably read my TRASHVILLE

TENNESSEE article like everybody else. America does have a garbage crisis. And remember, what America has today, the rest of the world wants tomorrow. There are over 3,000 landfills in America and they're rapidly filling to the brim. Over seventy percent of US garbage goes in those landfills, despite recycling efforts by a few brave eco-warriors.

I made a notation here about the local burger franchise offering to sponsor the healer if he endorsed their *Feeding of the five-thousand* promotion. Can you believe that? Sure you can, even though I made it up, because you know how crazy the profit motive makes people. Can you believe this though? The healer got his helpers to suggest that all the garbage-generating peddlers in the wilderness work with Unicef and Oxfam and Amnesty, and help feed the people who really need it - at their own expense! Imagine.

Hell no, that didn't happen either. But don't think I'm not sniping at you; everybody's to blame for being profligate. Most times the halos only get aired when somebody's watching. See, we consume the same way we behave in every other area of life: hypocritically, as if it's a whole bunch of other guys being greedy and competing with each other to gobble up the planet's natural resources like there's no tomorrow. Jesus Christ, guys, there'll be no tomorrow if we carry on looking for somebody else to blame. It's *you* who's greedy, *you* who's being profligate with something that was meant for everybody's life-support. *You're* the one shutting your eyes and your mind and pretending we got rich and comfortable and fat by being kind and generous and fair.

Yeah, it's YOU I'm looking at: Mister ME FIRST. The one hiding behind the alias of Mister Who, Me? when the finger points. It's YOU who thinks that doing a little recycling can make up for all the mindless gluttony that created this desperate need to recycle in the first place.

Believe it or not, besides all of the people out there who know they're Mister Greedy yet don't care, there are still more who don't possess enough brain cells to even realize that GIMME is their middle name. They're just not capable of thinking about the amount of stuff they're using up. Somebody has to legislate some sense into them. It's the only way.

The healer's primary concern, though, was how we waste our most valuable resource: ourselves and each other. Only he was speaking that special language of Reality, whereas I have to make do with being semi-literate. (It's okay. I know my limitations.) I'd just come up with a new Star piece: TRASH OR TOURISM? PLACE YOUR BETS. The opening paragraph said: 'Which gifthorse is your money on - a hole in the ground, or a holy man?' It was intended as a kind of mini-poll to discover whether locals making a pile from tourism would keep out the landfill and the jobs it could bring.

I was thinking about that when I met Andrew DeSoto, the Sheriff's deputy who was scared of cops. Andrew was okay right up until he saw the truck connect with J the B. Then something happened. The trauma translated into a conscious need for Andrew to relate with a member of the opposite sex and reproduce his genes while there was still time. Now he was wandering around the wilderness, seeing all of those people with other people when he was alone, and wishing he could meet Miss Right.

I'll let you look through my Reality Window. Somewhere in amongst all of those new visitors to Raiment County was Andrew's Miss Right.

The next person I stumbled over was Donna Hughes, telling some folks from up east just what the healer had meant by being generous with their own property instead of with other people's, because everything rightfully belonged to everybody - or words to that effect. Donna saw me and broke off from her explanation.

"Hi, Laurie." She seemed to be enjoying herself. "Some crowd we got here today."

The way she said 'we' made me think how much she'd changed. Maybe the 'little sister' had grown up some. Maybe there was copy in it.

"Some crowd. You mean this circus?" I said, thinking she might laugh, but all she did was smile politely as though I'd said something wrong.

I tried again: "Hey, I just caught the edge of your little talk with the folks there. You the healer's interpreter these days or what?" Suddenly I was lost in her company.

"I'm just helping any way I can," she said, as light as if I'd asked her if she liked ice-cream. Then she got melodramatically serious, which I thought was her horsing around, but wasn't.

"Some of these here folks are kinda embarrassed to go see him in person, Laurie, so they need encouragement. They're kind've scared to look him in the eye, the way I used to be, y'know?"

Used to be? Donna really had changed. But I knew what she meant by scared. That close-up of him I got through the camera still registered sharp in my memory.

"Mind if I ask you something straight out, Donna?" I was trying to hold a pleasant expression on my face. "The uh, healer…did he recruit you?" Knowing as much as the next person about the bad press given to religious

228

cults, I was still undecided about what the healer was trying to do. Hell, I was Laurie Hendricks, alias Doubting Thomas with a Masters in Cynicism.

Donna surprised me by laughing out loud and grasping my wrists and bringing my hands together and saying, "It's okay Laurie," so earnestly I almost believed it *was* okay. Then she let go my wrists and dropped her gaze modestly. When her eyes leapt back up to mine there were tears in hers, but happy tears.

"No, he didn't recruit me. I recruited myself."

If you could've seen my face at that moment, I'd sure love to know what it looked like. There was so much of my younger self in Donna that I was getting all choked up just looking at her. Hell, I felt *joyful* right along with her, and joyful was not part of my vocabulary. Only the seriousness of it stopped it being funny.

I gazed around at the sea of pilgrims religiously stuffing their faces with junk-food, chastising their rowdy kids, tossing their empty coke cans and Walton-family-size popcorn cartons everywhere.

I didn't really take in any of that though; the dark side of me was too busy torturing my sugar 'n' spice alter-ego into admitting the healer was a charlatan out for himself. I didn't believe somebody called God arranged for guys to come amongst us with divine messages.

I remember excusing myself and striding off someplace where I could continue fighting myself in private. I stumbled into and over people, wondering why didn't I have the presence of mind to capture on tape Donna's little sneak-attack on my credulity? Had something gotten to me? Or was I just angry at not recording what she said because I might've been able to use it for The Star, and maybe for this book too? I'd gone a little out of focus and it was hard to think clearly. When you're standing over a fissure separating tried and trusted reality from something you never experienced before, you should never look straight down. And I was doing just that.

TAPE 47

I keep talking about the 'big R Reality' of consciousness (as opposed to this small r material reality), but there are many levels of conscious development, so big R Reality is a relative term. Imagine a universal sliding scale of consciousness. The more you evolve, the higher you go on that scale, and the more consciously aware you become. I go into the various aspects of big R

Reality elsewhere. Right here I'm going to look at a practical aspect of big R Reality for general issue.

Okay. When you've evolved far enough to begin to appreciate that selfishness (and the other traits surrounding it) are just you looking out for your genetic ass, something interesting dawns on you: you realize that the *opposites* of selfishness - compassion, empathy, love and various other 'giving' things - are not what you thought they were.

For instance, you might think that compassion, empathy, love and etc - the requirements of genuine unselfishness - are *feelings*, right? *Emotions*, yeah? Well they're not. Recall what feelings actually are: sensations caused in nerves by chemistry looking out for itself, without even knowing it's doing that. Now recall what emotions are: The consciousness that's just passing through, confusing itself with those mindless sensations, becoming deluded and getting ensnared by the demands of self-centered biology.

Throughout the whole of human evolution, a physical body's survival demands have dictated what and how your mind should think. Driven by those survival demands, you refer to this matter-over-mind control as *being practical*. What you actually mean is, being practical about your own survival as genetic DNA. What could be more 'practical' than looking out for your ass?

But...evolve some more, overcome that downside-up notion, and you realize that Real compassion, Real selflessness and Real forgiveness, are created *not* by survival feelings in a material body, but by your consciousness acting *against* the feelings and urges in a body. (Example: when you help somebody else entirely for *their* sake, without needing any form of material reward or recognition, simply because your understanding of Reality bypassed all of that genetic interference.)

Real compassion, Real selflessness, Real forgiveness, Real tolerance, Real love and etc., are *not* subject to the vagaries of chemical-driven feeling. Deluding yourself they're the same thing is like imagining that material love (the instinct-driven circus devoted to keeping genes replicating) is the same as Real, non-physical love.

In this narrow genetic reality, trying to make Real practicality work in everyday life can seem like pushing water uphill. But in higher dimensions of Reality, practicalities like compassion, sympathy, love and stuff like that are the ONLY Reality, the building blocks of everything that exists.

Reality Window: It was when I made Ed explain those 'higher dimensions of Reality' that he presented me with the earlier explanation of our subtle 'bodies' made from different frequencies of consciousness energy. The Russian dolls thing? If that still sounds a might too fanciful (as in bullshit), be aware that this same system of energy levels in your body are linked by a series of energy channels that are used in acupuncture, reflexology and other therapies. It's only when something interrupts this energy flow that we develop illness, disease, pain.

While that threw a new light on these monkey outfits with their archaic plumbing and constant maintenance requirements, it didn't explain what happens after you transcend the need for a monkey suit altogether.

So imagine two people standing side by side. Both appear human, yet one can be hardly more than a hairless orangutan with a hundred rungs still to climb up the evolutionary ladder on this particular plane of materiality. (Each rung will require a trip back to this material plane, though not necessarily this planet.) But the person standing beside him has already climbed all of those rungs and is about to step off the top of that ladder into a more refined level, where its consciousness will dress for an even subtler plane of materiality, because this consciousness learned all of the lessons on this material level.

See, even on this level of materiality there can be a world of difference between how conscious people are, and so how they perceive and interact with everything.

Now I want to say more about Real practicality, and how on higher Reality levels before life and after death, everything is a natural function of Real compassion, Real empathy, Real love, Real selflessness and so on - Real practicalities, uninfluenced by genetic demands.

For you to make those Real practicalities work in the here and now, you have to become a living embodiment of what they stand for. Folks who're heading in the right direction don't think about words like compassion, empathy, love and selflessness, or sit around discussing the ins and outs of being those. They don't get together with a lot of other folks and march around singing about it. People who practice being a living embodiment of those Real practicalities - as far as you can be while in a monkey suit - just keep quiet and get on with doing Real practical things and setting an *unselfish* example.

Want a simple rule of thumb? In the same way selfishness encapsulates the downsides of being genetic, unselfishness encapsulates how anybody can be Really practical. As a piece of Real practicality unselfishness beats any amount of philosophizing, bible punching or hymn singing.

Religious or not, if you wanna see "a beam of light in the darkness", *make* one - be unselfish. Being unselfish means you're acting above the influence of materiality, above primitive human notions of God and religion. Much of religion has gotten shaped around our own best interests anyhow. And I'm taking about everybody's religion, because everybody is genes.

You want to talk sacred to genes? Talk ME, ME, ME. That's the subliminal language written in great big letters in your genome.

TAPE 48

You own a gun? If not, you're in the American minority, so chances are you wouldn't have liked what the healer said about the right to bear arms. I heard this from Matt after he put his own slant on it, but it originated with the healer, so you're getting it third-hand. (How many hands did your gun pass through on its way to you? How much blood was on them, I wonder?)

Am I subtle or what? Anyhow there was this young guy listening to Matt who objected to what he was saying.

"You agree with that stuff about guns, boy?" The guy could well have been younger than Matt, but he was using the down-home form of address to point-up his opposition. "You think we should rewrite the Constitution of these United States to satisfy a minority element? You think that's what democratic people should do?"

I could hear all the unspoken arguments of someone who doesn't take kindly to being asked not to do something that might erode his personal 'freedom' to get pleasure at the expense of another creature's life.

"Yes, I think we should re-write the Constitution," Matt told him. "A Constitution should *never* be an unimpeachable icon."

Damn right it shouldn't! (This is me talking now.) Why? For the same reasons that religions and notions of God shouldn't either (it impedes evolution). Especially if those Constitutions have Second Amendments giving people the right to bear arms. Check the homicide figures. But can you imagine what would happen if you tried amending that particular amendment to rewrite the right to bear arm out of it? Somebody'd probably shoot you. Planet Psycho? I said it.

After that stuff about Constitutions not being sacrosanct, Matt added: "Any life is more sacrosanct than a written Constitution, and legislation that says otherwise is failing in the most important part of its job."

232

"Well Jesus H. Christ, boy," the other guy came back at him, "What happens when the other fella tries to rob me, or rape my wife, or molest my kids? I just stand aside and let him?"

Before I go on with that I'm gonna say two things about the subject myself, surprise surprise. Don't panic; this is short and sweet. (Well it's short.) First, anyone who needs to be told that life was not created for us to go around killing it, shouldn't be let loose anyplace near a gun. And second, once everybody understands that we only ever kill anything because we're too dumb not to, they'll have a serious reason to stop making guns altogether. Now I can finish Matt's answer to that particular moron, which was as follows:

"The Bill of Rights legislates for people to have guns by saying a militia is necessary for the security of a free state, and for that reason the right of the people to keep and bear arms shall not be infringed. The few simple words in that straight quote may have made some kind of sense in 1791, but that was more than two hundred years ago, when a free state meant wearing swords and owning human slaves. Some of those misguided 'freedoms' have been phased out, but the freedom to bear arms has gotten way out of control.

"The Bill of Rights should not be an obstacle to the most important freedom anybody has - to stay alive without having somebody stick you up, or take pot-shots at you. Yet it seems the only way a piece of legislation can uphold that freedom adequately, without leaving the barn door wide open to natural human weakness, is by reversing that two hundred years old decision whose consequences couldn't have been foreseen.

"A society that doesn't have a policy aimed at phasing guns out of the civilian population should make it their policy. Without it, we're as good as at war with ourself. We have to be mature enough to curtail our own freedom to behave irresponsibly."

Jeez, and I thought I went on about stuff. I especially liked the 'freedom is a responsibility' idea. Anyhow I agree with all that business about any so-called 'legal right' that allows for guns to be acquired with the same ease as automobiles being a legal wrong, even if it is couched in something so grand-sounding as The 2nd Amendment to The Bill of Rights of The Constitution of The United States of America. This is a legalized lack of concern for life we're talking about.

As for all you brave 'hunters' out there who epitomize the 'free' spirit of a proud nation, and all of that crap, what you actually epitomize is the refusal to quit being a savage, or to grow up and get Real!

Did what Matt was saying make a dent in that young guy? Leave me alone! Guns were a religion with him, and nobody was gonna interfere with that gun-worship. Even while he was saying something entirely different, the message I heard loud and clear was, "Now don't argue with me on this 'cause I got me a gun too."

Okay, so I'm being flippant considering the gravity of the material, but life's too funereal anyway. (It would be a lot less funereal without guns.) And like I said, while Matt was saying his piece, I was watching the other guy and imagining I could see blind, stubborn resentment glowing dark red in his center. Where was all of that amazing smartness human beings are supposed to have that other animals don't? As for compassion, tolerance and the rest, that guy probably thought those were invented for him to negotiate with; to trade with for his own good if the need ever arose. More weapons that he could just open the closet and bring out selectively.

Think I'm being too hard on him? Listen, his own brand of 'compassion' would get dusted off if he saw some frail old lady who reminded him of his grandma, because she used to bake blueberry pie specially for him, and stuff like that. (The fact that she only did that because he had some of her genes is totally relevant here.) Other times, his idea of 'unselfishness' got an airing if he needed sex from his wife, and had to give her something in return. Like a house to live in, food on the table, and the prospect of sending her own genes down the line. There are countless other, less obvious but still contributory bits of icing on the gene-cake everybody wants their share of.

Even though I'm simplifying this so guys like him can understand it, which makes it sound simplistic to the more enlightened, people like him do exist in great numbers. Folks who wouldn't do anything with, to, or for anybody if they were not getting something for themself. Even the most brainless members of the animal kingdom look like they're doing things *for* their fellows, but that ain't even close to being Real unselfishness; it's just more of the same stupid, mindless, instinctive old replication process.

So I repeat: to be Real, altruism has to be for somebody else *regardless* of, or better still, *instead* of you and yours getting something out of the transaction. That Real potential is right there in everybody. It's recognizable through finally understanding that 'your' kids and other genetic relatives, and even you yourself, don't deserve any better treatment than anyone else and 'their' genes. Understanding that is the only way Real equality will ever happen. But it doesn't just fall in your goddam lap. You have to work at it!

234

Okay, I'm almost done here. So that young guy's argument about protecting himself and his family was precisely what I've been saying about genes. His family *were* his genes, but he'd never thought of it that way. Even if he did, it wouldn't have meant anything. His kids weren't DNA for God's sake! DNA was just something that gave people inherited diseases and stuff.

Clinging to ignorance that way is how and why supposedly sane, thinking people fight for, achieve, and protect selfish, subjective freedoms like the right of civilians to bear arms. Just never forget, accidentally or on purpose, that no matter how smart, or sensitive, accomplished, religious, sophisticated, handsome, cool, brave, or anything else you are, if you have a gun, you're also a potential killer. See, you *did* forget. Hey! *Wake up!* (Jesus Christ, doctor, I think we're losing this one!)

I'm not criticizing what some well-meaning people wrote in the US Constitution. What I'm criticizing is any and every decision, anywhere, that advertently or inadvertently downgrades or threatens human and other life.

Did I say dump The US Constitution? I did not. You know what I've been saying all along: start dumping the part of *you* that's responsible for maintaining lunatic, holy-cow Constitutional rights at the cost of something nobody has any right to violate: *life*. Until everybody does that, nobody's rights are unchallengeable. They have to be forever subject to improvement, never etched in stone. Legislation, like religion, should only ever be a means to an end, not the end itself. Mistaking the means for the end is one of humanity's BIG mistakes.

I wasn't altogether sure if I should use any of that material for The Star or this book. I know reticence doesn't sound like me, yet things were being said - like Matt wanting to change the US Constitution - that I felt pretty strongly about myself.

Aw hell, I cannot tell a lie. The real reason I thought twice about using this stuff was that by appearing to take a stance on such a hot-potato issue as the right to bear arms, and blowing holes in the US Constitution, I might jeopardize the sales potential of this book. Then I imagined what Ed would've said. I always do that when I'm uncertain about stuff.

TAPE 49

'*I think, therefore I am,*' is a quote from Rene Descartes, the famous French mathematician and philosopher. Descartes figured that our mind, though immaterial, is the only part of us we can definitely say is Real. He must've been reading my notes. Descartes also said that as minds, we're made from stuff called awareness. As awareness we're uniquely qualified to appreciate that our mind and our mental experiences are real. But being *only* the stuff of minds, we're not the material things that surround them (which includes bodies/brains), so we can't pronounce on the realness of those material things with any authority. Now read that over a few times.

Like me, Descartes was pointing up the fundamental difference between mindless material things that just 'are', and our uniquely conscious selves that 'know' we are, and are uniquely able to think about why. These notions are where the expression Cartesian Dualism comes from. (Dual = two: mind and matter.) When Descartes used the word 'mind' he meant consciousness. You're right, I did explain somewhere they're not the same thing.

Descartes wanted people to quit being doggedly determined to see consciousness and material things as part of the same 'reality'. Only by seeing them as two different realities that intermingle (and influence each other) can you appreciate the fundamental differences between the absence of meaning inherent in mindless material things, and the meanings that consciousness gives to those things. (Better reread that too.)

Your brain is a prime example. As fundamentally unaware components it was never meant to run by itself, any more than your car was. Like more primitive brains that do mostly run on auto-pilot, your brain is capable of plenty of autonomic (self-organizing) stuff. But like your car it would cause havoc without input from a conscious driver.

The important factor is not how the components of your brain work (or in most cases draw welfare). What matters is what that mechanical brain is capable of when the conscious YOU is in control of it. The less input there is from you, the more opportunity that brain has to influence your thinking.

It's true. The interface between non-conscious brain processes and our consciousness works both ways. Brain machinery can have just as profound an influence on our thinking, as our thinking has on it. Why'd you imagine religious nuts kill themselves and other people, thinking they'll be rewarded with a glorious afterlife? Worse yet, an afterlife where their lusts (the products of the most primitive earthly appetites) will be satisfied by a God who rewards depraved disregard for the very lives that He created! You'd be out of your mind to think that kind of twisted behavior was condoned by God. (Although I imagine the guy downstairs would approve wholeheartedly.)

To imagine that God would encourage you to commit atrocities under any circumstances is the result of trying to live as a collective of mindless and uncaring components that I call *the monkey suit*, and you, in your deluded state of reality, call *yourself*.

Coming back from the tangent I just went off on, it's because consciousness tries so goddam hard to be something that ain't conscious (a body/brain) that creates such powerful delusions, about all kinds of things. These delusions manifest as hatred, vengeance and homicide and the rest. I don't need to remind you how powerful these delusions are. Even when they tell us that murder is somehow the 'right' way to achieve peace, unity, progress, enlightenment or some glorious afterlife, we believe them.

Recall Ed's genetic morality? (Good for genetic survival is 'right', bad for genetic survival is 'wrong'.) That survival morality is behind the influence that a material body and brain have on our consciousness. In people with poor control of their body/brain, it can create the delusion that murder is right. (Legally sanctioned murder by judicial systems is itself the result of insufficient conscious understanding that the influence of these bodies and brains predisposes us to the primitive doctrine that says 'good for genetic survival is 'right', bad for genetic survival is 'wrong'.)

Going back to Descartes, you maybe heard the expression 'Ghost in the machine'. That was how a Brit philosopher named Gilbert Ryle described Descartes' notion that our mind haunts a biomechanical brain. Ryle thought Descartes was nuts. He knows better now. (Mom, he's dead.)

Being dead, aka between lives, is where you get to learn some Real home truths. People like Descartes, with ideas before their time, always get labeled nutty. Except that Descartes wasn't just ahead of his time, he was ahead of yours too if you still don't realize that consciousness ain't just something you have, it's what you *are!* Everything else is just propaganda.

Reality Widow. (There's that damn sticky 'n' key again.) Actually that Ryle guy was right about consciousness being a ghost in a machine, but if you don't believe in ghosts you won't believe in your own consciousness as a thing in its own right.

Well hey, when people talk about believing in themself, the *self* they're talking about is the ass that's guaranteed to up and die in a few years. They're so in love with that mindless ass, they worship it and everything it stands for. Living as that genetic ass is familiar, safe, reassuring. Merging into a crowd of genetic asses, all of them following an accepted tradition of self-interest, means that you don't have to admit you're being selfish. It's a hell of a lot easier than accepting responsibility for your selfishness.

Okay, I think that's enough about Descartes for now, therefore it is.

TAPE 50

Driving down to Tennessee took longer than P.P. had anticipated. He'd neglected to make an advance reservation so wound up driving around the poorly signed roads of Raiment County in search of accommodation, asking directions of ogling locals and getting lost anyhow. It was dark and he was tired, disoriented by a hangover from the previous night and desperate for a leak. He hadn't grabbed a burger as he had intended, or bought a tourist map. Or anything really. (He ended up peeing by the roadside someplace, the way you do.)

When he finally happened on the Hilton Motel, a run-down establishment which should not be confused with any chain of similarly named establishments, he climbed out of the Porsche not knowing where he was or even who he was anymore, but he'd remembered to bring essential supplies. In his wash-bag was a vitamin jar of white powder, and once in his motel room and freshly rewired, P.P. stripped naked, turned on the TV expecting a cable sex or killer movie and lay on the bed, his eyes glowing in the dark as brightly as the screen that flickered and jumped every few seconds as if unused to being watched by a naked man on drugs.

P.P. decided he felt the way an automobile did if it was allowed to free-wheel at speed with the motor running and clutch depressed: kind of racy but relaxed.

His gaze focused on the lines comprising the TV picture rather than the picture itself before he rubbed his eyes and realized he was not watching lifestyles of the slick and shameless, but a feature on the very person that had started him on this crazy jaunt to hicksville.

The voice-over was describing the effects on Raiment County from all the people coming to see the healer. It seemed that the healer, by design or accident, had brought much attention to the nation's poor relations. A sizeable portion of the region's vacationers were making their way to Raiment County, attracted by something more than the pursuit of leisure-time activities in beautiful surroundings. As the VO insisted, Raiment had none of the Smokies' visitor's centers, motels, campgrounds, park wardens or anything of the kind

238

because this was not a recognized part of the park; hell, it was not even a recognized part of the country. It was not so much a vacation area as one big, rundown back lot.

When P.P. decided his staying-power was all artificially-induced and it was time to crash, he killed the TV, wondering if he was just bright enough to know that he was intuitive rather than intellectual, with maybe the occasional flash of insight. Would the answers to his questions come as a result of thinking, or as one of those flashes? As he lay there, drifting towards oblivion, he imagined the surrounding darkness pouring into his open but unseeing eyes, thinking that all of this healer stuff was pouring into his brain in the same way. Except the healer stuff was not blackness pouring in, it was light…

Now about consciousness being a ghost in DNA's machine. Begin by imagining that my head is a room with a computer in it, 'kay? The computer is linked by miles of wiring (my nerves) to a bunch of electrochemical machinery (my body). What happens is that I - consciousness - wake up most mornings and walk into this room. (Some mornings I have to be carried in.) When I get in here, the conscious me sits down at the computer (my otherwise non-conscious brain) and I become the ghost haunting this machine known as Laurie Hendricks.

You know how computer operating systems have all of those tiny icons for controlling programs and documents in the 'brain' of your computer? Those icons are like the different functions of your brain that interface your conscious mind. I'm interfaced so close and tight with this brain, it's as if I am its molecules, atoms, quarks and etc. (Or, if you prefer, the probability waves comprising those.) By interfacing this brain on each of the levels of material reality described by science, my consciousness (in the form of those Russian Doll 'bodies' Ed talked about) damn near 'becomes' this brain. And, through its nervous subsystems, I become conscious of this body.

To help me make my point, just pause and think for a moment how little time we take to think about 'time'; it happens, and we go along with it. Right, but now that the conscious ME is interfaced so closely with this monkey suit, be aware of how unimaginably complicated must be all of the non-stop, ultra-subtle shifts between past, present and future in my mind. Think how my memories (past) or imagination (future) influence the decisions that my present 'self' makes moment to moment. Did I say complicated? And this never ending, phenomenally complicated past/present/future mental activity is only a small part of my conscious awareness. You can't imagine the full complexity of everything that's going on in the conscious ME.

Now, scientists insist that the only reason why any of it happens - the only reason why this biomechanical body/brain exists at all - is to survive in a highly competitive world long enough to reproduce its genes. For that all-important reason it would be evolutionary suicide (or insanity) for my past, present or future 'selves' to be active at inappropriate moments. (For my imagination of future events to be accessed in a situation where I'd be best served by my memories of past events. Or for facts about what's materially real in the present to be confused with falsehoods or fantasies woven into memories of the past, or an imaginary future.)

But brain scientists insist there's no fundamentally separate, autonomous agent called consciousness. They say there's absolutely no difference between this body/brain and 'me'. To them, my sense of autonomy is an illusion. They say our brain is so incredibly well-organized, so fantastically versatile, that it needs no ghostly agent to direct it. On its own a brain can juggle past, present and future time periods (and their relative realities) in the most incredibly dexterous ways. (For instance, it can simultaneously recognize fact from fantasy in each of those time periods whilst allowing fantasy to *merge* with fact, as in creativity, or as in the ability to run 'maybe' scenarios so it can choose possible courses of future survival action.)

In dismissing the autonomous ME of consciousness, scientists are factoring out the one and only phenomenon that could make it possible for a brain to perform the otherwise impossible task of supplying a logical and consistent stream of *meanings* and *reasons* for why all of these things are happening. And by meanings and reasons, you have to be more than flatline material to appreciate that I mean the indescribably complex soup of understanding, knowledge, insights, aspirations, hopes, dreams, fears, needs, etc. that are unique to our conscious awareness.

Without a ghostly presence calling itself ME, a brain built entirely from the uncaring nuts and bolts of material reality would simply have no conception of meaning or reason.

See all of that my way? Good. So in getting Real you have to quit seeing your body/nervous system/brain as a biomechanical device. A soft machine. An engine of cogs, wires, valves, transistors, microchips or whatever. (I know you've seen pictures of brains and they look more like rubbery footballs than engines, but how brains actually work is still so mysterious you're tempted to

240

fall back on mechanistic images that you can handle.) Resist the temptation. Your notion of a human brain as something mechanical - no matter how miniaturized and complicated - is not only inadequate, it's wrong. Those 'material' notions are forced on you by evolution. They're your stupid past telling you how things have to be. And besides, you didn't hear Ed's explanation.

A brain is actually a gateway between different dimensions of reality/Reality. Brains link this plodding, dense, restrictive material reality with the free, negotiable, 'anything's possible' Reality where consciousness is all. A brain is also a vehicle. But don't think of a car, train, boat, plane or starship. Think of a vehicle you never imagined before; one that can accommodate an aware, all-pervading force of understanding that's simultaneously a multi-dimensional jigsaw puzzle that's forever putting itself together in astronomically complex new ways.

I'm gonna embroider a sampler with that description on it. (Maybe I'll get my mom to do it.)

Incidentally, while I've been talking, your consciousness has been using an advanced function of the brain's multi-level, mega-complex operating system called *language*. Plain old words. You may have heard about it. As a more recent evolutionary development of the consciousness/brain interface, language enables you to juggle mental models of things in the form of abstract symbols (words) that compress and encapsulate cumbersome mental images of mindless objects into tiny packages of living, negotiable thought. Words let you manipulate, in any conceivable way, either part or all of your thoughts about those objects.

But you're manipulating something else when you use words: the molecules, atoms, quarks and (if they exist) strings of brain machinery. And by doing that, you're also creating an abstract representation of the way that other molecules, atoms, quarks, etc., comprise the object you're thinking about.

Now buckle up because I'm about to take you on a roller-coaster ride out of reality and into Reality.

While you're reading this, tiny quanta (quantities) of material energy in the form of particles of *light* (called photons) are bouncing off these words and hitting the atoms shaped into your eyes. (The light is coming from either the sun or some other form of illumination.) That light energy then becomes electrochemical pulses that travel into your brain along nerves shaped into yet more atoms.

While all of that activity seemed to be happening in hardware made from non-conscious material energy, somehow, along the way, the billions of ink atoms that form these words miraculously turned into ideas in your mind. And yet you take all of that for granted. You live your life on a one dimensional level without even realizing that all of this amazing stuff is happening all the time. And it happens all because consciousness enables your eyes and brain to do with plain old ink, what alchemists tried to do when they thought base metal could be transmuted into gold.

Gold my ass! That's a minor-league miracle compared with the way consciousness uses the energy of this material universe (light, ink, paper, eyes, a brain) as a tool for getting information from my consciousness to your consciousness. By reading and thinking about these words, your mind is translating dumb-level material energy into higher-level consciousness energy to make conscious use of something that started out in conscious form - my thoughts. Yet you're hardly lifting a mental finger to do any of that. You're not even aware you're doing it. All you're aware of is the meaning of these words in the non-material, conscious environment of *ideas*.

(A famous physicist called Niels Bohr once said: 'Anybody not shocked by quantum theory doesn't understand it.' But as practically nobody on the planet understands quantum theory, that explains why we don't all walk around looking shocked. I dropped that in so I could say anybody not shocked by *themself* doesn't understand themself.)

Words come instantly, automatically, far faster than any amount of mental images of the actual objects they represent, their speed and aptness decided only by your verbal fluency. That's because words are designed by the evolution of consciousness itself to be quicker/easier/better than making non-physical models of physically 'real' objects in your brain.

Plain old picture-images of material things are the evolutionary dodos of understanding and communication. Even pictures of things that symbolize other things are ancient compared with words. What the hell good would pictures of mindless material things on their own be to a sophisticated person like you, if you couldn't relate yourself and your ideas to them in the mega-complex way that your consciousness has evolved words to do? If you couldn't relate to the generalized and personalized meaning of what those pictures represent?

The more mind you have to appreciate implications and/or relationships, the more that words reveal about pictures. Words are 'encapsulated related implications that help us understand materiality in a conscious sense. (If your words fail to communicate properly, it ain't words themselves that are inadequate, it's your ability to wield them.)

Words hugely improve the operating system of that information processor called your brain. Since language happened, all notions of size, shape, time, space, movement - in a word, material reality - have depended entirely on how *consciousness* perceived those notions. The system that the early ancestors of these bodies had prior to language was grunts and body gestures. (They were trying to use their whole body as an information processor and it didn't work too well.)

You know anybody still using that old system? I do. (Me, on a bad day.)

TAPE 51

Our simple storyline progresses to a big room in the Passmore Town Hall with rows of uncomfortable seats facing a raised platform on which is a long table composed of smaller tables end-to-end covered with a few moth-nibbled sheets. An aged, resident microphone is center-stage.

If this were videotape running in fast-forward, all of the above would remain motionless while a series of blurs starts whizzing around the place. Figures appear for an instant, then disappear. Some shiny new microphones appear on the stage suddenly out of nowhere, their cables looping overhead and leading out through the doorway. A TV camera plinks into existence. Jugs of water and glasses plink on the table. There's more stuttered blurring as the seats fill with residents of Passmore and roundabouts who freeze to near-motionlessness. The only sound is a kind of twittering.

Now a bunch of blurs has hit the platform so I'm going to slow this to normal speed. We see people sitting at the long table with wads of paper on front of them. They've left a few empty seats in the center behind the microphones. Then Mayor Bobby Stevenson walks in with a tall man in an expensive dark suit, who happens to be the State Governor, looking distinguished in the way that money and power distinguishes you. They're closely followed by the Governor's aide, a harshly attractive young woman in glasses who, because you're human, you automatically suspect is the Governor's bimbo.

You know that stuff where a man and woman are alone after hours in the library (that's a place where they store old books), and he takes her glasses off and lets her hair down (no, I have no idea why he was wearing her glasses and hair) and he says, "Why Miss Jones, you're beautiful!" Well that was definitely not the Governor's aide-stroke-bimbo, who was already pretty obvious in most departments. But she did have glasses and was called Barbara. Barbara the Bimbo. So aside from anything else, she was alliterative. (The word bimbo also seems onomatopoeic in a funny kind of way.)

Governor Brian Cunliffe was here to answer questions that some of the local people had pre-recorded to save time and maybe embarrassment. This was a mixed crowd, some of whom were poor and uneducated so their questions needed a little grammar edited into them during pre-recording.

I'm not suggesting those questions lost anything in the edit, though some of the faces in that audience didn't look too happy with the translation. But the Governor's answers looked okay, and that was what mattered.

(You've maybe seen those old photographs of Soviet politicians - the before-and-after ones where some figures mysteriously vanish from the line-up? In the right hands recording tape is equally susceptible to that same magic.)

Magic is the art of creating illusions. Human life itself is just a lot of illusions so densely packed together they appear solid and real.

But nobody in that audience was under the illusion that Governor Brian Cunliffe - aided by his glamorous assistant Barbara the bimbo - was going to magic away their problems. In a free-for-all enterprise society, curing one person's ills automatically makes someone else sick. Not because resources on this little planet are finite. (They are, yet there are more than enough of them to go around if used even half-wisely.) No, the problem is that somebody has claimed ownership of all those resources, and will only sell to the highest bidder. And if that doesn't make you real mad, you obviously control one or more of those resources, or you'd like to.

Yep, it's all about control, which is driven by insecurity. (Hell, you figure it out. For reference see the tape on scientists who're scared of getting eaten.) Politicians are driven by it too. After all, politicians struggle and connive to become the ones who actually make all the major decisions affecting them personally. The fact that those decisions just happen to affect everybody else is coincidental, and means we're talking mega self-interest here. You might well find something resembling altruism covering that underlying bedrock of 'me-ism'...but then again you might just as easily find a kind of 'I'll be a little altruistic to you in exchange for you keeping me in office'. Not that I'm
244

criticizing politicians. I'm criticizing the entire human race, of which politicians just happen to be a particularly pushy sub-species. I guess you might describe politics as an attempt to establish some kind of order out of the chaos created by everybody looking out for their own ass. But orderly selfishness is still selfishness. And remember, by being selfish on your behalf, politicians are experts at it.

Another of those illusions is the one which has people convinced poverty and need and deprivation are not merely unavoidable, but right and fair and normal aspects of life's downside. I'd love to say this illusion is all the fault of a bunch of evil entrepreneurs, traders, businessmen, dealers, brokers, or tycoons: wicked extortionists who place a higher value on wealth/goods/resources than life. But I can't say that, because those are just ordinary people who grasped the same opportunities most other folks would in their place and turned them to their own advantage. (Is there no end to these indictments? That's up to you.) Anyhow I'm not saying Brian Cunliffe was evil or an extortionist. I'm just saying he was a rich politician.

He introduced his act with footage - mostly crowd and scenery - of the healer on a TV they'd set-up on the stage, then promptly forgot the healer and started talking about '...wonderful and exciting new tourism opportunities, and the dynamic turn-around in the business health and well-being of all his good friends in the County of Raiment, and especially the up-coming little town called Passmore. But hey, you don't need me or anyone else to give you the good news - you *are* the good news!'

Boy, and I thought I could bullshit. But now the applause has died I can relate how he conducted his answers to the pre-recorded questions, many of which were from commercial self-interest anyway. The few hard-edged and potentially embarrassing questions on health-care, education and other social misfits were either watered-down, lost in translation, or saved until the very last and cemented over with the usual stock assurances that we were getting there, and this new tourist boom would do the job for everybody in the community. You've heard it all before.

Governor Cunliffe appeared to be talking straight and getting down to brass tacks. He did that twice, for about three seconds each time. A sly and daring semi-expletive off-camera here, an 'honest' bit of self-effacement there helped the trick along. (He knew the tape would all be edited later.)

Cunliffe was a professional illusionist. He even had a glamorous assistant called Barbara to help him with his tricks. (See if you can find an item of underwear hidden in the name Barbara before the Governor makes it disappear again.)

No, wait. The real meeting happened after everything the Governor had meant for general consumption by a wider audience was in the can, courtesy of his very own TV lackeys, and when Mayor Stevenson thought he was winding up the proceedings. Only somebody in the audience had other ideas.

"How is that gonna help all the folks with no work, not involved in tourism, and never will be?" The speaker was me. "And isn't it true," I went on, "that the people I'm talking about are just a small proportion of around 30 million Americans on welfare right now, and what's being done to get jobs for those people?" From my eye-corner I saw the audience looking at me, then at the Governor.

The Governor said, "Would you mind identifying yourself, Mizz…?"

"Surely. Lauren Hendricks from The Star."

"Okay now Mizz Hendricks…" (I could see he wasn't logging my name for future reference because he already knew it, courtesy of the Mayor. I'd probably go straight on the FBI's most wanted list right after the meeting.) "…as you seem to know how many people are taking taxpayers' money in government handouts, you must also know that most of those people use welfare simply as a fill-in until they find another job. It's just a breather. Maybe even some of the folks down here visiting your neck of the woods are vacationing as part of that breather, who knows?" He looked pleased with himself.

"But Governor," I persisted, "isn't it also true that half of those 30 million people - the fifteen million not currently on *vacation* - aren't using their welfare money, which they paid in taxes, to 'fill-in', but are instead forced to stay on welfare for as much as eight years because there's no other job for them to find? And don't try telling these people otherwise because they've got hands-on experience."

At that, the Governor looked at the Mayor and said something with his eyes. Because I'm writing this book I can tell you it was: 'I thought we were all done? So much for your walk-through,' and, 'You never should've allowed her in here.' (That guy had *really* expressive eyes.)

After clearing his throat, looking modestly down at his hands and chuckling to himself because I'd made a joke, the Governor's eyes found me again.

"Mizz Hendricks, I think these people know that you're purposely ignoring the massive job training this government introduced, yes, and childcare during

246

that training for all those who need it. We're both quoting from the same source, except you're overlooking the facts that don't help your argument because that's the only way you can score points."

Me again: "You mean facts like those same people we're both talking about being forced to take the first job they're offered after your training - whatever that job might be?"

"'Sounds reasonable to me, Mizz Hendricks, after the government trained you at its own expense, that you accept employment in the field you've trained for."

"Okay," I came back, "So maybe you'll explain to these folks about all the jobs you're going to train them and their kids for in this part of Raiment County."

At that the Governor smiled like a shark and said, "Mizz Hendricks, you couldn't have been looking this way when we showed that little movie earlier…of all those tourists? I came to this meeting to congratulate you all. Your town's got new money coming in now and lots more on the way. It has a bright future. This is the land of opportunity, ain't it? Well here's your opportunity. Here's your - " he chuckled - "I, uh, believe you yourself called that healer fella a 'gift-horse' in your paper, yes? Now it's up to everyone to make the most of that gift-horse."

There was a lull in which the audience broke into a murmur, and while I didn't intend for that to be the end of our little exchange I had no chance to regroup, because while a smug Governor Cunliffe leaned across to check Barbara the bimbo's bosom – I mean notes - a small voice came out of the crowd and, though mostly inaudible, sent ripples of quiet spreading out around it until everybody was silent. A short, emaciated man in a grubby windcheater was on his feet and, when all eyes were on him, re-read the question: "How long's the tourist boom gonna last, or will it be just a flash in the pan?" He looked around nervously. "I have to know 'cause, well, I can't see this here 'gift-horse' doin' me no damn good at all. I could've gotten me a steady job on the landfill though."

He was looking from one face on the stage to another, brave as hell. I mean, he had nothing to lose. In the charged silence I could feel the rising pitch of agreement like an approaching thunderstorm. It began with a few spots.

"Yeah, how 'bout that, mister Governor?"

"We don't want your gift-horse."

"Give us somethin' more permanent than horseshit."

That was when the Mayor got up and, trying to quiet things down, said to the air: "Now excuse me one second, Governor, let's get something clear for anybody who might've gotten the wrong end of this here stick. The tourists are no flash in the pan. As for any damn 'gift-horse', compared to the gifts of nature we got around here - gifts from God Almighty Himself - this healer is just a sideshow. The beautiful scenery's always been here, an' that's why the good folks are comin'. The tourists have seen the rest of the National Park and, well, they've discovered finally that we're a quiet and peaceful corner of the most beautiful piece of real estate in the USA."

He waited for the roar of approval, but it would take more than wishful hypocrisy to appease this crowd now me and the brave little guy in the dirty jacket had stuck that bit between their teeth.

Somebody yelled, "Might be one or two folks makin' money from that, but what about the rest of us who've fell through the cracks?"

Another shouted: "Damn right! If prices keep on goin' up to pluck the tourists clean, us locals won't hardly be able to afford to live here no more."

A woman jumped up like a jack from a box. "At least a landfill would mean jobs - even dirty money buys a livin'!"

"An' a new sewage-treatment system," someone else piped in.

A man opposed to the landfill stood up and produced a placard as if by magic that said: *Say no to the landfill.* Then another three or four people were standing with placards saying, variously: *Don't dump on Passmore! Trashville Tennessee!* and *We don't want your garbage!*

By now it was obvious to Governor Cunliffe he had no friends in this audience. To a cry of, "We want real answers here," The Governor held up his hands for quiet. When things settled down he addressed the meeting sternly.

"Alright, okay. Here's the bottom line, and I'm giving it to you straight. Everything is dependent on money, yes? Nobody, and I mean nobody, expects to get something for nothing..." He never finished.

"Nuthin's what we got plenty of right now!"

"Yeah. What else ain't you gonna do for us?"

"That your economic strategy - nuthin'?"

Finding a rowdy rabble instead of the coached sheep he'd been led to expect, Cunliffe began, "Now come *on*..."

I stood up again. "No, *you* come on. The Medicare and Medicaid programs in this state are *your* responsibility, Governor. And what's being done about tax surcharges on the richer members of this country?"

248

My last question was hardly relevant but what the hell?

An old guy right behind me grabbed the back of my chair and started shaking it. "The hell with those fat cats; when's the next load of tax shit gonna get dumped on folks tryin' to run their own business? That's what this here meetin's all about ain't it?"

That began a fresh torrent from the audience. The town meeting was heading towards anarchy.

The Mayor jumped up and grabbed a microphone but was drowned in the ensuing uproar as Governor Cunliffe leaned across for a hurried word with Barbara the bimbo. Then she was unfolding her long stick-insect legs in preparation for a quick getaway while Cunliffe conferred with the Mayor. As the TV people started hurriedly dismantling their gear, Cunliffe straightened his tie, forced a superior smile, and with a barely perceptible movement of the head motioned for his driver. The two of them headed for the door with Barbara the bimbo right behind, wagging her tail behind her while trying to pull the creases out of her tight skirt. I remember thinking that she probably paid more for that outfit than I made in a whole damn year.

TAPE 52

The first thing P.P. saw when he opened his red-rimmed eyes the next morning was a copy of The Star somebody had left on the night table. He blinked a few times to bring his surroundings into focus then remembered where he was. He could see only part of the headline on the front page - TOURISM TOPS TRASH - and was not sufficiently interested to read further. (After all my hard work!)

P.P. rolled his head around and took a dispassionate inventory of the room, remembering it from last night. The way his things hung around the walls from anything that would hold them reminded him of someplace he'd been once: a female locker-room, waking up from a marathon binge to find himself smuggled in beside a cheerleader, both of them huddled together on the floor between the benches and lockers, wrapped inside an old Stars & Stripes. Had they done it? He didn't know until she woke up and suggested they do it again - for their country.

Yeah, he'd been there. Now he was here, and all of the stuff from the day before was beginning to parade noisily through his brain, making him feel pathetic. Just look at this place! P.P. lay back with his head against the hard wall trying to decide what he should do next. Well, he'd get out of this dump, pick up a tour-map at the next gas station and figure out the way to Passmore; they must have a lodge or something there; that was in the park, wasn't it? He wiped a hand roughly over his face and felt the muscles of his jaw tensing, the way jaws did in movies.

P.P. took that copy of The Star with him when he checked out. The weather was fine and bright, warm and getting warmer, making P.P. feel better about everything. He even forgot the night before and how he'd driven around a strange county in a strange state, unsure if he'd lost his way or his mind.

This morning, while sunlight flickered through the trees and the ground warmed under a soft mist, he was more relaxed about being in Tennessee, yet still no clearer in his mind about why he had to find this healer. Maybe he was making a protest, the way kids had forty or so years earlier in the Summer of Love when they registered their objection to an unacceptable system and its war. (Except his war was the unacceptable system espoused by his father the Senator.) Or maybe this trip was closer to what traveling hippies did around the same time when they took The Marrakech Express seeking enlightenment in the form of some quality hash. Either way, a dormant seed in him knew it was time to awaken and take action, and P.P. was simply going where it directed.

TAPE 53

No matter how big my trailer was, the junk would expand to fill it. That's a recognized physics law, of which my notes are a microcosm. (I didn't need to invent any imaginary mess for this book; the table in front of me really is a disaster area. The National Guard is in here right now looking for survivors.) Disaster area or not, I always know there's a table and a word processor under this debris. There may even be a book, who knows? Well you do because you're reading it. Unless you ain't, in which case, there ain't.

The fact that this organized confusion is pretty much like the inside of your head enables me to make a few points here. For instance, why d'you think thinking is so easy, any idiot can do it without you even having to think about it? No, it's not because you're secretly smart. It's because most of your so-called 'thinking' is just your brain doing its own thing. Once the ignition is on, that brain (responding to its body) can take you where *they* want to go, for *their* benefit. That's what they evolved to do.

250

The machinery in that brain is so unbelievably, phenomenally complicated, the Real, conscious you can easily get lost in all of the biological self-interest. Why'd ya think so many folks screw up their lives and the lives of those around them, even though they know they shouldn't, and later wish they hadn't? It's because they confuse their conscious self with the stupid machinery. Boy, if your mental environment is even a fraction of the mess my trailer is, it's no surprise you don't know who's running your mind.

True, some folks have tidier minds than others, though even tidy minds need concentration to stop 'em doing what the hell they like. (This is nothing to do with intelligence. Geniuses can be so mentally untidy they're practically nuts. They just happen to have a gift for looking deeper under the mess, and maybe a knack for seeing new stuff in the disorganization.)

But the problem isn't just untidiness, it's that the mindless machinery of your body/brain has no understanding of the Real things that ought to make your life worth living. Worse yet, brains recognize neither 'good' nor 'bad' in Real, conscious moral terms, only in terms of what's good or bad for the survival of DNA's body. So when your moral judgment is uncertain or compromised, that's the conflict between what the Real, conscious you suspects is morally right, and the genetic version of morality: good for survival is right, bad for survival is wrong. Conflict, because there's no uncertainty or compromise in the hardware; it's only ever out for itself.

Let's say your self-image is of a caring, home-and-family-loving person. You imagine the thoughts and conscious experiences in that brain are *your* thoughts and *your* conscious experiences. But the brain you inhabit doesn't know what consciousness is, or give a damn about you or your thoughts with their meanings, inferences, hopes, dreams and aspirations. The biomachinery you're so fond of protecting 'knows' and 'cares' about things - you included - in the same way your washing machine 'knows' and 'cares' about things.

Yet this same biomachinery established your (mostly subconscious) conviction that life, reality, your relationships with people, happiness, sadness, good times, bad times, winning and losing, etc., etc., are all really about you as a genetic organism.

By dropping my metaphors in a blender, I could say that being born is like waking up inside a fantastically complicated robot that's pre-programmed for its own survival. But that would be misleading because this is much, much worse. This is more like dreaming that you actually ARE the robot, without even knowing you're dreaming or pre-programmed.

So far as the mindless genetic furniture in the robot's head is concerned, your most erudite and intelligent mental activities, your best demonstrations of smartness, are there to assist genetic survival. All of your so-called physical or mental prowess was evolved, by genes, to keep them and their goddam body alive. The smarter you can be about how your ass responds to everything, the better for your ass.

Did somebody ask where do altruistic considerations come from? They come from the Real part of you. Nothing evolves for altruistic reasons in a genetic organism except consciousness itself. And then only by making a determined effort not to be genetic.

It could make you wonder how we ever managed to become in the least bit unselfish - but only if you forgot that our consciousness *ain't* a product of this totally, mindlessly selfish body and its brain.

And that's why, for you as consciousness, reality should be what *you decide* it is, by *thinking*, rather than what the chemicals of your ass decide it is, by *not* thinking. Your consciousness must refuse to let the mindless machinery run itself. We're here to give a conscious direction to all of these dumb components, right? *Right?*

TAPE 54

'To lose one parent, Mr. Worthing, may be regarded as a misfortune; to lose both looks like carelessness.'

That's from Oscar Wilde's *The Importance of Being Earnest*. (If you want to know who Worthing is, or what's so important about this guy Earnest, go see the play.) If you don't know who Oscar Wilde is, forget I spoke.

The Mayor and Maxine still had separate bedrooms, but these days the Mayor's was usually empty first thing in the morning when Willie started creeping around because the Mayor now spent his nights with Maxine. Willie would sneak out and put his ear to Maxine's door, trying to catch the sound of her voice in the midst of passion. Voyeurism was all Willie had left, though as his folks were, by nature, vocally undemonstrative, Willie was not rewarded with sound effects appropriate to the colorful imagery in his mind, and had to make do with anything he could get: Maxine's voice lowered in a word or two of unintelligible conversation, say, or a tantalizing creak of her bed. (Previously the only sound Maxine's bed made - through the kitchen ceiling as it groaned on the boards whenever Maxine shifted position - had gotten to be something both men took for granted. Now it was only Willie who had the privilege of listening to Maxine's bed groaning with a slow rhythm his father had never heard, and it made Willie feel sick and horny both at once.)

But while Willie had to rely on his imagination to tell him what his parents were up to, you have me to explain it in graphic detail. Except that as some things are best left to the imagination (preferably not Willie's), I don't think it's any of your business what Bobby and Maxine Stevenson did in private, which was only what other folks do. They slept mostly. They talked some. They read a little.

Oh okay, you might as well know that Willie's worst suspicions were true; the Stevensons did *it*. (You people and your morbid obsession with sex.) Incidentally *morbid* is a medical term meaning 'indicative of disease.'

Now some background. Willie hadn't figured in the original split between the Mayor and Maxine years earlier; they handled that all by themselves, as you'll maybe understand if you were ever married, even if you never actually got to the sleeping apart stage. It's a marvel that marital disintegration isn't more common when you consider that life itself can get pretty morbid sometimes.

See, Maxine came from a previous marriage childless, as I explained. What I did not elaborate was how Maxine didn't quit that first job of marriage; she was fired. For being frigid. (Frigid! Another goddam idiotically misunderstood word.) What Maxine actually was, was worried and upset, confused and frustrated because she wanted children as much, and maybe even more than that first husband. Except those thwarted feelings, drives and maternal instincts wound up giving her all kinds of ancillary psychological problems. Maybe you can understand how all of those worries and problems meant Maxine had a hard time even pretending in bed. Trouble was, none of Maxine's problems altered the Mayor's expectations of her, and he felt cheated. He'd married Maxine because he liked the look of her as a highly visible mass of chemicals encoded by genes. To hell with the Real Maxine as the consciousness that moved all of those chemicals around as a single unit; fact was, he wouldn't have been interested at all if she'd been physically unattractive, regardless of how attractive her consciousness was.

Even worse was the Mayor's expectations of Maxine's offspring potential, though not having X-ray vision he couldn't see that Maxine's genes had arranged for her reproduction chemistry to be a little different from most women's.

When Bobby Stevenson discovered she couldn't deliver on demand, he wasn't just disappointed, he was also concerned about how the negative results of her deficiency made him look in front of other people. His feathers were good and ruffled by the idea of folks thinking he'd bought him a dog that couldn't bark.

When Maxine saw how badly he was taking the discovery of her problem, she became even more screwed up, just like with husband #1. The lack of one thing led to the absence of another, and Maxine moved into the spare bedroom.

If you take a situation like that and leave it to simmer for a few years, you end up with the way things were between the Stevensons when the healer showed up and turned the whole thing on its head. Maxine found God, and the Mayor went along for the ride.

Did somebody ask how Neil Hughes landed a part in this picture? Hughes was never anything more than a can for Maxine to kick during her long walk down that lonesome road. I doubt that Maxine would've given Hughes a second look in a police line-up if his own screwed-up marriage hadn't inspired him to chase her. Add to that the fact that the Stevensons plainly had a problem, and Hughes' ego was the size of Texas, and bingo. (People get themselves paired up for the weirdest reasons, or hadn't you noticed?)

Homespun Philosophy Corner: It could be said that some relationships have only so far to run before they either wither and die of some wasting disease, or they come to a sudden and dramatic stop, and the people involved have to extricate themselves from the wreckage as best they can, walk away with whatever's left of their life and start over. On the other hand a relationship that seems dead might simply be in suspended animation, maybe to give the participants time to do some evolving. Maybe all they need then is a revitalizing catalyst to get them up and running again.

Now Willie being the kind of person he was, instinct told him that the most rewarding way for him to live his life required the use of cunning, deviousness and secrecy. Whatever Willie might've inherited from his real momma, most of his unsavory traits came from his father the Mayor. Those were honed by peers like Jeff Ackerley, and from watching all that mindless junk on TV. Manipulating his family the way he tried, Willie's feeling of power over his parents was the only good feeling he had about himself. But it was entirely illusory. To prove it, when Maxine suddenly got religion and the Mayor got Maxine, Willie was left with nothing. What made it worse for Willie was seeing

254

that all his efforts at keeping his parents apart had been futile. Worst of all, though, was his contrition.

Contrition is a good word to remember because not too many people know what it means. Contrition means 'crushed in spirit by a sense of sin'. I couldn't have put that better myself so I copied it straight from the Webster's. Besides everything else Willie was, he was that too now. Did he ever have problems! Contrition also means being penitent, or, if you prefer, remorseful, both equally fine words but lacking contrition's erudite edge. Penitent and remorseful also lack relevance in this instance, because Willie was anything but sorry for the way he'd treated his parents. Willie was only sorry for himself, making it hard to understand why he did what he did next. As it is, you'll have to wait until later to know exactly why he decided to become one of the healer's disciples.

My mom will be nursing a bemused smile at all of this stuff. She always thought I was a little weird, but only because I was a coalminer's daughter who wanted to be a writer. (I still want to be that, but at least I know what *bemused* means; my mom thinks it's a pretentious way of saying amused.)

Now where did I put the next goddam –

TAPE 55

...tape #55 is supposed to carry on from er...aw shoot, I don't know! Anyhow I'm inside the computer called your brain. I'm unscrewing a few panels so I can poke around to show you what's really going on. First I'll wrench off this grill and...well looky here! Dust inches deep and cobwebs everywhere. When I jiggle a few circuits - feel that? - I want you to *think* of something so I can check what happens. Knowing you, it'll be one of those old favorites: sex, money, fame, drugs, babies, football, food, booze, etc.

Uh-huh. According to the indicators in here you're thinking about ballet, but you can't kid me. That's just a front for sex.

Okay. When you think 'sex', it's as if you typed the instruction 'sex' on the computer keyboard of your brain and then hit the 'enter' key. Or you moved your mouse to the little 'sex' icon and clicked. (For anybody who doesn't know, that's how we tell a computer to go open the appropriate memory files.)

From inside your brain I can see your 'sex' thought, right in the middle of a bunch of wires that just caught fire. (That's why your eyes are glowing. If anything else is glowing I don't wanna know.)

Now be serious and get to the point, it says here. Apart from the temperature rising, does any of the activity I'm watching in this brain machinery look, sound, feel, smell or taste to you like the 'sex' you're imagining? Not in a million megabytes. How could it? Brains are nothing but stupid circuitry where electricity and chemicals interact. If that's your idea of sex, you must be a robot because boy, it sure ain't mine.

So let's keep getting Real. You have no more conscious a notion of what's happening inside the complicated machinery of that brain (when you think of sex or anything else) than you do of what happens inside a computer when you type in 'sex'. (Yep - because a brain's bio-reality is utterly alien to your conscious Reality.)

But if this biomechanical brain's relationship with the world is so alien to your conscious view of the world, how in hell do you manage to manipulate all of these dangerously complicated atoms, quarks and (maybe) strings to make thoughts? You don't know? So how do you know it's you who's running things in there and not your stupid brain? In case you forgot, the only way to be sure it's you who's doing the deciding, is to be *unselfish*. Anything else is what mindless genes want you to want, for them. But are you smart enough to do that? Hardly ever.

TAPE 56

The morning was already balmy and humid when P.P. took his diver's Rolex out of his pocket, amazed to see it was barely eight a.m. A gentle, cooling wind blew the scent of trees down the slope to the settlement. The sun was trying to extricate itself from some leafy branches higher up, making too-bright-to-look-at shafts of golden light in the shadowed mist under the nearest copse.

P.P. took in a long, noisy breath and let it out appreciatively, thinking this was pretty damn close to heaven as he watched McClure clearing up trash left over from the previous day's crowd and flexed his shoulders to feel the new lightness of spirit, the lifted burden of those suffocating values he'd left behind in Boston. God, but this was wonderful. Everybody should experience such freedom, preferably on a permanent basis.

Standing there in the dewy grass, enjoying not having some kind of hangover, he decided he'd become part of this settlement in just one night, and it felt more like home than The Glades had in all the seven years he'd lived there. His father had them move out of the previous house because it was not grand enough for a US Senator. It had been big enough, but lacked the Patrician elegance of The Glades.

Patrician elegance! It was vulgar as hell. But now all of that was starting to seem wonderfully meaningless.

P.P. wandered in through the open door of the settlement's dining room in the main hut and looked around. There was a stove, a range, cupboards, a sink, all of the usual kitchen equipment and one enormous refrigerator. He opened its door and was amazed to see the shelves packed with cartons and dishes and bowls and jars.

On closer inspection he recognized huge boxes of burger buns and cartons of uncooked burgers. They looked like the ones sold in the wilderness. He closed the door and found McClure behind it, beaming at him.

"Breakfast?" McClure asked.

Half an hour later, drawn by the aroma of grilling bacon, Matt showed up and sat down at the table opposite P.P. to renew the acquaintance they'd begun the previous evening. (Okay, so I forgot to mention that Matt from The Triangle lived at the settlement too. You try writing a book and see how many things you forget to mention.) Matt immediately found a plate of eggs and toast in front of him. He looked knowingly once at McClure, then to P.P.

"If you ever open a restaurant, on no account employ this man. He'll bring everybody off the street to eat whether they want to or not."

"I thought that was the idea?" P.P. said around a mouthful of bacon before he shoveled more egg into the same hole. This Tennessee air certainly gave a guy one whale of an appetite.

"Yeah, but him - " Matt turned to grin amiably at McClure's back, " - he'd bring them in the kitchen by the back door and there'd be no charge."

McClure, rattling pans in the sink, sang out, "No charge!"

"He'd have you undermine everything this country was built on," Matt said.

P.P. almost emptied his mouth and said, "Hey, Mike, you should read the book I'm working through. It's titled 'Clean Up and Clear Out'. Written by a coupla guys from a top Wall Street brokerage outfit. Just your kinda thing."

At McClure's renewed interest he flapped a hand dismissively. "Hey, that was a joke." Then he fell silent, having reminded himself of the P.P. Johnson who, just a couple of days before, had quit Harvard, along with the business studies and everything else. Now was the first time he'd allowed himself to think about what he'd done. To this point he'd been in a daze, only this daze was beginning to feel more like heightened sense, rather than its absence.

P.P. felt he'd become two people in one - an old self and a new self. His old half was all the weight of tradition and common sense, the material values of his past life: the parameters he'd lived by. Those were telling him his new self was crazy. And what was this new self anyhow? What did *it* have to offer? A finger of terror jabbed in his stomach; the lonely terror of suddenly knowing this new self was very different from the person he'd been for all of his nineteen years. Different from the way most of the people out there in the world seemed to be. He couldn't even describe to himself what this new self consisted of, though a feeling of disorientation definitely seemed part of it.

He caught Matt watching him, said, "Huh? What?"

"Aw, nothing." Matt was fairly sure that this new addition to their small group would work out okay, but there was someone he was not so sure about. Willie Stevenson was the reason why Matt had begun doubting his ability to judge people lately, not for his own sake but for the healer's. The notion of judging people on the healer's behalf brought a private smile, and Matt resumed eating. If someone had the healer's approval, that was enough. They were none of them perfect.

As if reading his thoughts, McClure, who took everyone at face-value, said, "Matthew, you interduced Peter to Mister Willie yet?"

When P.P. looked up, Matt said, "Pete's going to meet a lot of people today." He glanced pointedly out the window for P.P.'s benefit. "A lot of people." At P.P.'s mystified expression, Matt added, "In this 'brokerage' we deal in something more important than Commodities and Securities."

Later, when the mist cleared and the sun was high and hot, the crowds began gathering on the green hills above the settlement. Yet before the first of them arrived, all the usual services were in place - fast-food franchises and souvenir stalls, itinerant entertainers and side-shows - so now the smells of cooking and the sound of many people intermingled in the sunny air and drifted down the grassy slope to where P.P. Johnson stood at the open gate of the lean-to shack; inside sat the Porsche, now spotlit by bright points of light where the sun beamed through holes in the timber wall under a corrugated metal roof that leaked when it rained, and trailed newly-dislodged cobwebs over the blue bodywork.

P.P. had just removed his tuxedo from the excuse for a rear seat and was wondering what he ought to do with the Porsche. A battered pickup seemed to be the property of the settlement. There was McClure's trail-bike and a couple of pedal-bikes. As McClure said, what else did you need?

Then Matt suggested just putting the car in the shack and letting things take their course, meaning that it would be there if P.P. decided he'd made a big mistake.

P.P. still had no idea how he'd broken through the fence keeping him inside that old way, but now he was out, would he be able to go back if he wanted to? Or was it like growing; once you'd started you couldn't *un*grow? Who'd want to do that anyhow?

Trying to make sense of the jumble of half-ideas flying around in his mind, he figured you'd only oppose growth in the first place if you didn't want things to change. You'd want the future to be an undisturbed continuation of the past only if you had a vested interest in keeping things *your* way, for *you*. If you did advocate change, it would only be in the hope that things would change *your* way. He was thinking how pointless and futile that final, apocalyptic row with his father had been.

He closed his eyes and grimaced, thinking about how what started as a minor disagreement between himself and the Senator had blossomed into a full-blown critical assault. A surge of jagged-edged misery rushed up under his heart at the memory. His shoulders tensed defensively. The fight had been entirely one-sided, as all of their exchanges were. His father had the weight, the reach, the experience.

P.P. groaned, not liking this analogy because it was too goddam accurate a description of the old man raining a series of verbal blows on him that left great mental welts. P.P. saw and felt it now, plain as day. Hell, a fist-fight would have been preferable to that.

He rolled his head, felt the tension in his neck, recalling the malicious disappointment shining in the Senator's eyes at having such a weak son, his mouth twisting into ugly shapes with the recriminations and accusations, designed to justify his own ideals and values while pointing-up his son's inadequacies. Maybe the Senator had been fighting against himself, angry and frustrated at seeing his blood-line aspirations dashed.

P.P. came back to the present, aware he was gripping the hard bulge in the tuxedo pocket. He brought out the vitamin jar of white powder, turning quickly as a shadow fell across him.

"I doubt you'll have much use for that down here." Matt's backlit face was unreadable. He took the tux from P.P. and held it up for inspection, then he nodded to the crowd gathering on the hill above them. "Though I guess you'd sure stand out up there."

TAPE 57

Let's do *Qualia*.

What the hell is qualia?

According to neuroscientists and philosophers of the mind, your conscious awareness is made from qualia. It's the collective name for the tiny pieces of awareness that combine to create the conscious *you*.

The notion is that when tiny amounts of electrochemical information come into your brain from the outside world, different areas of your brain (the ones that process your senses of taste, smell, sight, etc.) take those bits of information and move them around, weigh them, compare them, and use them to create your conscious experience of everything. They call each of the *degrees* of this conscious experience a *quale*.

Dear mom, you already know a quantum is a tiny quantity of energy, (countless numbers of which form into the objects and forces that you experience *physically*). Well a quale is supposed to be a tiny quantity of your *conscious* experience of those material qualities. So when you smell a pineapple, for example, your conscious experience of that unique smell is created (so they say) entirely by material components in your brain exchanging bits of electrochemical information. Same goes for your conscious experience of the feel of that pineapple in your hands. Or your conscious experience of the taste of it, etc.

The qualia notion, if you didn't already guess, comes from the same people who think that brains can somehow manufacture consciousness out of non-conscious components.

What I'm saying is that you, being consciously aware that your body is experiencing sensations caused by the material qualities of things, doesn't mean that your brain is *creating* your consciousness, does it? No Laurie. It just means your consciousness is *aware* of those sensations caused by the material qualities of things.

The problem with qualia is the same problem you get with a brain creating consciousness from non-conscious parts: One moment all you have is a bunch of mindless matter in the shape of a body and its brain…then suddenly there YOU are, consciously aware, knowing, understanding, etc. Exactly *how* did those brain atoms cross over the line from being mindless, to become the conscious 'you'? The answer is, they didn't. *Qualia* are just one more way brain scientists try to reduce the conscious 'you' to tiny amounts of fundamentally mindless materiality by saying that you, the mind, recognizing things, is *the same as* all of those tiny amounts of materiality in that brain recognizing things.

When the material senses of that body you occupy come in contact with a goddam pineapple's material qualities, it's just atoms interacting with other atoms, all the way up to, and including, everything that happens in that brain. All of it is non-conscious material activity.

No matter how many different groups of chemical components you have comparing, exchanging, quantifying this material information, no matter how subtle or complex their comparisons, the components and the information would only *ever* be different amounts of *unconscious* matter…if you didn't have a special something *more than* plain old matter to make *conscious* sense of all these different amounts of material information…otherwise all you'd get is a goddam computer!

Consciousness is the material sensations being perceived by something that *knows* it's *different* from those sensations. Something has to be different from them just to *experience* them *as something different from them*. Otherwise you wouldn't know, consciously, that you were appreciating, judging, quantifying and qualifying any of that mindless material activity as *material* activity.

If we, the consciousness, were not a uniquely separate phenomenon, then all of that hugely complex interplay of material information would be forever confined to the same goddam unconscious, material level as the information itself! So how the hell would you even begin to understand, or be aware of understanding, not just the material implications of the material information you receive from outside of yourself, but all of the *conscious* implications of that material information?

TAPE 58

Since his new awakening, P.P. Johnson sensed that something new had come on-stream inside of himself. He imagined having come up from underwater but hadn't yet gotten as far as taking off the diver's helmet. (P.P. was fond of aquatic metaphor; don't ask me why.) More abstractly, he had the peculiar notion that he was seeing and thinking of himself from outside of himself. (I appreciate how that notion, and the diver's helmet, are an ill-fitting pair, but who said notions have to be comfortable with each other?)

Now he was walking up the rise towards the wilderness crowd with Matt, anticipation growing in him as the weight of human numbers and the invisible wave of their massed voice - like a fairground, a carnival or a football game - rolled downhill towards them, and a part of P.P. went out to meet that wave like a surfer. Without knowing why, he felt an incomprehensible desire to communicate. Maybe he wanted reassurance about who he was now, and it scared him. Hell, he was no big communicator. He had gotten used to letting his family's money do that for him.

"Jesus Christ, there's so many of 'em," he told Matt.

Without looking at him Matt said, "Closer to, they're just plain folks. Some think they're vacationing, but others are looking for something deeper. Seeing the healer on TV was only the beginning, the way it was for you. Remember how you felt - curious, skeptical, apprehensive?"

"Who, me?"

"And maybe something else. The doubts are you imagining how you *ought* to feel. That's the 'old you' you were telling me about. All that the 'old you' is good for now is telling the '*new* you' how most of these people must be feeling. But you're one-up on them; you know there's another Peter Johnson."

P.P. said nothing. It still sounded like heavy shit. He wished he'd taken Matt's advice and left his jacket in the car. It was hot down here - or maybe that was nerves.

Matt said, "Whatever reason these people have for being here, they need a sounding board to help them work out what that reason is. It won't be the same reason you're here, but if they heard your reason, they might find a place to begin figuring from. People might seem to be going in different directions, Pete, but we're all coming from the same place and going to the same place."

As they walked, Matt smiled and nodded at people while P.P. tried not to step on anybody or trip over the kids running loose everywhere. While his heart was in this thing, his stomach was not. The drifting aroma of food made it worse.

The real problem, though, was in his head. He felt as if he'd begun wading towards the middle of a deep lake without knowing how to swim. Just because other people said you could do it, that didn't mean you could. Who was this healer anyhow? *What* was he? Maybe he'd hypnotized P.P. into doing this! And Matt and McClure. No, that was stupid because of McClure. Or maybe McClure was the one they were still working on? Yeah, and -

He walked through the middle of somebody's picnic and was busy apologizing when his eyes met the healer's. The fact that there was fifty yards between them, most of it occupied by people who became more numerous and closely packed the nearer they got to the healer, made no difference to the rush P.P. felt right then.

And something else happened. Later, he'd wonder if he imagined the voice as he stood in the middle of that picnic. Maybe he overheard somebody in the crowd. Any explanation was easier than admitting what he *knew* he'd heard - the healer's voice saying, "You *can* do this."

The voice still fresh in his mind, P.P. found himself negotiating a party of free-range musicians and performing artistes who, judging by their outfits, had escaped from their cages backstage of *Cats*. When P.P. looked for the healer again, he'd been swallowed by the crowd, but P.P. found Matt seated amongst a group of little black kids with their schoolteacher or somebody, all of them looking so grave that P.P. wondered what the hell they were talking about. Then all the little kids laughed out loud, and there were white teeth everywhere. In that momentary interlude Matt turned to P.P. and winked. It was all just so goddam unreal and magical.

First time I clapped eyes on P.P. Johnson he was the wide-eyed and well-dressed young guy coming up the hill with Matt. Being a reporter and an inveterate snooper who was also writing a book around the healer, and a friend of Matt, I naturally took an interest in P.P. Besides, I knew the healer was gathering disciples, and a new one of those was an item of curiosity.

What did P.P. Johnson have the look of? A young man who thinks he's been everywhere and done a lot, but hasn't. You know, kind of see-through cool - until his feet joined in that family's picnic and brought him back to earth.

As my fact-gathering mission meant noting all of the boring and mundane things people did in case somebody decided to do something interesting for once, I trailed around after P.P. awhile. (If it helps keep your disbelief suspended, I didn't even know he was called P.P. Johnson then, but having him introduce himself to some guy from Delaware gives me a perfect opportunity to let myself overhear him say his name. Which, as if you didn't know, was Peter Paul Johnson.) After that I let myself listen to the conversation with this guy from Delaware where they discussed the finer points of capitalism.

While Delaware asserted that a country where everyone worked for the common good was a recipe for personal and national prosperity, P.P., with a brand-new bee in his boxers and the zeal of the newly half-converted, chose the 'money controls people' route to go down because he had first-hand experience. P.P. soon realized he was arguing not with a guy from Delaware, but rerunning the set-to with his pa, and kept on seeing the Senator's face on this guy from Delaware. Not only that, he seemed to be standing outside of himself again and listening to everything they were saying in a somehow clearer yet inexplicable way. Yet again, P.P. wondered if his 'new self' was just another term for going bananas.

"Where'd you think this country would be today without healthy competition?" Delaware told him. "If we didn't have each other to push against? What happens when you got nothing to push against is that you don't go anyplace, isn't that so? In my book that's stagnation."

In *my* book, what P.P. actually heard was his father saying: "Where in hell do you think you'd be right now if I hadn't got out there and hustled, huh boy? If I hadn't made myself a winner by walking over the opposition? Hell, Johnson, I need that opposition; I thrive on it. I get off on winning, on being first every time, the same way this goddam United States of America gets off on it. If I had my way there'd be legislation to make *not* walking over the opposition a federal offence."

So there I was, earwigging on P.P.'s conversation, seeing that Delaware had a long way to go before the new P.P.'s side of things made any sense to him. First Delaware would have to learn how to listen to - and actually think about - viewpoints that didn't just agree with his own.

I decided to leave P.P. Johnson there because I didn't get any breakfast. Now it was noon and the whiff of onions frying, the sight of kids walking by with burgers and fries reminded my stomach it was used to food dropping by at least once a day.

That's why I had mayonnaise plastered all over my face when Donna Hughes tapped my arm and said hi, and we exchanged the usual small-talk before she asked me if I'd noticed some guy in a phony tropical-style outfit sniffing around. You know, the light coarse-weave pants and Hawaiian palm-trees-and-parrots type of print shirt, loafers but no socks, all topped off with a Panama hat and stuff? Okay, so there was no hat, and I exaggerated the outfit, but apparently he did have reflective sunglasses. You know, the kind that repel cosmic rays.

People who wear those always seem to be incognito, right? In fact wearing such glasses when you actually are incognito only draws attention to the fact and destroys the whole purpose. He was on his own too, which made him even less incognito. (Or should that be more cognito? I don't speak Spanish.) But hey, imagine my ears flapping at the news of a government agent covering

264

the proceedings. Well what else could he be? If it was true, I figured he was not there to brighten anybody's day despite the happy shirt.

Waving the remains of my burger at her I told Donna I'd catch her later and rushed off to find the agent. A government man checking out the healer was a tasty morsel twice over: once for this tome, twice when I built the covert surveillance angle into The Star's next issue under the headline: HEALER NOW BIGGER THAN LANDFILL.

Why would the FBI be interested in the healer? Maybe because some folks were unhappy about his ideas. I noted the first adverse reactions just by pushing my little recording device in various faces and asking questions like: "Sir, how'd you feel about the healer?" I got answers ranging from the pathetically obvious: "I'm a might unhappy 'bout his dislike of our constitutional right to bear arms," through the slightly more parochial but equally self-oriented: "It just ain't natural and proper for somebody with no officially elected status in this community to start criticizin' the way we run our business operations," and ending with: "When some guy livin' out in the woods starts modifyin' the holy Christian scriptures that this God-fearin' country and its people were raised on, hell, lady, I get *reeel* mad."

TAPE 59

The story that had originally brought Deeks and CNLB News to the wilderness - a bunch of drug loonies besieged in a house outside of Boone, just across the State line - had also gotten the attentions of the local FBI, who had then picked up on the healer phenomenon.

That's just some background for you because, for *moi*, listening now to those snippets of discontent in the wilderness from Joe Blow, was the first intimation that something was wrong with the state of the union.

My suspicion was confirmed when I caught up with the FBI man in the Hawaiian shirt. I was expecting a middle-aged gentleman, balding, portly, sweating some in that hot sunshine and kinda damp around the coconuts who takes off his sunglasses and mops his brow before slipping back into uncomfortable anonymity behind the shades.

Wrong. He was very, and I mean very, young for a job like that. Almost as young as I was, and I have to say he looked as cool as anyone there. But furtive, definitely, to my trained eye. Furtive in a cool way. When I found him he was in conversation with some tourists. He kept glancing around so I couldn't get near enough to eavesdrop without a cover, and short of slipping one of the hot-dog vendors a few bucks to let me borrow his cart - which only happens in movies - I was stuck.

That was when I saw someone who looked vaguely familiar lunching on a burger. It took me a few minutes to place this young man as the same hot shot whose ancient red Camaro practically ran me down the first and last time I visited the Mayoral residence. In those few minutes I also knew he was watching me, too, though when somebody is wearing sunglasses it's hard to tell. I strolled over to him and watched him tense up. Even his part-masticated burger slowed to a momentarily motionless mouthful before he could begin acting innocent.

"Still drive a Camaro?" I said.

He swallowed hard. "Who's askin'?"

"That vehicle of yours very near got an impression of my butt in its fender the last time we came close, is who." You could tell he didn't expect this approach from a stranger, so I gave him one of my disarming leers. "Hey, relax willya," I told him, "I'm not a talent scout for Playgirl." I took off my dark glasses and rolled my eyes in the direction of the Hawaiian shirt. "But I'm not so sure about that guy over there. The one you've been watching for the past ten minutes?"

"Who, me?"

This was getting nobody anywhere so I did something that I'd always wanted to do - I reached up and removed his sunglasses so I could see what he was thinking. "Okay, you're under arrest," I told him. "You have the right to remain silent and all of that crap, 'kay?" Jesus, what you have to do to get through some people's armor.

His thin lips teetered on the threshold of a grin finally. "C'mon, you're no cop. You write f' The Star."

"So you heard about that, uh? Lucky for me I don't got to depend for information on people like you or I wouldn't have a lot to write about. Yeah, I'm the famous Lauren Von Hendrickstein."

He snorted, and from beneath lowered lids examined my shoes, and, I might add, my legs, pelvic area, chest and the rest. Sly-boy.

I handed back his glasses and found out he was Willie Stevenson, which you already knew. You could've knocked me over with a feather when I found out he was also one of the healer's disciples, which you also knew. (You know more than me and I'm writing this!)

266

I surreptitiously showed him my tape recorder and told him that I, too, was working for the healer, indirectly, but the tropical dude definitely wasn't.

"Okay Bill. You must know Donna, right?" He did. "Well she informs me that Joe Coconuts over there is a government spy. I'd like to know what he's asking people and I need you to (I nearly said to cover my ass but thought better of it) be my cover while I move in. You game?"

He eyed the agent. "I guess."

I took his arm and strolled him around in a wide semi-circle until we nudged the people next to the people the agent was with, all the while talking my head off to Willie about nothing in particular, laughing, and generally hamming it up for the both of us because Willie was about as casual as a goddam Wookie.

And you know what happened? Just when I was practically close enough to pick up the agent's loud shirt on my pocket snooper I heard him say, "Danker, fraulein" like a native and suave as hell to the young German lady he was talking to. Then he turned around and placed a very cool smile right in my face before adopting an intercept course for me and Willie.

"Miss Hendricks?"

I tried to look surprised.

"Hoped I'd bump into you, Miss Hendricks." He removed his reflective glasses out of politeness, then became professionally shamefaced. "No, I'll come clean," he said. "I knew you were here, and would have found you if you hadn't found me first."

You know how you take to some people right away? Well this guy was definitely not Willie Stevenson, whose arm I didn't need telling to leave go of. On this guy's arm, jungle shirt or no, I'd have been a different person.

"Alright, so we found each other after all these years. What happens now?"

"An exchange of ideas maybe." His uncertain smile and twinkly eye-movements said Willie was not to be part of the deal.

Willie, looking offstage, didn't see the instruction.

"Bill - thanks," I told him.

My new friend said, "Hey, Bill."

But Willie, obviously receptive to atmosphere, said he'd catch me later and ambled off in a haze of awkward vibrations. I felt sorry for him then because I am sometimes a human being as well as a journalist, strange as it may seem.

"Boy, I thought we'd never get rid of him," I said when Willie was gone.

Mister nice-guy, looking slowly around at everything, said, "So what do you think about all of this?"

Then he was examining my face as though he was thinking about kissing it. I mean that was weird.

I'll tell you what it was like. You're on a first date with somebody you like a lot and want to make an especially good impression on, which involves not letting them do certain things because they'd get the wrong impression of you. Only they don't even try to do those things because they know that's the way it is even before anything happens, and you know they know, and - Yeah.

I said, "Don't tell me - you're with The New York Times, here to offer me a job because everybody up there has heard what a damn good reporter I am."

His eyes were still nuzzling my cheek as he said, "No, I'm with the FBI," as casual as if he was from the phone company. He even showed me his credentials, which was unnecessary because I'd seen his shirt already.

"Okay, so I believe you. Now what ideas did you want to exchange?"

"From your pieces in The Star I assumed you'd know all about the healer."

"I thought you guys were trained not to make assumptions? And why would the FBI be interested in me knowing about him? You're looking out for his welfare in the interests of national security, right?"

His face stopped smiling but his eyes carried on. "Take it easy Miss Hendricks, we're on the same side. The Bureau's presence here is more out of habit than anything."

"This country has a lot of expensive habits," I suggested. "Ever thought of getting a proper job?" (Tough huh? The better the adversary, the tougher I get. You can say stuff like that in a book.)

He just laughed a little and eyed his own reflection in his sunglasses. "Look," he said, "As I'm your next Star story, I was hoping you'd help me out with some background material to pad-out my report. It's really just a formality, believe me." He looked away and back quickly. "Now I'll just bet when somebody says *believe me*, that's the last thing you do, yeah?"

It was my turn to watch him and say nothing.

He shook his head and gave me a rueful look. "Uh-huh, me too."

"What were you talking to those people about?" I said.

"Just passing the time of day."

"The hell you were. How old are you?"

He blinked because that always throws people if you say it right, especially young ones who imagine they're real smart.

"Something about you tells me you're not all bad," I told him. "So here's what I'll do. You give me the lowdown on what you've been asking people

268

today, I mean the truth, and I'll make sure you get to read my next piece in The Star. Whaddaya say?"

He grunted, but quite nicely. "That's a deal?"

"It's all you're getting from me."

He thought that over before putting his shiny glasses back on so I figured we'd reached a stalemate. His mouth crept a millimeter wider on each side and his eyebrows peaked above the frame of his glasses so I could see he was kind of amused, and for a while he seemed to be looking for something on the ground between us.

Then he said, "Miss Hendricks?"

"What?" I expected him to be rude or something.

"I like you...hope we meet again." He started backing away and nodding gently before he turned and mingled with the hot crowd once more, and either (A) I had the feeling we would be meeting again, or (B) that was just because I wanted it to happen. Only I didn't have time to dwell on the exchange because who should I see next but Mayor Stevenson. And who was that walking with him? Why, none other than the exotic Mrs. Maxine Stevenson, and boy, had she blossomed all of a sudden - if you call looking like a walking advertisement for hormone replacement therapy *blossoming*. Worse, she had on some of those skin-tight pants and a real frilly pink top that just didn't team at all. Her mind may've convinced itself she was getting younger, but it couldn't make her body believe it. Women of any age - even the ones who imagine they're cheating time with chemicals, implants and scalpels - still only ever grow older. (Okay, men too, but Maxine just happens to be a woman.) Having found religion - hell, the healer had actually, physically *touched* her, so religion had found her - Maxine was now using religion like a detergent to try and clean away the years of misery she'd carried around because of childlessness.

Maybe it would work. Though regardless of how Maxine looked, her appearance would've been improved enormously without her Mayoral escort. Had he also turned out for the healer on this sweltering day in early Summer? Like fun. The Mayor was there so people would see *him*.

On the surface of things the Mayor was pretty goddam irate about the healer spreading reactionary ideas against the proposed landfill project. The Mayor's problem was that he'd accepted a cash incentive from somebody on the landfill board way back when, and had no intention of relinquishing that incentive. Furthermore, the landfill would bring welcome jobs for voters in addition to any tourist income.

As I mentioned a few pages ago, the Mayor wasn't the only one taking the healer's name in vain that day. Resentment amongst the populace at large was growing steadily - hardly surprising when practically everything the healer said was, in some way or other, critical of self-interest. And wherever there's a buck to be made, self-interest is there in abundance. Also, if anything is guaranteed to rub the buck-makers the wrong way, if they're not too busy raking it in to care, it's somebody reminding them of their greed. Consequently as he processed through the crowd that day, Mayor Stevenson received a number of complaints, most of them from locals, but some caught in passing from complete strangers, because the healer's message was aimed at everybody and anybody who ever reached out their hand to take something.

Tagging along behind the Mayoral couple, licking on an ice-cream cone, was a sullen sheriff Hughes. I swear that man had put on ten pounds since I last saw him. Seeing Hughes made me uncomfortable because not once did his eyes leave Maxine's behind, and the way his tongue was going into that ice-cream…!

TAPE 60

The hastily erected wilderness public rest rooms were supplied by a builder in Zeno who'd made a donation to Mayor Stevenson's personal savings account for the privilege of landing the contract. He'd even come up with a new-style on-site disposal system that involved allowing all the effluent to seep into Blackwater Creek, which had suddenly and magically gotten designated a natural beauty spot. Whether it was from pollution of the creek, or from a threat to the local drinking water supply, one way or another the above situation would all eventually come right back in the Mayor's face.

Inside the female half of those toilets, an army of perspiring women of all ages, colors and attitudes to personal hygiene created a heady mix of conflicting odors. One was Donna Hughes, examining her face in the communal mirror and deciding she felt good about herself, proud of her transition from robot to disciple. Gazing into her own eyes she told herself that being one of the healer's helpers put her above these robots around her. Then the woman beside her dug a sharp elbow in her ribs as an 'accidental' incentive to move over, and Donna's mouth came open, a rebuke ready. She caught the woman's eyes in the mirror, recognized in them her own robot and felt a hard smile come onto her lips. The woman looked away quickly and

270

carried on fixing her hair, and when Donna stepped back to leave, the woman expanded instantly to fill the space she'd left, pointy elbows jutting in readiness for the next adversary. Donna felt even better about her own superiority.

Outside it was just about hot enough to fry ham, eggs, onions, tomatoes and a burger on the hood of your car. As Donna squinted against the brightness, her self-satisfaction faded at the memory of having told the healer how good she felt for overcoming her old robot. Personal growth was not a matter for pride, but humility, he'd said. Pride was just her old robot seeking to reassert its control over her.

The memory brought a rush of mixed feelings and made her shiver in the hot sunlight. She replaced her sunglasses and concentrated on the difference her short hair made to the feel of her head, because that was easier than self-reproach. Short hair gave her a new sense of lightness.

With the sun hot on her skin she suddenly wanted to tell other people how good she felt. She wanted to go out into this crowd and sell God. Except that the healer also made it clear he was not in the business of selling God. He said enlightenment, spiritual or otherwise, was free to all. He said it was too easy when you were just starting out to think you had all the answers upfront. Truth was, you yourself would be learning from the same enlightening process you were part of.

In pushing that thought aside, Donna caught sight of the familiar cop-colored shirt, the overweight shape inside it, the big, rounded shoulders, the head on which perspiration had plastered wisps of blond hair. Instantly she felt her insides clench, then other disturbing physiological changes that reminded her of the coloring-up of an octopus.

The sight of her father, ambling between these people, affected her whole personality. Because of this man she'd known all her life, she was unexpectedly tempted to see herself as a kind of healer groupie, acting the devotee and playing disciples.

She'd grown to dislike her father for all kinds of reasons: because of the leering way he looked at her with his dirty eyes; because he represented all the men who ever looked at her that way. But this man had a special power over her. After all she'd done to try and change, he could still make her feel like a guilty child, still undermine everything she was trying to do to change herself. It all crowded in on her at that moment, along with the knowledge that if she couldn't cure herself of him, she couldn't ever move on. Raw anger flushed through her at his ability to make her feel like this now she was a grown woman! Along with her teeth grinding on each other, Donna felt her hands bunched into small, hard fists until the pain made her stop squeezing. The anger was a confusion of both fear and fury.

God! For the first time since she quit The Triangle she wanted a stiff drink! And a smoke. Oh…oh Jesus and God! The robot was flexing its claustrophobically muscular wetsuit around her again.

She made herself look in her father's direction again because he seemed to represent everything she was fighting; all of the bad things she was trying to outgrow: the wayward, hard-nosed, determined-to-go-against-his-authority tramp. (Jesus. folks always said their parents made them what they were and it was God-almighty truer than they realized.)

Donna had the bastard's genes and she hated the realization. She was just too much like him. They really were two of a kind - only she must've gotten something else from somewhere. Well sure she did. She couldn't help but have his genes, but she sure as hell had her own mind, and she was going to beat those tainted Hughes genes!

She closed her eyes and from someplace within found a new insight: Dumping the robot was not the simple thing she'd imagined; that had only been the robot itself telling her it was simple, fooling her into thinking she'd made great strides towards a new way of feeling about everything. In truth she was still under its control; a new regime of robot control of a subtler and more dangerous kind. This sneaky new version of the robot had been walking around right along with her all the time - even while she'd been with the healer! Now that she was fighting it, it had hunched down into a smaller, more concentrated and potent version of that earlier and less complicated, easier-going, unthreatened self.

But right then and there, like a warm, comforting embrace in her mind, she heard *his* soft voice saying: 'Think of yourself as part of me, and of others the same way. Inseparable parts of the whole.'

Donna blinked, wide-eyed, suddenly newly aware of the sounds, the smells, the moving, dazzling, shocking force of so many people around her. It was like coming out of a dream, back from a journey inside of herself where she'd reviewed old thoughts, feelings and fears. She had - God almighty! - been back inside her old persona. But the healer's words stayed. Even though her father was still a dark shadow in her thoughts, she felt excitement and a new determination...

272

Here's a scenario to chew over. Don't spit it out simply because you were indoctrinated with another idea; try thinking bigger than your indoctrination.

As little pieces of an overall evolving consciousness, one short trip to this earthly level of material reality would hardly scratch the surface of everything there is to know and learn about. So we make repeated trips, each time learning something new, building on what we learned the times before. As we learn, we evolve, and our consciousness becomes more refined. This process of constant refinement is what gradually alters our view of material reality so we no longer see life merely as a ME, ME, ME thing. (And you imagined you were here just to get laid, or to see how fat you can get? Shame on you!)

I guess you know that the name for these repeat journeys is *reincarnation*. But why would a multi-level universal consciousness, already very old and knowledgeable, need to educate itself? Simply because you can never have too much education, no matter how smart you think you are. (And the smarter you get, the more you realize that.) Evolution *is* education, and learning new stuff is the most fulfilling experience - as you'll discover when you quit being a squid. The more times you re-learn stuff, the more new things you learn from it. And I'm not just talking about 2+2=57, I'm talking about everything you can possibly learn by evolving.

Huh? You think 2+2=4? Listen, 2+2 can = anything you want it to when you learned and evolved enough.

According to Ed, when we dump the monkey suit (when it dies) we revert to the state of disembodiment we had before we were born and we go someplace between the lives we experience on this planet. In that 'someplace' between lives we can check out what we learned (or not) in the life we just had, and decide what we need to learn during our next bit part in a monkey suit to help us continue evolving consciously.

In the place between lives we have counseling and advice from more advanced consciousnesses about precisely what kind of lives we still need to experience, which gender we need to be, rich or poor or whatever.

Hell, you know how life is. It seems excessively hard and unfair for some folks, right? Well those lives are the ones they chose for themselves, believe it or don't, during counseling between incarnations. In that enlightened state, we can appreciate that we need to go through specific experiences so we can learn specific lessons. (Seemingly easy, privileged lives can contain just as many lessons as the harsh lives - if we choose to use them that way instead of sitting back and taking it easy.)

Regardless of how painful or pointless a life looks from the outside, on a far more meaningful level of learning above this one, none of these experiences is wasted. Your Real, essential self (whether you call it your soul/spirit, higher self or something else) is indestructible; it learns from *every* experience. Even the most abominable-seeming tribulation is, ultimately, beneficial.

Whatever kind of life you land in, you know the unchanging rule of thumb for every situation: quit being selfish for YOU and YOURS. If you must be selfish, be it for somebody else who could use a break.

Incidentally, all of this information has been common knowledge and in the public domain for millennia - for anyone who's ready to go looking. If you have trouble with these notions, at least be prepared to think about them rather than shutting your mind. (And remember: no matter how smart you think you are, you know a heck of a lot less than you think you do.)

You heard of *karma*, aka reaping what you sow? Okay. People often think of good karma as being something you accumulate by being 'good', and bad karma what you get by being 'bad'. And being genetic, we then think bad karma is God or somebody wreaking vengeance, retribution or punishment on us, while good karma is material pleasure or rewards. Forget those notions. When you're between lives - before you slide back into the monkey suit that's most appropriate for your next trip into materiality - you get to see and experience a record of the way you lived your previous lives. This is a kind of review of your less-than-perfect behavior during each human life.

Every single moment of each life is recorded in the fabric of your higher consciousness, as it happens, and is replayed to you - *through* you - so you can re-experience your selfish mistakes, or the rarer moments of benevolence. The big difference is that between lives, you re-experience all of those moments as your Real, conscious self, unprotected by the cushioning stupidity of a material body/brain. And in re-experiencing the way you treated other people, you get to feel, for Real, the parts of yourself that need correcting.

Feeling how you caused other people to feel is another aspect of the learning process. We're all part of one big consciousness, so what you do to another part of that consciousness is the same as doing it to yourself.

Reality Window: Even between-lives, most folks' consciousness isn't evolved enough to get by without needing to create around itself a semblance of the earthly materiality they've gotten used to as a human being. So their mind creates familiar surroundings to make them feel at home. Like I said, we all create our own reality with our mind.

274

Anyhow, while you're reviewing your behavior in previous lives, that behavior is being assessed without emotion or criticism by more highly evolved consciousnesses, for whom only the practicalities of our personal evolution matter. You're then advised on how best to use your next life to help other people further their conscious evolution, and in doing that, to help you further yours. Though once you step into your next monkey suit, it's necessary that you promptly forget about other levels and other lives you've lived, otherwise you'd get completely confused. What you're not supposed to forget are your obligations to others.

Yet the fact is, most people find too many reasons to forget what they were counseled about on that higher conscious plane between lives, and instead allow themselves to be influenced by all of the material things that happen to them in gene-land. As human beings, from day one we're constantly presented with stuff that tempts us to be selfish. Being selfish means avoiding pain, hardship, deprivation or disapproval - genetically-created experiences - and instead succumbing to what this material body wants first and foremost. That usually winds up causing pain, hardship or deprivation for somebody else ultimately.

While we might conveniently forget why we're Really here, what never forgets is the part of your Real, conscious self that's always linked to the motherboard - the overall superconscious. If you're sufficiently evolved - and choose to evolve further - your earthly consciousness will access that higher level where details of your 'karmic' obligations are stored, and you'll remember, to a greater or lesser degree, what you and everybody else Really are: immaterial, eternal consciousness, rather than just a bunch of goddam monkeys. As a result, you might just get a bit more Real.

Recall those Real practicalities I talked about earlier? Love (the Real version, free of monkey suit influences), selflessness, forgiveness, tolerance and the rest? Exercising those Real practicalities is precisely how we re-establish contact with our own and each other's Real selves even though we're all dressed as monkeys.

TAPE 61

Donna didn't have to make a point of smiling because the woman smiled at her first.

"You seen the healer yet, ma'am?"

"What?"

"Beg pardon, I said have you been up to see the healer yet?"

"Why no. Should I have?"

"Most folks come down here just to see him."

"They do? I thought this was part of the park. We're touring."

"Mighty crowded little corner for a national park, don't you think?"

"Well now you come to mention that, I suppose it is. This is not my idea of a picnic stop, but the boys wanted to come up."

"You mean you ain't even heard of the healer?"

"No. What does he do? No, that's a silly question. He heals people, yes?"

"In a way, yes he does. You mind if I kind of sit down here a moment?"

"Go right ahead. My husband's just over there with the boys getting ice-cream."

The queue for ice-cream was a mile long, it seemed. "They been gone long?"

"Just a couple of days."

Donna smiled at the woman. "Yeah, that's 'bout right."

When Donna had settled down on the grass the woman said, "Well I must say, honey, for a hot day like this one you certainly seem cool and collected. And I do like your sweet little top. Did you buy that locally?"

"No, I made this."

"Really? I'm hopeless with my hands. But why do I get the impression you're dying to tell me about the healer?"

"That obvious, uh?"

The woman scrutinized her with a gentle smile. "He means a lot to you?"

"Oh yes he does."

"What's your name?"

"Donna Hughes."

"Local, Donna?"

"Yes ma'am, Passmore."

The woman decided Donna belonged to a religious sect. Well maybe that was better than doing a lot of other things, and maybe it wasn't. She hoped this young woman wasn't immersed in something dangerous; that would be such a shame. "So tell me about the healer."

"Well, he talks about how we're all part of the same God, whatever our religion, so we shouldn't go imposin' religious barriers between each other because that's like choppin' God into different little pieces an' sayin' we got the right piece an' you don't."

276

The woman wondered if this girl, still in her teens, had any real appreciation of what she was being fed, or if she was simply repeating what this healer said through misplaced devotion.

"But surely people have a right to preserve their own traditions, their own unique culture? Doesn't that include their religion too?"

"Well there's a problem in that, isn't there, an' a lot of room for excuses? Too many folks have a tradition of hatin' the people of other cultures for ancient reasons that nobody would even recall or care about if those reasons were not preserved and kept alive in their different ideas about religion. Havin' a different religion gives you a reason for thinkin' you got God on your side, while the folks you hate don't. That religious difference just reminds people of bad stuff that happened long ago. Ain't that just a way of keepin' old wounds open…an excuse to go on hatin' each other?"

"Religion - a way to keep old wounds open? I always thought religion was meant to make us more caring towards each other?"

"Well it might, if folks didn't keep those religious walls up between each other. They're not real walls, just symbols of old differences between them. While you got those religious symbols, you got reasons for stayin' different, 'cept there's no real differences between people - it's only the *idea* of a difference keepin' those old fears and hatreds alive in their mind. Without the walls we make in our minds, we're all the same."

"Well yes, I suppose we are, but - ."

"Ma'am, we *are* all the same. It's just that some folks have such strict religious traditions symbolizin' those imaginary differences, an' they just won't give an inch 'cause, uh, maybe they're scared to. The only differences are ones *we* make. We all came from the same beginnin' and we're all goin' to the same end. How we get there is what this is all about…an' if we think some of us have more of a God-given right to get there than others, it's just gonna take *all* of us longer to get there."

The woman felt a little overwhelmed, but that didn't stop Donna.

"See, we're all part of the same idea. You might say it was God's idea, but God didn't invent prejudice. Prejudice is all our idea. The healer tells us that prejudice and inequality and all of those things are products of fear and misunderstanding."

"Tell me why inequality is a product of misunderstanding."

"It's because we don't understand ourselves an' what we're doin' here, mostly. If we have more wealth than other folks, that's just God givin' some of us the responsibility of usin' what we got for the good of everybody, not so we can keep it all for ourselves."

The woman looked thoughtful. "The healer said all that?"

"Yes ma'am, and much more besides, 'bout all kinds of things."

There's more on this tape about why we reincarnate over and over. The plain and simple reason is that you just can't learn everything in one life. According to Ed it takes countless different lives and experiences, lived as all kinds of people with different genders, in every kind of circumstance you can imagine and plenty you can't. And not only on this planet; through all levels of material reality, consciousness is constantly evolving and reincarnating. That way you get to experience EVERYTHING.

It sure makes a lot more sense than experiencing just one lifetime. If you believe you're alive so you can learn stuff, why stop after you just got started, when you can be forever moving upward, becoming ever more, uh, refined? Why shouldn't it go on forever? What do you know anyhow?

And don't expect to get a break from learning during your many trips to the betweenlife. Ed said there's plenty of opportunity to work on projects you maybe worked on while you were on this planet, or on ideas you'll be developing on your next trip down here. (Though even in the betweenlife there are folks who just sit around, mentally speaking.) The smart ones, they want to grow.

See, when you arrive in the betweenlife there's no longer a monkey suit influencing you and confusing matters. You have a clearer picture of what you Really are. On reviewing who you were and what you did earthside, in earlier lives, you're more able to appreciate how much you still have to learn, and what you need to do to learn it. (Think of the betweenlife as the place where you get your head straight about what needs to be done, and this life as the place where you get the opportunity to put that information into practice.)

Reincarnation figures in the belief systems of millions of people just as sane as you, remember. To many of them, consciousness is just the working extension of their soul.

Let's pick this thing up where you're in the betweenlife, about to be re-born in your new human body. You've been shown scenarios of earlier lives and situations where you still have responsibilities to fulfill. (Maybe you mishandled relationships with people or failed to complete your 'mission' on earth in some other way.)

278

Then you're shown more scenarios of opportunities to complete those responsibilities in the coming life. These are future scenarios where you'll get the chance to interact with the same consciousnesses involved in those past relationships. (For example, if you were mean to somebody in an earlier life, you'll be shown opportunities to make amends.)

If you're wondering how you're able to see future scenarios during the betweenlife period, recall tape #33 about how time is entirely negotiable when consciousness is free of materiality. Okay?

Like you, the consciousnesses you'll be interacting with from your earlier lives will be in new monkey suits in your next life, though you might still recognize something familiar about them. But the part of your conscious self on that higher level of Reality will know them, and record your progress with them.

Next, your consciousness is born into a new monkey suit. This involves the different levels of consciousness that together make the Real YOU, forming an interface with all of the so-called *material* waves/particles that comprise the monkey suit. A diagram in one of Ed's books showed the seven frequencies of consciousness energy that create our subtle bodies. (Remember the Russian doll image of a series of more refined energy layers that correspond with our physical body/brain?) The consciousness energy in these subtle bodies is governed by seven intersections - called *chakras* (it means wheel) – that constantly adjust the energy and circulate it around and through your body/brain via a complex network of channels, okay? (Seven is supposed to be a highly esoteric number. Think of Snow White and the seven dwarfs.)

As you evolve during each lifetime (*if* you evolve), the seven levels of consciousness interact and adjust through the chakras, accommodating changes in your personal evolution, and also maintaining a direct link with the higher part of your consciousness (called the *superconscious*) that keeps a record of your life.

Superconsciousness is actually all of the consciousnesses in everyone and everything, on every evolutionary level, all of it combined to make the overall consciousness, aka Ed's corporate consciousness, aka God, okay? This superconscious maintains a connection between itself, your subconscious, and your everyday consciousness.

Well certainly it's complicated – while you're in a monkey suit.

Now I want to expand on what Donna said to that woman about religious indoctrination and the divisiveness it creates, and not just in more obviously

279

repressive religions. Oh-ho no. Even in democracies, where freedom of thought is prized so highly, kids don't get to decide for themselves what they want to believe. Tradition and ritual often win out over freedom of thought, and by the time kids are adults, they're stuck with someone else's ideas about stuff that could influence their behavior for the rest of their life. That's what it's meant to do, right? And it's wrong. Indoctrination only helps maintain the narrowness and divisiveness of religion. If kids are taught 'this is the one and only way to believe', already you've closed their mind to everything else. Not only did you restrict their freedom of thought, you also made them unwilling to see people with different beliefs as equals.

Why'd you do it? Because somebody indoctrinated you the same way, just like they were indoctrinated. And so it's gone on, right back through human history and even before that, starting with the way those first smart monkeys got their beliefs - from their own primitive imaginations. I know that's hard to accept, but what shouldn't be hard is seeing how unreasonable, how negative this indoctrination process is for everybody.

And yet how many folks would even consider telling their kids: 'Don't just adopt my beliefs - go think about other beliefs, keep an open mind, then choose.'? Precious few, because most religions just want to see life in terms of *their* narrow rules, *their* restrictive principles, *their* repressive dogmas.

I already explained how religion per se is designed to *resist* integration with people from other regions rather than welcome it. Yet those other people are as much like you as anybody could be if you took away the illusory cosmetic differences of skin color, ideology or religion. Inside we're all the goddam same, in the best way. But often we don't want to know about that way because we're all the same in the worst way also. And that worst way is overruling the best way. (If you don't believe me, read this book.)

That's how vital it is not to indoctrinate kids with ideas set in holy concrete. That way, they wind up nursing the same old superstitions, grudges and bigotry, when they could have been taught to question those dogmas. Boy, it makes me mad to think how many millions of people have gotten ruined by some narrow-minded fool with a chip on their shoulder, deliberately denying them the chance to see a bigger picture.

The healer talked about that bigger picture. He also said it's not some superior being called God who writes bibles filled with complicated rules, arcane ritual and divisive rigmarole. Those are all human inventions, traceable right back to imaginative monkeys.

280

At the wilderness that day, the healer was also spreading ideas about kindness, generosity, unselfishness and respect for life - concepts that come from people wanting to evolve, rather than from their monkey origins. And what happened? If those simple ideas didn't fit in with people's indoctrinations, they either weren't interested or they got mad. Some of 'em got real mad. Some just got confused over the whole business.

Like Andrew DeSoto. Remember I mentioned awhile back that Andrew wished he could meet Miss Right? Well that's exactly what happened. The Wright family had driven down from Chicago in their motorhome especially to see the healer. Miss Rebecca Wright, a few years older than Andrew, hadn't been too overjoyed about making this trip for personal reasons. Not that it's any of your business, but her period had just started the morning they were setting out, and Rebecca Wright felt about as romantic as a damp bedsheet until the day she met Andrew DeSoto at the ice-cream vendor. Then she saw a pair of eyes almost as sad as her own, and those hungry little genes of hers all started jumping up and down, waving their arms in the air and yelling at the top of their voice: *Reproduce us.* Though to be fair to sexual equality, Andrew saw nothing wrong in reproducing his genes either now he'd found Miss Wright. After all, the sight, sound, smell, taste, feel and idea of Miss Right - or Mister Right - is just one big chemical circus designed by mindless molecules for the sole purpose of persuading you to party.

I stood and watched Andrew and his new-found beloved listen to P.P. Johnson tell a group of Japanese tourists they were worshipping the wrong God. I got it all on tape, so as there's nothing of me in it I'll be out back making coffee while you read this, and I'd be obliged if you'd yell when you're done so I can insert the tape containing the next part of this story, 'kay?

TAPE 62

P.P. Johnson had graduated some in public speaking since I last saw him. Old P.P. probably had more of his father the Senator in him than he cared to admit. The difference was that P.P. was seeing the arguments his father used to bully opponents into doing things, from the opposite side of the fence. With his fertile imagination, P.P. was able to put himself in the shoes of the downbeaten underdog. From there, with his knowledge of the kill-or-be-killed world of high finance, he also understood how money is used to keep the underdog under.

Though what was really running through P.P.'s mind while he spoke to that party of nice Japanese people was how he'd phoned Susan E. out of the blue and said he'd quit Harvard, and in the next breath that he'd quit her also.

I won't make a big thing of P.P.'s bust-up with Susan E., other than to say she was unhappy about it. Well okay, if you read what I said about P.P.'s father's reaction to his son's rebellious new attitude, you'll maybe have some idea of the way Susan E. reacted, her being so much like P.P.'s father and all. I don't think P.P.'s left ear ever fully recovered from that conversation. Susan E.'s pain went real deep: all the way down to the roots of her pride.

The English poet and dramatist William Congreve wrote: 'Heaven has no rage like love to hatred turned, nor hell a fury like a woman scorned.'

Anyhow, Susan E. didn't waste too much time thereafter getting to P.P.'s parents to do some scorning. In fact she saw them just so she could scorn the pants off of them, with an aside about how their beloved son had also quit Harvard. By then P.P. was out of it, with no notion of the storm he'd kicked up, because his exit didn't simply involve Susan E. and his parents, but Susan E.'s parents too, who were pretty influential in their own right, though not so much as the Senator; they just had a lot of financial muscle without the political edge.

No, things didn't end with the loud noises money makes; not with all of the hopes and dreams of the Johnson family's dynastic genes riding on old P.P. His Senator father was a hard man, and that extended to his treatment of his own son. As the Senator would have explained, he was only doing it for P.P.'s own good, the way all parents do. He was teaching the boy how to survive in a tough world. But when P.P. turned around and dumped on the family's good name and their expectations, to say the Senator was disappointed would be like saying a rattlesnake can give you a real nasty look.

Even a parent like the Senator tends to be more forgiving of judgmental errors in their own genetic issue. Only when the issue stray so far from the accepted route they pose a danger to the survival of the species does infanticide become a serious option.

Yet before it need come to that, there are other options. The healer was the Senator's other option. To people like Senator Johnson, the healer was just a pseudo-religious publicity seeker at the heart of all of his family's troubles, and Senator Johnson was a past master at removing unwanted options.

Thinking on all of the stuff about chakras and reincarnation in those earlier tapes, I figured that for a lot of people, simply being unfamiliar with those

282

things might automatically invalidate them. Even more people are unfamiliar with quantum physics, but does that make quantum physics invalid? No. And what about your own consciousness? Even neuroscientists can't pin that down, but nobody says consciousness is invalid.

Then there are people who're *clairvoyant*. It means clear-sighted. These people can 'see' into dimensions of Reality that ordinary folks can't. There are people who're clairsentient (clear-knowing), clairaudient (clear-hearing), and so on. These folks used to exist on the fringe of accepted reason, like spiritualist mediums and mind readers. Then the new age happened, and now anything goes.

Hoaxers aside (you get those in any business), clairvoyants are attuned to the unseen vibrations created by consciousness. Such people can actually see other levels of reality above this material one.

Being more sensitive this way is something we're all capable of, and a perfectly normal aspect of everybody's evolution, yet is unaccepted by science because their instruments can't detect it. It's not the extra sensitivity that's crazy, it's the non-acceptance. Like not accepting the crazy notion of TV before you even understand what electricity is.

There are millions of 'ordinary' people who glimpse more of Reality than is supposed to be 'normal' - through premonitions, near-death and out-of-body experiences and so on. Are they all nuts, or might 'normal' not be confined to the frequency that matter vibrates at, in a tiny segment of the energy spectrum that monkey suits can access? Right.

What really surprises me is that most of the billions of people who want to believe in a soul, an afterlife and God, are so goddam skeptical about the unexplained stuff of life. They're like kids living in a house filled with unexplained noises and half-glimpsed movements out the corner of their eye. Even when folks like *moi* offer explanations for these things, what do they do? They cower in fear of them and/or worship them. Or they let the skeptics tell them these things don't exist, and that they're nuts to even want to believe in unexplained things.

Too many people confuse 'healthy skepticism' with 'not thinking beyond strict boundaries'. Yet the boundaries are all products of our own ignorant past. By sticking yourself with rigid scientific or religious dogmas, the former bound by what can be 'proven', the latter by superstition, and refusing to think outside of those, you cut yourself off from so much knowledge and information, so many profound ideas. Those two major opposing dogmas –

religion and science - force kids to make an either/or choice, when we should be giving them enlightened guidance that *re-minds* them they're only a small part of an infinitely wider Reality where dogma only serves to inhibit Real progress.

Enough. I'm gonna walk away from all of this and come back in a couple of martinis.

TAPE 63

There was no phone at the settlement so Luke Lawrence couldn't call to fix a meeting with the healer; he just had to turn up and hope for an interview, or whatever you called seeing this guy one-on-one. And this morning it was really throwing it down, the rain a continuous spread of small caliber gunfire on the roof of his rental car as he negotiated the empty backroads, deliberately driving through waterlogged depressions in the road to wash the mud off. Not only were there no splash-guards on this model, its bodyshell seemed to have been designed so road dirt would deposit a dark streak up the front doors.

As the wipers cleared a repeated swathe through sheets of rainwater, Luke decided that his dislike of badly designed bodyshells was the tip of an iceberg: his dislike of thoughtlessness. Carelessness. Lack of consideration in all its forms. People not taking enough care over what they did. Somebody didn't take enough care designing this car to stop it being a mud magnet. Maybe people only took real care over something when it was for themselves. There was less incentive to do their best when it was for somebody else.

What had gotten him thinking along these lines? His job. Did he take care over the way he did it? Sure he did. Certainly. The problem wasn't with him, it was with the job itself. Like the way they neglected to tell him he was here today to set the healer up.

This was how it often happened; it was one of the things that had disillusioned him about his job. The gray areas. The secret knowledge. The deceit through omission.

It hadn't started out as a setup. Initially he was just eyes and ears; passive information gathering. Then it dawned on him what was really going down. He'd seen this assignment move through a series of subtle shifts in emphasis and now he knew precisely what his role had become: He was the mechanism that would unlock the door so they could walk in and take the healer...and he was *taking care* over it because it was his goddam *vocation*. Because he couldn't
284

help but take care over what he did, even when he disagreed with it. That was his nature.

Being FBI had once seemed a vital, worthwhile and honorable thing. Not anymore. The vocation had gotten to seem like a burden. There were too few arguments for, too many against. Too often, what barely seemed morally justifiable to one half of your brain, was practically an outrage to the other half. That was the nub of this unhappiness with his vocation. Well hey, the public executioner had a vocation, but if you happened to disagree with the taking of human life, even under socially accepted circumstances, calling an executioner's job a vocation or anything else didn't make it right. After all, this was more than just his job; this was his life!

The wipers rolled from side to side but the thought stayed in the front of his mind. Ten minutes later he stopped the car at the dead end of an unmade track next to a rickety lean-to shed and let the window down a couple of inches to enjoy not being out there in the rain. And there he sat for a while in the rainy silence, waiting for the right moment to get out, not realizing that inside this dilapidated wooden lean-to, under a thin veil of dust, reposed the Porsche belonging to a Senator's son.

Was anybody up this early? How early did the healer rise? It was twenty after eight; somebody must be up and about. Boy, just look at this place. It was a miserable sight in this weather. If the healer was raking in the donations from a devoted following, he was not spending it on luxury accommodation.

Okay, time to review procedure. He was Special Agent Luke Lawrence, here as an envoy from the government with an official notification of discredit, dressed up to look like recognition of the healer's status as a spiritual leader. The ploy was to tempt him with a promise of protection from factions who wished him harm. The promise was, in fact, a statement of intent. The machinery was already in place for his removal.

Luke felt a mounting discomfort at this thing he was party to. Never mind about the First Amendment of the US Constitution stating that 'Congress shall make no law respecting an establishment of religion, or prohibiting the free exercise thereof; or abridging the freedom of speech.' That had never gotten in their way before if they thought somebody was misusing that freedom. It wouldn't this time either. Luke Lawrence was here to make sure of that.

"Hi."

Luke's head snapped sideways. He didn't jump out of his skin because that was not his style. His stomach tightened and his skin prickled.

Looking in at him over the lowered glass was a grinning, gap-toothed mouth with a beat-up face loosely arranged around it. The hair was flattened onto the skull by running rain and the shoulders of his parka were slick like a wetsuit, but this guy's grin said he didn't mind. Luke knew this was Michael McClure, one of the healer's so-called disciples.

"Good morning," Luke told him.

The grin unchanged, the guy looked sideways up into the falling rain that forced him to blink happily. "It's good for me. I like rain."

Luke had to grin back. "I can see that!" He started to open the door, watching McClure back off so he could get out. "Luke Lawrence. FBI. I'd like to see the healer. He around?"

McClure wiped water out of his eyelashes. "Sure he is. Yeah, I know." He walked away, then turned back. When the man wasn't following, McClure said, "C'mon," and set off again.

Luke started after him, silently chastising himself for not having had the foresight to outfit himself properly for this weather. Before they were half-way to the long hut, which had to be their destination because there was nothing else over there for Christ's sake, his tan loafers were soaking wet and his socks and feet right along with them. Suddenly he knew that he hadn't brought rubber boots or an umbrella because he didn't want this assignment.

A dripping McClure showed him into a sparse hangar of a place smelling of mildew and cooking. The long hut had been partitioned off so all Luke could see of the interior was this inhospitable dining area with its long table and chairs around it.

"Hey!" McClure was pointing to Luke Lawrence's shoes, still grinning. It didn't seem to bother him that his own tattered sneakers were leaking.

"Like I said, I'm here to see the healer. Mind telling him?"

A jittery anticipation had begun inside Luke. He was here to see the same healer he'd gotten a good look at up there in the wilderness. He'd listened to the guy talking to people in that real quiet voice he had, using those strangely structured sentences that somehow moved your thoughts around in new ways. His words kind of parted your old ideas, Red Sea fashion - corny, but true - then he'd bring other concepts through the middle with those intriguing sentences.

Yeah, it had really happened. The healer had been saying something about…

"Mr. Lawrence - *Luke?*"

Luke turned towards his name and recognized Matt.

286

"Morning. He's waiting for you, when you're ready."

Luke frowned. "You were expecting me?"

"You want to follow me?" Matt said.

"Sure. Okay." Luke became conscious of his wet shoes again and looked down.

Matt said, "Take 'em off - he won't mind."

Luke looked up, knowing there was no way he'd remove his shoes for this meeting and heard himself say, "Uh-huh. Maybe I will." He picked the loafers up, wondering what to do with them.

"Allow me." Matt took the shoes that Luke was reluctant to let go of and handed them to McClure, to whom they might well have been a small puppy from the way he handled them.

Luke and Matt were going through the inner door by the window leading through to the body of the long hut when McClure called out, "You only get these back after I fix you some breakfast."

TAPE 64

Recall my theory: *Reality is what you think*. Maybe you got it and maybe you didn't. So what if I hand you a flower and a hundred dollar bill and say you can keep whichever you think is more real. Why would you take the money, knowing for a fact that flowers and dollar bills are both the same kind of 'real'?

The answer is, because something is distorting your understanding of 'reality'. Something is making the money more 'real' for you than the flower. But being a smartass you'd argue that this wasn't about 'distorting reality', or one thing being 'more' real that another. This was about the practical, common-sense reasons why we put relative values on things. Everybody knows why money has more value than flowers.

Right. So why does it?

It's because money represents the material survival of you and yours. That's the only reason why money has any value whatsoever to you or anybody else. Could something as important as your survival distort your understanding of reality? It wouldn't need to if it *created* your understanding of reality in the first place.

Now consider the intriguing fact that materially real things are simultaneously getting less real for us, and more real for us, all the time. To insist that reality will forever be confined to the way you currently perceive material things and their meanings, assumes that your consciousness won't evolve any further *in relation to* material things. That assumption is as nutty as thinking that our consciousness won't evolve any further period. Yes, I know some folks think that the natural selection pressures that drive organism evolution eased off for us so much that we practically stopped evolving. We didn't. There's more competitive selection pressure now than ever, but it's on our *conscious* evolution as we rely more on our mental abilities than our physical ones.

Now mom, sane people like us know that mindless material things don't get more conscious do they?

No Laurie. Mindless material things stay mindless. The only thing that gets more conscious is you *in relation to* material things. Everything evolves, but whereas material things merely change into other material things, only consciousness becomes more conscious. And as it does, it recognizes that materially real things are both less real - meaning less solid - and more real - meaning we understand more about what they really are. This also applies to our materially real brains.

Earlier I said that our consciousness evolves and, just by thinking, influences the brain's evolution as well. But being made from fundamentally different stuff , consciousness and brains evolve not just in different ways, but in different *realities*. (Consciousness is aware and can think, whereas everything else isn't and can't.)

A good word here is exponential. (Go look up exponential in that dictionary you keep hidden in case somebody suspects you can read.) In this instance, exponential means that while external influences cause mindless genes to design bodies/brains to suit themselves, consciousness - merely by thinking and without realizing it - is designing bodies/brains to suit *itself*. As consciousness evolves exponentially in relation to brains, it slowly takes over from genes in the design of brains and the way they work.

This process began long before living organisms knew it was happening. Even the poor excuse for consciousness in the simplest nervous systems influences their design and operation by working to a slightly different agenda than the chemicals around it.

So. The Real you (of your consciousness) becomes more Real in relation to the mindless material things around you, including your body and brain. Hell no, the things around you don't *seem* any less real to you. You only get a few

288

score years in each life to observe any changes and that ain't long enough to notice anything.

"But Laurie, if this amazing conscious evolution is happening anyhow, why are you beating a book out of all these tiny tapes?"

Because of the eternal downside. No, I don't mean you having to read this book. I mean that we're not simply dragging our primitive past behind us in the shape of DNA's ass, we're pushing it ahead of us by trying to *be* that ass. We got the Descartes in front of the goddam horse!

TAPE 65

Under the banner HEALER GETS FBI BODYGUARD, my next Star piece wondered who was going to protect the healer - or anyone else - from organizations like the FBI. I did it as a joke, not realizing how prophetic it would become.

Anyhow this short chapter is in here so I can bring you up to speed with what our other characters were doing.

I just bet you were wondering what happened to my friend whether he wanted to be or not, Rudy Deeks? Well, after I met him in the wilderness that last time, I didn't hear another thing until he showed up outside FBI headquarters in Washington, doing the piece that would get him fired from CNLB. But more of that later.

Did somebody mention Ed? Remember I used to call him Ed the Logger just to annoy him? Well it didn't, and that annoyed me. You know the syndrome: you see that someone is better than you so you try to find fault with them. The clinical term for that is 'jerkoff'. And all because you admire something good in somebody other than yourself. Is that sane or what? (Ed went off to live someplace in Alaska, and who could blame him?)

On the subject of marijuana, after Jeff Ackerley's little crop failed he tried a little pushing until Matt banned him from The Triangle. Ackerley then tried the same thing in the wilderness, only that's another part I haven't reached yet, and neither have you - unless you're reading this book back to front. It might make just as much sense. Don't let's get bogged down in tradition here.

Harvey Brown, proprietor of the Gun 'n' Tackle store in Passmore, was still dying from the inside out. If you ever saw anybody do that, man, it's an awful thing to behold. I don't know if you believe in ghosts, but I'd say Harve was half-way there without waiting for his heart to stop beating, haunting his own life the way ghosts haunt the space between this life and the betweenlives state. Even the upturn in sales at the store couldn't prevent old Harve's premature demise; his mind was made up.

Rosemary Brown, on the other hand, was coming to life after all those years thanks to the healer, but you already know that so I'll move on to something you don't know: how hard Andrew DeSoto, sheriff Hughes' deputy-cum-dawgsbody, was struggling with himself over his recent acquisition, the waif-like Miss Rebecca Ruth Wright. I call her waif-like because of her big, sad eyes. Maybe she knew - without actually knowing she knew - that her new love Andrew was not to be her husband and the father of her children as she hoped, regardless of her parents letting them use the Winnebago for their pre-marital sex while the rest of the family were out at the wilderness enjoying theirselves in other ways. Hey, don't ask me why they tolerated such licentious behavior; I'm just telling it like it is. Who knows, maybe they thought that by letting the cop knock their daughter up, the marriage would be in the bag. They'd been trying to offload her for years.

I'm going to leave you hanging there and go onto something completely else. Such as how Susan E.V. Raleigh, recently spurned ultra-rich spoilt brat ex-girlfriend of P.P. Johnson, was continuing where P.P. left her: superficially outraged for her pride's sake, secretly excited by the prospect of parading her high-profile available status for the bidders, interested only in netting the highest.

Playing the field is always more rewarding when you've known, as Susan E. did, that everyone who'd been wishing you were on the market, would now get their chance to play for the prize. Needless to say Susan E. had all-but forgotten about someone named P.P. Johnson. If anyone asked, her dumping him had resulted in his seeking solace in some kind of dropout hippie commune.

Now about Maxine. Being reunited in God meant it was alright to sleep with your husband again after goodness knows how many years of marital celibacy, because the healer had finally taken away her misplaced sense of guilt and the stigma of being devoid of baby-making equipment. It wasn't just the sex; having her family happy again was the real blessing. Well heavens above, her son (she never used the expression stepson) was even a disciple! God had shined a light into her life again.

God had also shined the same light into Bobby Stevenson's life. He'd decided that it didn't matter one way or the other if Maxine couldn't reproduce; his real rake-off from this particular blessing was finding out just how good sex could be after all those years.

In fact I'm gonna be unchivalrous and say the Mayor was making a pig of himself courtesy of that divine light. Only now I'm making myself feel uncomfortable because I like Maxine, whereas I don't care for the Mayor at all, and just visualizing them together, well…If you think that's distasteful, I'd best not say anything at all about sheriff Neil Hughes, other than that he was still smarting.

Then there's Mrs. Catherine Hughes. *Oh my!* Mrs. Hughes was last seen playing the vodka bottle, and it wasn't even good vodka. (The Polish stuff is pretty good.) She was enjoying every inebriated minute of her holy confusion. Both text and illustrations in that bible of hers had taken on some quite lurid and fantastical configurations, but then bibles are like that when you think about it. Not that you will, their being sacrosanct and you a Godfearing person. Maybe even in the same way Catherine Hughes is.

And finally there's Senator Robert Johnson, otherwise known as P.P.'s father. (P.P.! I mean to say, didn't his parents realize the cruel names he'd get himself called?) Misinformation is a polite way of describing what the Senator handed to the FBI about the healer and everything that was happening in the wilderness. Bare-assed lies is a more succinct way to put it, but as that's so crude I won't say it. And boy, was the Senator one ace bare-assed liar, which is twice I didn't say it.

Enough marker-buoys. Back to the story.

TAPE 66

On this tape I want to say a little more about how the Real, conscious you becomes more Real in relation to the material things around you (including your body/brain), but I'm in a lousy mood so this'll be brief. It'll also be very simple but you will need a few basic pieces of equipment: A mind, a tire-iron to force it open, and something to wedge in there to stop it slamming shut again. The triple-strength martini is optional but I happen to like it.

Let's go. Your expanding consciousness is a unique environment of multi-dimensional awareness exploding slowly in every conceivable direction, and some inconceivable ones. Because the Real, conscious you is composed of different, interacting facets of awareness, the actual process of conscious evolution involves you gradually learning to understand what each of these parts of your conscious self is and does, and how to integrate them as the whole, evolving you...kind of thing. (I'm trying to keep this brief and understandable. It ain't easy.)

In plain words, what happens is that you slowly become more conscious. But that's not all that happens. In evolving consciously, the relationship between your consciousness and material things evolves as well.

Because you're currently using a material brain and body to manipulate material things outside of yourself, you probably think that's the only way it can be done. Not so. As human consciousness evolves exponentially in relation to material things, it's able to interface and, increasingly, to manipulate, other forms of matter besides the monkey suit it's in. And I do mean remotely, without needing to touch them.

You do that routinely each time you're out of an earthly body/brain (between lives). But you forget you had that ability when you get back down here in material reality.

Yeah, I know - remotely controlling matter with your mind sounds like a dream, but that's what some dreams are: the Real, conscious you, acting out scenarios in the more refined dimensions of reality that you visit during sleep.

The more your conscious self evolves, the more *real* seeming these so-called 'dreams' become. Far enough down the line you'll learn how to by-pass the need for a material brain and body altogether, and to manipulate the material universe without having to dream to do it. You'll learn to interface an ever greater part of materiality directly, at finer levels, without the need for a middle-man monkey suit.

Okay. So as I was saying before I interrupted myself, your expanding medium of multi-dimensional conscious awareness is exploding slowly in every conceivable direction all the time. (I have trouble thinking of my mom doing that, but even she is part of this process.) In doing that, your mind constantly bumps into new ideas about things.

You know what happens when you meet a new idea, or extend an old one. As DNA's brain evolves more consciousness-handling capacity, you get (A) more new ideas/extended old ideas coming your way, but (B) you're also able to think more *deeply* about them; to make more connections between ideas; to go further outside of yourself knowledge-wise. And with ever more knowledge of new ideas about reality coming into your growing mental environment, you become not just aware of a greater proportion of reality, you also come to a more profound, more complex, more meaningful *understanding* of reality -

292

embodied in questions like why, how, when, where, and even *if* the stuff of reality is the way you previously thought, and what else it might be if you thought some more. (You know what I mean so quit looking deliberately dumb. It isn't deliberate? Okay.)

You know the old saying (which I just made up): 'You have to start stupid to learn how not to be.' Well, the difference between being stupid and learning how not to be, is the same difference between your expanding consciousness simply pushing new ideas out of your way and ignoring them (narrow-mindedness), or thinking them over and assimilating them as knowledge. Knowledge increases your understanding of the overall Reality those ideas are part of.

Even though DNA's influence keeps minds narrowed for its benefit in a metaphorical sense, consciousness, by its very nature, just goes on assimilating an increasing number of ideas about reality, and growing. You become more conscious of what it means to be consciousness. If you still think it means being a survival tool for genes, you just ain't as conscious as you thought you were.

Now look at this conscious expansion process another way. We don't simply meet new ideas and assimilate them; as our consciousness expands, we *become* those new ideas. That new knowledge becomes the raw material of what we *are*. (It's the 'you are what you eat' principle, and it works in exactly the same way when your mind imbibes ideas as it does when DNA's body imbibes chemicals called food or chemicals called illegal.)

Everything in the material universe that impinges on human evolution helps determine what we become. Just 'knowing' about things causes not only our material evolution, but our conscious evolution also.

By 'knowing', I mean we 'know' the events that created us as parts of our own nature. (When a thing is created by events, and the whole of its development caused by those events, the thing created is an *expression* of those events.) The events that directly cause and influence your creation and evolution become you.

Your eyes, for example, were made by a long, complex stream of interactions between evolving matter and evolving consciousness, which is like saying that your eyes now 'know' that stream of interactions. If you're having trouble seeing that, imagine your body (and every other material thing) as material features on a map drawn from all the events and interactions that made them. While these material bodies/brains are the 'map' of all the material events that made them, our consciousness is a metaphysical map, made not from material events but from our thoughts about those events, and the way we relate to them.

Our consciousness becomes a 'thinking representation' of all of this knowledge. We then cause our bodies and brains to evolve faster by putting that knowledge to use. This means that what you consciously choose to think about, determines an ever-increasing portion of the structure of your brain and how it works.

No matter how complex you see this notion - even down to brain maps and the mega-subtleties of the conscious interface inherent in those billions upon billions of connections - it simply means that we can choose what we absorb, how we absorb it, etc., and why. We can choose what we want to become. This ability to choose our own destiny by deciding the shape of our minds and bodies, is the ultimate expression of our freedom from the iron grip of material laws.

TAPE 67

By midday it was raining again in the wilderness, just heavily enough to make sitting on the ground about as sensible as peeing in your pants. The smell of wet grass and damp earth mingled with other aromas drifting through the crowd: burgers and wet hair; fries with warmed clothing confined under plastic; hotdogs with wet dogs; limp, perfumed kleenex to wipe a kid's ketchupy mouth. Smells that seep out of home videos to help color the memories.

Luke Lawrence would never forget how the wilderness looked and smelled that day. Its memory seemed to have registered in a brand new way of perceiving things. Before, this crowd were not individuals; his sterile professional attitude had made them an amorphous, inhuman whole, a slowly shifting mass of movement, an all-pervading atmosphere of sound, a statistic that could be manipulated without emotion. Now they were people again.

As he walked amongst them, their magically individual images, their real and animated features, their distinctive actions and mannerisms, unique quirks and one-off combinations of all those, were mirrored facets of himself. The vivid, rain-washed colors of their personalities were reflections of his own, and that made him one of them, instead of the superior, detached observer. He even felt awkward in the Burberry trenchcoat he had coveted for months before feeling justified in spending that kind of money on what was, after all, just a raincoat. It had fitted who he used to be, but now felt like the robes of an order whose values he no longer believed in. He also had on a pair of P.P. Johnson's old galoshes. Lucky they had the same size feet.

The time Luke had spent with the healer that morning was divided into sharp and brilliant insights, and periods of what now seemed like deeply satisfying blankness. He felt that same happy blankness right now, moving between these people in a contradictory emotionless daze of heightened awareness. He smiled. Crazy, but this feeling was almost like being in love…

Wow! Yesterday he would have been embarrassed to admit something like that, even in the privacy of his own mind. It was…like trying to compare the satisfaction of being with someone, with the completely different satisfaction of…of wanting to be *like* someone, and words simply did not do justice to the ideas and feelings dancing around inside of him right then. And the thought: 'You imagine God doesn't know what's in your mind? God *is* you. You *are of* God. There is no difference; no separateness.'

At first he had decided the healer was a hypnotist or a psychologist. The guy had worked one on him the way clever fortune tellers do, picking up on nuances, subtle clues, building a profile that could apply to anyone. 'You didn't want to come here today', the healer had told him. And even though Luke had known that, the notion of not wanting to be here *had* seemed like the healer's idea…

Luke smiled, watching the shiny green toes of P.P. Johnson's galoshes plodding through the wet grass. Somebody grabbed his arm to stop him walking into them, and because he was still smiling when he looked up, the person smiled back awkwardly.

…Moreover, when he actually started to believe that the healer was genuine, that itself was part of the same trick. Like when he'd agreed - not that Luke had told him anything to agree with - that Luke should treat his employers with respect and report back with a full and accurate account of their meeting. Nothing so all-fired perceptive about that - until you remembered that the healer was not supposed to know what this visit was for.

Luke had told McClure he was FBI. Matt had known before McClure said anything about it. Come to think, McClure, mister pumpkin-head, had looked as if he'd known even before Luke told *him*. Those two guys had not left Luke's sight from the moment he'd met them, yet the healer knew his name and the organization he represented. Of course there were simple ways for these people to collect all this information, but even so, it should not have been that way around. Luke was the intelligence. These people were just *hicks*. That, too, made Luke smile.

'There's nothing to fear, not for anyone here, nor for yourself', the healer had told him. That was before Luke had shown him his FBI credentials. A lucky guess? Maybe the guy had hypnotized him. He'd seen those eyes before; they were hypnotist's eyes all right. Yet - ha! - the healer had chosen *not* to stare into Luke's eyes.

Luke had never heard of anyone mesmerizing a subject by deliberately *avoiding* their gaze. Those were not the shifty eyes of the felon, the weak-willed or the frightened. He knew that for certain when their conversation was ended, and those eyes had finally settled on him, held his gaze for interminable moments. Maybe that was when the hypnosis happened?

Aw Jesus! Luke closed his own eyes tightly and raised his face to the rain, realizing with amazement how trivial everything else seemed in comparison with those moments spent with the healer.

"Kinda sweet, ain't it?"

Luke opened his eyes, the tears on his cheeks hidden amongst the raindrops, and found an old man doing the very same thing he was, head back, eyes narrowed to keep the rain out, mouth wide open to let it in. Without looking at him the man rapped him lightly on the chest with the back of his hand.

"Go on - open up, son. Let it pour in."

So he did, thinking the word 'yes' over and over, without knowing what he was saying yes to. When he opened his eyes again, a woman was leading the old guy off into the throng. Before they vanished, the man looked back and gave Luke a sly wink.

Luke halted at the edge of the designated wilderness area by a lone cypress. He touched the tree, felt the black, wetly abrasive bark drag at his fingertips, and a single, cold, heavy drop of water fell on the top of his head, right where his hair was thinnest. Next moment an extra wide trickle of rain ran down the side of his face.

Luke did as the healer had said he should and sent his report down the line. After that, feeling kind of light-headed, he wandered around the wilderness awhile, frowning a lot with a bemused smile on his face, feeling stupid. What he'd really been doing was trying to avoid himself, half-afraid he might revert to the person he had been up until meeting with the healer. He was scared to death he might still be FBI.

296

At around five-fifty that afternoon he finally got in his car and pointed it in the direction of Zeno and his hotel, where he took a shower, slept for an hour, woke feeling as if he was still dressed in somebody else's skin, and packed his things ready for his return flight to Washington. In the bathroom he took one last look into his own eyes in the mirror, recalled the healer saying something along the lines of this not being man's wishes, but God's, then settled his check and drove to the airport.

At around eleven-thirty p.m. that evening McClure began setting the long pine table in the settlement dining room ready for the evening's communal meal. P.P. Johnson ambled into the kitchen and blew a sigh so McClure could ask what it was for, and P.P. could tell him it had been a long day and that he was looking forward to falling into bed. To prove it, he stretched out full-length on one of the wooden bench seats and closed his eyes.

Then Matt and Donna Hughes came into the kitchen, Donna sniffing the air, trying to decipher the ingredients of the evening meal. When Rosemary Brown appeared behind Donna she was barely able to walk. The pain in her back was worsening daily, aggravated by all the walking she did in the wilderness.

McClure was by her side at once, practically carrying her into the room and lowering her gently onto a chair. The tight smile on her lips matched perfectly the sharp gleam of determination in her eyes, the hairlines of controlled pain around those eyes.

As McClure started probing her back, Rosemary closed her eyes and breathed in gasps. When she opened her eyes Willie Stevenson was standing by the window, watching her, chewing on a carrot, his own eyes as expressionless as Rosemary's were expressive.

"You should have the healer take a look at that," Willie told her.

Rosemary lowered her gaze to the native American rug she'd contributed to the hut's floorboards and flinched at McClure's mercilessly understanding fingers grinding away in a slow rhythm. "He knows," was all she said.

Willie swallowed a mouthful of carrot and sniffed. "Knowin' ain't doin'."

When Matt rewarded his comment with a disapproving frown, Willie shrugged as if to say 'well, why not?'

"That Lawrence guy - what d'you make of him, Matthew?" P.P. asked, listening to his stomach rumble and wishing McClure would put some food on the table.

"He's just learning who he is."

From the kitchen area McClure called out, "Cool dude, him. Real cool."

"He's got a ways to go before he catches up to you," P.P. yelled back.

McClure came over with a plateful of discarded vegetable stalks and showed them professionally to P.P. "Should I put these out back in your doggy dish?"

Donna said, "When you're all done with him, when do we get ours?"

McClure looked concerned. "We ain't gonna eat on our ownsome, is we?"

Matt checked his watch, wondering if he should go invite the head of their table to supper.

And then the subject of Matt's thoughts was there in the open doorway, and conversation, activity, even thought, was stilled as if a wind of tranquility had passed through. He looked at each of them in turn, then went to Rosemary. He smiled without smiling, and when Rosemary tried to return the smile, found her mouth quite free of the tension her pain had etched around it. Her whole face opened and brightened now there was nothing to keep it in. She straightened - the pain was gone.

"What's cooking Mike," he said to McClure, who beamed back at him with unalloyed happiness.

In a flash McClure began bringing food to the table. When at last they were all seated, and only then realized that Willie was absent, the healer told them Willie was on an important errand, with his blessing. Then he closed his eyes and the others did likewise in a silence that linked them all.

A couple of miles outside of Passmore, a battered red Camaro slowed and stopped, its headlights illuminating an otherwise dark road, its engine idling unevenly.

Fifty yards off, at the mouth of a track that disappeared into the vegetation, the long grass growing up its center nuzzled the undersides of two anonymous black Plymouth sedans with their lights off. A gray panel van loomed behind them, the silence of their presence exaggerated by cricket calls.

The Camaro's headlights blinked off and on three times. Then its motor roared and its tires squealed like a scared creature of the night as it took off round the next bend and was gone, headlights flickering into darkness like an echo. Before the sound of the Camaro had died away the sidelights of the lead Plymouth came on, followed by the other two vehicles. In convoy, the three of them turned into the Passmore Road, in the opposite direction to which the Camaro had gone, and headed back towards the Blackwater Creek bridge.

298

See if you can get your head around this: Because of its unique, non-material nature, our consciousness can no more 'belong to us' than the knowledge and understanding we accumulate can belong to us, okay? Consciousness doesn't belong to you, it *is* you. There's a big difference. As small pieces of an infinitely more comprehensive consciousness, by rights we all belong to each other. (No, dummy, not in a personal possession sense; that sense is entirely survival derived, genetic, and confined to the material level.)

It's too easy to think of the knowledge individuals have as being their personal, private possession, but it ain't anybody's to possess. Knowledge is the inherent qualities of, or interactions between, subjects or objects that your consciousness logs or initiates in idea-form. Knowledge is also the *potential* inherent qualities of, etc. That includes anything that could possibly happen, and that you could possibly know about.

Here's the part I like: Only by actually being an object/subject, while simultaneously not being it, can you possess total knowledge of it. Take yourself as an example. There's the subjective view of you (the view of yourself you get by being you), and there's the objective view of yourself (the view of yourself you'd get by being somebody else).

To have a *total* view (of both your material and conscious selves), you'd need to be all of the material parts of yourself (in both a material *and* conscious sense), and simultaneously conscious and separate from both your material and conscious selves. (In other words, you'd have to be you, and not you, both at the same time.)

How can you have a view of yourself from outside of yourself? You can't while you're in a monkey suit. Only by dumping the monkey suit and merging with other consciousnesses, so you're no longer this isolated, genetically oriented, egocentric 'you', can you come anywhere close to a Real view of yourself from outside of yourself.

But that would only be a view of your conscious self. To have a conscious view of your material self, your conscious self would have to know what it was like - in a conscious sense - to 'be' quarks and atoms and genes. Easy enough for a highly evolved consciousness, but never mind about that for now. I'm supposed to be talking about knowledge as something nobody can own.

It would be kind of like saying you can own the quarks, atoms, genes and stuff of that monkey suit you're inside of, when in fact quarks, atoms and genes are part of this material universe. (They're all energy, and energy can't be lost, only moved into some other form.) You can't 'own' the material components of the universe. If you were conscious enough, you wouldn't need a material body, so you wouldn't want to own stuff anyhow.

Boy, just think: if we could own knowledge and understanding the way we imagine we own property, somebody could put patents on those things. That would be the same as putting a patent on consciousness! Yeah, people try such crazy things all the time without having the slightest notion of what they're monkeying with. In some cases it appears to work in this small r reality, but I'm hoping you can see how ridiculous and futile it is in a Real sense.

The reason why I'm going on about this is so you'll stop thinking of consciousness as something made on production lines in little factories called brains just to benefit the brain's owner. Instead, think of more consciousness as something that already exists, waiting for us to evolve greater access to.

Hell, let's throw caution to the wind and say that if we go on accessing/absorbing knowledge and understanding (the food of our expanding consciousness) this way, we'll be like a black hole, swallowing everything that comes within its gravitational range. When we've swallowed every particle of knowledge eventually, our consciousness will equal everything that exists...which is what some people imagine God is, right? (Well at least try and look like you're thinking about it.)

Okay, let's make camp for the night. Besides, I just spilled tea over my notes, but that's not your problem. (And this ain't tea.) Now before I go do something else for a while instead of talk to this machine, here's something to think about: If, after billions of years of evolution, the only thing you can do with that amazing consciousness is think of more efficient ways to screw other people, then (to paraphrase Descartes) you could say: 'I'm gonna carry on thinking for genes, therefore *I* might as well not be'. (Ouch!)

TAPE 68

The people who came out of the night in anonymous black sedans to get the healer didn't refer to it as an arrest, they called it protective custody. Fact is, they were only trying to protect their material reality from the Reality he was spreading. The healer was seen as a force for change; that in itself was enough to hang him, because we only want change if it means a more efficient way for us to live the same selfish way we always did. As an intruder from another world, the healer was messing with our dyed-in-the-genes traditions, threatening the material infrastructure of our virtual reality.

300

You know how the human body's immune system protects it from invading viral intrusions. More to the point is that it reacts with equally ruthless vigor to the donation of healthy material - if that healthy material doesn't fit certain criteria.

Even as I write this, I doubt that many people are prepared to go inside themself - metaphorically speaking - and search for the selfishness-circuits. To re-route the pipework and the electrochemical conduits. To strip-out the cybernetic hardware, decommission the old self-destructive gene-robot and try to behave like their Real self.

Taking the covers off of my favorite analogy yet again, the automobile is still going where the sum of its parts wants it to go, instead of where the goddam *driver* should be taking it, because the goddam driver is *asleep!* As this analogy has legs (or rather wheels) I can add that the driver is asleep because she/he thinks she's/he's just another piece of the automobile. She/he has her/his foot stomped on the gas. She's/he's going too fast to think. She's/he's afraid another competitor (sure it's a goddam race) will pass her/him. The freeway is all she/he ever knew. The race is her/his *life*.

If that was a fantasy movie you'd think it was crazy, yet your whole DNA-life *is* the movie. But you can wake up. You *can* lift your foot off the gas. You *can* stop the car. You *can* get out and stretch *your* consciousness, and start to experience the wider Reality of what you are and what you're doing. Just keep on telling yourself you're *not* actually, physically a part of that genetic vehicle. You can only evolve further as a conscious being if you quit competing with other people and their consciousness. What you should be competing with is the thing that has no consciousness, yet runs your life for its own benefit: your genetic ass.

Only then will you begin exercising your own conscious free will, instead of doing what mindless biomachinery wants. That's when you'll discover that 'free' will is something completely different than you imagined.

We all start out being controlled entirely by what a genetic body wants. After that we only achieve a conscious will that's truly free of genetic self-interest by evolving *beyond* the need for a genetic body/brain altogether.

Evolving that far is either sci-fi or just plain nuts to people who can't cope with the idea of life ever being anything but genetic. But even they'll evolve sooner or later, and one of the facts they'll learn when they do is that pro-active *un*selfishness is as natural to your more highly evolved, conscious self, as selfishness is natural to your underevolved genetic self.

Nobody expects you to suddenly stop being selfish and become pro-actively *un*selfish. It's a gradual process. It begins only when you become aware that other genetic organisms besides you and yours have a right to exist. (Though some people obviously didn't even evolve that far yet.) If you don't work that out for yourself, those other organisms soon point it out. Interacting with them and their determined right to exist creates cooperation, sooner or later. Without cooperation the only alternative is opposition and aggression, which after awhile you learn just ain't a viable option.

As the genetic need to treat other people as competitors lessens, you begin to perceive them and everything else as part of something less destructive, less antagonistic, less wasteful than genetic competitors. Now add a little more consciousness and you realize that shedding the instinct to be a competitive survivor is a natural part of your evolution. You also begin to dump the need to be greedy, and mean, and sneaky, and unfair, and more than equal, and the entire Pandora's Box of ways a genetic body enslaves your free will.

As your conscious evolution continues, you start to realize all kinds of things, in ways you never dreamed of before. (Unless you did dream some of them, but kept waking up and thinking that stuff wasn't real.)

Something else this growing enlightenment changes is your notion of what *reality* means (which we already covered). Your notion of reality was always changing, but so slowly you weren't aware of it. Now, you might just be conscious enough to recognize that it is changing. For an organism to recognize that its view of reality is changing is pretty damn profound, because even though we're all right in the middle of it, right now, we take it for granted as 'the way things are'. We take all the best parts of our amazing conscious self for granted, and instead get all worked up about things that wouldn't even deserve to be called 'alive' if not for the spark of consciousness in them.

Okay. So what happens to your famous free will while all this evolving is going on? Shut up and I'll tell you. This is pretty damn profound too.

You always understood 'free' to mean 'independent', right? (That usually means independent of the needs of those outside of your chosen group.) But as your conscious notion of reality starts nudging Reality, you begin to see beyond that stupid old idea of 'freedom' as a state of independence; you begin to see it as something that seems to *contradict* independence: the chance to achieve a state of *unity* with *everybody*. One-ness, of the kind that only this gradual shift from genetic selfishness, through cooperation, to conscious *un*selfishness, can achieve.

302

Instead of being separate from, and independent of, other consciousnesses, you finally achieve a state where we all have our act together. Not like acting onstage, as separate actors inside genetic bodies, but as consciousness acting together, over and above material barriers. That's what we're all meant to be - part of the same conscious act, on a stage that transcends the material, rather than playing a lot of genetically competitive bit parts.

Before any of that can happen though, the ghost in DNA's machine will have to realize that wasting time trying to *be* the goddam machine is the very opposite of freedom. The more determined you are to be genetic, the longer you'll be a prisoner of that monkey suit. (A prisoner in a cell is free to do anything he wants inside his cell, but you'd hardly call him *free*. Now include in this analogy what would happen if he was born in there, with no means of knowing he was in a cell, and therefore no way of knowing what was outside that cell, or if there *was* an outside.)

Here's something I recorded at the end of a multi martini evening: In this Land of the Free, how do we use the precious freedom we're prepared to fight and kill other people for, and in the process maybe even die to preserve? We use it to compete more fervently than any other nation on the planet for the right to chase a buck. 'Freedom' lets the more equal exploit the less equal, not covertly but in your face. Yet this is praised and worshipped by everybody. (Communists might secretly aspire to the ways of selfish capitalists, but at least they got the decency to *pretend* to despise them.)

So exactly what kind of a species does that make us? An instinctively hypocritical one. I wish you could tell me I'm wrong, but most of the injustices on Planet Psycho are *supposed* to be offensive to us. We admit they're created by greed and selfish materialism. And while we're admitting that, we actively promote, condone and advocate them, like always.

This is an unfair assessment, right? The way you see it, there's plenty of material 'wealth' to go around. Capable and caring people are out there working for the good of all, generating this wealth so everybody has more to share out between them. That's real magnanimous but crap, because 'freedom' doesn't work that way. The most predacious always wind up with the booty. A few get far more than they need and flaunt it as the spoils of war, consuming and wasting conspicuously while others just waste away conspicuously.

Everybody wants to be like those predators. They're the exemplars of freedom, envied by everybody in a struggle - okay, a society - where life itself is often up for grabs, while down the bottom of the heap the disenfranchised are left to pick over each other's bones. (Am I being metaphorical again? You tell me.) This struggle is as small as Manhattan and as big as the world. If Manhattan can't get its act together, what chance is there for a world where millions somehow manage to miraculously multiply faster than they can die of malnutrition, disease or infighting?

Did you ever notice how legal systems protect the rights of individuals no matter how selfish or wealthy or ruthless they are, just so long as they play by society's rules. Trouble is, those rules just happen to include gaping loopholes - 'freedoms' - allowing anybody to totally ignore the basic human needs of other people. To ignore a guy lying in the street who's dying of starvation, just because he's what we call a 'vagrant'.

Forget starvation. One millionaire's neighbor could be another millionaire who just happened to get mugged and left bleeding on the sidewalk. His neighbor is under no 'legal' obligation to do a damn thing to help, right? This 'civilized' society leaves it to the individual to decide whether or not he, she or it is gonna *care* about somebody other than ME & MINE. (In that example, you'd be more liable to get a trash-dumping fine for leaving the guy on the sidewalk than for your lack of concern.)

A genuinely civilized law would include a statement saying you are legally obligated to help your fellows. And yet that supposedly progressive document on democracy, The Bill of Rights, works against it by legislating for all of those even more important rights of the individual to be free to think of ME & MINE FIRST.

There is no written law forcing us to help each other as conscious entities or as little pieces of a corporate God, because that would infringe our freedom to survive as gene-machines. Anybody is free to become a millionaire in this 'civilized' society, while people sleep on the street; while in the rest of the world many are as good as dead before they're born because they've got nothing. (So what did they have to live for anyhow?)

I guess it must take real guts to live in luxury, knowing others have nothing. But we need every red cent we can grab just so we can compete with our peers who're all being equally gutsy. So our employees, or our electorate or our audience know even an honest, God-fearing Joe like us can make it to the top. We've shown them how to do it - to each other.

This far into the book you know that living together in peace, happiness and harmony so we can all share the cake fair and square, is a nice idea that can't ever work where evolution still means competition. Where the very concept of life itself appears indivisible from the concepts of winning, material success and exploitation.

This state of affairs only persists for us because survival of the fittest still rules. So we go on thinking our struggle to get a bigger share of the cake for us and ours is how a fair and democratic society should operate.

Or maybe we say: 'What else can we do? Some poor suckers have to be down so the rest of us can be up. Somebody's got to be more equal - that's life'. It sure is, and all because ME & MINE come first. Being created equal in the sight of somebody called God means nothing to the walking chemical plant you're wearing. But chemicals didn't patent the concept of inequality. *You* did.

Properly developed, your consciousness has more power than you can even begin to imagine. Like the power to shape the universe. (I don't mean by voracious global corporations expanding their selfish interests into the cosmos disguised as advancing 'civilization' so we become multi-galactic material resource exploiters. Man, that is a disgusting notion - Interplanetary Pillage & Rape inc.) No, by 'shaping the universe', I mean as enlightened consciousness.

Just imagine what could happen with a bunch of DNA-crazed dorks rampaging through the galaxies, grabbing whatever they can. While it sounds like progress to all you gene-survival machines, we'd be doing it by DNA's will, wielded so potently through DNA's ever-more-advanced brain. We'd still be trudging down these same narrow evolutionary avenues, professionally mugging and raping each other and everybody else for a living. A genetically engineered new master race of 'beautiful people', stripping out the heavens in starships. Except the beauty would be only skin-deep, a result of parents feeling compelled to ensure their offspring were equipped to compete with everybody else's kids and their modified genes. As walking sacks of competition we'll go on imagining we're our own master, plundering this virtual reality in the name of Competition Psychosis, determined not to see the wood for the trees in this pathetic, genetic jungle. Remember my Dr Jekyll/Mr Hyde analogy? It's on page # 7. Go back and read it.

So. The powers that be heisted the healer. They made sure everything was covered, asswise, so there'd be no question of any statutory freedoms being infringed. I heard they even brought representatives from the World Council of Churches as observers. There'd be no comebacks. Nobody would think about improper and unnecessary use of powers, funds, force, or the infringement of personal liberty or - oh hell, I don't know all of those stupid titles they use for trying to appear like terrific human beings, when all they are is criminals, plain and simple. When you make the rules, the worst excesses of criminal activity can so easily become patriotism and freedom and stuff that you cease to recognize any difference. The drugs they had Willie plant in the healer's trailer were just the icing on the cake that proves my point.

TAPE 69

The first I heard about it was when my bedside radio brought me out of a dream where Katherine Hepburn was down on her hands and knees cleaning my kitchen floor, complaining in that whine of hers that something sticky had spilled by the refrigerator and my cat's hairs were adhering to it in the most disgusting manner.

That was when a man's voice from the local radio station said threats had been received from unnamed terrorist sources and the healer had been given the full protection of the intelligence services. The healer was now safe under the dubious cloak of the FBI. And what's more, I don't even have a cat!

I guess the news media had been waiting for something like this to happen. Obviously I wasn't the only one who'd noticed a parallel with the first 'Coming' and, human nature being what it is, it inevitably followed that, for news people, the best thing after discovering him was renouncing him. After they'd fed off him awhile, they almost had no choice but to hope the worst would happen (which for them was the best that could happen).

But what am I saying - I still had my piece to write for The Star, and the best place to get copy was the wilderness. Even before I got there I had my headline written - HEALER HEISTED, (OR HAS HE SOLD OUT?) - though from the way those vendors were carrying on in the wilderness, you wouldn't have known anything had changed.

The first concern of everyone who might have been affected materially by his disappearance was: What am *I* gonna do now? If their income was affected, the question was: How much am *I* gonna lose? If you'd been there you'd have asked the same question. Where just months earlier there'd been only grassy hillsides, we now had a ramshackle business park with a sizeable dollar turnover.

Sure there were those who fantasized that his departure wouldn't make any difference to the commercial health of the area now it was up and running.

The Mayor for instance, who was one familiar face I bumped into that first healer-less day.

For Mayor Stevenson everything seemed normal because he wanted to see it that way. It confirmed what he'd been determined was the case all along - that tourists really were heading to Raiment County for the many wonderful amenities, and not for one quietly-spoken man in jeans and a tee-shirt who lived in a silver trailer.

I hadn't intended to get into conversation with the Mayor because I was looking for real feelings in response to the healer's removal, not professional lies. And there was Mayor Stevenson, strolling amongst the crowd, smiling and chatting as if he was the reason they were there. I almost expected him to pick up somebody's baby and kiss it, you know the kind of crap. (I'd certainly think twice about letting him kiss my baby, or my anything else.)

His smile soon died when he saw me. He even turned his back on me and pretended to talk to someone, which was a red rag to my bull.

"Mister Mayor? Mister Ma - "

He wheeled and hit me with a plastic smile for the onlookers. "Mizz Hendricks. And what brings you out on such a fine Summer's day? Not annoying these good folks I hope when they're having themselves a good time."

"Well, Mister Mayor, I came to find out how 'these good folks' feel about the healer getting himself taken into protective custody." I made quite certain everyone for miles around heard me.

Watching the people around me for their reactions, I saw doubt on the face of a young woman, which the guy beside her seemed to find contagious. They began talking about it, but I only heard them out of the corner of my eye because I was still jousting with the Mayor.

"Things will change after the side-shows and financial backup and everything that came here because of the healer packs up and leaves now he's gone," I told him. "What will you tell everybody 'bout that?"

Stevenson's smile was cracking around the edges. "You're living in a different world to the rest of us, Mizz Hendricks. If any of these folks have had the dubious pleasure of reading your material, they'll have gotten a pretty good idea of the world of scandal and smut you an' your imagination inhabit."

He was playing to the crowd but getting mixed reviews. It was obvious that I'd started something off for some of them with my little revelation, though equally clear that others couldn't care a twopenny darn whether the healer was still there or if he'd decided to go down to Florida for a spot of alligator wrestling.

Before I had the chance to come back to the Mayor, a lady with false lashes round her glassy bird's eyes and carelessly applied overbright red lipstick asked me: "Miss, is that there the truth? The healer's gone?"

"Oh yes ma'am," I said seriously into my midget tape-recorder, then let her chew on it.

"Gone where? Where'd he go?"

"The FBI or CIA took him away for his own safety, so they said on the radio."

She looked back at the old wreck of a guy she was with and shook her head. Then to nobody in particular said, "But that's just awful. I mean that's terrible, the CIA takin' *him* away. What's he *done?*"

Quick as a flash I brought the Mayor back into the conversation. "Maybe our good Mayor would like to answer that question for you, ma'am, in his official capacity. Mayor Stevenson?"

The way he eyed me, I decided that maybe it would be a good idea if somebody took me away for my safety.

"Now you folks don't need to go worryin' yourselves," he beamed. "You just carry on enjoying this beautiful countryside of ours an' all of the other amenities we've got here and in Passmore. Hey, you're on vacation! Enjoy!"

I had to hand it to him. The Secret Service had just cancelled the Second Coming, and the Mayor had every confidence he could patch things up.

But you've seen people like the Mayor, persisting with something regardless of whether it's good or bad. They've got something in their head and they'll die before they give up. If they want something real bad but can't have it, even the most sophisticated and mature people can fall back on pig-headedness.

Hell, you see it all the time everywhere you go. Maybe you call it stubbornness, or determination. Maybe even a strong will. And all of a sudden, Jesus! Pig-headedness has a desirable quality to it.

See that? Let's look at it again in slomo: Pig-headedness...is actually stubbornness...which we interpret as determination...meaning you're strong-willed. But what are you being strong-willed for? Yourself. Pig-headedness, and those 'desirable' disguises it wears, are just you looking out for you.

Why should you do things for other people free of charge if they're not wearing the same brand of genes you are? There's no survival value in that. Now go to tape #1 and start reading this book over again.

308

Okay. Want to know what a genuine Second Coming would Really be about? Forget all of that archaic eyewash in bibles. The Second Coming is a purely *symbolic* return of what Jesus Christ Really stood for. It's about a more Real approach to life, but *we* have to make it happen. It's not some goddam gift that we're handed on a plate.

While we're running around like inmates of a lunatic asylum waiting for God to get on down here and make it happen, God's waiting for us to wise-up and figure out that we can only make it happen for ourselves. That's the way God's worked so far and I don't see Him changing His plans at this crucial stage. I sure wouldn't.

I'm all done waffling for now so I'll watch the Mayor walking away from me in my memory and wonder if he'd forgotten about that dangerous tape I still had of him, gleaned on the Passmore Town Hall steps that night when he referred to those good folks who'd taken the trouble to drive down to the pimpled and unwashed backside of the country as 'new-age dopeheads looking for a handout.' I was holding The Sword of Damocles. Maybe that was why he was relatively easy on me that morning.

TAPE 70

I guess where Willie Stevenson went wrong was in thinking remorse wasn't a part of his makeup. It was there alright, but masked by jealousy, envy, frustration and the burning need for vengeance. All of those feelings, and lots more besides, are side-effects of DNA's survival armory; they're part of the neurosis produced by what Shakespeare called 'the slings and arrows of outrageous fortune', otherwise known as life.

So where, in a gamut of self-serving feelings, does a misfit like remorse come in? Where, in all of those other twisted urges spawned simply by the urge to stay alive long enough to replicate for your genes, does the unhappy notion that you're sorry for committing a sin against someone else, come in? I'm not talking about the fear of being caught and punished (because then it's no different than any other self-serving feeling). I'm talking about a genuine regret that someone else has been hurt or deprived in some way.

I guess having the imagination, empathy or whatever to put yourself in that other person's shoes means you're halfway to feeling remorse. It also helps to know the difference between genetic right and wrong, and Real right and wrong. So let me remind you: Genetic right is whatever's good for genes and their bodies, genetic wrong is whatever's bad for genes and their bodies. Real right is whatever's good for people other than yourself (who don't share your family genes) as something *more* than genes, while Real wrong is whatever's bad for those people.

It is kind of awkward-sounding, but it covers an important difference that has nothing to do with what religion says is right or wrong. Or what the government says is right or wrong. Or what scientists, parents, teachers, cabdrivers, policemen or opinion polls say is right or wrong. No amount of religious torture or coercion or indoctrination can teach you the essential difference between the right and wrong versions of right and wrong; that difference is something you only learn by evolving as your Real, conscious self.

Willie Stevenson had yet to learn it, and that's why he did to the healer what Judas Iscariot did to J.C. by betraying him to those who wanted him out of the way. (I didn't mention Judas in relation to Willie before as I figured you'd recognize the inference unaided.)

Then there were the drugs Willie planted, courtesy of Sheriff Hughes' mule, Jeff Ackerley. There was no antidote to the remorse Willie was experiencing after *that* particular career decision.

Willie took his remorse back to the wilderness with him that day and to the settlement, barefaced as you please, not just to keep up appearances but because he had nowhere else to go. His one consolation in all of this was that only Jeff Ackerley knew what he'd done. That was no comfort at all.

When I ran into Willie at the wilderness he looked like he'd swallowed a dollar and shat him a dime, as my granddaddy used to say. When I asked him what had happened the previous night and if he'd been at the settlement when they came for the healer, he looked sicker than ever. No, he said, he was gone by then and knew nothing about it, though being the astute judge of character I imagined myself to be, I could see more was bothering him than the healer's 'protective custody'.

"Did they just walk in and take him?" I asked.

He didn't know.

"Was anybody else with him when it happened?"

He didn't know that either.

"What do you think will happen next?"

That was when he showed me a side of his nature I hadn't known existed. His eyes lost their fishy listlessness and became hard as marbles and his lip curled up like a dog's. Then he told me, with real venom in his voice, why didn't I stop going around asking such fucking idiot questions and hadn't I made enough trouble for people as it was? Okay, so he was upset. Some people behave irrationally in a crisis. Then he wandered off in no particular direction and I was left with a crowd of curious onlookers gawping at me like stupid cattle. Boy, that really gets up my nose. One guy had even recorded our little set-to on his video camera just for something to do now the healer was gone. I guess the rest of those buffoons most likely thought we were just rehearsing an episode of some mindless soap. Maybe we were.

Recall me finding deputy Andrew DeSoto wandering in the wilderness awhile back, looking lost before he found his Miss Wright? And who did I find wandering in the wilderness and looking lost again? Andrew DeSoto, still with the sheriff's office but soon not to be.

Andrew started out as one of those unformed characters; there's plenty spinning around inside of them and you keep catching a glimpse of it, but nothing seems to have settled into a definite, conclusive pattern yet. You might call people like Andrew 'late developers', or you could be less charitable and call them shiftless, indecisive, dithering, or various other names that reflect failings in yourself because you're denigrating someone just because they're not a perfect human being. The more you criticize other people just for the hell of it, the less perfect you become. (I'll just slip a *hallelujah!* in there, 'kay?)

Helping somebody to help themselves - now that's a complete other story. Go on and try it instead of criticizing them. Just don't try so hard you interfere because that'll simply be another of your own failings showing through. (Boy, do you have a lot of failings!)

The truth was that Andrew DeSoto was an intelligent and aware young man who simply didn't know he was intelligent and aware when I first met him, and getting himself entangled with Miss Wright only confused matters more. The reason why so many relationships break down is because people start out on them thinking everything's wonderful, when the truth is they're thinking with their reproductive organs (aka their entire body/brain) instead of their conscious mind. And that was why Andrew and Becky went right ahead and jumped in the sack the way everybody else does, because that's the grown-up thing to do, right? If you're a grown-up monkey, that is...

Any of you monkeys still reading? If yes, it's my opinion that Andrew half-knew he'd be reaching out to the healer sooner or later and was maybe having one last fling before it happened. I could be mistaken (see, I can be modest) but I don't think I was. Listen, when practically everything in life is geared to sex and money, it's one strong character who can resist the temptation.

Instant reminder: The only reason why sex is enjoyable is because genes evolved all of the physical equipment that makes you keep wanting sex. Genes evolved that machinery without planning or knowing that 'enjoyment' would result. Genes can't foresee anything. They work from feedback. If the feedback gets the right survival results - meaning if it helps genes replicate more efficiently - they build it in. That's how all of the biomachinery for registering sensations of pleasure, pain, happiness, sadness, and everything in between came to be.

Unless, of course, you believe that something else is behind all of this: Something beyond all of the self-satisfied ME-ism generated by mindlessly humping for hormones. Something that is merely using the genes, the materiality and the universe that you're in to help your and Itself evolve. What then? Would that mean you should just carry on helping uncaring chemicals go on being uncaring chemicals? Get Real.

Reality Window: the above was me thinking aloud while I searched for the dialogue tape of my conversation with Andrew DeSoto that day. Do you have any idea how many of these midget audio tapes it takes to compile a thing like this? Me neither. I know I lost a few along the way. I also think there's a family of badgers living someplace in the middle of this junk called my kitchenette…

It's tomorrow now and I still haven't found that goddam tape! (I mean tomorrow in real life, not in this story.) However I do remember Andrew saying something had clicked inside him when he learned the healer had been spirited away. Strangely enough Andrew didn't appear overly upset in the normal sense at the government-engineered snatch. Andrew was *spiritually* upset, if I can possibly describe it that way. Well I have anyway, and you confirmed it by having just read it, so it must be possible. (Somebody remind me to erase that stupid sentence.)

Being spiritually upset isn't the lunatic indignation of being offended on God's behalf I once spoke of, like when you're on the lookout for anybody being blasphemous. Spiritually upset is more like getting disappointed on someone else's behalf. That makes it practically an emotion, except that this is no more emotional than it is intellectual because –

Hell, let's say that being spiritually upset is a product of the *heart*, but the word heart in this context belongs to a more metaphysical explanation and has little in common with a twitching organ in your chest.

312

I suspect that Andrew had unintentionally encapsulated the very same reaction that the other disciples were to express to me later that day. Except that Andrew wasn't a fully-fledged disciple yet. None of them were. (I might have implied that becoming a disciple takes forever, and I mean forever in its biggest sense.)

Each of the healer's disciples was spiritually upset. Sure, they knew it was supposed to happen because he'd told them it would, and that it was all part of something bigger. But they were also emotionally and intellectually upset, still being gene survival machines in some measure.

Maybe DeSoto was destined to meet and 'fall in lerve' with Miss Wright, in the same way he was destined to fall out of it again almost immediately. All I know is that in becoming a disciple DeSoto had found his calling in life. Only then did he realize his mistake in letting his genitals go to his head, though they do say mistakes are a very sure way to learn, don't they.

I had a most illuminating conversation with DeSoto that late morning in the wilderness, which is how I happen to know so much about his circumstances. How I know, for instance, that Miss Wright was a virgin when she arrived in Raiment County. I also know just how eager a beaver she'd been to change all of that.

Andrew himself had made every excuse he could think up to get himself out of the sheriff's office and into the Wright family's camper where Becky would be waiting for him, already undressed and in bed, the sheet practically turning brown and crumbly with the heat!

I mean to say, when a young guy you hardly ever spoke to before starts to give you the most intimate, aromatic and sordid details of his sex life, you almost feel obligated to relay that information to your readers.

Do you know, Andrew and Becky spent practically all of their time together in bed? I gather people often do, especially if it's their first relationship. He did assure me they were in lerve - well, he'd thought so at the time - but you know my feelings on that score. I think Andrew would probably agree with me now.

I don't know why Andrew DeSoto decided to spill all of that private information to me of all people. Maybe he was a secret exhibitionist? More likely he was trying to purge himself of the deed for God or something. He needn't have bothered; unlike people, who take pleasure in administering vengeance, God has better things to do with His time. Pity you don't.

But I'm driving with two wheels on the sidewalk again. Perhaps Andrew hoped that by writing about what was on his mind during that episode, I'd be going some way towards explaining it to Becky's parents. Oh yeah, I didn't mention how they reacted to him jilting their little girl, did I? Okay, so I'll just remind Becky's parents if they're reading that Andrew became a disciple. If reading that doesn't make them any more kindly disposed to the man who stole their only daughter's honor, I'll also remind them it was with their full, if tacit, consent.

So that was Andrew DeSoto. Sorry I couldn't find all of my notes on him, but as the guy was kind've incomplete within himself anyhow, it leaves you with an oddly accurate picture of him. Perhaps a lot of the folks I spoke to that first day of the healer's absence were suffering from that same deficiency; like they were missing something that most of them hadn't even been aware was there to begin with. I could describe the general disposition I encountered that day as *dreamlike*, because that fits neatly with my contention.

I was gonna put a Gurdjieff quote at the beginning of this book: '*Life is only real when I Am.*' To the casual reader that statement might be gobbledygook. Admit it. You think: 'Someone here is trying to be too smart for their own good.' Or for yours, right? But it's necessary to try and make words exceed their jurisdiction in small r reality.

Yet despite Gurdjieff being a true weirdo, and a might too fond of peach brandy on occasion, even more than Descartes he was a great believer in waking people up to the wider Reality. But boy, before you can wake somebody up, you have to convince them they're asleep. Incidentally, mystics refer to finding Reality, or the state of having finally woken all the way out of the Big Sleep, as *being realized*, but that's just another way of saying your immaterial consciousness has fully outgrown DNA's material world. Yeah, I know I've said that before, and if I edited out of this book all the times I reran myself, it would be only half as long as it is. After you'd forgotten half of the things I said, that in turn would reduce its value to a quarter what it is now, but no way would the publisher have reduced its price correspondingly. So all things considered, me repeating myself is actually saving you money.

TAPE 71

Funny, but I'd started thinking of the healer as belonging to me, the same way that guy in The Triangle did. (The one who told an out-of-state visitor: "That there's *our* goddam healer, boy, and don't you forget it.") I'd begun to understand exactly what he meant as I stalked those unsuspecting people, trying to build a story around his not being there anymore.

See, even I'd changed. If I'd still been the same Laurie Hendricks who'd sell her children to white slavers just to get a story, I'd have used what Andrew told me about the things him and Becky got up to in her parents' camper, in the wilderness parking lot, just inches from families with little kids enjoying their picnic lunches.

But I didn't. I felt I had an obligation to the healer to get the Real story. I had the same obligation to people I thought of as friends, and others who practically were friends. Donna and Matt, and P.P. Johnson, McClure, Rosemary Brown, and even DeSoto. Oh yeah, and Ed…I'm getting better about Ed. Thinking about him this time I only stared out the window for a moment and felt my nostrils twitch. Eventually I'll maybe be able to think of him and just smile fondly, without all of that hotness around the eyeballs, dammit!

Okay. Enough of that stupid junk. Here's a tape of short interviews with folks who I invited to give me their views about what happened to the healer. I'll transcribe them straight, without adulteration, the same way I did with everything else in this book. Honest.

The first was with a youngish woman struggling to change a baby's diaper without displaying the outcome to everybody around her, which was pretty ripe judging by the catch in the back of my throat on this tape. I couldn't help wondering where that outcome would wind up after it went in the trash. How do you recycle a package filled with baby-crap? The answer is, you drop it in a landfill, along with the billions of others just like it - another happy picture of life on Planet Psycho. Anyhow I held my electronic snooper at arm's length and stood as far back as I could to introduce myself and asked her what she felt about the secret police taking the healer away for his own protection. She looked up at me just for a second with an expression that said her olfactory nerves were battle-hardened but still not entirely happy, before turning her full attention to the job in hand.

"Yeah, I heard about that on the news this mornin'…ain't fair is it…he weren't doing any harm?" She looked up, all done. "He weren't doing nobody any harm," she repeated to prove she knew what she was saying the first time. "Was he?" Okay, so she didn't really know what she was saying after all.

"Well I don't know 'bout that. 'S'why I'm out here today, ma'am. So you don't think he did anything to get arrested for?"

She was keeping one eye on the baby and checking out my shoes with the other, because they were looking kind of tired if you want the truth after all that tramping around in the wilderness. Besides, after I've used up all of my income on basics like gin and cocaine and filling up the gas tank of my Ferrari, it doesn't leave a whole lot for luxury items like footwear.

"Arrested? I thought you said it was for his own protection?"

"That's one of the things I'm looking for opinions on."

Now she was checking out my pants; they'd seen better times too. She'd started trying to form an answer I'd be happy with, but couldn't decide if she was happy with it. I know because I'm writing this story.

"I don't know," she finally got around to saying, which is always gratifying to have an interviewee tell you, because it means you're wasting your precious and valuable time for nothing. It also meant there were people in the wilderness without any opinion on the healer's arrest. The next person I talked with confirmed my suspicions.

"Sir...*sir?*" Either this guy was deaf or he was deliberately ignoring me because he thought I was selling something, or he'd been approached already by one of the wilderness hookers. "I'm a reporter sir, from The Star? In Zeno?"

That got his attention.

"Oh-ho, hey, hey, no need to shout y'know."

"Well why didn't you answer the first time you deaf old bastard?" That's what I'd like to say to some of the people I interview, believe me. In fact I said, "Sorry, pardon me." My tape recorder was where he could see it, not where I would like to have put it. "You know about the healer's arrest by the FBI-stroke-CIA?"

"Who's gettin' stroked by who'd you say?"

Luckily his wife or somebody with him saved the day. She popped a piece of candy in her mouth and said around it, "He'sh jusht being awkward, honey. It'sh hish way."

"Right." I smiled painfully.

"Maybe I cad help you."

"The healer?"

"That's the young fellow who gets a crowd around him? Talks a lot but you can't hardly hear what he's saying?"

"Sure. The healer. The one that started all of this thing here in the wilderness."

316

Surprise. "Really? I thought this was part of the Park? We came over through…"

I don't recall what else she said because I'd decided to save my battery for somebody with paydirt. So two and a half down and I was getting ready to be struck-out when I noticed this family of five watching a tiny portable TV and all of them looking like the third world war just broke out and they didn't have any weapons stock in their portfolio. Call it instinct, but I just knew they were catching an update on the healer. I didn't ask how they felt; I didn't have to; their reaction to the news of him being rerun was plain enough.

This family obviously thought he was something special judging by the kids crying, and the dark faces of their parents, and their disapproving conversation.

"Pardon me, folks, but you seem kinda unhappy about what happened here last night."

"Is that any of your business?"

Uh-huh. The healer had gotten to them but evidently left before completing the work.

"Hey, I'm on your side, really. Anything you care to say I'll make sure The Star prints if it's relevant. It's one way of registering your disapproval."

The parents thought that over in silence, then he said, "Well alright."

He was still pretty tetchy, but you would be if somebody arrested your messiah. Bear in mind that a lot of people truly wanted the healer to be a genuine messenger from God. Well yes, many of those people naturally expected more of him. You know – a few minor miracles at the very least. They didn't have the sense to realize razzmatazz or power and glory ain't God's way. All of that stuff is human invention with its origins in the way DNA constructed the human psyche out of fear and calamity. If God ain't threatening hell and damnation, going supernova and hurling thunderbolts, people just don't bother looking up from their replicating and reproducing.

The First Coming probably didn't seem like all that big a deal at the time either. Only later, after the PR people moved in, did any real significance became attached and a profit-and-loss religion got itself up and running.

"So," I kept on at him, "Did you agree with what the healer was saying?"

"Yes we did. Oh Lord, yes. Everything. Every single word."

"Er, and was it God's word?"

"I believe it was God's word. I - we - believe this is the Christ returned to set the world aright and to show mankind the way ahead."

"And what's going to happen next, d'you think?"

He was streaming tears now. "I just don't know…" Shaking his head and watching his wife's bottom lip tremble while she tried to look brave for the kids because they'd only start off again otherwise.

"Ma'am, you want to say anything about this?"

She opened her mouth but all that came out was a squeak, and she changed her mind and brought her hankie up to dismiss my attentions. I wandered away. Hardened hack I may be, but the sight of folks crying is like funerals. It's contagious. But you got the general idea about their feelings.

What else? Oh yeah, here's an opposite view. This from a family of six; at any rate I think that was the IQ of the father. A not-so-old woman was bad-mouthing the three kids into line and an older woman looked like somebody's grandmother. But not mine; she's been dead these past four years. (I've edited the expletives out of this.)

"Sir? Laurie Hendricks, The Star. You have anything you want to say about the healer getting arrested last night?"

"Like what?"

"Well, how you feel about it?"

"I feel just fine. In fact I feel more than fine if you got to know. It ain't enough to have them Jeehova's Wetnurses and crazy Mormons annoying my wife all hours of the day, banging on the goddam door of my house, but we come down here for some peace and relaxation, and f*** me if those bastards ain't bothering us here too. Jesus f***ing Christ and everything, I'm telling you those healer dealers were tarred with the same f***ing brush as the rest of them holy pests. F***ing parasites is all they are. An' him too. Now you go an' let people read that in their stars."

Wasn't that just delightful? And while I could have gone around recording people all day, I guess I had me enough with a further half-dozen comments culled from a cross-section of opinions and nationalities, races and creeds. There were people so up in arms they were intending to petition their Congressman. Others were relieved because the antichrist had gotten his come-uppance, and yet another loony bunch were certain the end of the world was nigh. Reactions covered the full spectrum from suicidal outrage to brain-dead indifference. But there was an uncomfortable crackle in the air if you stopped and listened carefully enough. Like an approaching hurricane maybe.

It was while I was listening to my thoughts that Sheriff Hughes snook up behind me and just about scared the you-know-what out of me. The last time

318

I saw Hughes was awhile before that, in the wilderness, wandering along behind the Mayor and Maxine. Then he seemed heavier than when I interviewed him in his office, as if he'd been pigging-out to compensate for something. Now he looked distinctly ill-at-ease, touchy and fidgety, with strain-lines I hadn't noticed on his face before. Even the old Hughes smirk looked like he'd brought it out from underneath a load of soiled linen in the laundry basket. I might just as well apply that comparison to Hughes generally.

"Laurie Hendricks, now what brings you out to the wilderness? An' I know it can't be the healer, or ain't you heard?"

I already had the tape recorder in my hand so I thought I might as well try the old battery trick.

"Shoot! Wouldn't you just know that when I wanted to get me an on-the-spot interview with Passmore's popular Sheriff the damn batteries died on me." I even removed the little cover and showed him the offending items, brand new that morning.

"Well, that's what you get working fer a shoestring outfit."

I kept the machine in my hand as if I'd forgotten it was there. "So, I might ask you the same question, Sheriff Hughes, or is it too long since last time for me to call you Neil?"

That pumped a touch more blood into his grin. "It'd never be too long for a nice young woman like yourself, Laurie," he managed, unable to resist the bait.

He hadn't changed. If anything he was more susceptible than ever to bullshit. I felt sorry for the guy. He'd been deprived of life-giving compliments for so long it seemed his self-esteem was practically trailing along on the ground behind him.

"Well *thank*you, Neil. And now I might as well ask you the same question I've been asking everyone else here today…"

He pulled out all the stops and laughed. "Hell, no wonder them kiddy batteries of yours is all fu- , uh, shot."

With a knowing-hack twinkle in my eye I said, "Yeah. So anyhow, how'd you feel personally about the healer getting lifted by the government's legalized terrorists?"

The life oozed back into his ego before my very eyes just having a woman to show off for. His face became more animated and his voice along with it.

"Aw, now that's no way to talk 'bout them fellas after all they've done for our national security an' all." He even winked to show me he was being sarcastic.

"No, seriously," I persisted. "After all, none of these folks would ever have come to Raiment County if it hadn't been for him."

Hughes decided to turn professionally serious and reflective, looked off into the crowd and told me that he was "Sorry I have to be so honest but the healer brought the wrath of the people down on himself by setting hisself up as some kind of a new-age messiah, and even goin' as far as gatherin' those goddam deesciples round him." Then he thought a little harder and changed tack. "Shame he got took when everybody was doin' so well."

He put his hands on the rolling ring of fat where his hips should have been while the toe of his boot toyed with a flattened Diet Pepsi can. As we both watched the can, he said, "Hell, I'm no churchgoer, but even I objected to some of them things he came out with. I mean, just who'd the man think he was - *Jesus Christ almighty?*"

He turned his gaze on me. "Hey - it was *you* that started all of this second comin' stuff off in the first place!"

I scrutinized the people around us. "Brought this place alive though."

"Oh-ho, you sure did that! He started shaking his head and couldn't seem to stop. "Yessir, you certainly did that. Could be this town won't never look back. Hell, Laurie, you changed Passmore's history, you know that?"

"Yeah, didn't I just. And look what happened."

I think I must have grown a scowl or something because that was the excuse he'd been waiting for to touch me; thank goodness it was only my arm.

"Hey now, Laurie? It weren't your doin' the healer got above hisself. You couldn't foresee...I mean, well *hell!*"

He still had a hold of my arm, the one belonging to the hand holding my recorder, and I'd just caught a glimpse of P.P. Johnson through the heads of a coach-party of Muslim women in their cover-up outfits. (I used to think I'd just hate being forced to wear that symbol of repression until I actually heard a young Muslim woman say it wasn't that way at all and she was proud to dress like that.)

Well that's just fine, but I still can't help thinking about religious indoctrination whenever I see a person dressed that way. Then one idea leads to another and I wind up thinking of suicide bombers and all of those fanatics who give an entire religion a bad name. Yes I know all of that 'Onward Christian Soldiers' stuff ain't a whole lot better. 'Fighting the good fight' is metaphorical, but a lot of people don't seem to appreciate that. Devotional scriptures are filled with martial talk, but the only fighting that needs to be

320

done is with yourself. The healer never once used fighting talk. Mostly it was stuff like: 'Before you expect others to be perfect, become perfect yourself', and 'Don't judge others unless you want them to judge you.' He was simply reiterating what old JC said first time around. Like JC, the healer was not about religion, he was all about stuff like understanding, harmony and tolerance - the very things that religion's extremists don't seem to have any interest in.

Like I keep saying, there's no mystery behind the extremist problem. Those people have gotten it into their head that God upholds the same materially-based values that people do: the sanctity of property, of procreation, of competition, tribalism, oppressive tradition and the code of vengeance when those things are threatened.

"Well Neil," I wrestled my arm free of the Sheriff's big sticky hand and forced a smile onto my face. "I have to go replace those ol' power cells." I waggled the machine at him, trying to relocate P.P. with the eyes in the back of my head.

Hughes gave me one last visual examination, as though I'd earned it, and said, "An' I was enjoyin' our little chat, Laurie. But I do got all of these people to watch over, sure enough. Catch you later now."

"Am I some kind of disease?" I said. That's one of those pathetic parting quips designed to help you get away when you can think of nothing else. I let myself be swallowed up by the jungle of vacationers, thankful for their cover.

When I found P.P., boy, did he look different. I'm sure his hair was going gray, but that wasn't the real difference; it was his eyes. This is hard to describe so listen. Where previously the superficial sheen of juvenile, happy-go-lucky casualness had been, there was now the light of understanding. His rich-kid carelessness had hardened into the intelligence of new-found wisdom. (Hell, I know that's no description of anybody, but I'm just a small-town hack; if you want real prose, read some Elmore Leonard.)

Then there's the way P.P. sounded. Let's say you've just graduated from happy-go-lucky to disciple all in the space of half a day, then the government arrests your spiritual leader for subversion. How would you sound? Well that was pretty much the way P.P. sounded: resolute, tempered by adversity, possessed of an unshakeable faith - all of those qualities were right there in P.P.'s voice when I asked him the stock question, with a subtle sensitivity that takes years of practice:

"Hi P.P. So the healer got himself arrested, huh?"

His unsettling new gaze turned on me and the second-hand voice of the healer said, "No, he wasn't arrested. It was his idea, before they ever thought of coming here."

"I don't understand."

"I'm not sure I do either, but understanding him isn't what this is all about. It's about understanding ourselves."

See what I mean? Before he came to the wilderness P.P. Johnson sometimes had trouble recognizing himself in a mirror, and now here he was, talking about whatever he was talking about. I still get a mild headache thinking about how P.P. could've altered so much so soon.

"Uh, tell me, P.P....what did happen last night? I mean - "

"I don't know."

"You don't know? You were there weren't you? You and the others?"

"No, we were up here."

"What? All night? What were you all doing up here for Christ's sake?"

Yeah, he smiled at that. "You really want to know?"

"No, I not really P.P. I'm not in the least bit interested. *Jesus!*"

"Praying."

"You were praying while (I almost said while Rome burned, I swear) he was getting arrested?"

"He sent us up here with instructions to pray for him and not come back till sun-up."

"He did that...so the whoever could just walk right in and take him?"

Now he was looking at me with pity. "Sure. We would only have gotten in the way."

I think I was uncommonly wise for once to steer the conversation in a different direction with my next question.

"So where do you all go from here?"

At that, P.P. turned his shining eyes on the crowd and looked even more resolute. "As far as we have to," was all he said. That gaze had softened into a kind of warm glow - like women sometimes get when they look at babies, only instead of being in his hormones, P.P.'s glow was in a part of his mind someplace higher than his head.

"You intend to carry on, uh, spreading his message?"

"Sure."

Dumb as I am, I knew P.P. had acquired an esoteric knowledge that I was as yet unfamiliar with.

322

"Are you speaking for the others? For Donna and Matt and McClure?"

"I think so, yeah. Rosemary, too. And Willie…"

Something had changed in him all of a sudden. Maybe his aura flashed a different color and I felt its effects without knowing, who knew? Aura's are not my department.

"*Willie Stevenson* was with you, up here in the wilderness? All night?"

Somehow I couldn't see Willie *praying*. Maybe there is such a thing as female intuition, but I didn't believe Willie was a real disciple. I hadn't actually thought about it if you must know; I had better things to do with my thoughts than allow somebody like Willie Stevenson to wander unaccompanied through them, however pious he professed to have become.

"No, Willie went home to his family." P.P. seemed reluctant to think anything bad of Willie. "Rosemary went home as well."

But we both knew Rosemary was not Willie.

"You all out here in the wilderness today?" I asked, wondering if I ought to go searching for Donna to see how she was taking it, immediately deciding that maybe I wouldn't.

"Sure we are, Laurie. Where else would we be?"

I didn't give him the obvious answer, which was *in jail with the healer*. And so much for my inside story. If the disciples didn't know, nobody knew - outside of the secret service. Now Luke Lawrence - that's who I would like to've spoken to just then.

"Okay P.P., I was hoping for a story here today. People will want to know what happens next. He's important to some of them."

He gazed off into space for quite some time before lowering his eyes to mine, but I could tell already this was not about to be the exclusive that would lift Laurie Hendricks to the elevated heights of media stardom.

"I think the best thing you can do now, Laurie, is wait and see. Just wait and see, huh?"

And that was it. We were done. Or rather he was, and I was left with my tongue hanging out, wondering how Wait And See could possibly be wrought into a headline worthy of the healer's arrest.

TAPE 72

In the midst of a dream Rosemary Brown struggled to raise herself up from the hard, makeshift bed on its unyielding board, unaware that her back no longer pained her. That pain had been a part of her for so long that even in sleep she experienced its memory like the phantom sensations in a lost limb.

Still dreaming, she stood at the small square of undraped window, watching the first chill light of dawn on the horizon as if through thick water. Then she was in the downstairs parlor, where the clock on the mantel said five-twentysomething in this hyper-world. Clouds of furniture rearranged themselves around her until the clumsy leadenness of being awake thawed her senses. She stood at the door of Harve's workshop, outlined in light from within, the smooth doorknob refusing the pressure of her just-woken hand.

She opened the door to find Harve seated, stock-still at his bench, his short body sagging like an unplumped cushion, his visible eye more glazed than the jeweler's glass still clenched in the other. Harve was a spotlit waxwork in the tiny lamp's private light, his surfaces closest to the lamp in fierce contrast with his shadows, like a man in space.

Rosemary reached out to him. The touch of his shoulder didn't feel like anything she recognized, but then she'd ceased to recognize Harve a long time ago - as a husband, a friend, even as a human being. She hadn't touched Harve for so long it was like reaching into the unknown, but her fingers found their own way to Harve's shirt-collar, felt the frayed linen where the liner showed through, then the smoother, pitted warmth of his neck, the white bristles of his jaw, the - oh! The pulse. Well my God, hadn't she expected to find one?

After all the wonderful new sensations that had been bubbling up and altering her perceptions, she realized that whatever she'd thought about Harve till now had all centered on *her* life; it was all about how *she* felt, how *she* wanted to change. Her entire point of view had been back to front! She'd been looking inward at a reflected image of everything around her so the image was reversed and second-hand, her first consideration always *herself*. The wonderful, cleansing bloom of righteousness she'd felt for the world and everything in it, had been *self*-righteousness. In her sudden insight she understood that this was what the healer had meant by the only way to herself being through others.

And now a great balloon started expanding inside her, forcing out the breath and the tears; causing the sheath she'd molded around herself to crack and shatter like clay, to begin falling away until her vision was free of the cataracts that life had grown over it, and she could see that not needing Harve because he had nothing left to give her, that was the illusion. The *reality* was that Harve needed what *she* had to give to *him*. So simple a change of viewpoint, so easy a notion to understand, yet so hard to put into practice. Even the tears dried up now she understood that they, too, were self-regard. That was all she'd known throughout life. *Her* life.

He was looking up at her, blank-eyed, unaware of all that was happening inside her. This was still the same old Harvey to whom she must appear as a piece of life-furniture. She was nodding gently at him, unaware of the half-grim, half-amused shape to her mouth, wondering what she might do next. Maybe take that stupid eyeglass out of his face and put it on the bench to begin with...

Well just look at that! Surprise or what? And why not try ruffling that spiky excuse for hair, what little there was left to ruffle.

There. *Amazement.* Well hell, maybe he needed amazing after all this time.

She had taken a hold of his upper arm, same old meaty Harve sure enough, and hauled him to his feet. Another surprise because Harve was pretty heavy, and yet here she was, moving him around with ease! But the biggest surprise was, there was not the least sign of complaint from her back...

Her goddam back! That had been her excuse for so many things left undone. Could that really have been how it was? Could her bad back have been just a symbol for everything else? *No backbone!*

Now she'd gotten him through to the parlor and would sit him in - no, not that same old chair - this one by the window where the light was starting to come in.

The customers had already started staying away from the store and Rosemary knew why, even if Harve didn't: The healer was gone. Whatever anybody else thought or imagined had been happening in this corner of Raiment County, the truth was that he had been the beginning and the end of it. Except that what was the end for some was just the start for others.

She had the coffee pot on and burping away before even she knew what she'd been so busy with. Harve watched her from behind a different set of eyes now, the circular mark from the eyeglass still there like a monocle, making him look like an old Prussian General, what with his square, white, spiky-haired head and bulldog jaw. The amazement was gone, replaced with a look Rosemary never saw before - maybe because he was looking at somebody he never saw before. She was only getting started. He was going to see a lot more things he never saw before if he kept looking at her.

The business would go back to what it had been, and what it had been was dead if the truth were told. If Harve was not to die right along with it - the way he'd been headed - something drastic would be required. From her. This new wakefulness was the beginning of her new life of giving, and she damn well did not intend to let her old self get in the way. Hell no, Harve wouldn't change, not in any dramatic way, whatever she did, but there was no reason why he should shrivel up and die just because he was no longer selling guns. Jesus Christ, that in itself was reason for celebration!

TAPE 73

Remember how someone on TV compared the wilderness at the high point of its popularity to that ancient rock concert-stroke-mud-wrestling festival called Woodstock? The wilderness also had elements of an amusement park with the added attractions of drug-peddling, prostitution, fringe-religions and what have you. In a few magical months the place had become a community in its own right. Yet already I could see signs of the healer's absence. I'm not suggesting a divine hand had any involvement in the wilderness fortunes. What I'm saying is, I wouldn't have believed it could happen so fast, and nor did those entrepreneurs. It was like a giant snowball rolling down a steep mountainside, gathering everything into itself. And then it was gone someplace else.

Maximizing your bottom line has gotten to be an exact science. Somebody twitching can tip the balance-sheets of entire companies. That's how it was - on a small scale - in the wilderness after the healer had a foreclosure notice served on him. Even ordinary people noticed - especially when they couldn't get a burger because hey, somebody took away the burger vendor! And to conserve my writing-time and your reading-time, for the burger vendor read ditto everybody else those wilderness visitors had grown used to having right there when they needed them, along with the makeshift pharmacy, paramedics, child-care-facilities, etc. The empty spaces left by the successful businesses got filled by smaller, less fastidious concerns. Business stank. Nobody looked after the public restrooms anymore. They stank. A lot of the people walking around stank. There was nobody to undertake the occasional fatality, so there were corpses lying around that also stank. (Not really; I was just amusing myself at your expense.) But you get the general idea. Boom-town to shanty-town in a few interesting days. And what did the tourists think about this sudden downgrading of facilities? They downgraded too. There were a lot fewer of them, moreso after the seamier side of everyday wilderness life emerged from beneath the rug: the bottom-end hookers and the pushers and suchlike.

TAPE 74

Now I'll insert another tape and bring Sheriff Hughes in here to remind me what I'm supposed to be talking about, though before I run this section by you, here's a Reality Window so you'll understand why Hughes was sporting so long a face. This particular Reality Window is somewhat gynecological so anybody this doesn't concern better close their eyes for a couple of sentences.

Okay. I'm parting the lace drapes on this one so we can see all the way into Maxine Stevenson's womb. Relax, everybody's got one. (The only people who don't are called men, which may account for why they're so determined to get into somebody else's.) We're looking in Maxine's womb because it contains an embryo. There, see it? It's not very big and looks kind of like a hairless mouse. Maxine knows it's there, and then some. She also knows that the Mayor must've put it there. What she doesn't understand is how come, when she had no plumbing to accommodate it.

But wait. Didn't the healer touch her? Yes he did. Well alright then, that's good enough for Maxine. Maxine is pregnant through the power of faith. The Mayor also knows about it, and now the two of them are swinging along side by side down happiness lane again. She's been tested; the equipment is all there and working normally. The reason why Sheriff Hughes was pissed off was that mister Mayor had felt the need to divulge his happy secret.

As just another character in this tale I knew nothing about Maxine's joyful miracle, yet I was aware of other reasons for why the Sheriff was less than pleased. For one, Mayor Stevenson watched the wilderness's prosperity draining away before his eyes, and with it his popularity and re-election chances. He had the impossible job of simultaneously trying to hold everything together whilst pretending nothing had changed - not easy when he was getting complaints every five minutes from the few 'decent' visitors who were left, not just about the disappearing amenities and malodorous condition of those remaining, but about folks being constantly harassed by junked-up hippies, and alcoholically-impaired bums. Or having their cars and trailers broken into.

What with the trash blowing and kicking around under their feet and the unlicensed shoestring traders who now graced the vacated plots with their downmarket goods, and downmarket methods of purveying them - it was all too brutal a reminder to the Mayor that what had so recently gone up was now headed right back down again.

I knew all of this for myself, but I still had to stand there and have it all unpicked and re-embroidered by Neil Hughes.

"Just will you look at these people, Laurie. Yessir, this thing is fine'ly showin' itself fer the old whore it always was, hidin' behind the pious disguise that holy hippie dressed it in. Kind've like a hustler done up in a nun's outfit."

A disillusioned downturn had crept into the lazy drawl, and even his famous old greedy gaze had turned kind of inward-looking, as if he were feeding off himself. That fitted his gaunt-faced appearance. Hughes was starting to remind me of nothing less than a balloon with a slow leak. Ever see someone with a cancer? I mean in the earlier stages when a loss of energy, a general lassitude and suchlike are taking a hold? That was Hughes.

"I reckon folks round about're goin' the same way, some of. The panties are off now. It's all comin' out the closet."

Jesus, now he was ceasing to make sense. When he looked at me I had to look away.

"You been kept busy out here in the wilderness, Neil?" It was a clumsy query, but I didn't know what to say to the guy. I was wishing he'd go away.

"I'm sick of this goddam place an' that's the truth Laurie.."

Hear it just then? The pathetic absence of conviction. He seemed unable to get any wind behind his words. A discomfiting cloak around him was suffocating the old Hughes sauce; there was no suggestion of him being already inside your clothes without an invite. Even that would have been preferable to this! I was even hoping he'd make a suggestive remark. Together, the healer's departure, Maxine and the Mayor had pulled the plug on Hughes and without a battery backup he was fading fast.

Something else he was doing that I didn't like was, he kept touching himself 'down there'. I don't think even he was aware of it. And when he wasn't doing that he constantly checked his holstered sidearm. (I could've woven those things into a joke but at the time it wasn't funny.)

That was when I learned how DeSoto had gone all religious on Hughes. The story was highly exaggerated, Hughes being Hughes, when all that had actually happened was, deputy DeSoto heard somebody repeat what the healer said about the one true religion being love, and then made the mistake of telling Hughes he agreed with the notion.

328

Hughes then fell silent, allowing me to catch the outer edge of a long drawn-out wail, only as I'm transcribing this from the very same audio tape I had running at the time - the tape that chose that exact moment to expire - both my train of thought and that wailing have just been cut off abruptly.

Now it's tomorrow for me (and no time at all for you). The sound of somebody wailing was Mrs. Catherine Hughes. She was drunk, staggering and falling down in all of that waste paper blowing around in the wilderness, then getting up and waving what I soon discovered was a big bible that took two hands to hoist aloft, immediately overbalancing her so down she went again.

To be honest her performance was nothing to write home about. What made it special was seeing the Sheriff's face and feeling the waves of pathos and ridicule from his wife echoing back off of him. Seeing her, and seeing his reaction and everything, the nice part of me wished I could be elsewhere, while the reporter was thanking God I was not. Nobody took much notice though; they'd all seen drunks before; some of 'em were drunks; others only had to live with drunks.

After I surreptitiously stuck in a fresh cassette (not that Hughes would've noticed if I'd squatted down in the mess and taken a pee just then), I followed in his wake as he advanced on his wife. I couldn't see his face but I'd detected what could well be the propensity for a temper in back of his psychotically debonair demeanor, and now I imagined all kinds of things happening in his state of mind. Not that I was watching Hughes; my full attention was on Catherine Hughes, who appeared not to have noticed what was bearing down on her, being so intoxicated by her preaching.

Well what did you imagine she was doing with a bible in one hand and a lightning-fork and matching thunderbolt in the other? Her voice was not so much high-pitched as storm-tossed, the words awash with religious indignation and slurred from booze. Verily she'd taken over from the healer! This was real eighteen carat delusion with the bona fide biblical text to back it up. Go get your family St. James's and check it out. (If you favor one of the new, textually-sanitized, politically correct rehash bible editions you'll lose much of the genuine fervor. It just ain't the same in new English.) Here goes with a gist:

"I am ready to go with thee to jail, and to bed." No, it doesn't say that in your bible; this is the official Catherine Hughes 50% proof vodka version. And furthermore: "I got two swords...I'm tellin' Peter 'bout his cock crowin'...don't tempt me...jus' don't tempt me - "

Next second she was down on all fours but miraculously kept a grip on her bible and got it right up against her face to read: "Judas…Judas, you bastard! Kiss me boy! Oh kiss me kiss me!" She was weaving about like a snake right there on her knees, eyes rolling and spittle flying from her lips when Hughes tried to grab a hold of her and she went scuttling away through a filthy heap of crumpled, rain soaked newspaper and fast-food wrappers, scattering them like startled chickens before she flipped over on her back, legs kicking and tears streaming from her eyes, still reciting: "Where's my angel to strengthen me? Are thou the Christ? Sure I am…*I am the Christ!*"

Now Hughes had her around the neck, then the waist, hoisting her bodily as the illustrated bible fell face down on the scrub, bounced over easy onto its back the way Catherine Hughes had, flapped a few of its pages in the breeze, and that was more or less the end of it.

I'm now seeing Hughes' rounded hulk striding stiffly away, a betrayed rag of a woman under his arm. He looked straight ahead and she at the ground, strings of saliva trailing out from her face, the sermon reduced to an incoherent, jogging croak. What a great couple the Hughes's are. Do anything to entertain a crowd.

After I rescued Mrs. Hughes' bible from the ground I just stood on that spot and watched the police cruiser in the distance bouncing in slomo off the tarmac lip of the wilderness parking lot before vanishing behind the trees in a drifting cloud of dust. My eyes held on that for a long moment, like in a movie. Only then did I remember to switch off my recorder.

Later, when I switched it back on in my other capacity (as the disembodied author of this story who doesn't always need to be on the scene personally to know what's going down), I reran the tape, transcribed it to the screen of my PC, then downloaded it onto the disc that became this book, and…But I guess I oughtn't to get too real for the sake of people who'd rather believe this is fiction.

Okay. Now you're all going to jail because that's where this story's going next, and if you want to follow it I suggest you give yourself up and come quietly.

TAPE 75

The body of Andrew DeSoto was slumped in its usual chair in the outer office looking exactly as if it was still alive. Which, of course, it was, if you can

330

use the term *alive* to describe somebody who thinks their spirit has given up the ghost. A lot had happened to Andrew lately, as it had to Passmore and Raiment county, and Andrew was having a hard time keeping up.

Despite the healer having reassured his small band of disciples that it was foreseen and for the best, they, regardless of his blessing, and being merely human, still had forebodings: not only about what would happen to him, but about what would happen to them. Andrew especially had forebodings.

Look at him, slumped at his desk while the boss's wife dries out in a holding-cell in back, (right alongside a couple of other miscreants) when Lord God Almighty, who should happen to walk in but the boss's daughter. Andrew's relationship with Donna had experienced a holy evolution; they didn't even need to speak to communicate these days, a phenomenon that gave DeSoto a pretty shrewd idea of what was about to transpire.

Donna Hughes was mad as hell. Things had been changing greatly for her too, and she was having just as hard a time keeping up with her new self as Andrew was. Nobody just becomes a disciple, end of story; like everybody else they still have the ugly fat of their old, impure self to work off. Donna was still toting her robot around, not yet in control of it.

Maybe you guessed that Donna's daddy, having dumped Donna's momma in the jail, sandwiched between a minor pusher and a vagrant, was not in Donna's good books. Not that he ever had been anyway, but Donna had discovered an Achilles' heel - a new-found need to appear respectable, particularly after everything the old robot had made her do. The receding echoes of that would be with her for some time to come.

By the time she was close enough for DeSoto to see the tears sloshing around in her eyes he was already braced for action, but before he could get out from behind his desk Donna was halfway through the Sheriff's office, her head performing odd elliptical movements on her neck, eccentric planetary orbit-wise, as if she was determined not to focus on what was in her mind this close to it.

Okay, we're in the back room now where the cells are, switching between Donna's subjective viewpoint and close-ups of her face. It's dark in here, and just under that thin top-layer of disinfectant are smells you don't want to think about.

Donna is moving along the short corridor trying not to touch the bars or to look into each cubicle but doing it anyway. Her head is lowered and wobbly, lips kind've contorted, the way they go when women are about to lose it. Her eyes are blinking through the tears, searching the twinkling, liquid gloom for a familiar face until she gets to the same cell John the Baptist once occupied.

And now, along with that smell nudging at her memory, there's a barely conscious recognition of herself in here that earlier time, at these very same bars. Even more deja-vu is DeSoto, standing right behind her. Yeah, and let's make it uncomfortably warm in here for good measure.

Donna's thinking: 'Oh Christ! How could that bastard leave her in *here?*' That's what DeSoto reads anyhow, except that all he can see of Donna's face is the back of her neck and her ear. Even in this murk he notices the three pinpricks where there used to be tiny gold studs above the lobe.

Now his eyes go inside the cell to Mrs. Catherine Hughes, sitting quietly in the far corner, head dropped right down on her chest so she can watch her hands try to strangle each other. Her knees and feet are together but her shoes are gone. Her hair's a mess. There's a toilet roll on the bench next to her. I think there's a tightly compressed wad of the stuff in her hand.

For the moment everything's deadly, seriously quiet. Man, this atmosphere in here is heavy as hell! Like the densely textured tones in an Edward Hopper painting. (I think that's the artist's name. I know for certain it ain't Hedda.)

I'm going to change tenses because that *here and now* stuff strikes me as kind've affected, but you have to have a shot at these things now and then.

The door between the cells and the office was heavy and soundproofed so nobody heard anything until it got banged open and Hughes came in, cussing hard under his breath - maybe because DeSoto wasn't on the desk. Maybe because Donna was in here. Then Hughes sort of slowed and stopped as though the two female members of his family formed an opposite polarity and were repelling him.

Let's just freeze everybody there so I can take this opportunity to tell you about the young guy in the cell to Mrs. Hughes' left; the one in there for petty theft and vagrancy who was innocent of the former and merely a victim of the latter. You'd have looked at this young guy and called him a hippie or a student or new-age dropout, or some other descriptor depending entirely on your fixed opinions. And being quiet and unassuming, and actually just about as straight and honest as they come, this young guy wouldn't have said anything back; nothing that an opinionated person like Hughes would be prepared to listen to.

The way he didn't listen when the proprietor of the Electric Wizard Mystical Bric-a-brac-and-Literature Emporium called him from the wilderness to say this scummy-looking guy had lifted a few zodiac rings from the display, and he should get out there and arrest his ass. Boy, you don't need me to tell you that Hughes had had more than enough of young bums flouting the rules of their elders and betters. Especially when he turned up and discovered the accused looked like the healer's twin brother. Now this young guy was innocent but in jail because Hughes didn't like the look of him, and because he didn't offer any explanation for why he didn't steal those rings. I know he shouldn't have needed to offer any such explanation but Hughes wanted one just so he could vent his spleen on somebody at that moment.

I'm telling you all of this because Hughes was not there to get mad, but because all three of his cells were occupied and he needed one vacated so the hooker he'd left outside in the cruiser cuffed to the door would have a place to sleep alone that night because she could be under-age. Hell, she looked no more than twelve years old to Hughes, but that was probably more wishful thinking than fact.

Hughes had also chosen to swallow the story - about someone having left the drugs in his car by mistake - from the minor-league pusher currently residing in the suite next to Mrs. Hughes. The fact that it was a flimsy lie doesn't figure in this equation because since when was this a fair world? So Hughes was going to release minor-league when his 'lawyer' arrived, whereas in a fair world he should have released the other prisoner - the healer lookalike - for being innocent.

Now we'll unfreeze everybody from the throat-catching aromatic gloom of the holding-room because somebody else just came in. This was a short, balding, bespectacled man who seemed to have his eyes fixed on a point two inches in front of but slightly above his nose. Right behind him, yet practically also in front of him owing to her being so tall and her nose so inquisitively long, came a woman who had to be his wife. She dragged a sullen young woman along after her. The wife couldn't seem to decide whether to shield the girl or present her as exhibit A.

Oh yeah, I nearly forgot. There was a younger boy tagging along in back of this triple-act lugging a real big stereo that he suddenly decided would sound great at full-volume. It was pleasing Hughes no-end now everybody had started treating his jail like it was open-day and could simply walk through and make themselves at home.

Hughes was in the middle of thinking he might just accommodate them when they all started yelling at once. See if you can follow this:

The little bald guy, still watching the point in front of his nose, started asking, "Who of you might be the Sheriff?" in an overly-formal voice. Halfway through the question his overtall, longnosed wife also started asking, "Who of you is the Sheriff?" Kind of like when people sing staggered duets. They both meant who was the Sheriff out of Hughes and DeSoto, except that they knew exactly who DeSoto was because he'd been giving it to their daughter at every opportunity until suddenly deciding he should become a disciple.

Uh-huh, *that's* who these folks were. And while this was going on, the look in eyes of sullen Becky Wright said she was undecided whether she wanted to kill DeSoto or turn and run so she could go bawl her eyes out because she wished he were still in lerve with her even though she hated his guts. But still lerved him too.

Now the Wright parents' staggered duet has some new words:

"What you gonna do 'bout him an' our little angel?"

"What are you gonna do?"

"What use is a young woman without her maidhood?"

"Yeah, a young woman's finished without her maidhood!"

"Right there under our noses, in our own goddam Bluebird Motorhome!"

"Right under our very noses in our motorhome - what you got to say about that mister easy-come-easy-go?"

And on it went. While that was happening, and Becky struggled with her love-hate eye-contact with DeSoto, and master Wright's death-by-heavy-metal rock radio forced his parents to shout (all of this with three stunned prisoners looking on), Donna found herself digging up some skeletons of her own.

Maybe her mother's arrest had catalyzed something for Donna that had awaited such a moment, because at the sight of her father's bulk, with the same rounded shoulders and thick neck she'd known all her life, the same large head with its perspiring brow and wisps of once luxuriant thinning blond hair, something made Donna's insides clench the way they always did when he was around. She'd often wondered why he had this effect on her. It had been this way ever since she could remember. Except that now something was different. This was a more enlightened Donna pondering the reaction. This was her most secret self going on red alert; an old instinct prickling to protect her from a nameless dread that accompanied his presence.

Hell, just thinking about him did this and always had - like an instinctive warning had grown up with her, become so familiar she accepted it as normal.

Even now she was a woman he still made her feel like a guilty little kid who didn't understand what she'd done wrong.

Donna felt her hands bunch into the familiar small, hard fists with the onset of this mysterious fear. Jesus, could it be a pheromone thing? Was the smell of him not only making her fearful but angry?

Now, for the first time ever, she found she was able to look right at it...*and she knew*. What? What did she know, with all of this pain and anger and fear whirling around inside her? *What?* Images...memories...imagined?

No! Oh God! Oh Jesus *God!* The sight of her father, the sound, the *smell*...the hot, old-straw smell of him...the unnaturally slippery hand with its other smell...(That was Vaseline; she suddenly, unaccountably remembered the blue label on the little round jar.)

But why was all of this coming together *now?* Why was she determined to disinter this thing that she'd secretly understood? That he'd literally had a hand in making her the way she'd become: the wayward, hard-nosed, determined-to-go-against-his-authority little tramp? Jesus! He hadn't simply passed on his genes to her. He'd lavished his unspeakable attentions on her with his Vaselined fingers and fucked her up for life!

No more! It was too much. The scene before her - these other people, the gloom, the fetid warmth - was suddenly all too real, like TV in her mind, the picture buzzing and flickering and making her dizzy, about to faint and make a fool of herself right here-and-now -

Then something else happened. She thought of the healer's soft-voiced reminder to 'Think of me, not of yourself.' He was right here with her, a billow of warmth rising inside of her, lifting her above all of this.

In that moment Donna opened her eyes in a new way. It was like coming out of a real heavy, numbing daydream. She realized she had just spent an ageless few seconds on a journey inside herself, deeper than ever before. The healer had held her hand and they'd made the journey together. *He* had helped her understand the darkness that had clouded her life. He had brought her through it and into the light again, and she had finally beaten it. She had *won!*

Coming right square in the middle of all that racket and accusation and everything, nobody hardly noticed when Donna went up to her father, looked around his rocky, uncomfortable face for a moment before plunging over the edge, deep into his eyes.

"This is harder for me than for you," she told him, "but I know what you did all those years ago...and I forgive you."

I can't even begin to describe her voice just then, but she turned and walked out of the jail, leaving her past behind her once and for all. On her way out she passed the guy who'd come to collect the pusher. Drawn through the empty front office by the sliver of noise before the heavy door closed itself behind Donna, this guy strolled cockily up to Hughes and asked, "Who the fuck's s'posed to be in charge around here?"

I don't think Hughes had the answer to that question just then.

TAPE 76

Those who're so inclined say *The Lord's Hand Works In Mysterious Ways To Perform His Wonders*. Except those wonders wouldn't have anywhere near so mysterious a working environment if more people shook themselves awake and got Real. The more Real you get, the less mysterious everything becomes, including God's Hand Performing Its Wonders. Now clear your mind and allow me to set the scene for this short chapter.

It's late at night, about half a mile up the road from the wilderness, where cold air is making the hot iron of Jeff Ackerley's pickup tick itself off in the silence of a little-used romantic pull-off.

You'll appreciate how little-used when I say the design on the discarded Pepsi cans practically make them museum pieces. There's a fresh trail of urine just to the rear of the pickup where Ackerley relieved himself; that trail's cold now, though Ackerley's personal trail gets warmer if you make your way back onto the minor road, then follow it to where the dirt track dives to the left and finds the Blackwater Creek bridge, its stinky water mumbling to itself down there in the dark. You should be able to hear that now you're standing on the bridge. Take a deep breath and smell the dampness, the water, the night-time trees. Feel the coolness of the breeze poking through your underwear.

So what I want to know is, why are you out here in your underwear at this time of night? Man, you are weird!

This is the bridge you cross to reach the healer's settlement. (Not to be confused with the newer road they threw down to take all of the visitors to the wilderness; that's further around the far side of these low hills. The settlement is separated off from the wilderness by a fence just so visitors will appreciate this group of shacks is not part of the 'leisure complex'.)

Ackerley's trail stops around back of the healer's silver trailer because Ackerley himself has stopped there. As I speak he's spattering more urine up

336

against the trailer, having come here straight from an all-evening stint in The Triangle. Matt barred him from The Triangle some time ago, but Matt no longer works there, and the new owner - the one who made old Woody, the previous incumbent, an offer he was no way in the world gonna refuse after all those years wishing he'd never bought the place in the first place - doesn't give a god-damn who buys his booze. They can't be much worse than he is anyhow.

Now that the healer's in protective custody, McClure is more or less full-time official caretaker of The Settlement. P.P. Johnson lives there with him, and the other disciples come and go as they please. None of them is around right now.

But Sheriff Neil Hughes is; I can just about make out his bulk, dark gray and indistinct in the night. He's standing real still and quiet - just one more piece of stillness and quietness out here - hat in hand, a couple of hundred yards up this gentle hillside, his huge gut swelling over the front of his pants and the perspiration drying on his face. He's looking at the black shapes of the few ramshackle buildings that comprise the settlement without understanding why he's doing that or what he's feeling, or even what brought him out here to the wilderness at this time of night when there's more paperwork than usual waiting in the office, and hunger is setting off those hollow rumblings in his stomach, which in Hughes' stomach sounds like a Mac truck shifting gears. Hughes is aware of his eyes narrowing as though he's thinking. I wonder what he's thinking? Let's go inside Neil Hughes' head and see what's happening in there.

I don't believe this. Neil Hughes, coming out here to *pray!* Yep, the same Neil Hughes who interfered with his small daughter and spent the past dozen or so years trying not to think about that, but occasionally thinking about it anyhow - especially when Donna is around. Hughes is now trying to digest an extra large helping of guilt, especially after his wronged daughter forgave him. You saw it happen. Being forgiven for a crime like that is the only thing worse than committing it…moreso when you know you didn't earn that forgiveness. When you know that maybe, under the right circumstances, you'd commit the same crime again because you've already considered doing it. Hughes keeps on feeling the shape of more of those same bad thoughts start to rise up. He *wants* to think about Donna that way, bad as it is, even while he's loathing himself for it. It makes him grimace - a genuine, tormented agony of confused doubt and self-loathing.

He starts down the hillside towards the settlement to try and keep his mind off itself, breathing hard through his teeth, feeling the muscles of his face writhe, conscious enough of the desire to feel his crotch to resist doing so.

He goes for his gun instead, hard and cold in his hand, and draws it from the holster. He really wants to shoot at something but there's nothing to shoot at and it'd make just too much noise in this special quiet. Hell, it wouldn't do any good anyhow unless he were pointing the gun at his own head. No, he's not the suicidal type. Hughes would rather blow some other sucker away for his own guilt.

Jeff Ackerley made this trip to the wilderness for much the same reason Hughes did: no reason that he understood. It surely couldn't be the fascination of being around this same silver shape he'd tried to torch not so long back, because that was one episode Ackerley would just as soon forget, yet was uncomfortably reminded of it with each epileptic seizure, the onset of which had begun that very same night.

There was a childish element of satisfaction to be had in pissing up the sidewall of the healer's abandoned quarters. It said, 'Fuck you, you're gone but I'm still around'. Even better than just being around, Ackerley had become a pusher for the main local supplier. Best of all, the wilderness was rapidly gaining a reputation as the state's mecca for that commodity.

Whatever, Ackerley still had to work hard to suppress a sense of daring just by being this close to where the weird dude had made his home for awhile. It was the same stupid discomfort you felt being around a house people said was haunted, even though you didn't believe in fuckin' ghosts. (Fuckin' ghosts? There had to be a word for that: *spookaphilia* or something?)

Ackerley fumbled two-handed with his zipper and nearly toppled over trying to land a kick on the side of the trailer. It was only a glancing blow that made hardly any sound…

…But Hughes heard it. In the silent night, the practically goddam holy night, the muffled hollow boom was just loud and different enough to separate itself from the sighing of leaves, or Hughes' own whispering footsteps in that dewy damp grass. He stopped to hold his breath, awaiting a repeat of the sound that mightn't have been anything.

This time there was no mistaking the sound of breaking glass. Fine. He was already headed in the right direction, gun in hand and a need to use it. And here's where you could probably complete the rest of this tape yourself; you've got all the ingredients. (How much did you pay for this book? And now you

338

have to write the thing yourself?) Well hell, everybody who can put one letter after another is writing books these days, so why not you? It's just a matter of dumping words on paper, and one of the most important factors is continuity. I don't just mean remembering that Hughes' first name is not Cecil but Neil, I mean remembering how you've shaped his personality throughout (and Ackerley's too) so as to steer them (and your readers) towards a satisfactory conclusion, rather than have Hughes suddenly decide not to blow Ackerley away, even though he had a few reasons to do that. Because Ackerley made use of Donna, for instance. Or because Hughes felt so guilty from having abused her as a child, he now felt he ought to recompense her somehow, and perforating Ackerley would go some way towards accomplishing that.

Hughes also knew it was Ackerley burned down that black family's house a few years back. And let's not forget that Hughes was the one who practically blackmailed Ackerley into planting LSD in the church. Ackerley has too much on Hughes. Then there were those sandwiches Hughes personally prepared for John the Baptist; Ackerley was the one who gave Hughes the acid. I guess that was a manslaughter case and Hughes knows it. He also knows that Ackerley knows it.

Being smart, you'll have figured that Hughes doesn't yet know it's Ackerley in the trailer, but after everything I just said, you figure he soon will know. So nobody is expecting him to replace his weapon back in its holster and go on home for supper. What actually happened was as follows.

Ackerley had gotten inside the trailer and was stumbling around in search of anything at all that he could either damage or steal. Ackerley's sensibilities were all shot to hell these days so he didn't make any effort towards stealth. Nor did he bring a flashlight or anything, being terminally stupid, so while he stumbled around inside there, everything struck him as being in the wrong place. Except that the one thing in the wrong place was Ackerley.

Advancing on the silver trailer, knowing somebody was in there, in the dark, making more noise than seemed legal, you can see how easy this was going to be for Hughes. I mean, he could sit down and wait for the intruder to emerge, then *bang!* Or he could put a few rounds through the silver skin; that stuff is only thin. He might get lucky. And you just know, knowing Hughes' mind, that he is not going to yell 'This is the Sheriff so come on out with your hands in the air.' That would be too fair and square.

No, on second thoughts that's a good notion. When Ackerley comes out, sheepish and grinning, imagining his one-time partner in crime (and secret half-brother) the Sheriff will show camaraderie, Hughes can enjoy the surprised look on Ackerley's face, illuminated by the muzzle-flash.

So that's what happens, and Hughes is going to remember the sight of Ackerley's face in that final instant for the rest of his life, though I don't guess it'll cause him too many sleepless nights.

TAPE 77

The next day they pulled Willie Stevenson's old red Camaro out of the river at the ford below the Baptist Church. Willie was in the driver's seat, dead through asphyxiation, although the length of plastic hose he rigged to run from the tailpipe through the window had gotten dislodged at both ends when the handbrake failed to hold the car on top of the hill opposite the church, and it had run sedately backwards to finish up half in the river. I guess you could say Willie got himself and his Camaro baptized. I expect they had to open up the other half of those Pearly Gates to allow him to drive right on in.

It was not so long after that that Mayor Stevenson's heart attack left him bruised all down the left side of his face where it had impacted the kitchen floor. Not a fatal attack; if I wanted to be real mean I could say that Bobby Stevenson probably didn't have enough heart to attack. Besides, he'll have to help take care of some new family pretty soon.

People are living longer these days, and more are being born than ever before. Maybe you'd be interested to know where those new people are all coming from and why. (I mean all of those *souls*.)

Yet a far more pressing question here is, where are we going to stack 'em all? I'm sure there's an infinite amount of room for accommodation where they all come from and go back to, but while they're here, having folks queuing to live on this already crowded little planet causes more trouble than you probably care about.

Sure it takes more food, which all costs money to grow, as does the technology that lets people grow more food on less land. But they don't only want to eat better, they want to live better in every sense. They want more disposable income because that's what civilized, sophisticated societies mean by living better.

A steadily growing number of people (on a small planet) all wanting a steadily increasing standard of living, are simply going to swamp the world with materialism in all its forms. The place will be covered in highways by all the extra people wanting more and more cars. The skies'll be filled with a growing number of airplanes, so more land will be used for runways and terminals. All of the natural resources under their feet will be mined avidly, turned into material possessions. More factories, more pollution. More waste to dispose of, organic and inorganic. And all the time the land is getting eaten up by more houses, factories, cities, agriculture, landfills…

You know that all of the people involved in this accelerating race to live better are doing it for their DNA-selves and their genetic offspring, before any other consideration. The ME FIRST survival ethic we inherit from a bunch of chemicals is getting ever-more-efficient at turning this world into the solar system's, and maybe the galaxy's, or even the universe's, materialistic center.

Now I've gotten that quota of disenchantment out of my system I'm ready to talk about what happened to me next. I had a call from Ed, all the way up there in big old Alaska. Yeah, he sounded terrific, like the Ed I remembered, telling me how pleased he was about me going ahead with the book. He even demanded a copy the minute it was published, you know how people do. That can become boring when everybody you ever knew in your entire goddam life starts demanding you give them a copy. I was only sorry me and Ed didn't get to have much of a conversation.

Well okay, I didn't actually get to talk with Ed, but he had a real good conversation with my answering machine. He never said a word about himself or what he was doing up there in Alaska.

Hey, I'm okay now, really. Right now I'm gonna tell you about another message that was on my answering machine that afternoon. From Luke Lawrence. At the FBI.

TAPE 78

Luke Lawrence called me from a public callbooth not far from the FBI's headquarters in Washington DC to say the healer was dead. (Or would you prefer me to break the news to you gently?) Okay, I'll start again.

Luke Lawrence called me from a public callbooth not far from the FBI's headquarters in Washington DC with some bad news about the healer. It seems the protective custody he was being held in was not designed to protect him, but to protect the people who put him there. As if you didn't know.

Anyhow (said with a mammoth sigh) Luke's news, coming so unexpectedly out of my answering machine, was like a fist in the gut. After I recovered from the initial blow it started seeping through me like poison, or a black fog. Poison *and* a black fog. (If this explanation is kind of disjointed and weird - yes lady, like the rest of the book - it's because I recorded the original right then at the time, and I was not feeling exactly fabulous.) I thought writing the story up for The Star immediately after getting it in the face would imbue it with authenticity.

So what did I write? HEALER DEAD.

What Luke said was that somebody - probably a professional plant - got to the healer and just took him out. Luke explained it briefly with professionalism of his own, being one of 'them', but I won't burden you with the details. I suspect Luke was being professionally terse and succinct to conceal his shock because you and I both know he'd become a disciple himself. Didn't I mention that? Okay, so consider it mentioned. He had to break the news to me surreptitiously because the FBI wanted to keep a lid on the shooting for as long as possible. Yes, it was a shooting. A crucifixion might have offended people's religious sensibilities.

As with Ed, Luke and me didn't get to have a conversation, nor was there any way I could call him back on this. Not that I had any need to - here was that big story I'd wished I'd gotten the exclusive on earlier when the healer first appeared. Except that now I'd gotten it I didn't want it. There's no excuse for being glad somebody died, and especially this particular somebody. (Okay, so a small, snake-like part of me wanted it; this was my Big Story after all.)

This is a couple of mornings later. I thought I'd maybe feel better now but I feel just as bad in a different way. I must've been real traumatized for the past few days because I didn't even take a drink, which is just as well because boy, would I have been suffering. A hangover on top of everything else?

When I recovered sufficiently to start putting this book together and had my nose glued to the screen of my PC, the phone rang. I just let it ring because I was working on my own time and nothing was going to disturb me - except me. That's what happens when you're writing a book: you make a gigantic effort not to let big things distract you, then you go right ahead and distract yourself for no reason at all.

When I finally checked to see who'd been calling, Donna's processed voice said, "Hi Laurie. Are you home or - well no matter anyhow 'cause I got something real amazingly wonderful to tell you."

She had too because, though I didn't know then what it was, the excitement in her voice was next door to tears - of happiness. She said to my machine: "I don't know if you'll want to put it in the paper or what but Oh! It's just…it's so wonderf - " (Then she got choked on her own joy.)

It'll make everything a lot simpler if I just say Donna wanted to see me in person at the healer's settlement to tell me the good news. And if you second-guess me before I've told it, well so what?

I haven't said much about the weather in this story because nobody buys a book so they can read about some made-up weather in Tennessee. But just in case you did, here's the part you've been waiting so patiently for. That afternoon was hot and sunshiny, too bright for your unshaded eyes if you happened to look at anything reflective, and it got you perspiring if you tried anything exertional. Oh yeah, it was humid too. Had enough weather yet?

So arriving at the settlement I found Rosemary Brown sitting out on an old chair by the door of the big hut, mending a pair of overalls. It was real quiet there, and the hot sun on that old wooden shed released a comforting odor. So did Rosemary: spicy and homey kind've, with a hint of plain soap.

Without looking up she said, "McClure (she always calls him McClure) can surely do this better than I could but it's the thought that counts so I'm saving him a chore. 'Sides, he's got enough on his plate." She snorted. "I mean he's cookin'."

Being the person who created McClure and his proclivities I knew just how much trouble he'd be taking. I wedged myself in the open door-frame and flapped the front of my shirt to cool me, suddenly deciding I was getting lethargic - a combination of the hours I'd spent writing this stuff, and that balmy weather. I'd left my sunglasses in the car and wondered should I get them, or would wearing them out here with Rosemary be kind've rude. Yes I do have a thing about wearing sunglasses in company. Eye-contact is part of conversation.

"Nice day, Mrs. Brown."

She gave me a sideways look. "It's *Rosemary*, not Mrs. Brown."

I thought how weird for a character I'd invented to be scolding me nicely for not using her first name.

"Okay Rosemary," I told her, watching her face for more clues as to her inner personality so I could relay them to you, because to me Rosemary Brown is just as real as you are. Moreso considering I created her, whereas I never met you in my life.

I could see - in my imagination - that she and Harve were finally on better terms after so many wilderness years - excuse the pun.

"Anybody around?" I asked, smiling into the sun with my eyes closed.

"There's the guy owns these pants...the deputy..." She was listing them and leaving a space in between as if she were examining them in her mind. "...Mister Johnson. Matthew's inside..."

"I was, uh, expecting Donna would be here."

"Oh she's here - I was keepin' her till last, her bein' the child."

Some child! Donna had already outgrown most adults I ever knew and she was not yet eighteen years of age. Strange, but I never had thought of these people as disciples or characters or any other group in a collective sense. To me they were all individuals. (And that's in both the literal and literary senses.)

Another strange thing was, the healer being dead didn't appear to bother Rosemary. She seemed more peaceful and together than in her entire life. As though...well, what happened next is explanation enough.

After a warm, easy space in the conversation she said, without looking at me or pausing in her work: "*He's* here."

"Who's here?"

"...*The healer.*"

A jolt went through me. I hadn't actually expected myself to make her say that. I'll be perfectly honest with you. I was daunted at the prospect of having to go in too close to him as *him*. Wouldn't you be, after I suggested that we might be talking about a reincarnated version of Jesus Christ? And now I'm faced with the fact that he's just around the corner from where I'm standing as a character in my own book.

Yeah, I know I've already seen him at a distance and on TV, but that's not the same as knowing he could just walk out through this doorway into the sunlight at any moment and speak to me.

Or maybe Rosemary just meant he was there in spirit, in each of the disciples?

No-ho, that won't work. I'd be letting myself off the hook by doing it that way. He was there alright, large as life. Only I'm not going to have me get to finally meet him face to face because I'm not ready yet, and nor are you.

Boy, that was a relief.

Donna came outside at that moment, somewhat calmer than on the phone and explained to me about how he'd told them he'd be back. She even wanted me to come in and meet him, but I'd already decided it would keep until another time. Somebody who did come out and surprise me was Luke Lawrence, looking cool as always.

It was surreal just standing around jawing with those folks in the sun, everybody feeling that special kind of high that I was not a party to, being an outsider. Though even I felt all of that gloom and doom leaving me now.

End note: Owing to the sleight-of-hand involved in putting this tome together, I still have yet to write this story into the book you just read. All I have are notes and a million tiny cassette tapes that I recorded over the past months.

I'm not starting work on it yet because the tub is running and I poured in some exotic bubble-bath. (Some dried-up old gunk I discovered behind the cistern but it smells okay when the hot water hits it.)

Know what I'm going to do now? I'm going to pour a couple of inches of English gin in a glass, drop in some ice, no olive because while those things are fine in a salad, I don't want them bobbing around in my martini, thankyou. Then I'll set the phone on autopilot, and me and my martini are gonna climb in the tub and get to know each other better.

LH

Printed in the United States
117745LV00003B/339/P